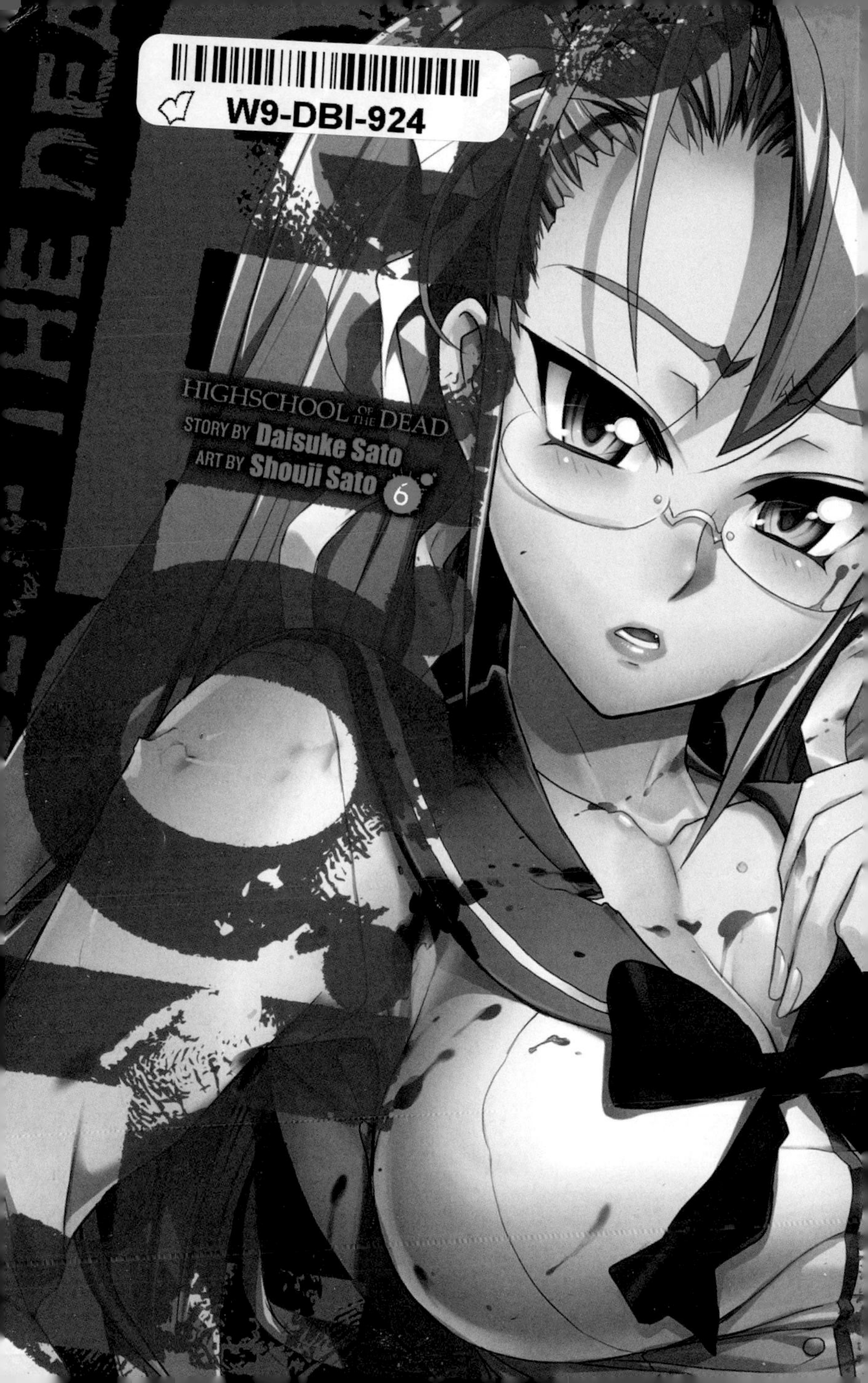
HIGHSCHOOL OF THE DEAD
STORY BY Daisuke Sato
ART BY Shouji Sato
6

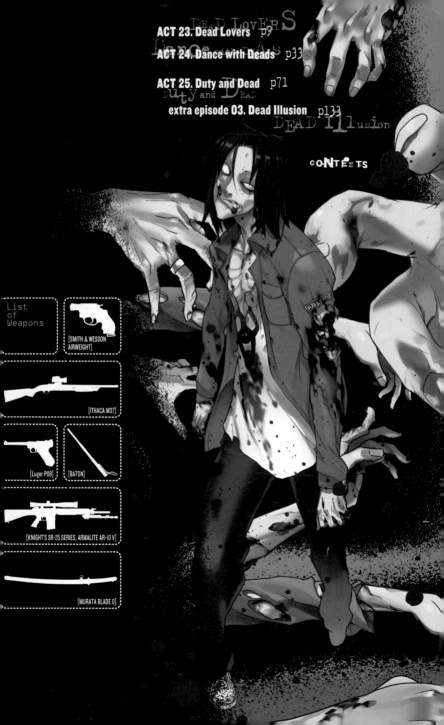

CONTENTS

List of Weapons

[SMITH & WESSON AIRWEIGHT]

[ITHACA M37]

[Luger P08]   [BATON]

[KNIGHT'S SR-25 SERIES, ARMALITE AR-10 V]

[MURATA BLADE O]

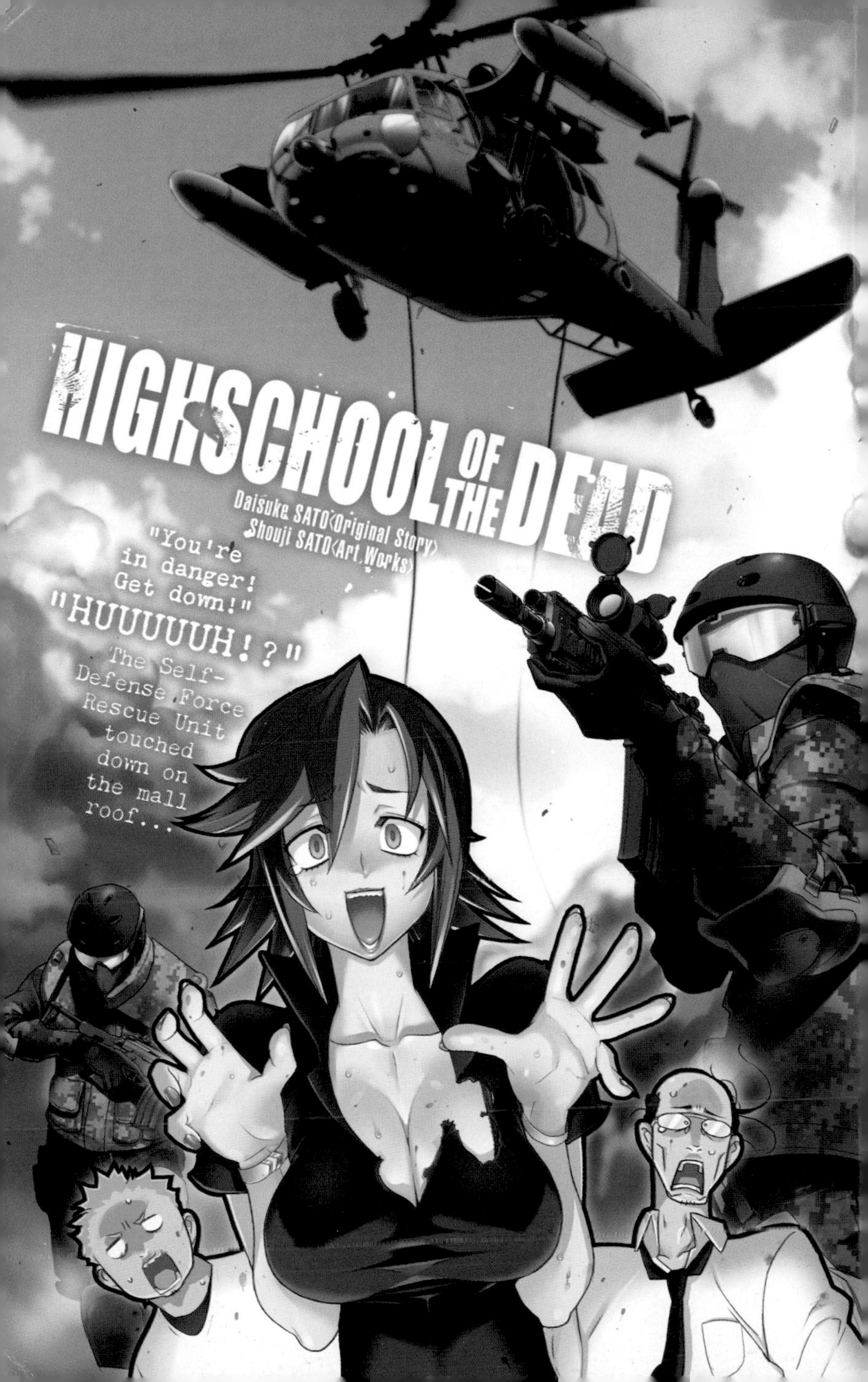
HIGHSCHOOL OF THE DEAD
Daisuke SATO〈Original Story〉
Shouji SATO〈Art Works〉
"You're in danger! Get down!"
"HUUUUUH!?"
The Self-Defense Force Rescue Unit touched down on the mall roof...

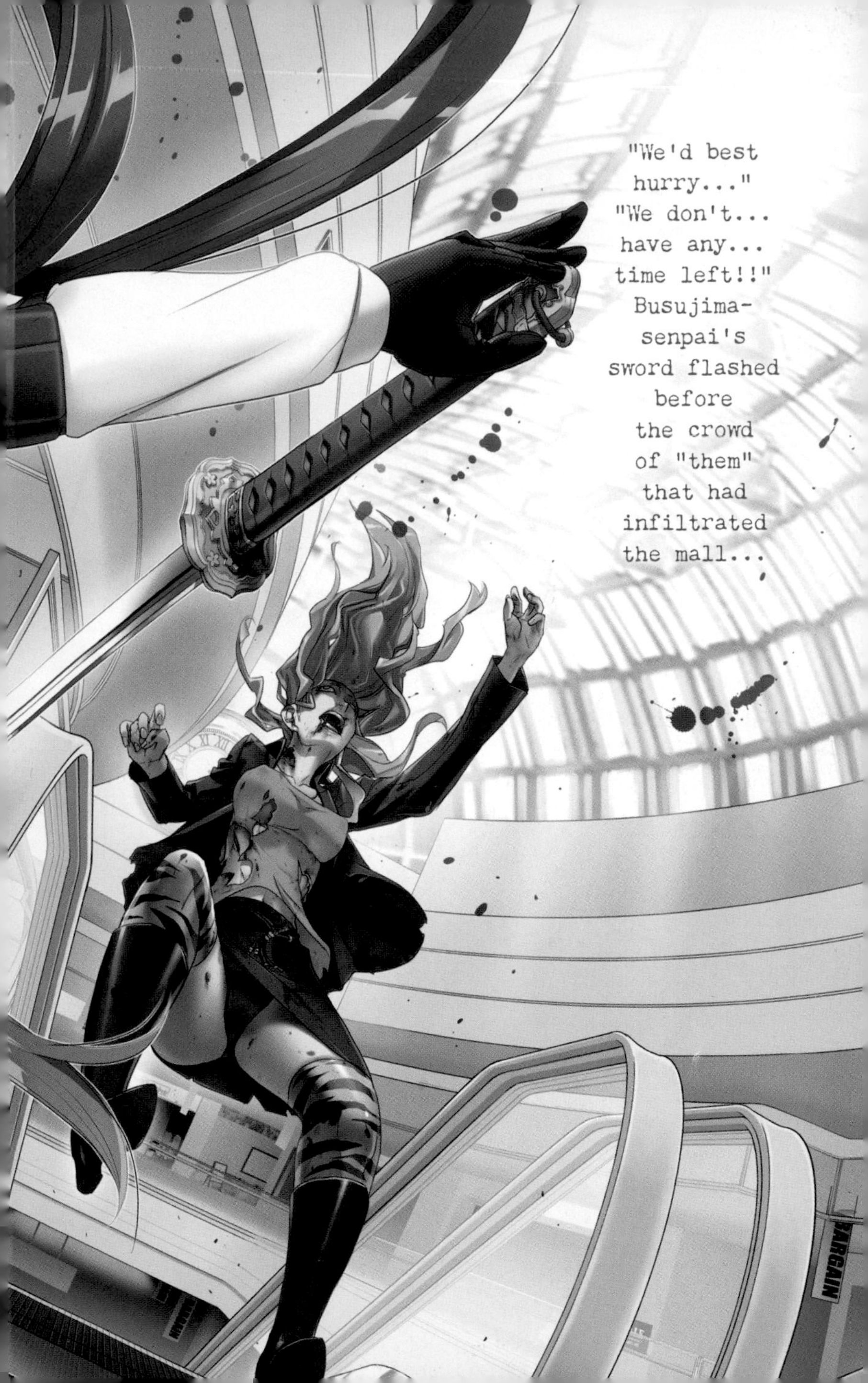
"We'd best hurry..." "We don't... have any... time left!!" Busujima-senpai's sword flashed before the crowd of "them" that had infiltrated the mall...
BARGAIN

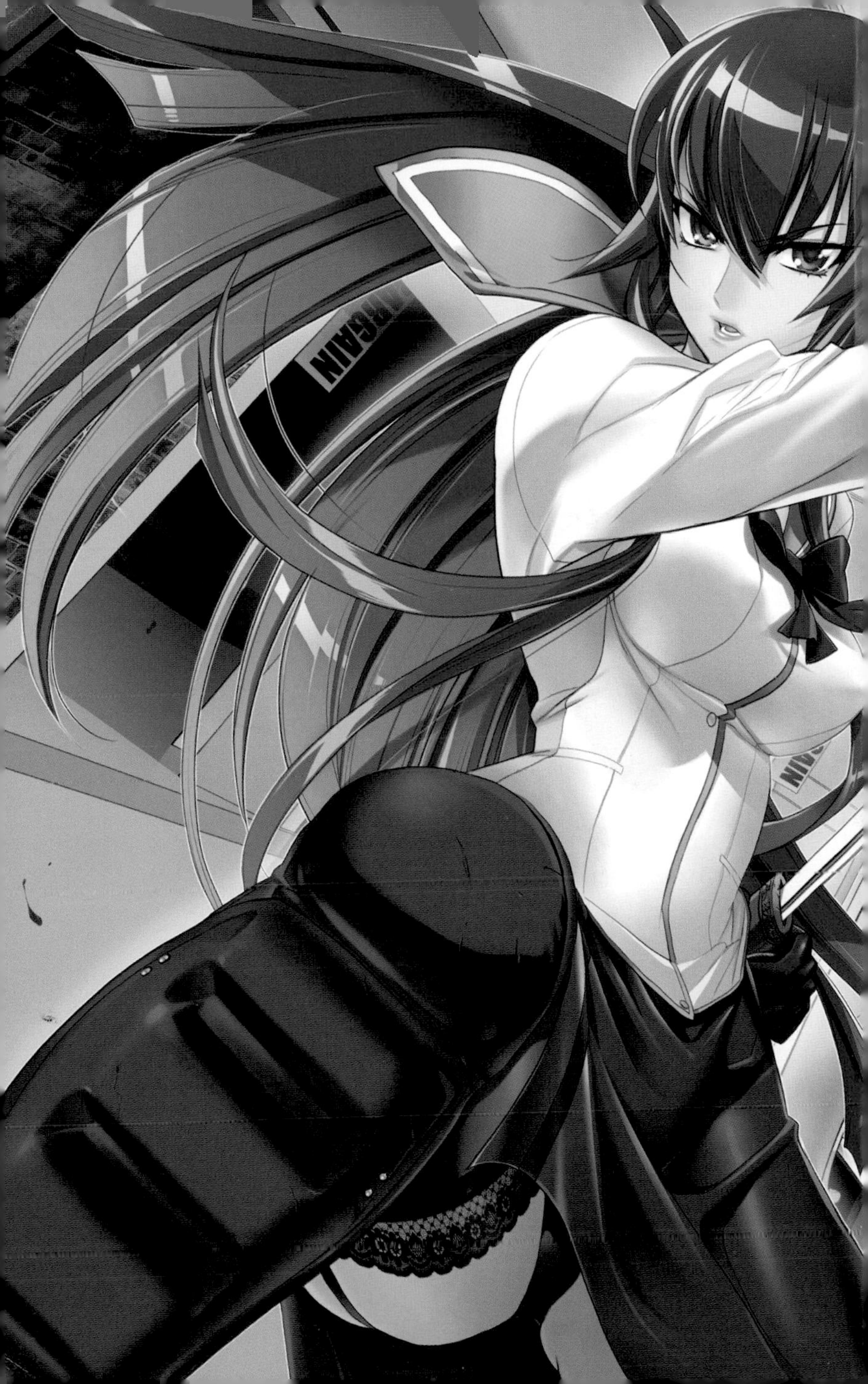

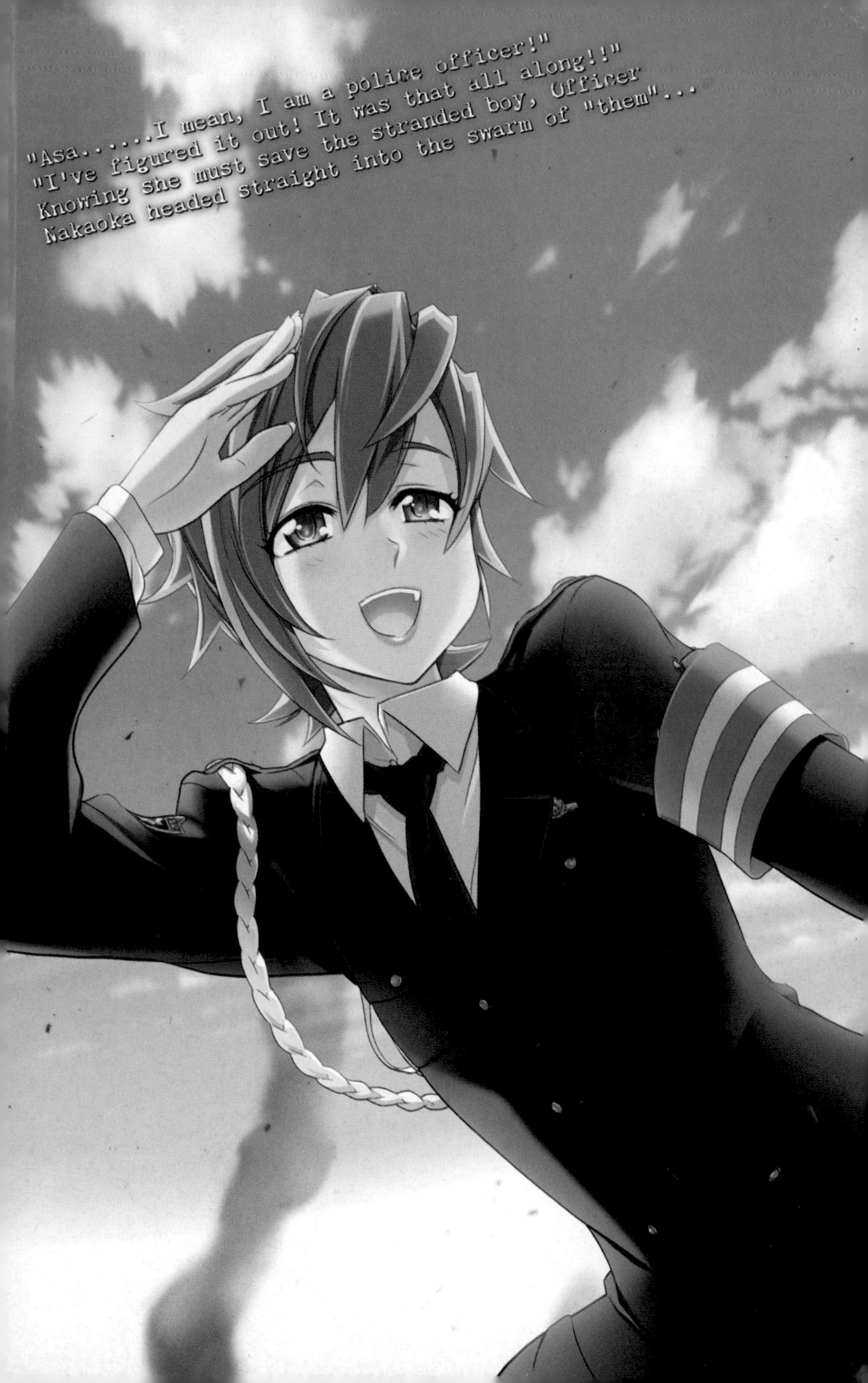
"Asa......I mean, I am a police officer!"
"I've figured it out! It was that all along!!"
Knowing she must save the stranded boy, Officer
Nakaoka headed straight into the swarm of "them"...

HIGHSCHOOL OF THE DEAD

6

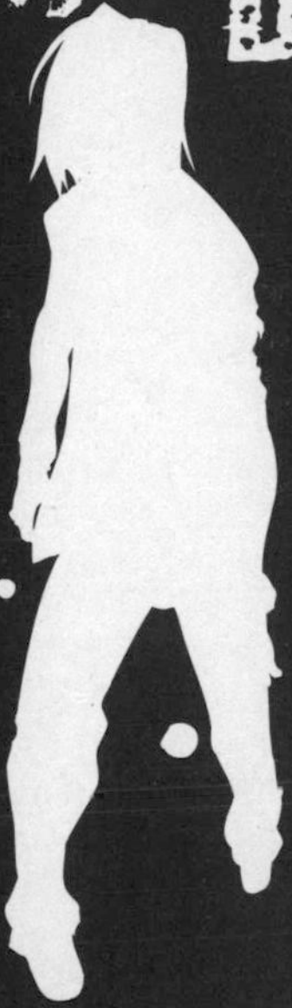

STORY BY
Daisuke Sato

ART BY
Shouji Sato

That was the day our once peaceful world
fell apart. A second-year at the private
school Fujimi High, Takashi Komuro escapes
from the living dead, known as "them," when
they suddenly storm his campus. He and his
childhood friend, Rei Miyamoto, join Saya
Takagi, Kouta Hirano, Saeko Busujima, and
the school nurse, Shizuka Marikawa, and flee
the school, seeking refuge in the home of
a friend of Marikawa-sensei's. Late that
night, they rescue a little girl named Alice
Maresato and welcome her into their group.

The next morning, the team heads to the
Takagi estate and is saved along the way by
Saya's mother and offered temporary sanctu-
ary in the Takagi mansion. Not long after,
a suspicious instructor from their school,
Shidou, arrives, and Rei finally exposes
the twisted relation he has to her, eventu-
ally driving him off the property. At the
same time, while the world powers panic over
the outbreak, an EMP attack is launched.
All electrical devices in the area cease
to function. In the ensuing chaos, "they"
breach the Takagi estate. Takashi and his
friends must leave Takagi's parents to
escape with their lives. In a town overrun
by "them," Takashi and Saeko make themselves
decoys to allow the other members to reach
the safety of the shopping mall, and the two
rejoin the group a short time later after
briefly taking shelter at a shrine.

At the mall, they encounter Officer Asami
and another group of refugees and manage to
avert a disaster between the two. The inci-
dent leads Asami to begin to develop feel-
ings for Kouta. In order to save a senior
among the refugees, a small party travels to
a nearby clinic, resulting in another vic-
tim. To make matters worse, the officer who
had gone out for help, Asami's senpai, has
been turned into one of "them," filling the
air in the mall with a sudden sense of doom.

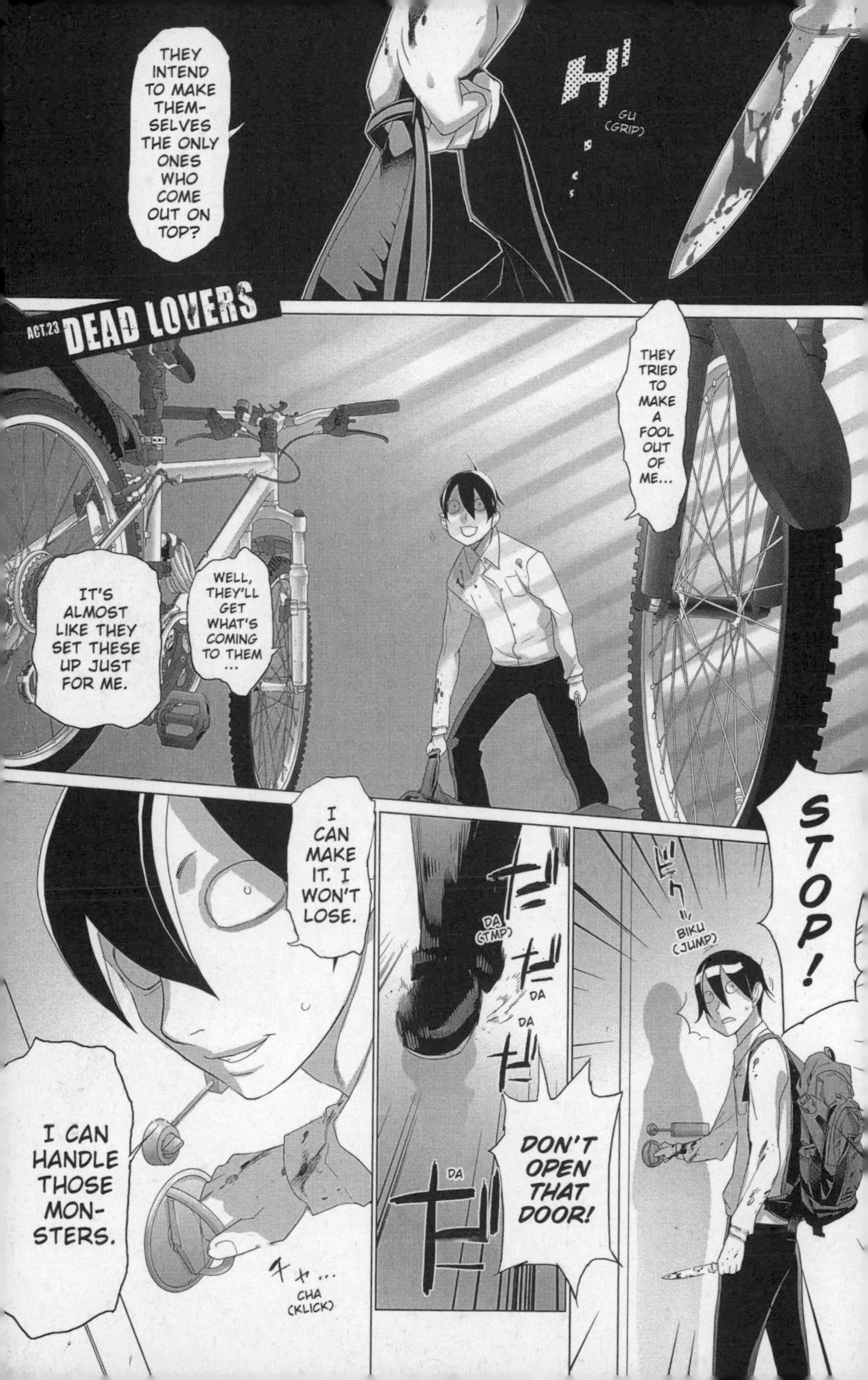
GU (GRIP)
THEY INTEND TO MAKE THEMSELVES THE ONLY ONES WHO COME OUT ON TOP?
ACT.23 DEAD LOVERS
THEY TRIED TO MAKE A FOOL OUT OF ME...
WELL, THEY'LL GET WHAT'S COMING TO THEM...
IT'S ALMOST LIKE THEY SET THESE UP JUST FOR ME.
STOP!
BIKU (JUMP)
DON'T OPEN THAT DOOR!
DA (TMP)
DA
DA
DA
I CAN MAKE IT. I WON'T LOSE.
I CAN HANDLE THOSE MONSTERS.
CHA (KLICK)

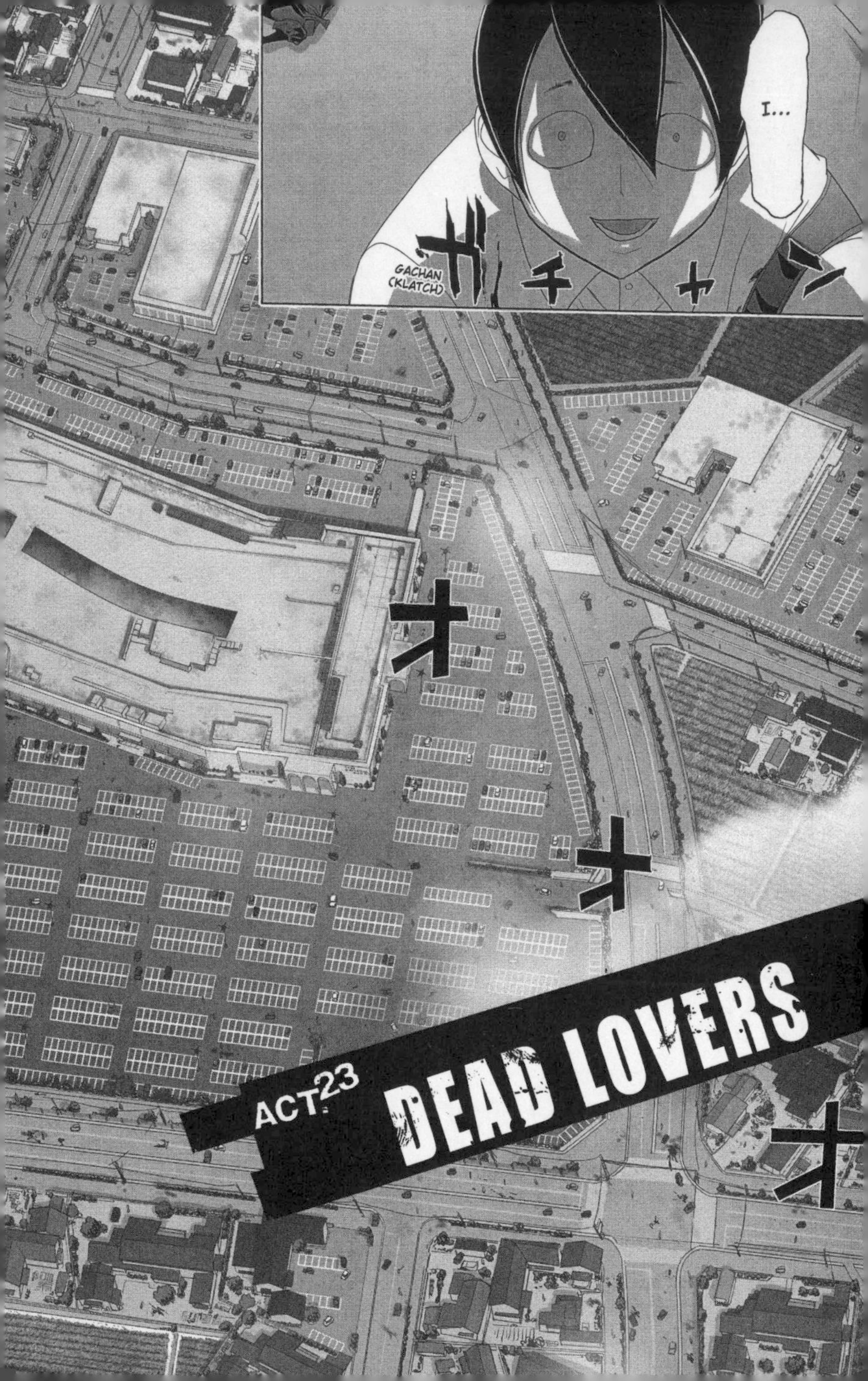
I...
GACHAN (KLATCH)
ACT 23
DEAD LOVERS

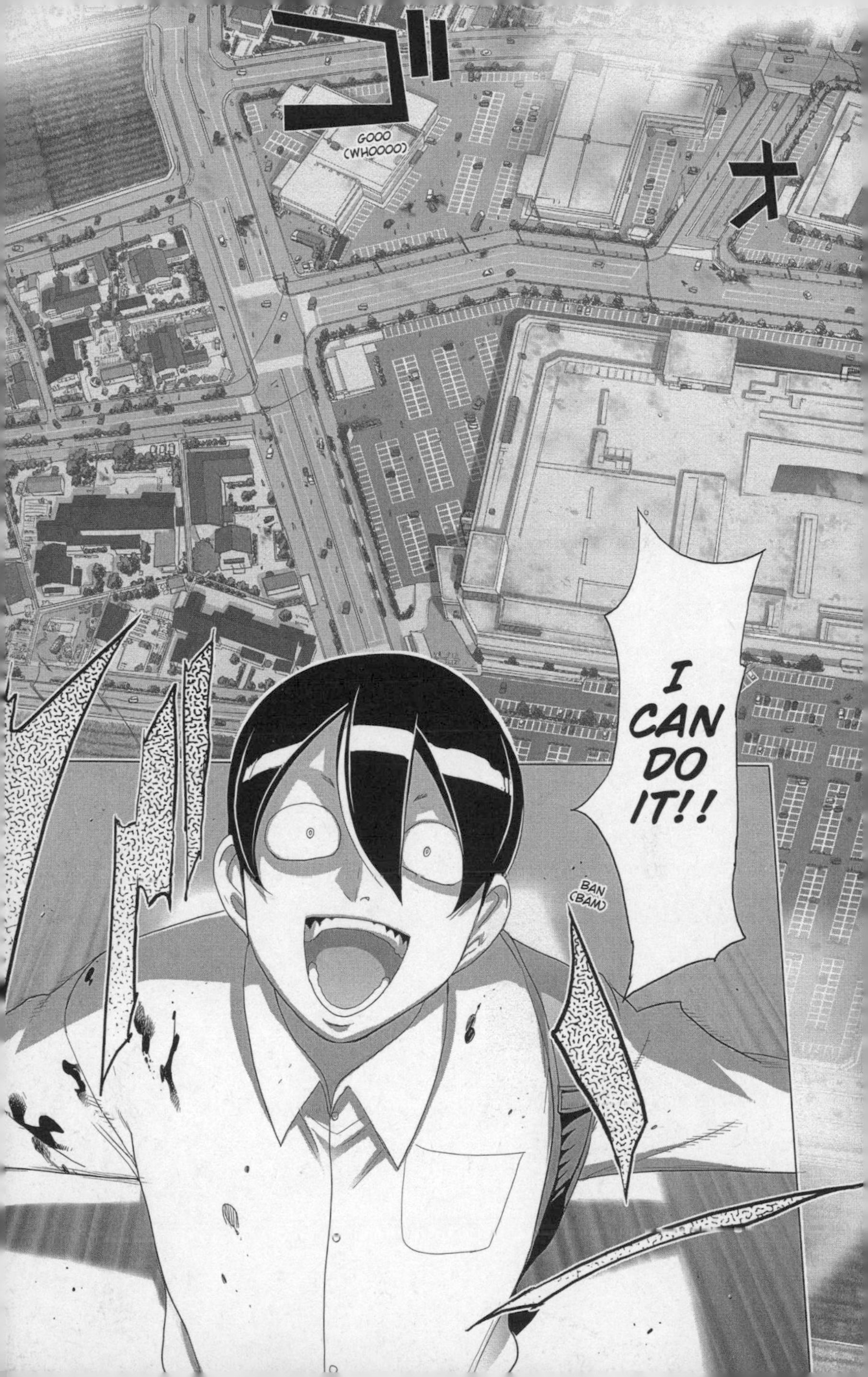
ゴオ
GOOO (WHOOOO)
I CAN DO IT!!
BAN (BAM)

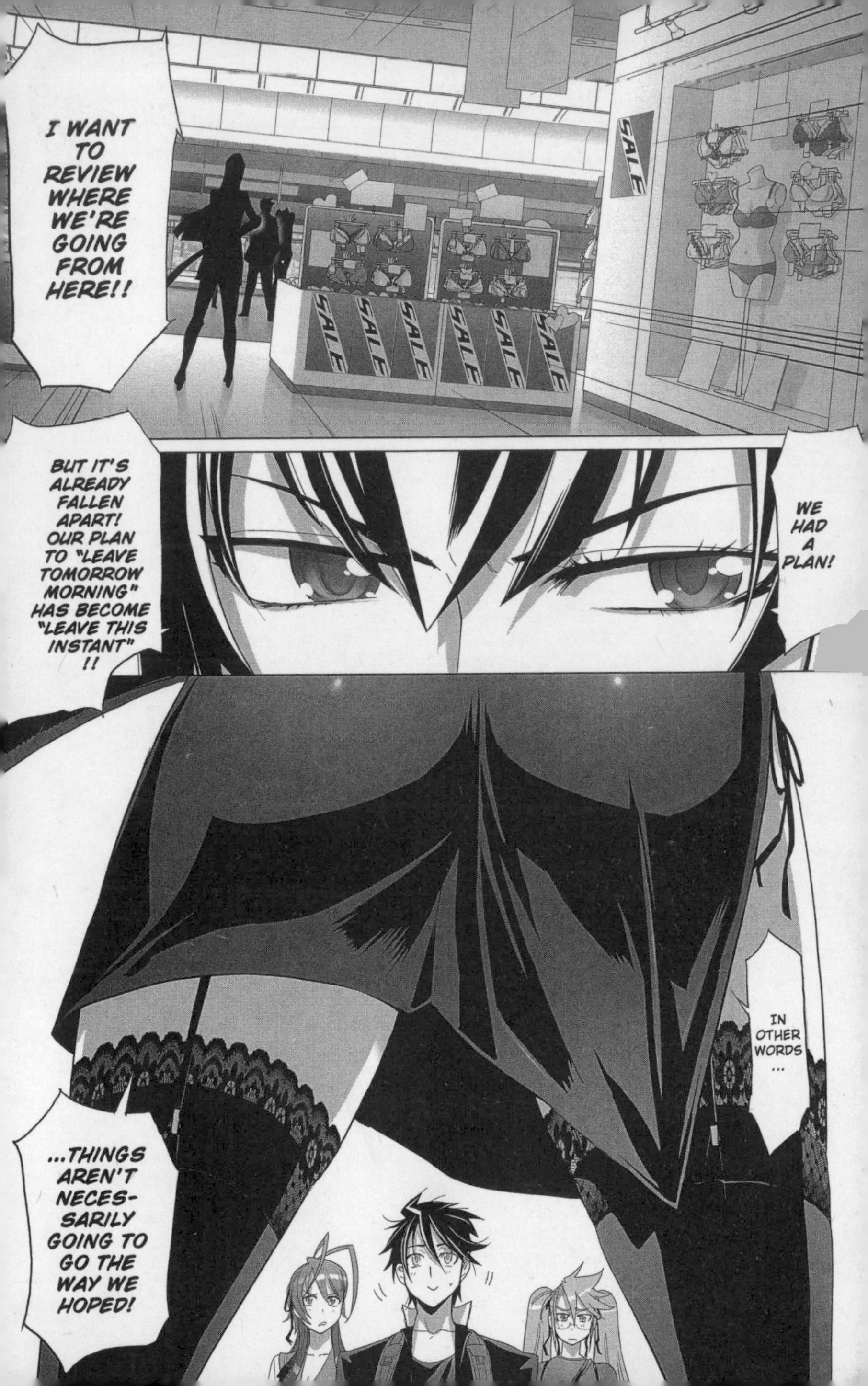
I WANT TO REVIEW WHERE WE'RE GOING FROM HERE!!
WE HAD A PLAN!
BUT IT'S ALREADY FALLEN APART! OUR PLAN TO "LEAVE TOMORROW MORNING" HAS BECOME "LEAVE THIS INSTANT"!!
SALE
IN OTHER WORDS...
...THINGS AREN'T NECES-SARILY GOING TO GO THE WAY WE HOPED!

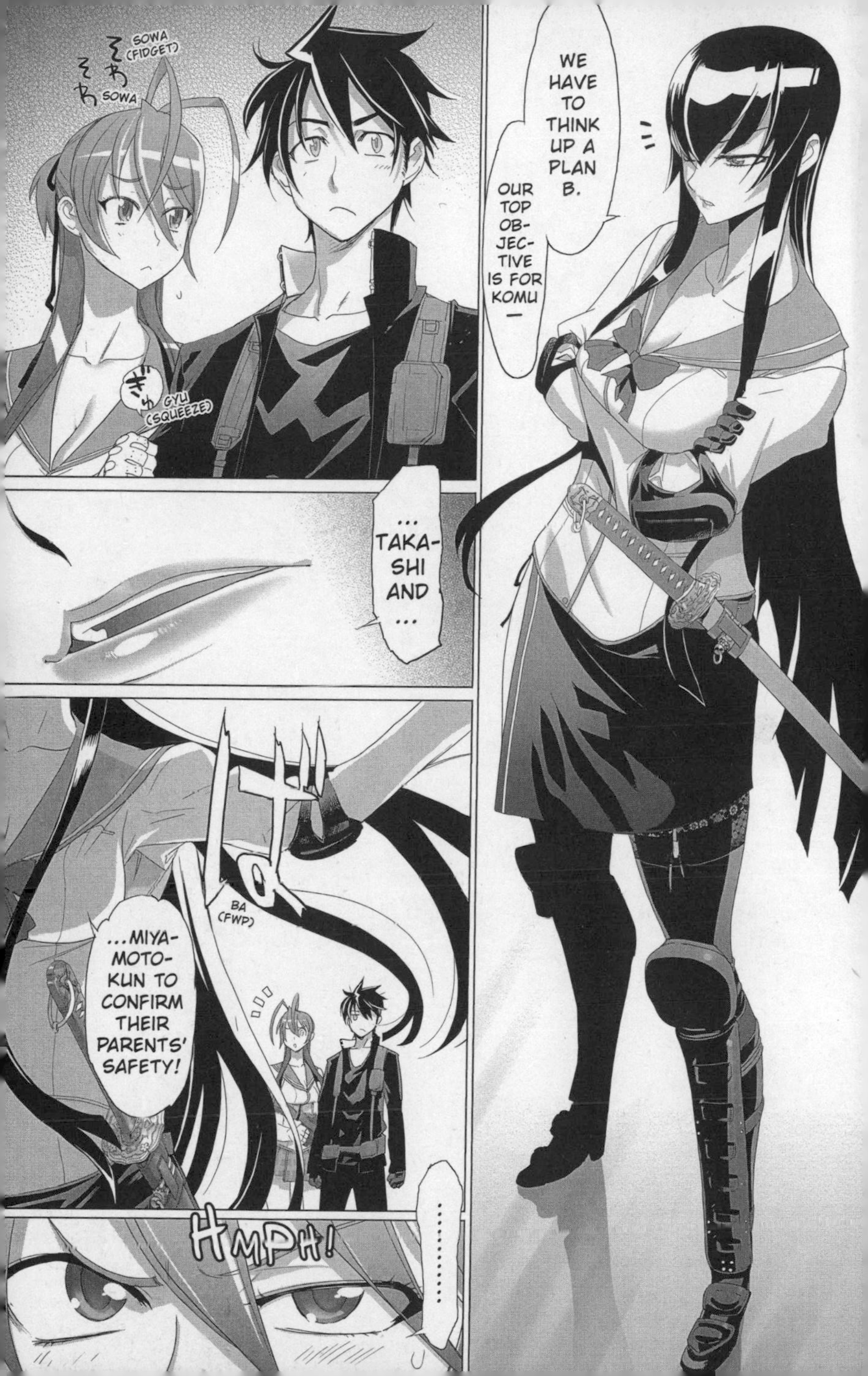
WE HAVE TO THINK UP A PLAN B.
OUR TOP OBJECTIVE IS FOR KOMU—
SOWA (FIDGET)
SOWA
GYU (SQUEEZE)
...TAKASHI AND...
BA (FWP)
...MIYAMOTO-KUN TO CONFIRM THEIR PARENTS' SAFETY!
HMPH!
......

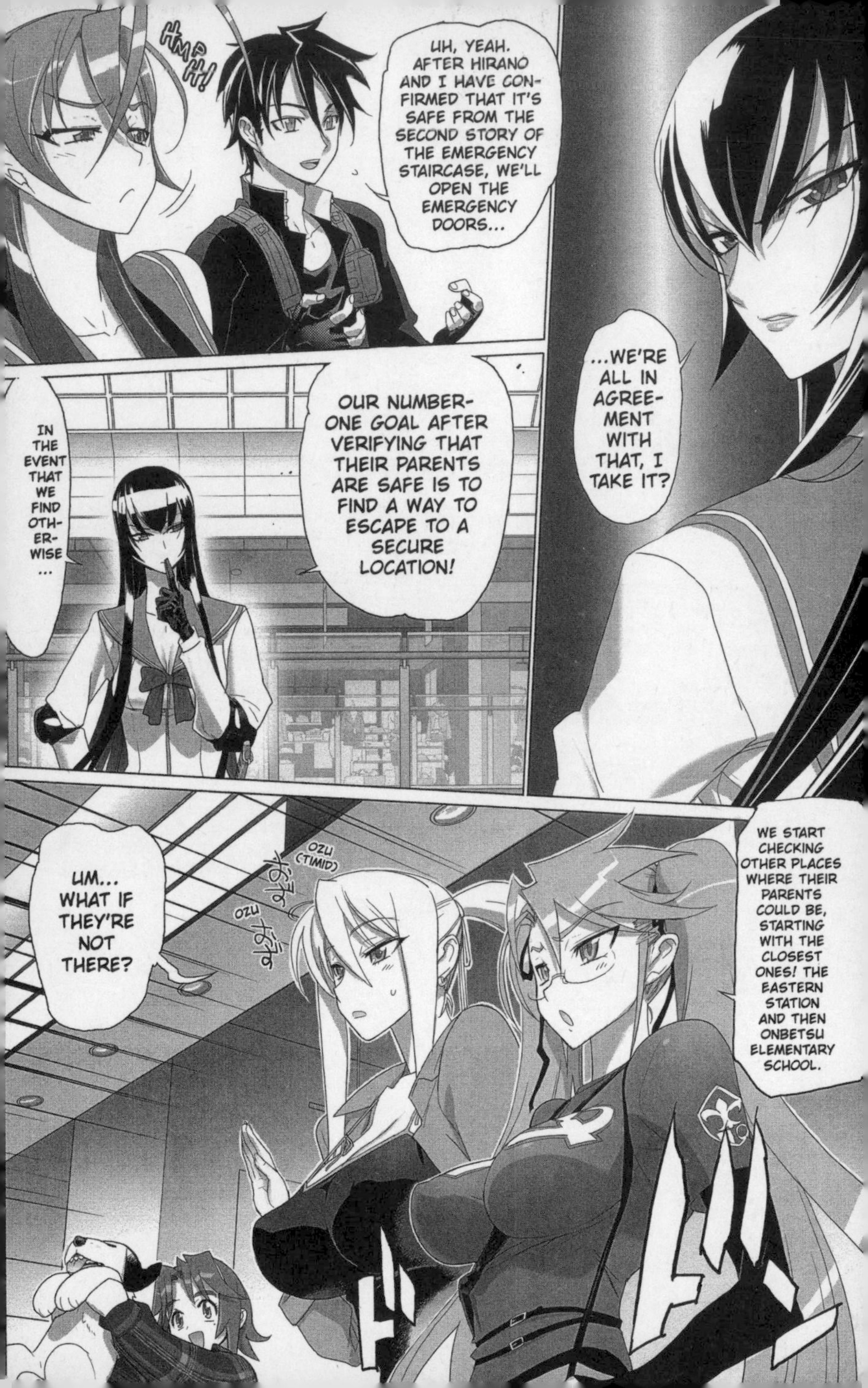
...WE'RE ALL IN AGREEMENT WITH THAT, I TAKE IT?
HMPH!
UH, YEAH. AFTER HIRANO AND I HAVE CONFIRMED THAT IT'S SAFE FROM THE SECOND STORY OF THE EMERGENCY STAIRCASE, WE'LL OPEN THE EMERGENCY DOORS...
OUR NUMBER-ONE GOAL AFTER VERIFYING THAT THEIR PARENTS ARE SAFE IS TO FIND A WAY TO ESCAPE TO A SECURE LOCATION!
IN THE EVENT THAT WE FIND OTHERWISE...
WE START CHECKING OTHER PLACES WHERE THEIR PARENTS COULD BE, STARTING WITH THE CLOSEST ONES! THE EASTERN STATION AND THEN ONBETSU ELEMENTARY SCHOOL.
OZU (TIMID)
OZU
UM... WHAT IF THEY'RE NOT THERE?

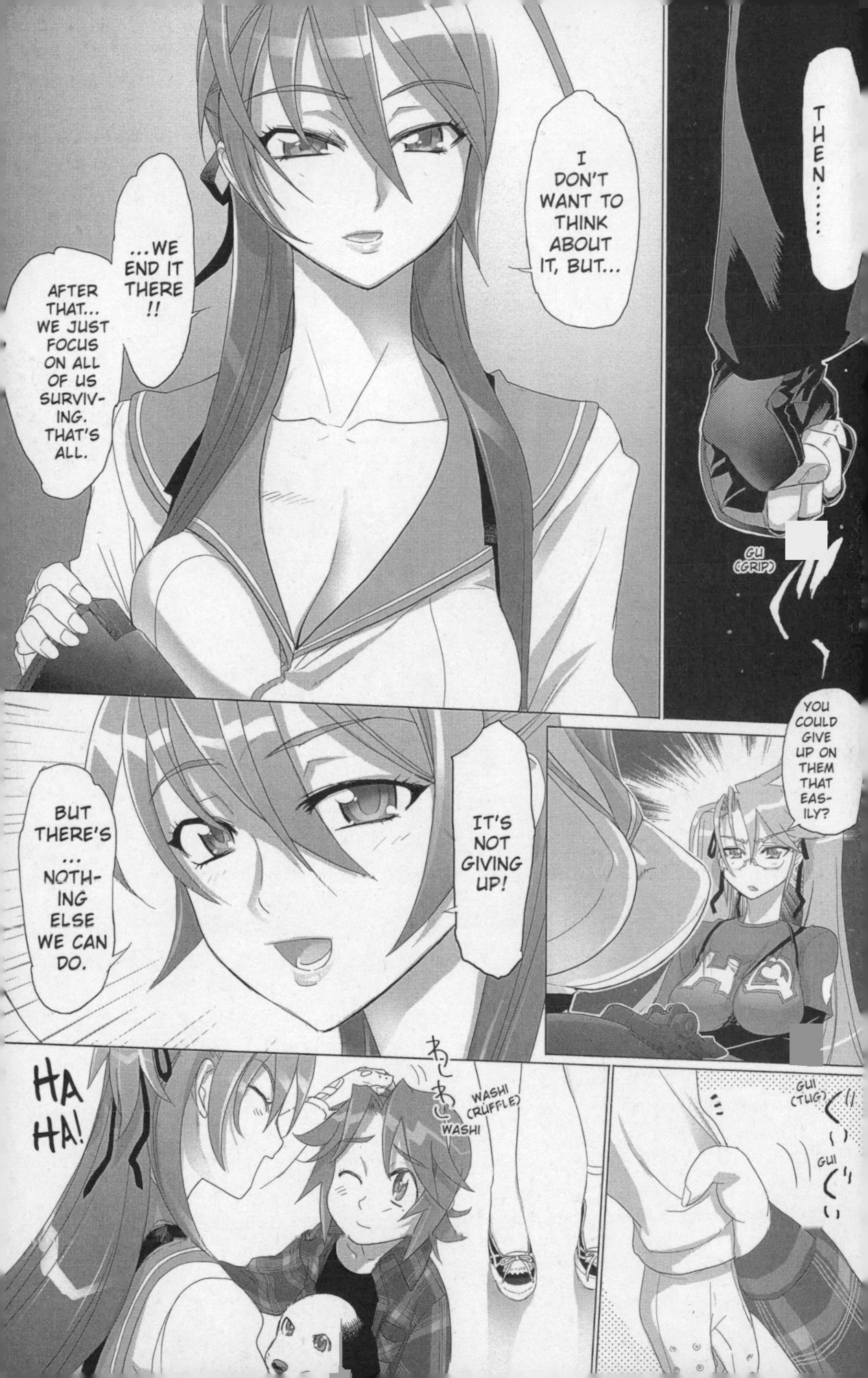
THEN......
GU (GRIP)
I DON'T WANT TO THINK ABOUT IT, BUT...
...WE END IT THERE!!
AFTER THAT... WE JUST FOCUS ON ALL OF US SURVIVING. THAT'S ALL.
YOU COULD GIVE UP ON THEM THAT EASILY?
IT'S NOT GIVING UP!
BUT THERE'S... NOTHING ELSE WE CAN DO.
...
GUI (TUG)
GUI
わしわし
WASHI (RÜFFLE)
WASHI
HA HA!

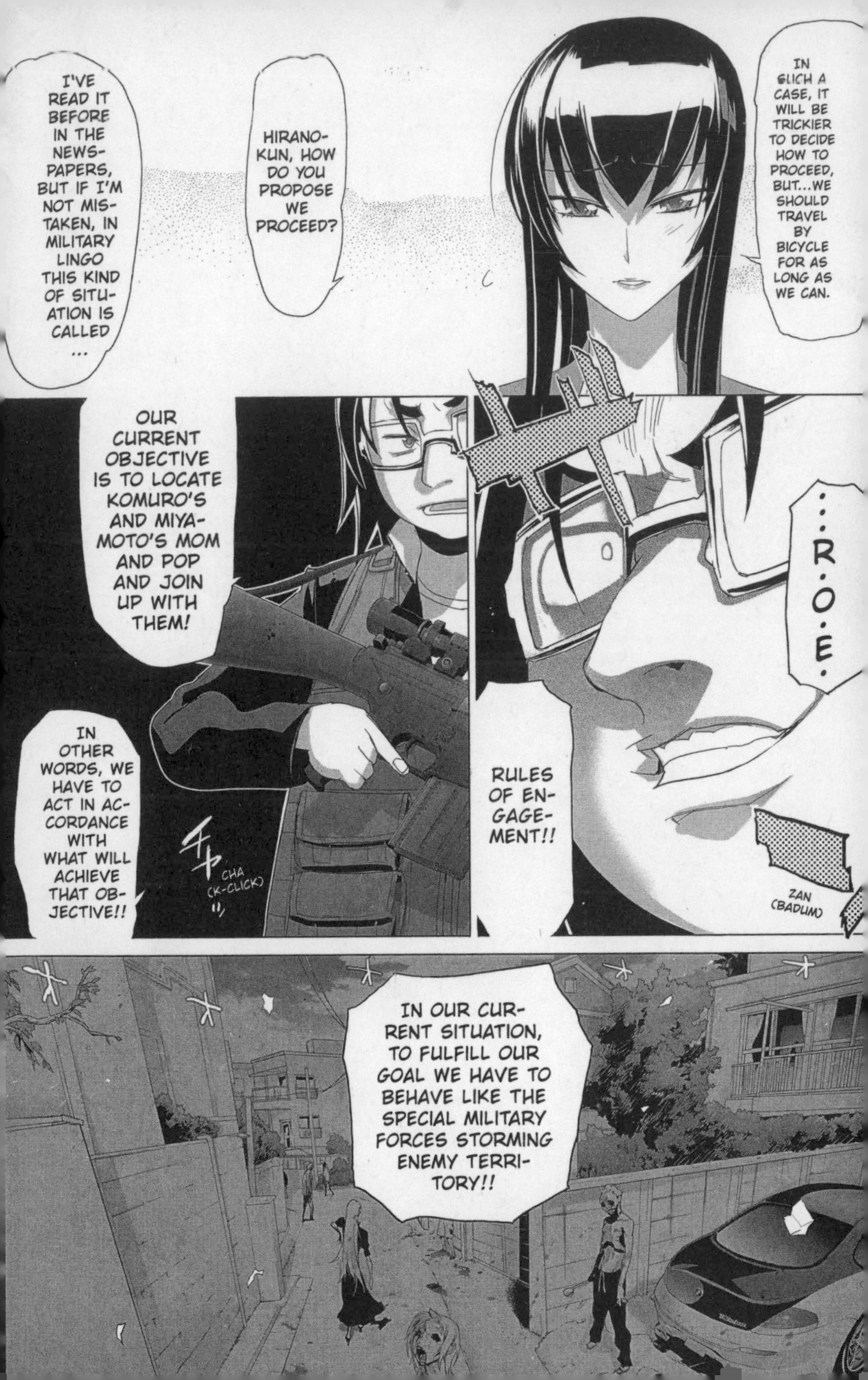
IN SUCH A CASE, IT WILL BE TRICKIER TO DECIDE HOW TO PROCEED, BUT...WE SHOULD TRAVEL BY BICYCLE FOR AS LONG AS WE CAN.
HIRANO-KUN, HOW DO YOU PROPOSE WE PROCEED?
I'VE READ IT BEFORE IN THE NEWSPAPERS, BUT IF I'M NOT MISTAKEN, IN MILITARY LINGO THIS KIND OF SITUATION IS CALLED ...
...R.O.E.
RULES OF ENGAGEMENT!!
ZAN (BADUM)
OUR CURRENT OBJECTIVE IS TO LOCATE KOMURO'S AND MIYAMOTO'S MOM AND POP AND JOIN UP WITH THEM!
IN OTHER WORDS, WE HAVE TO ACT IN ACCORDANCE WITH WHAT WILL ACHIEVE THAT OBJECTIVE!!
CHA (K-CLICK)
IN OUR CURRENT SITUATION, TO FULFILL OUR GOAL WE HAVE TO BEHAVE LIKE THE SPECIAL MILITARY FORCES STORMING ENEMY TERRITORY!!

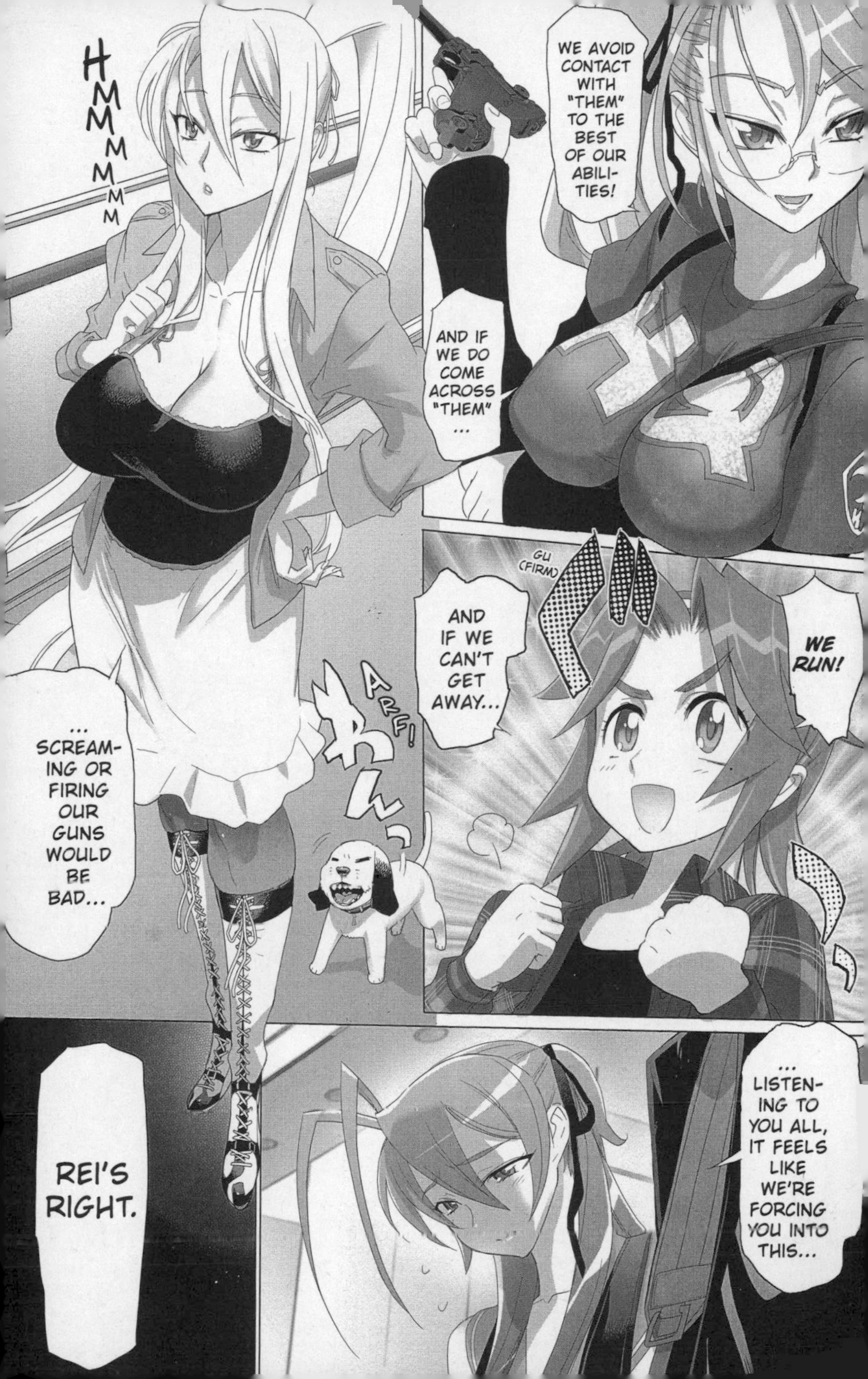
WE AVOID CONTACT WITH "THEM" TO THE BEST OF OUR ABILITIES!
AND IF WE DO COME ACROSS "THEM"...
GU (FIRM)
WE RUN!
AND IF WE CAN'T GET AWAY...
HMMMMMMM
ARF!
...SCREAMING OR FIRING OUR GUNS WOULD BE BAD...
...LISTENING TO YOU ALL, IT FEELS LIKE WE'RE FORCING YOU INTO THIS...
REI'S RIGHT.

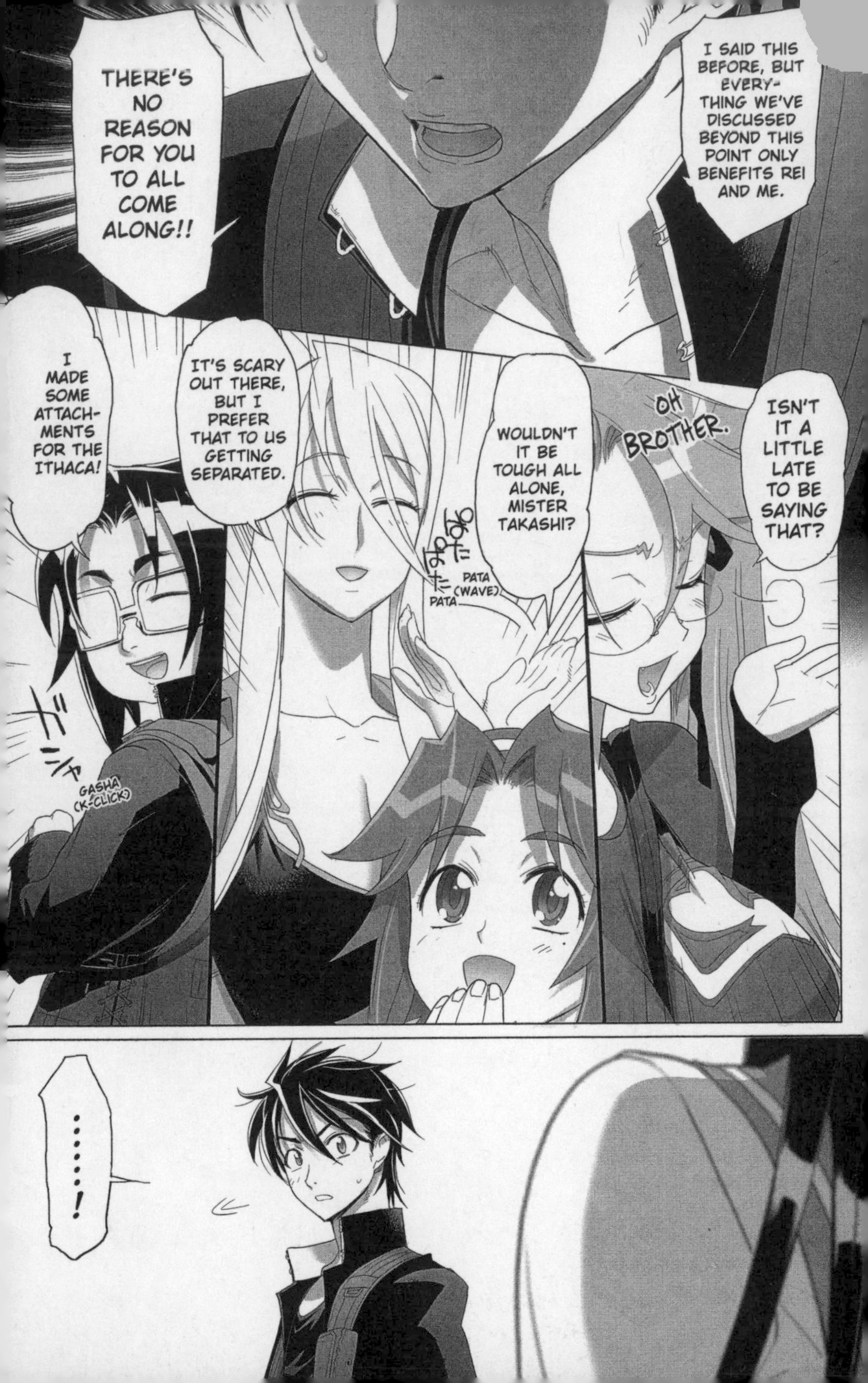
I SAID THIS BEFORE, BUT EVERY-THING WE'VE DISCUSSED BEYOND THIS POINT ONLY BENEFITS REI AND ME.
THERE'S NO REASON FOR YOU TO ALL COME ALONG!!
ISN'T IT A LITTLE LATE TO BE SAYING THAT?
OH BROTHER.
WOULDN'T IT BE TOUGH ALL ALONE, MISTER TAKASHI?
ぱたぱた
PATA PATA (WAVE)
IT'S SCARY OUT THERE, BUT I PREFER THAT TO US GETTING SEPARATED.
I MADE SOME ATTACH-MENTS FOR THE ITHACA!
ガシャ
GASHA (K-CLICK)
......!

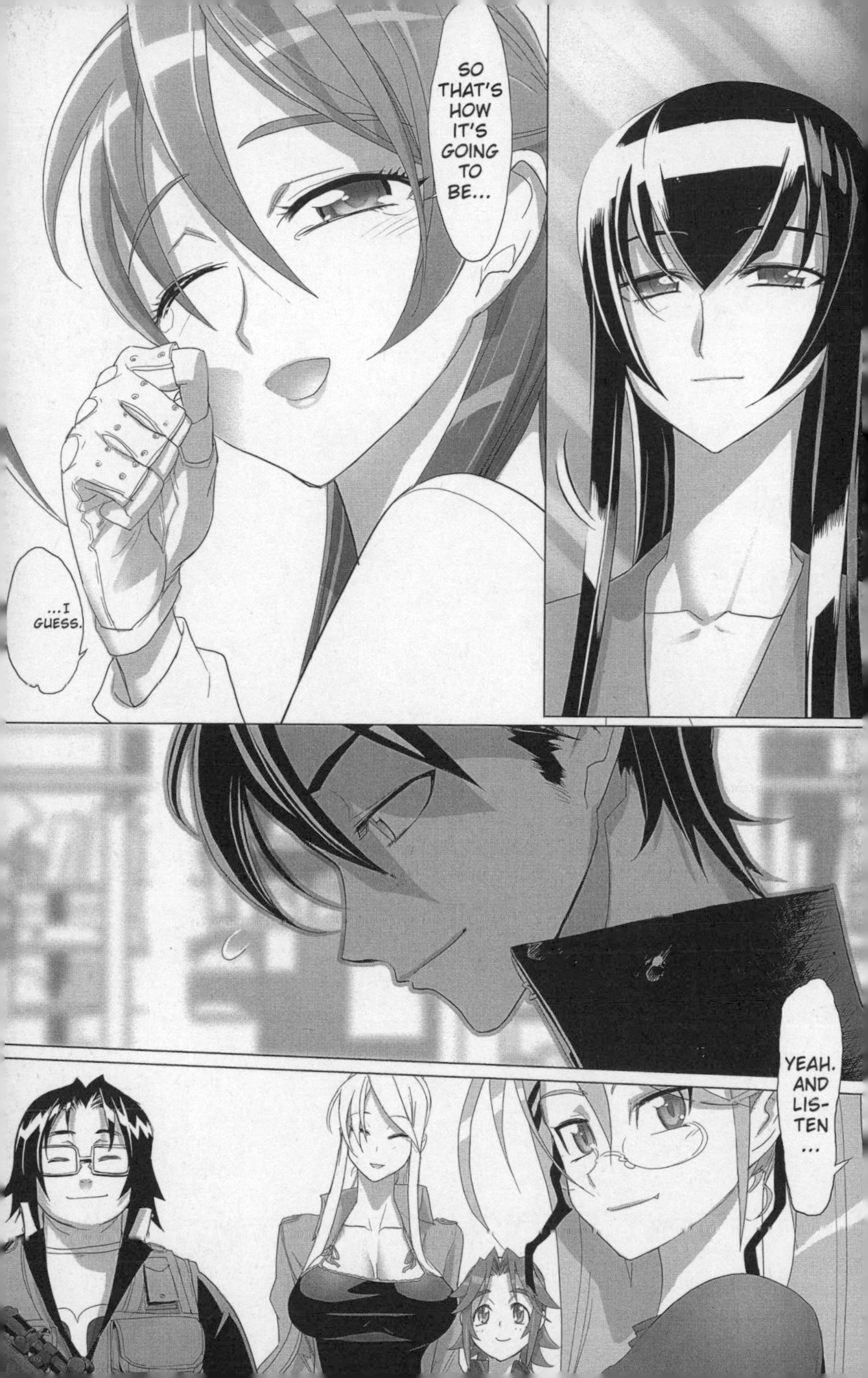
SO THAT'S HOW IT'S GOING TO BE...
...I GUESS.
YEAH. AND LIS-TEN ...

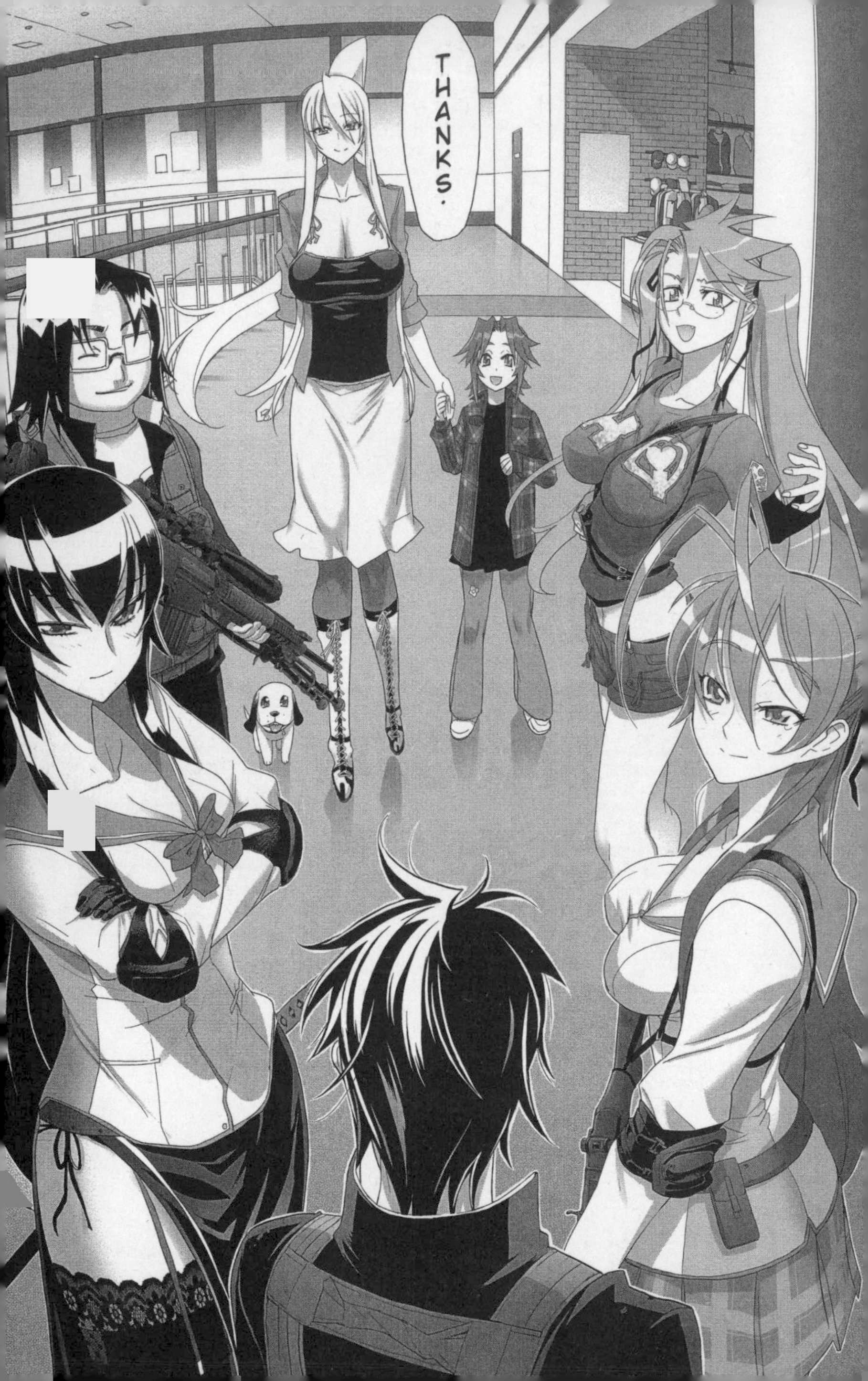
THANKS.

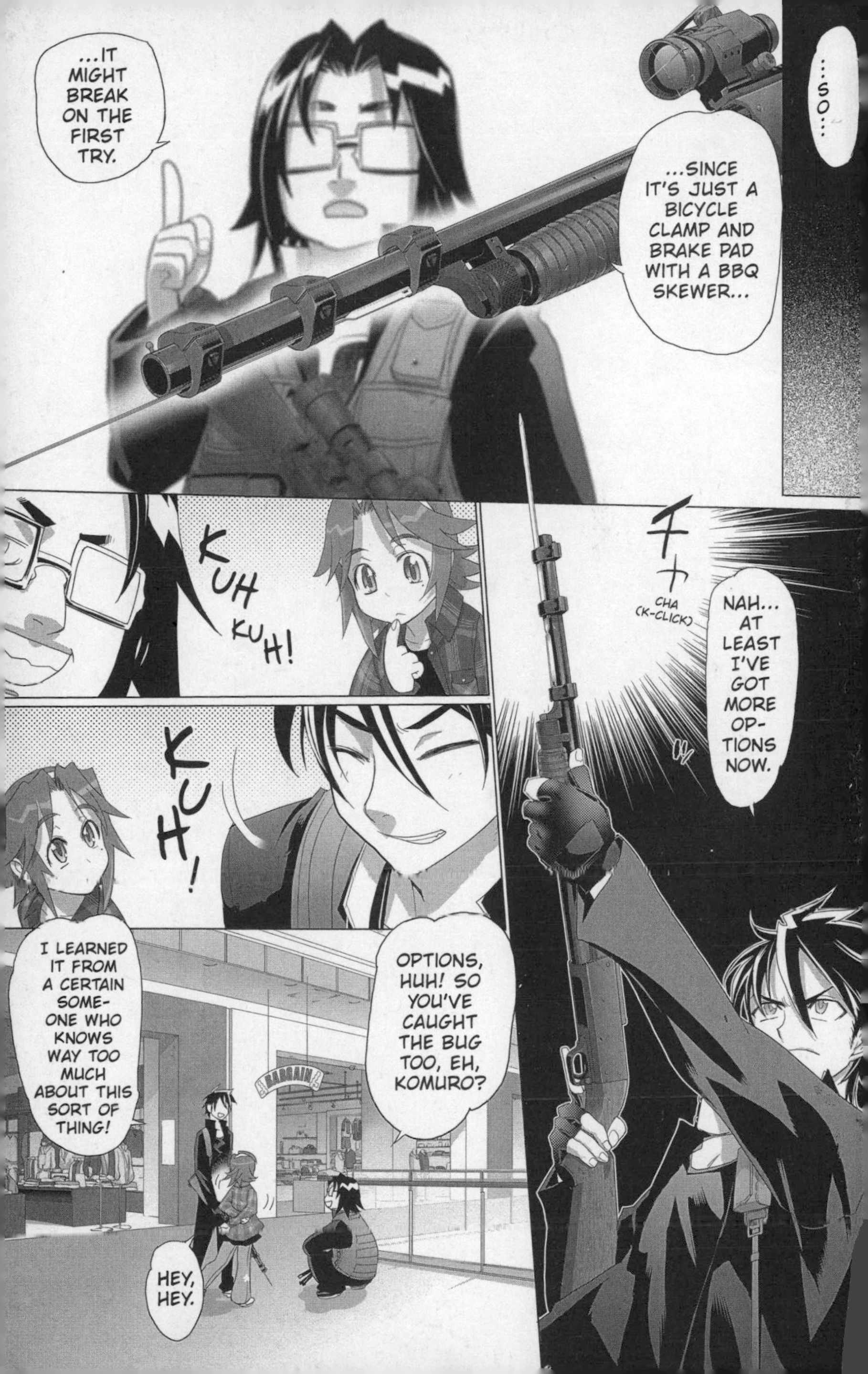
...SO...
...SINCE IT'S JUST A BICYCLE CLAMP AND BRAKE PAD WITH A BBQ SKEWER...
...IT MIGHT BREAK ON THE FIRST TRY.
チャ
CHA (K-CLICK)
NAH... AT LEAST I'VE GOT MORE OP-TIONS NOW.
KUH KUH!
KUH!
OPTIONS, HUH! SO YOU'VE CAUGHT THE BUG TOO, EH, KOMURO?
I LEARNED IT FROM A CERTAIN SOME-ONE WHO KNOWS WAY TOO MUCH ABOUT THIS SORT OF THING!
BARGAIN
HEY, HEY.

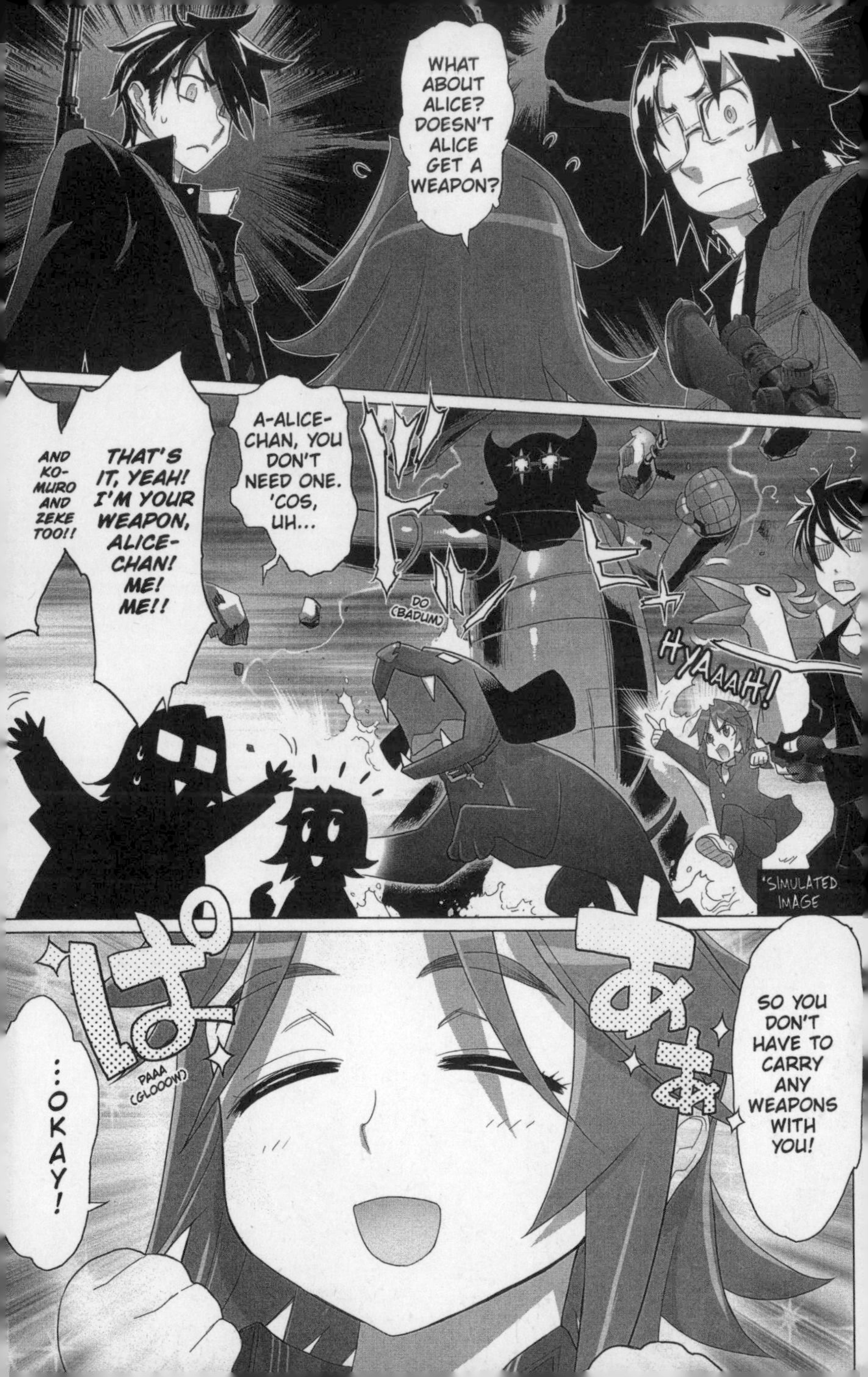

WHAT ABOUT ALICE? DOESN'T ALICE GET A WEAPON?
HYAAAH!
DO (BADUM)
A-ALICE-CHAN, YOU DON'T NEED ONE. 'COS, UH...
THAT'S IT, YEAH! I'M YOUR WEAPON, ALICE-CHAN! ME! ME!!
AND KOMURO AND ZEKE TOO!!
*SIMULATED IMAGE
SO YOU DON'T HAVE TO CARRY ANY WEAPONS WITH YOU!
ぱあぁ
PAAA (GLOOOW)
...OKAY!

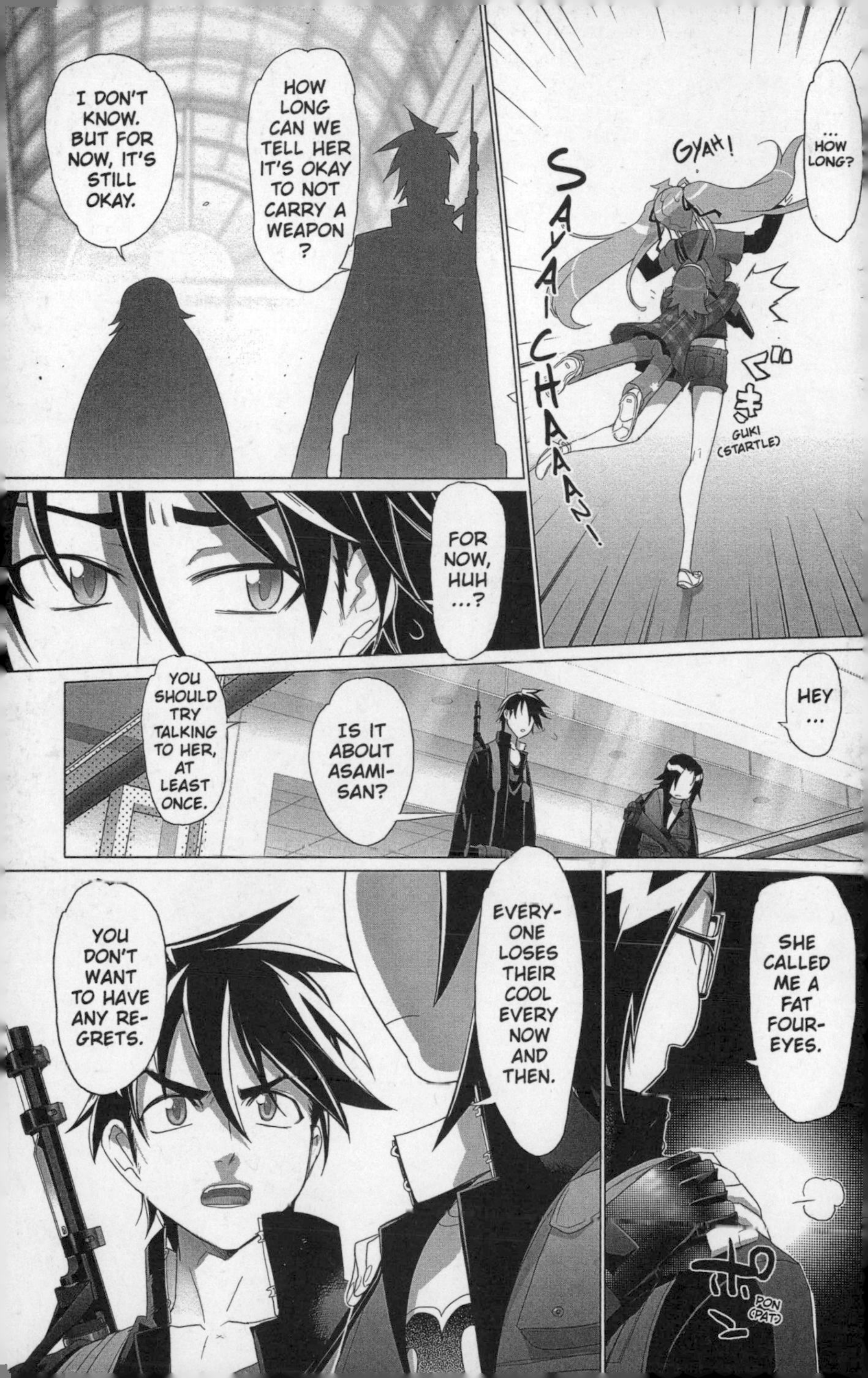

...HOW LONG?
GYAH!
SAYAI CHAAAAAN!
GUKI (STARTLE)
HOW LONG CAN WE TELL HER IT'S OKAY TO NOT CARRY A WEAPON?
I DON'T KNOW. BUT FOR NOW, IT'S STILL OKAY.
FOR NOW, HUH...?
HEY...
IS IT ABOUT ASAMI-SAN?
YOU SHOULD TRY TALKING TO HER, AT LEAST ONCE.
SHE CALLED ME A FAT FOUR-EYES.
PON (PAT)
EVERYONE LOSES THEIR COOL EVERY NOW AND THEN.
YOU DON'T WANT TO HAVE ANY REGRETS.

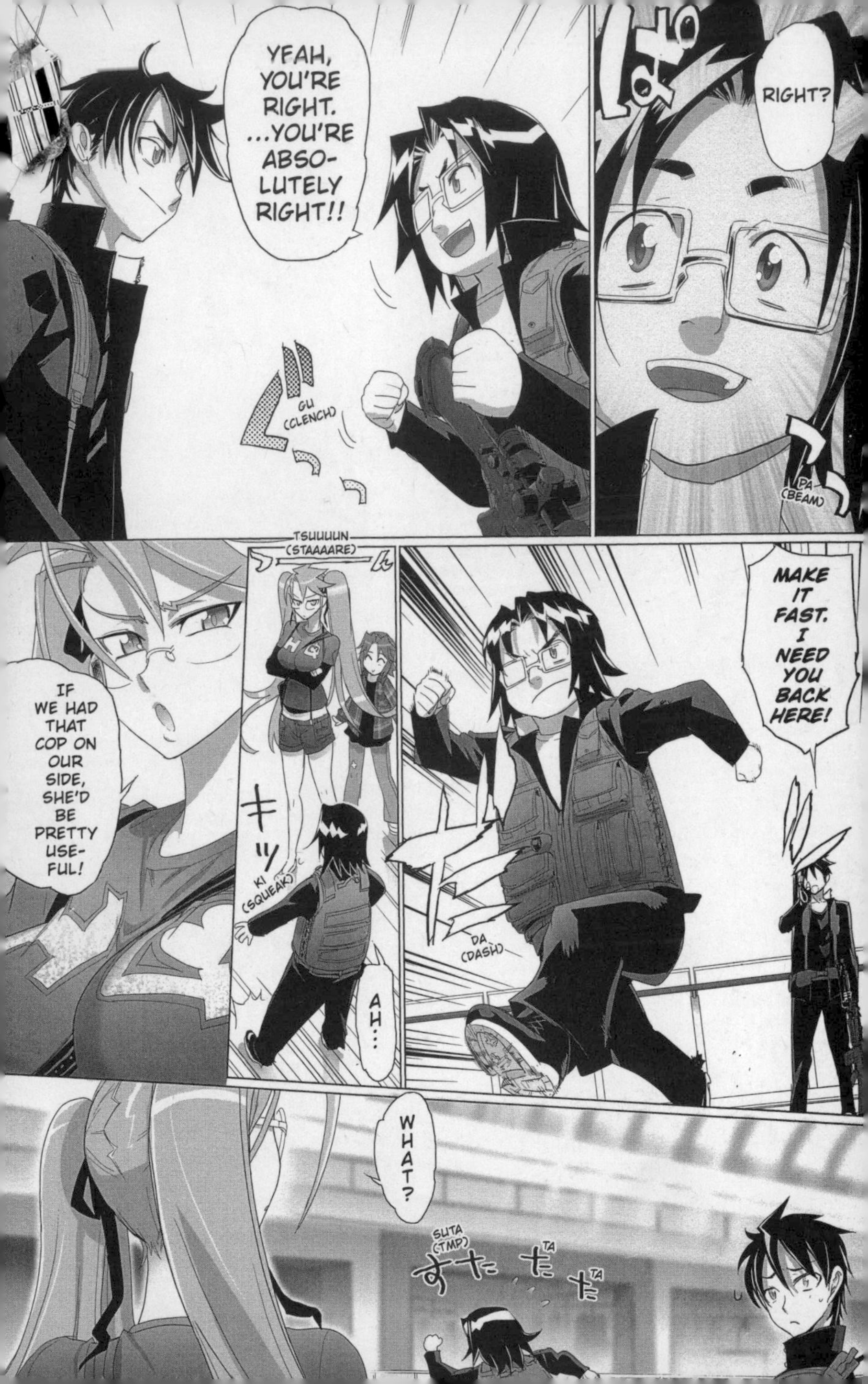
RIGHT?
PA (BEAM)
YEAH, YOU'RE RIGHT. ...YOU'RE ABSOLUTELY RIGHT!!
GU (CLENCH)
MAKE IT FAST. I NEED YOU BACK HERE!
DA (DASH)
TSUUUUN (STAAAARE)
KI (SQUEAK)
AH...
IF WE HAD THAT COP ON OUR SIDE, SHE'D BE PRETTY USEFUL!
WHAT?
SUTA (TMP)
TA
TA

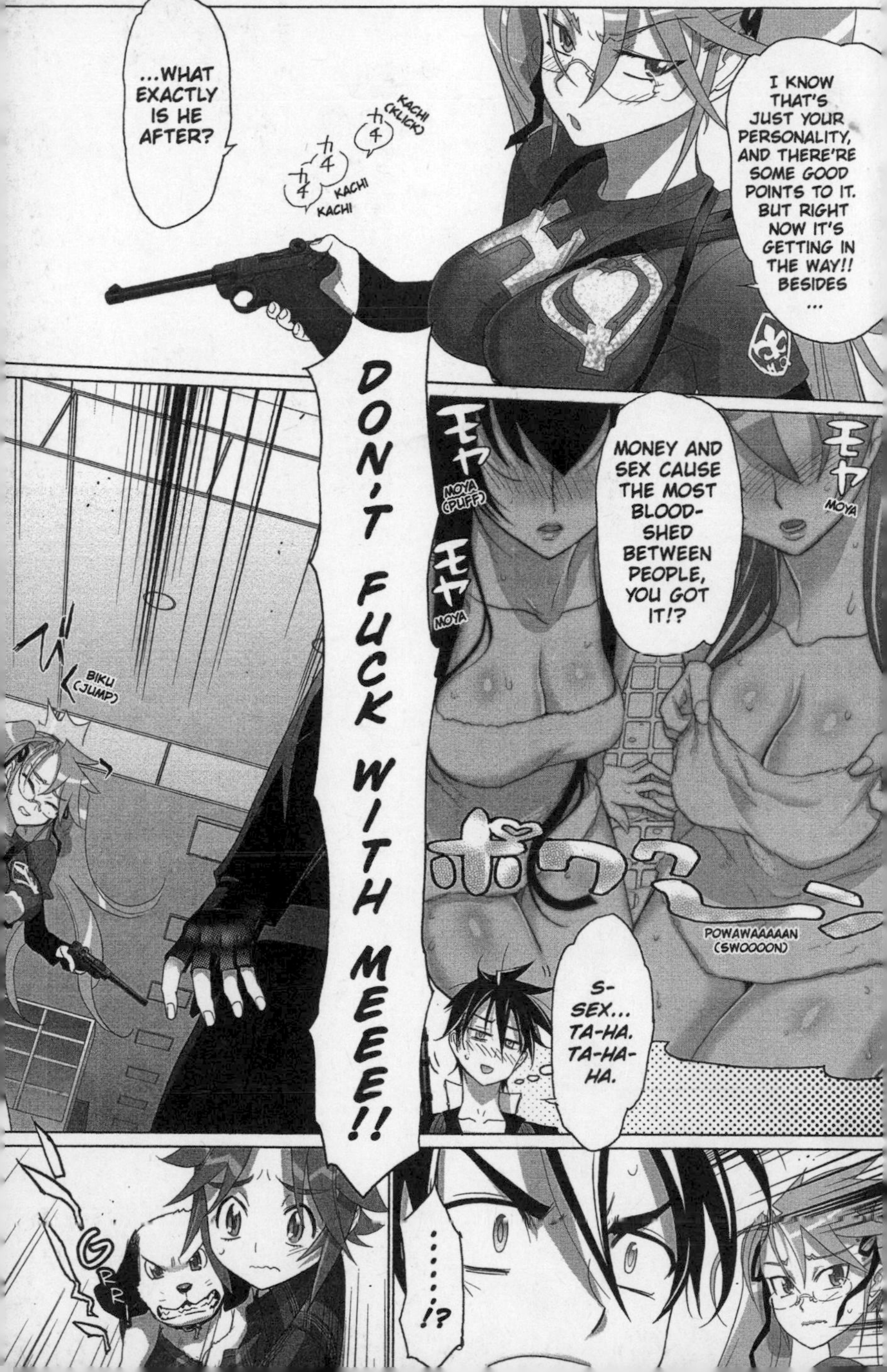

I KNOW THAT'S JUST YOUR PERSONALITY, AND THERE'RE SOME GOOD POINTS TO IT. BUT RIGHT NOW IT'S GETTING IN THE WAY!! BESIDES ...
KACHI (KLICK)
KACHI
KACHI
...WHAT EXACTLY IS HE AFTER?
MOYA
MONEY AND SEX CAUSE THE MOST BLOOD-SHED BETWEEN PEOPLE, YOU GOT IT!?
MOYA (PUFF)
MOYA
POWAWAAAAAN (SWOOOON)
S-SEX... TA-HA. TA-HA-HA.
DON'T FUCK WITH MEEE!!
BIKU (JUMP)
......!?
GRR

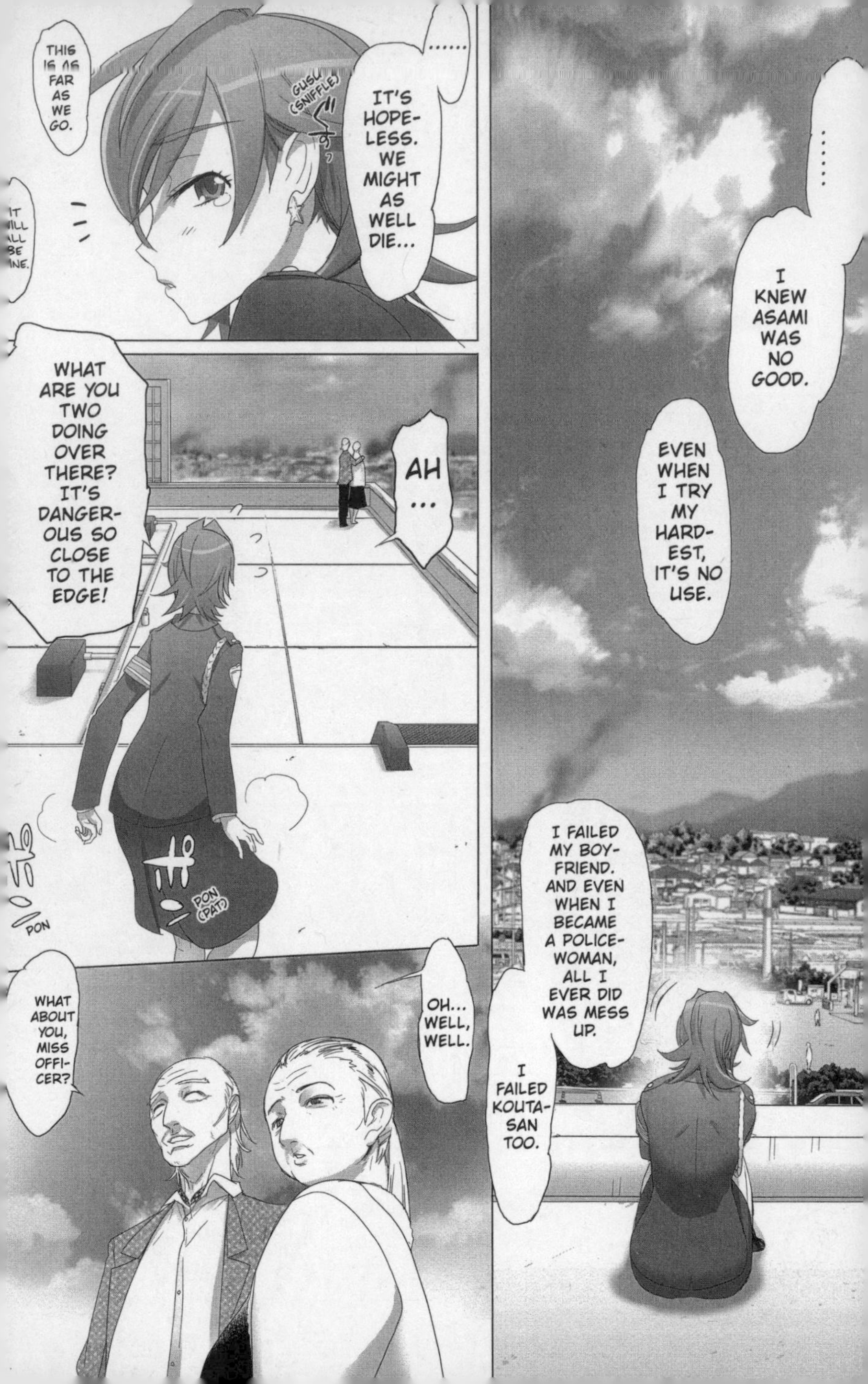
......
I KNEW ASAMI WAS NO GOOD.
EVEN WHEN I TRY MY HARDEST, IT'S NO USE.
I FAILED MY BOYFRIEND. AND EVEN WHEN I BECAME A POLICEWOMAN, ALL I EVER DID WAS MESS UP.
I FAILED KOUTA-SAN TOO.
......
IT'S HOPELESS. WE MIGHT AS WELL DIE...
GUSU (SNIFFLE)
THIS IS AS FAR AS WE GO.
IT WILL ALL BE
AH...
WHAT ARE YOU TWO DOING OVER THERE? IT'S DANGEROUS SO CLOSE TO THE EDGE!
PON (PAT)
PON
OH... WELL, WELL.
WHAT ABOUT YOU, MISS OFFICER?

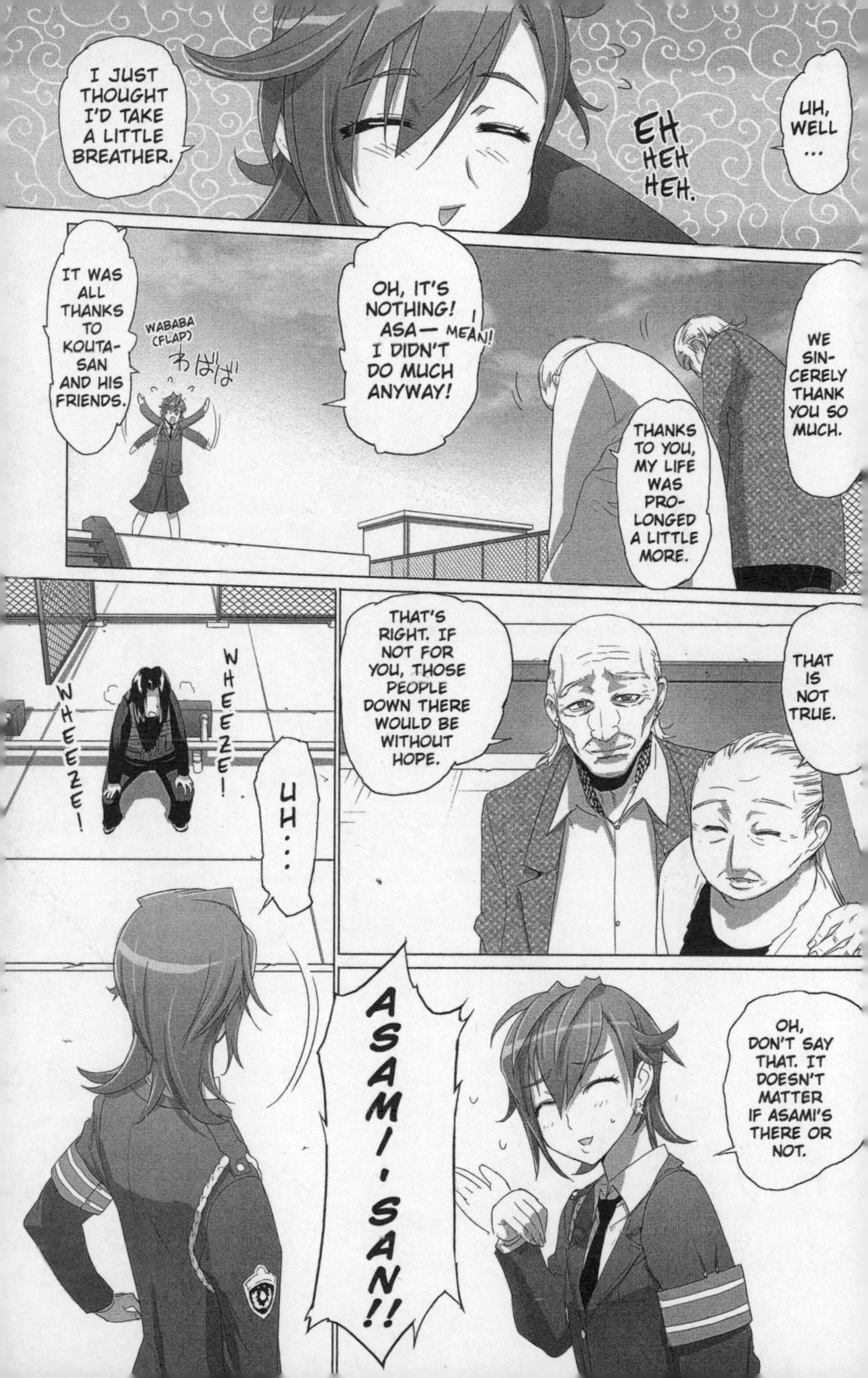
UH, WELL...
EH HEH HEH.
I JUST THOUGHT I'D TAKE A LITTLE BREATHER.
WE SINCERELY THANK YOU SO MUCH.
THANKS TO YOU, MY LIFE WAS PROLONGED A LITTLE MORE.
OH, IT'S NOTHING! ASA— I MEAN! I DIDN'T DO MUCH ANYWAY!
WABABA (FLAP)
わばば
IT WAS ALL THANKS TO KOUTA-SAN AND HIS FRIENDS.
THAT IS NOT TRUE.
THAT'S RIGHT. IF NOT FOR YOU, THOSE PEOPLE DOWN THERE WOULD BE WITHOUT HOPE.
OH, DON'T SAY THAT. IT DOESN'T MATTER IF ASAMI'S THERE OR NOT.
WHEEZE!
WHEEZE!
UH...
ASAMI-SAN!!

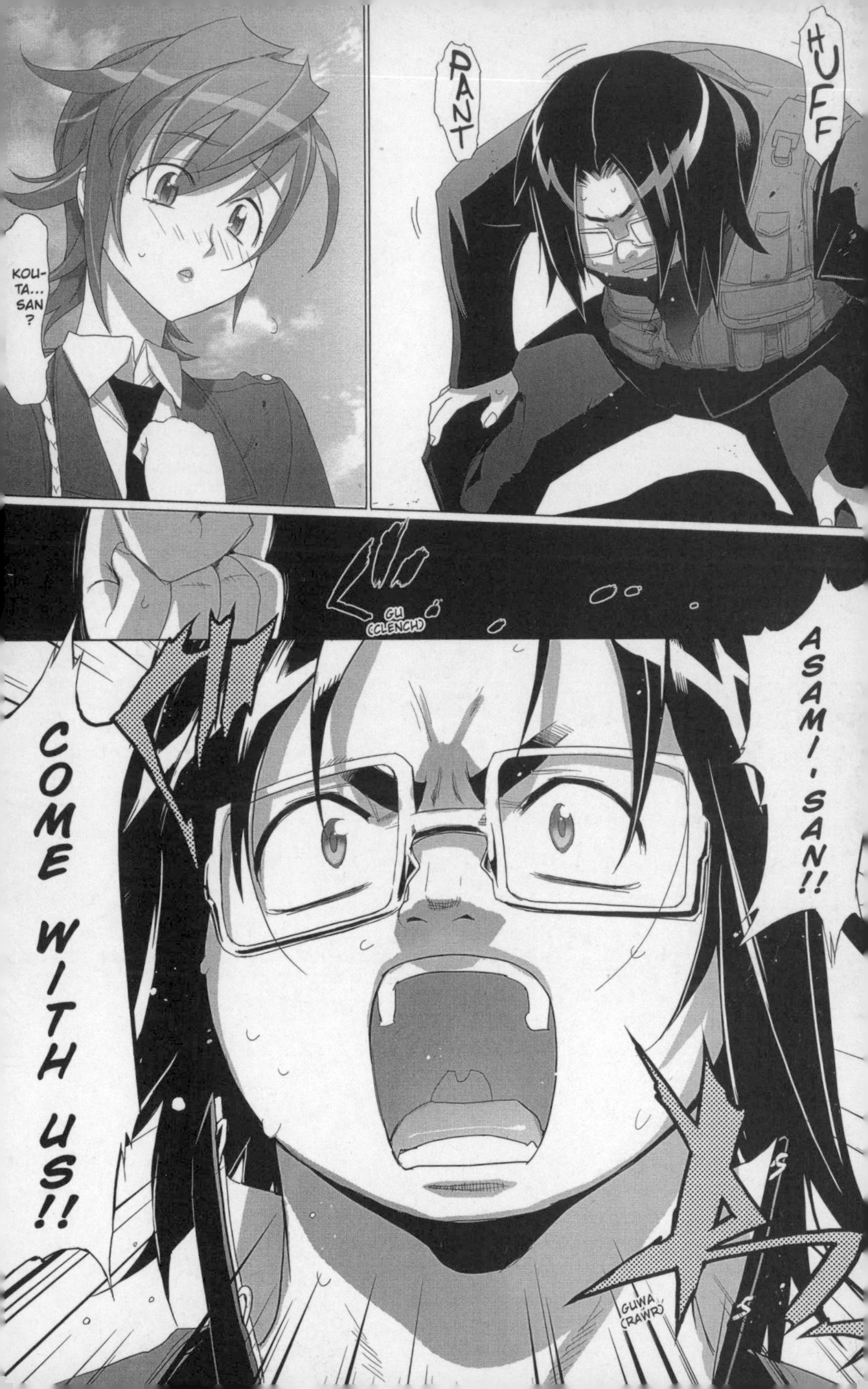
HUFF
PANT
KOU-TA... SAN?
GU (CLENCH)
ASAMI-SAN!!
COME WITH US!!
GUWA (RAWR)

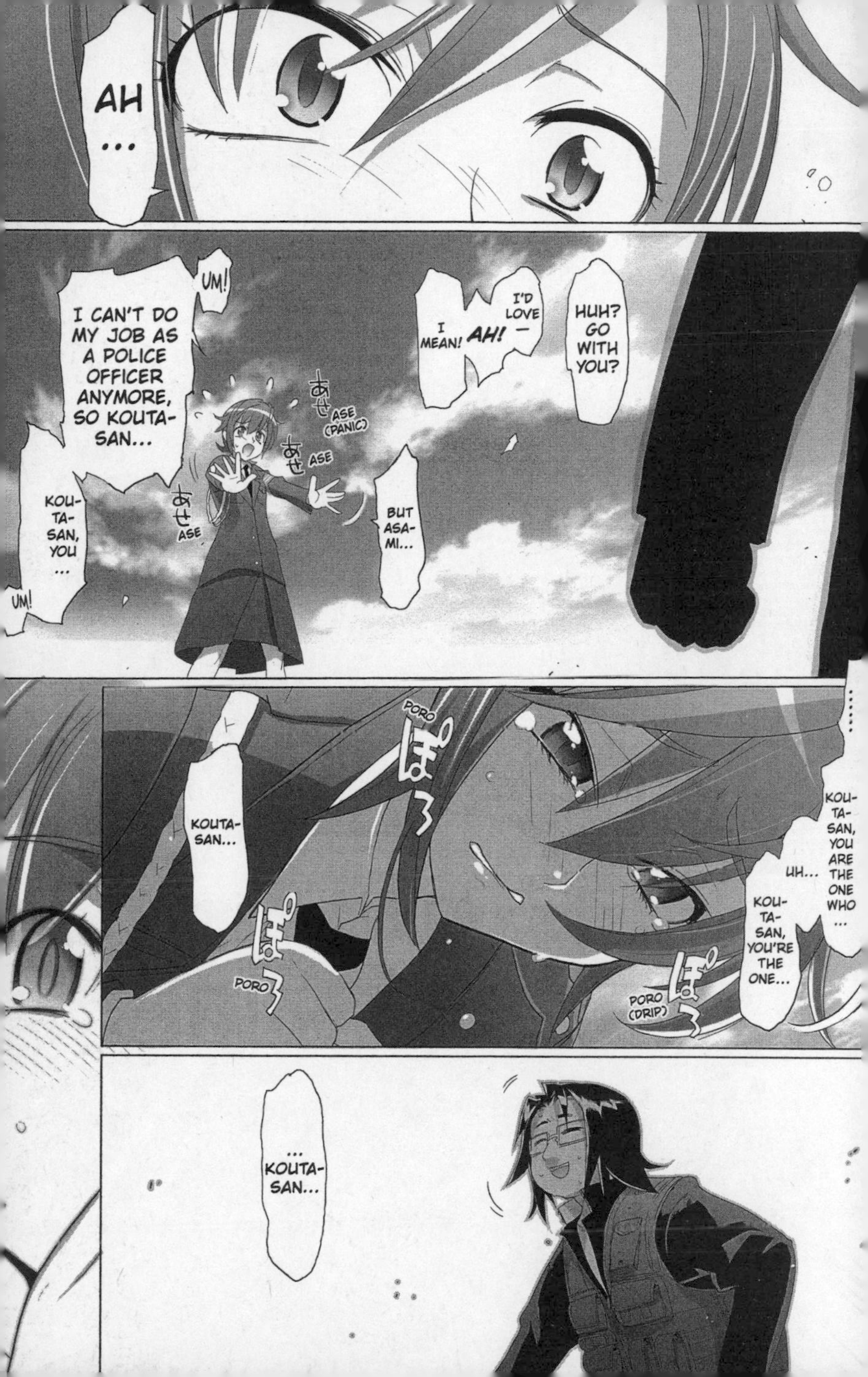
AH ...
HUH? GO WITH YOU?
I'D LOVE —
AH!
I MEAN!
BUT ASA-MI...
あせ ASE (PANIC)
あせ ASE
UM!
I CAN'T DO MY JOB AS A POLICE OFFICER ANYMORE, SO KOUTA-SAN...
あせ ASE
KOU-TA-SAN, YOU ...
UM!
KOU-TA-SAN, YOU ARE THE ONE WHO ...
UH...
KOU-TA-SAN, YOU'RE THE ONE...
ぽろ PORO (DRIP)
ぽろ PORO
KOUTA-SAN...
ぽろ PORO
... KOUTA-SAN...

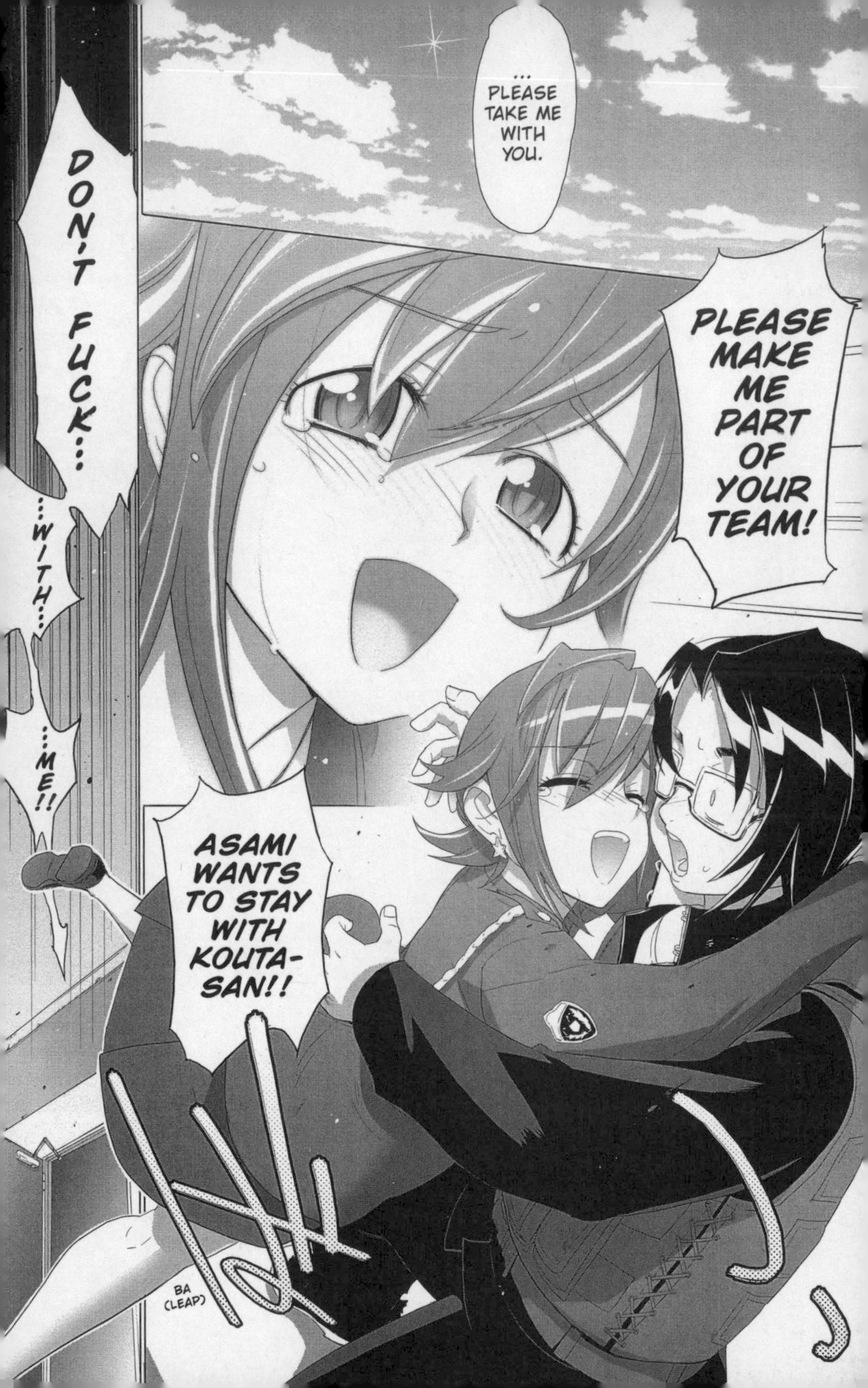

... PLEASE TAKE ME WITH YOU.
PLEASE MAKE ME PART OF YOUR TEAM!
ASAMI WANTS TO STAY WITH KOUTA-SAN!!
BA (LEAP)
DON'T FUCK...
...WITH...
...ME!!

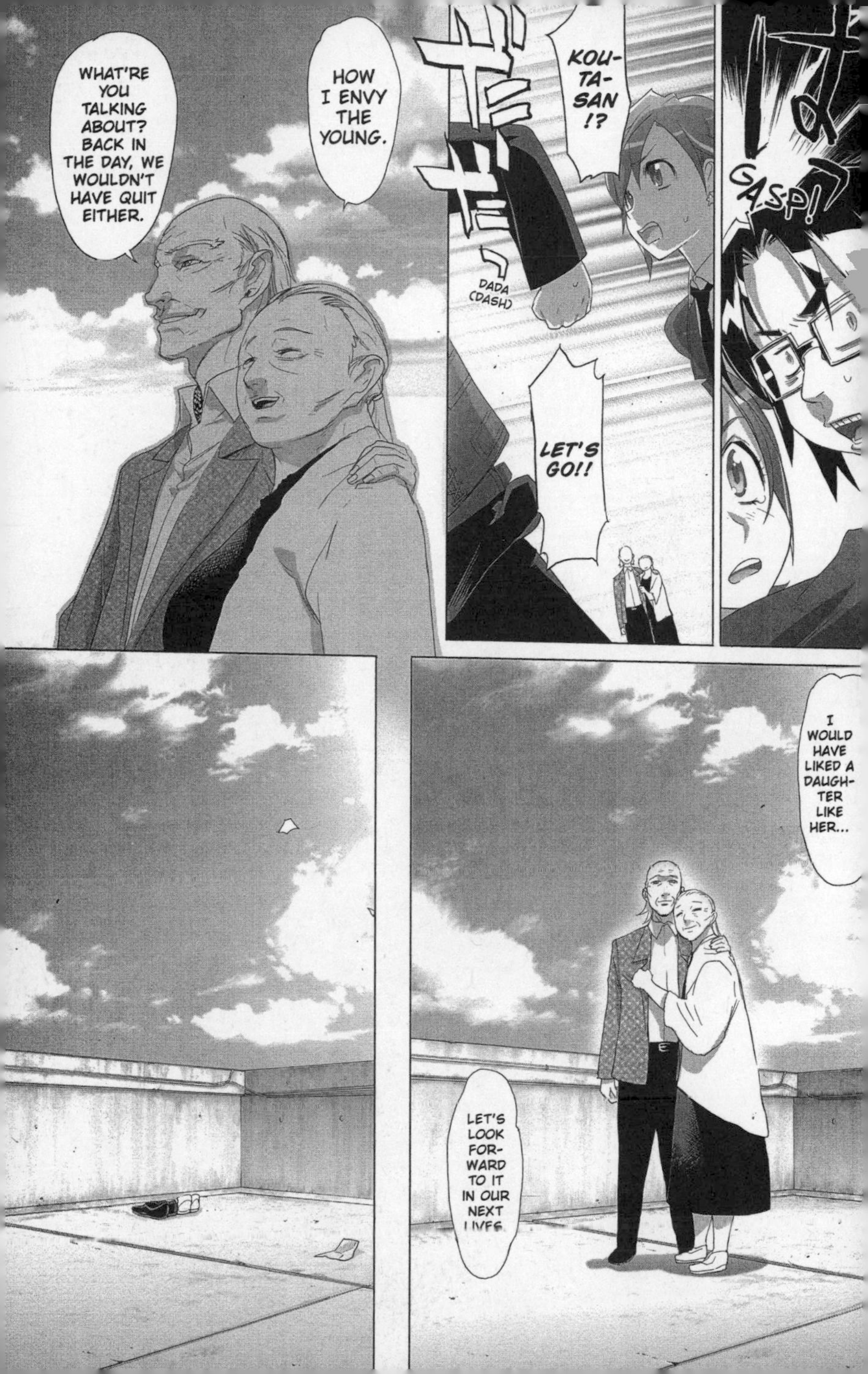
GASP!
KOU-TA-SAN!?
DADA (DASH)
LET'S GO!!
HOW I ENVY THE YOUNG.
WHAT'RE YOU TALKING ABOUT? BACK IN THE DAY, WE WOULDN'T HAVE QUIT EITHER.
I WOULD HAVE LIKED A DAUGHTER LIKE HER...
LET'S LOOK FORWARD TO IT IN OUR NEXT LIVES

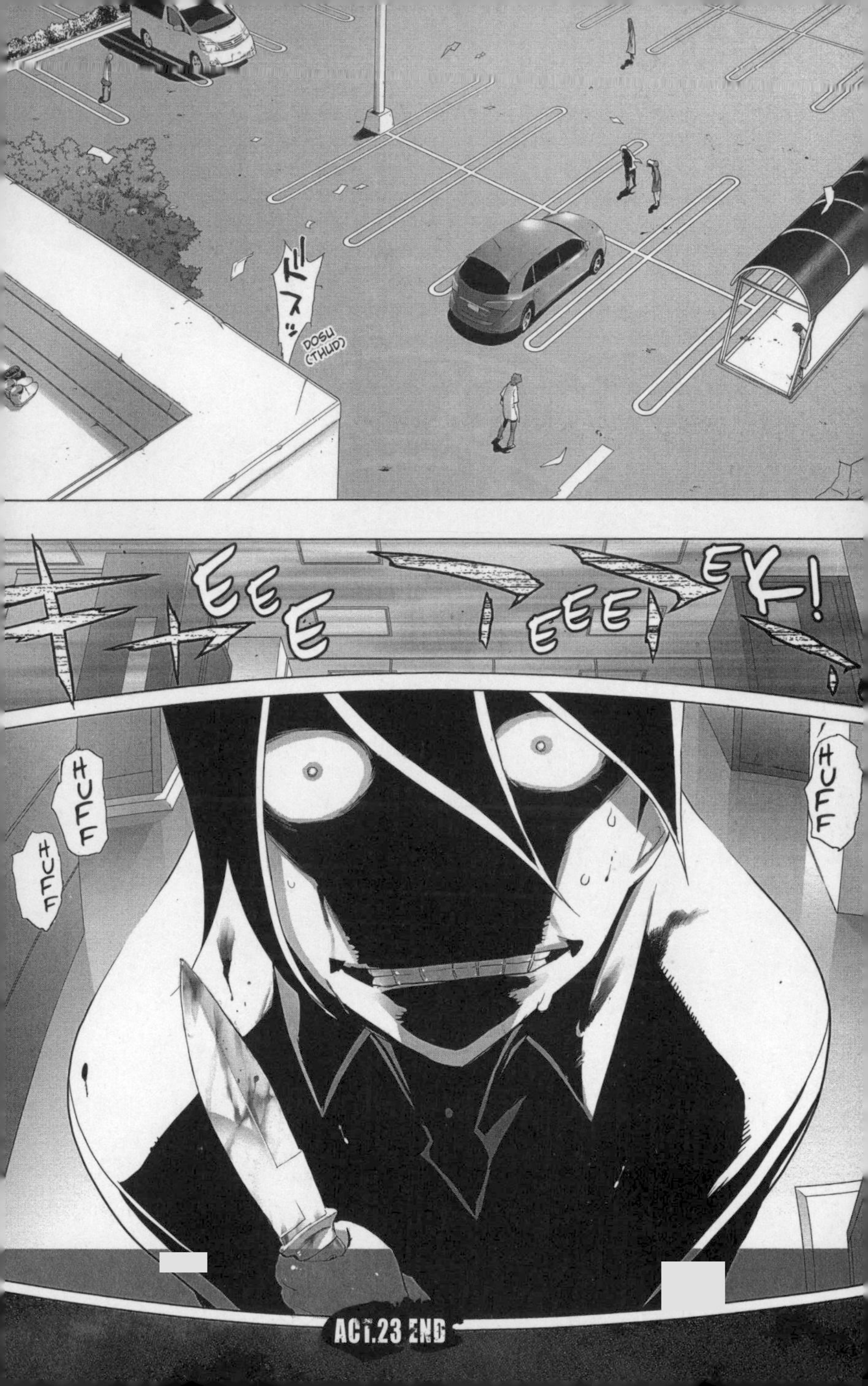

ドスッ
DOSU (THUD)
EEEEEEEK!
HUFF
HUFF
HUFF
ACT.23 END

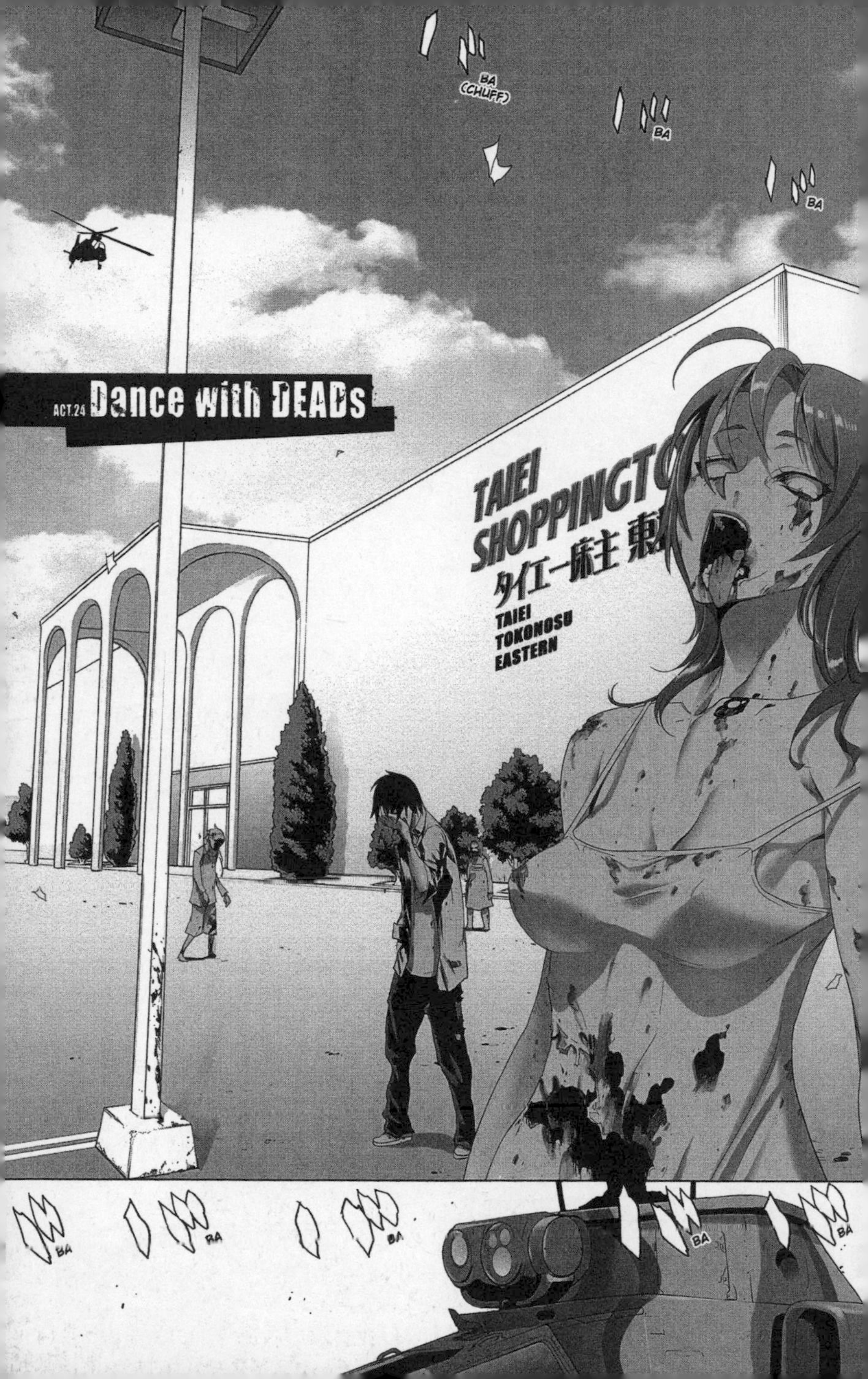
BA
BA
BA
(CHUFF)
TAIEI
SHOPPINGTO
タイエー床主 東
TAIEI
TOKONOSU
EASTERN
ACT.24 Dance with DEADs
BA
BA
BA
BA
BA

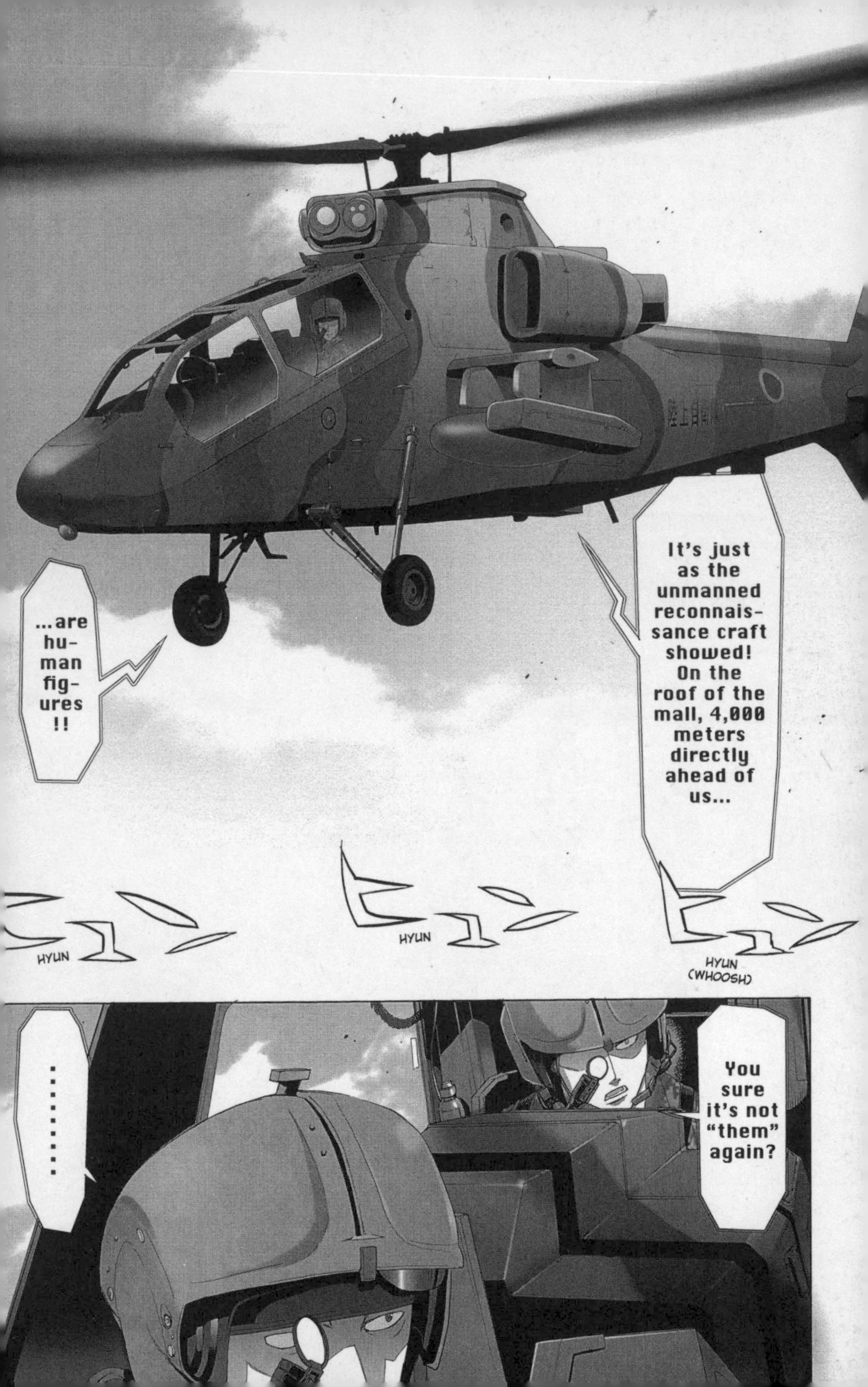
It's just as the unmanned reconnaissance craft showed! On the roof of the mall, 4,000 meters directly ahead of us...
...are human figures!!
HYUN (WHOOSH)
HYUN
HYUN
You sure it's not "them" again?
....

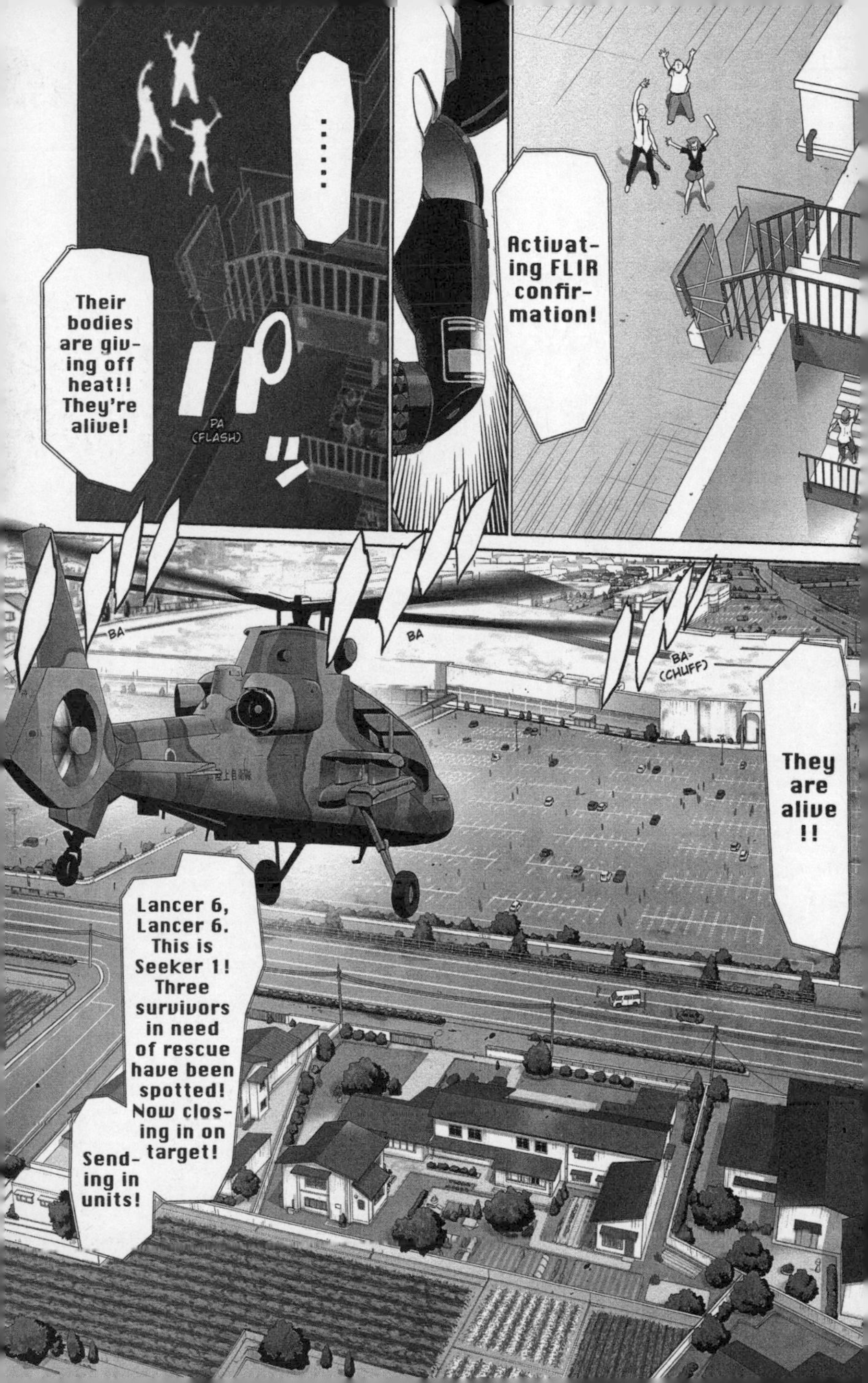

Activating FLIR confirmation!
......
PA (FLASH)
Their bodies are giving off heat!! They're alive!
BA (CHUFF)
They are alive!!
BA
BA
Lancer 6, Lancer 6. This is Seeker 1! Three survivors in need of rescue have been spotted! Now closing in on target!
Sending in units!

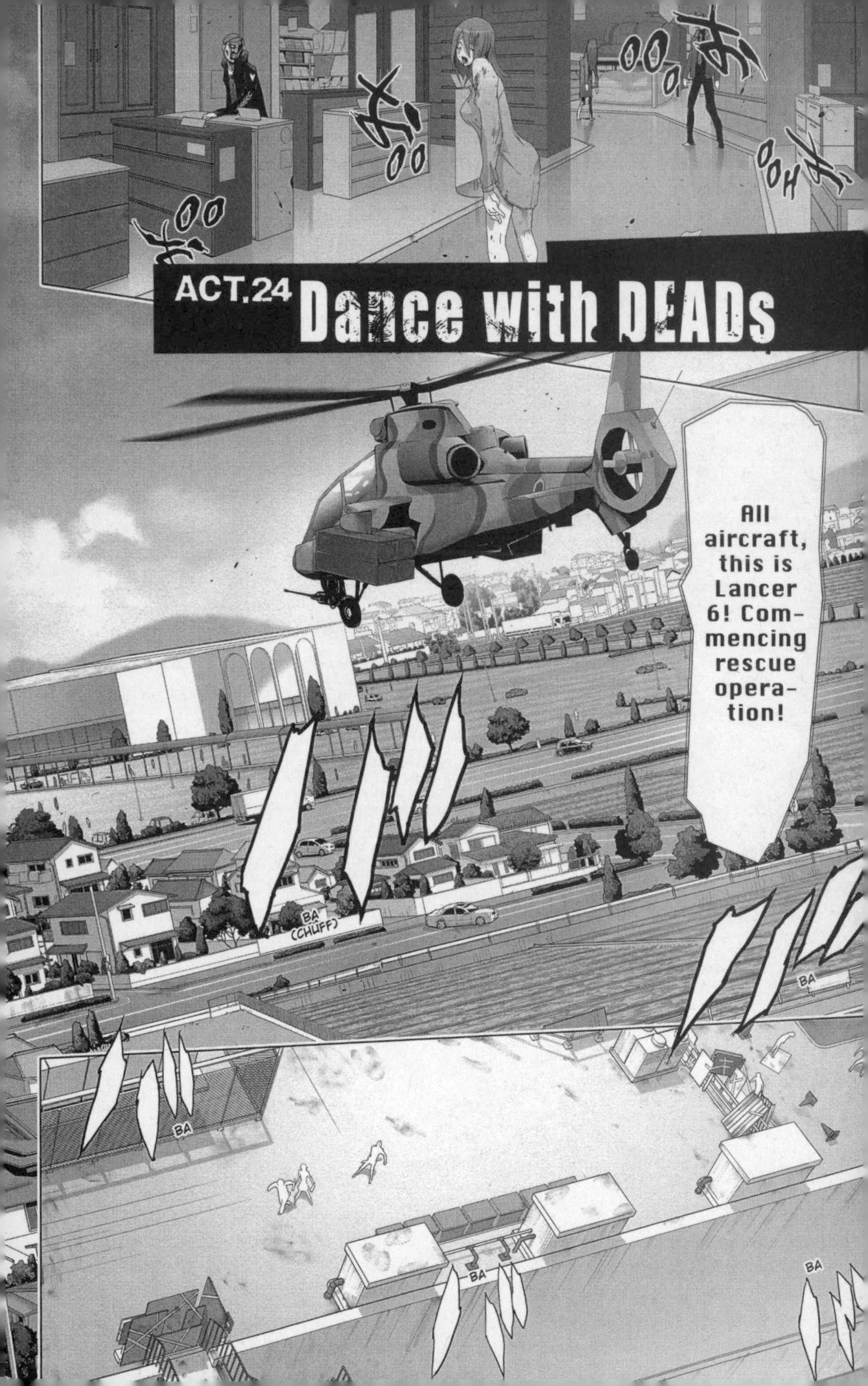

OOH
ACT.24 Dance with DEADs
All aircraft, this is Lancer 6! Commencing rescue operation!
BA (CHUFF)
BA
BA
BA
BA

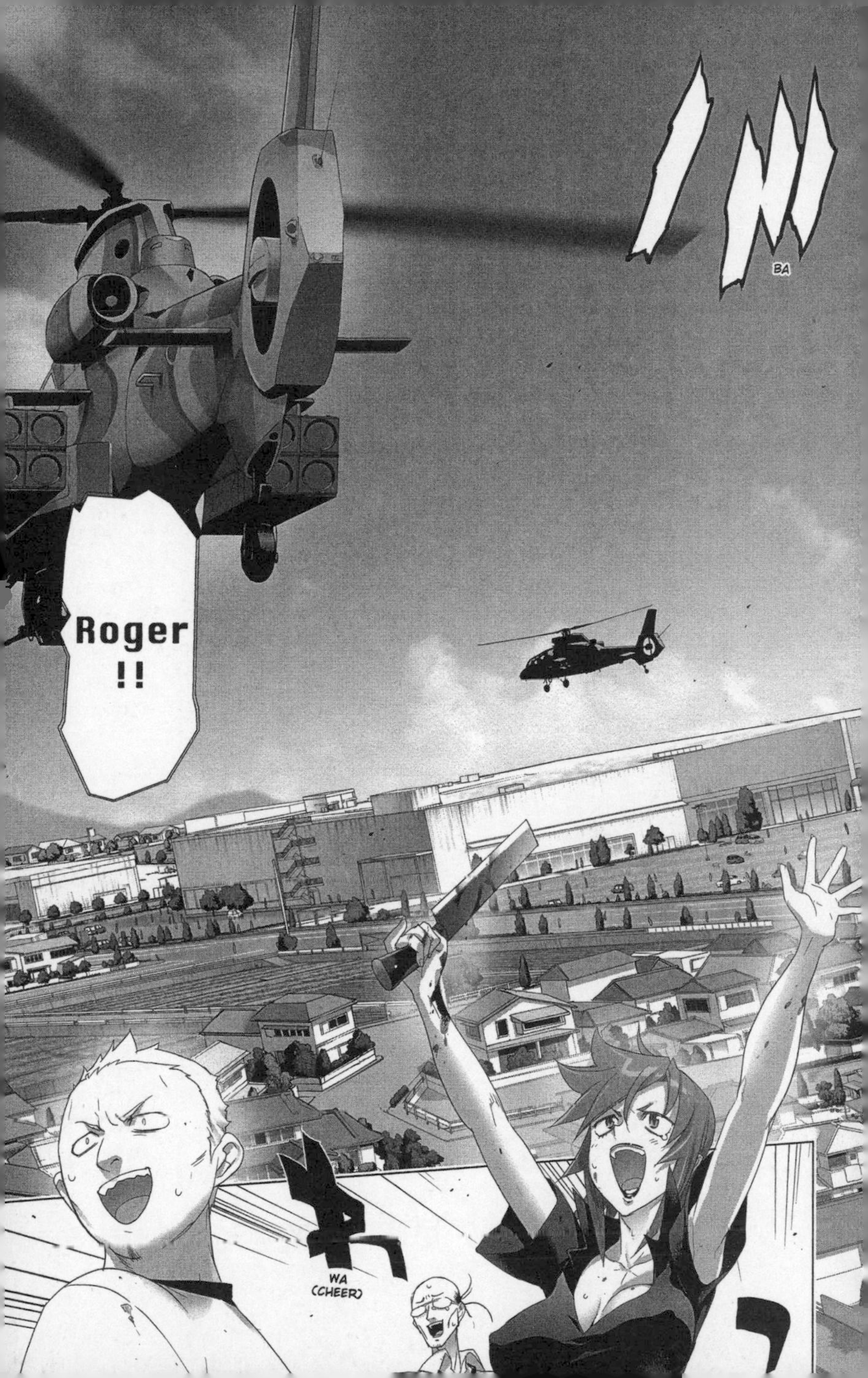
BA
Roger !!
WA (CHEER)

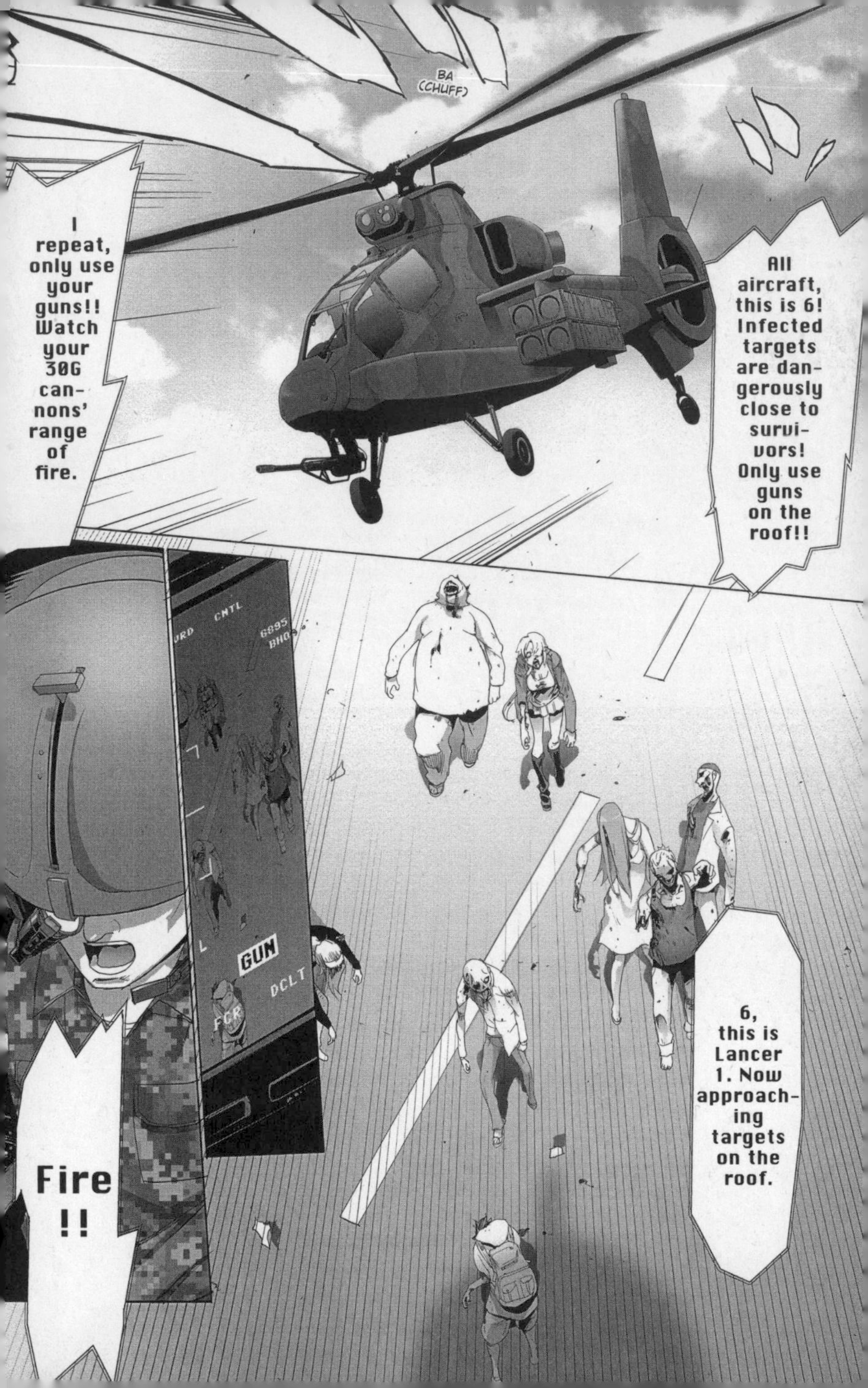
BA (CHUFF)
All aircraft, this is 6! Infected targets are dangerously close to survivors! Only use guns on the roof!!
I repeat, only use your guns!! Watch your 30G cannons' range of fire.
6, this is Lancer 1. Now approaching targets on the roof.
CNTL
GUN
DCLT
Fire!!

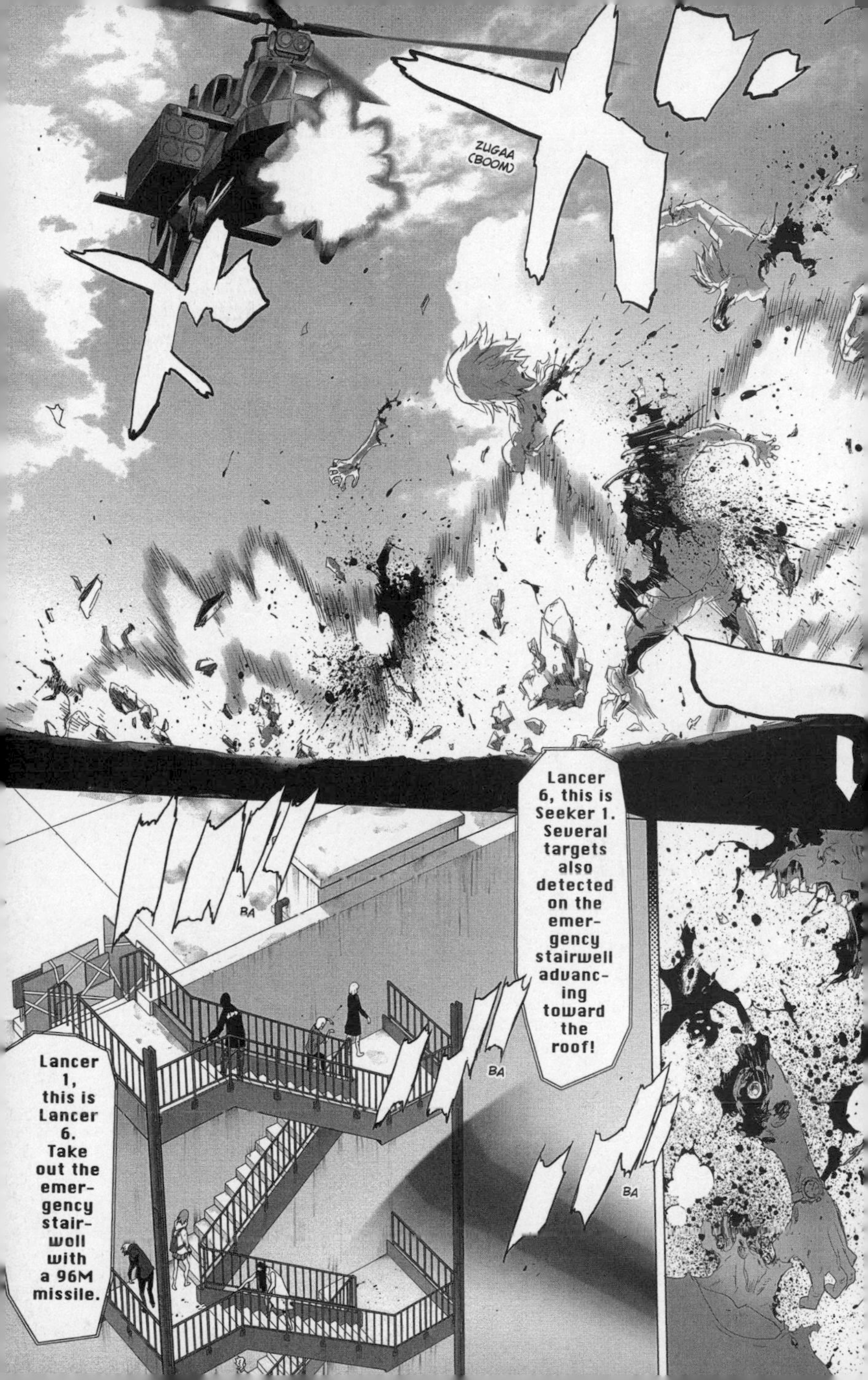
ZUGAA (BOOM)
Lancer 6, this is Seeker 1. Several targets also detected on the emergency stairwell advancing toward the roof!
BA
BA
BA
Lancer 1, this is Lancer 6. Take out the emergency stairwoll with a 96M missile.

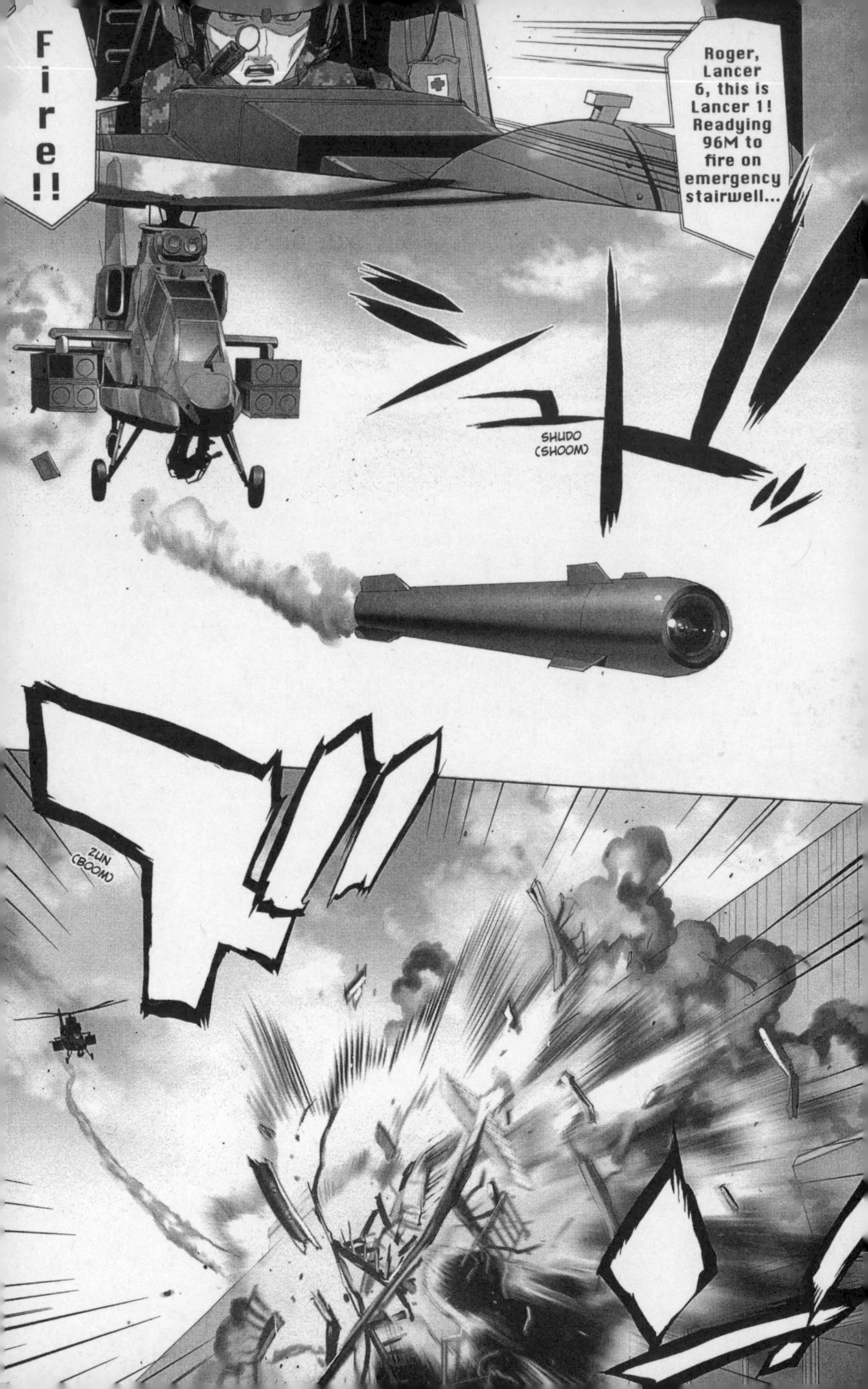
Roger, Lancer 6, this is Lancer 1! Readying 96M to fire on emergency stairwell...
Fire!!
SHUDO (SHOOM)
ZUN (BOOM)

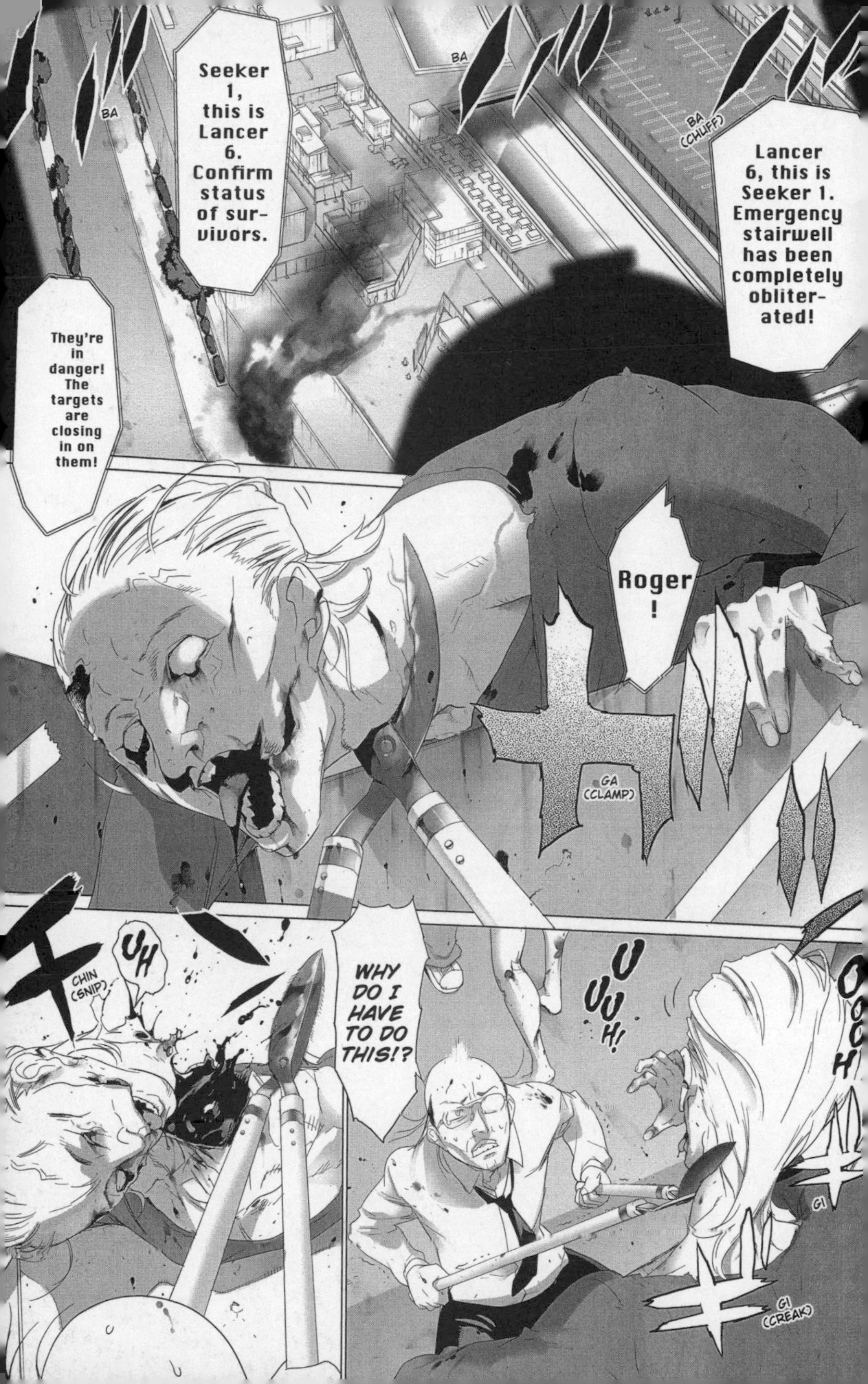

BA (CHUFF)
BA
Lancer 6, this is Seeker 1. Emergency stairwell has been completely obliter-ated!
Seeker 1, this is Lancer 6. Confirm status of sur-vivors.
BA
They're in danger! The targets are closing in on them!
Roger!
GA (CLAMP)
OOOH
GI
GI (CREAK)
UUUH!
WHY DO I HAVE TO DO THIS!?
UH
CHIN (SNIP)

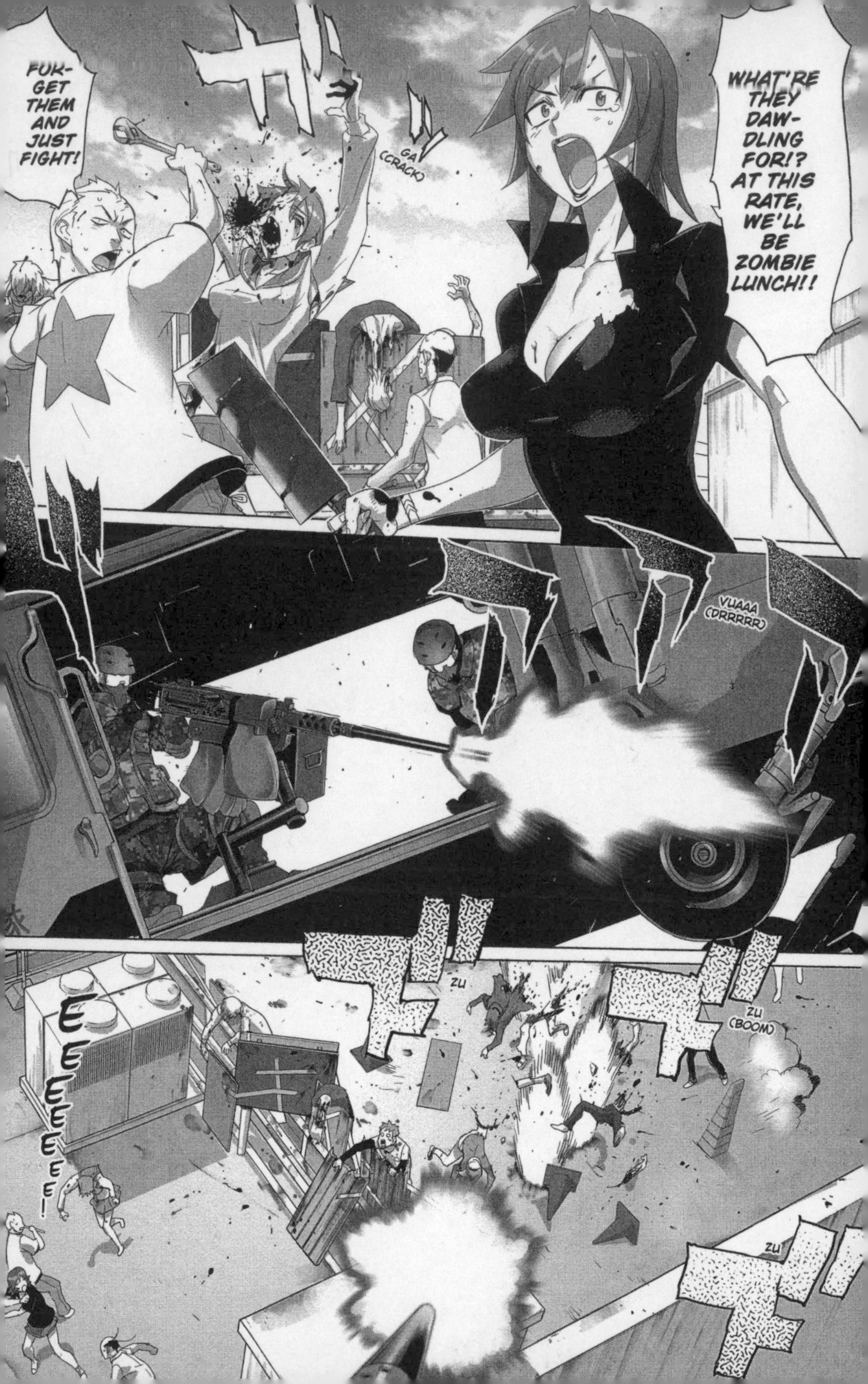
WHAT'RE THEY DAW-DLING FOR!? AT THIS RATE, WE'LL BE ZOMBIE LUNCH!!
GA (CRACK)
FUK-GET THEM AND JUST FIGHT!
VUAAA (DRRRRR)
ZU (BOOM)
ZU
ZU
EEEEEEEEEE!

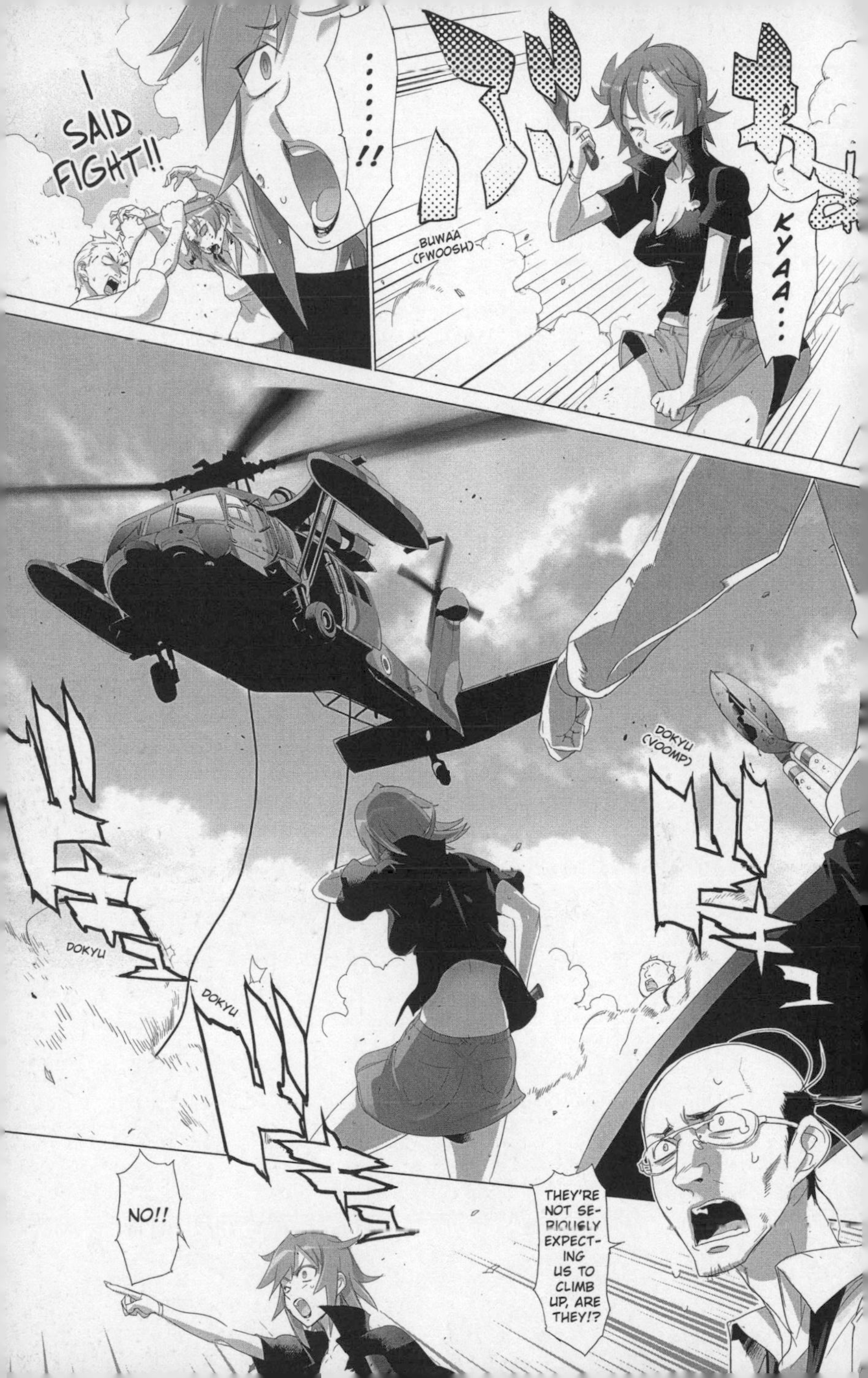
KYAA...
BUWAA (FWOOSH)
......!!
I SAID FIGHT!!
DOKYU (VOOMP)
DOKYU
DOKYU
THEY'RE NOT SERIOUSLY EXPECTING US TO CLIMB UP, ARE THEY!?
NO!!

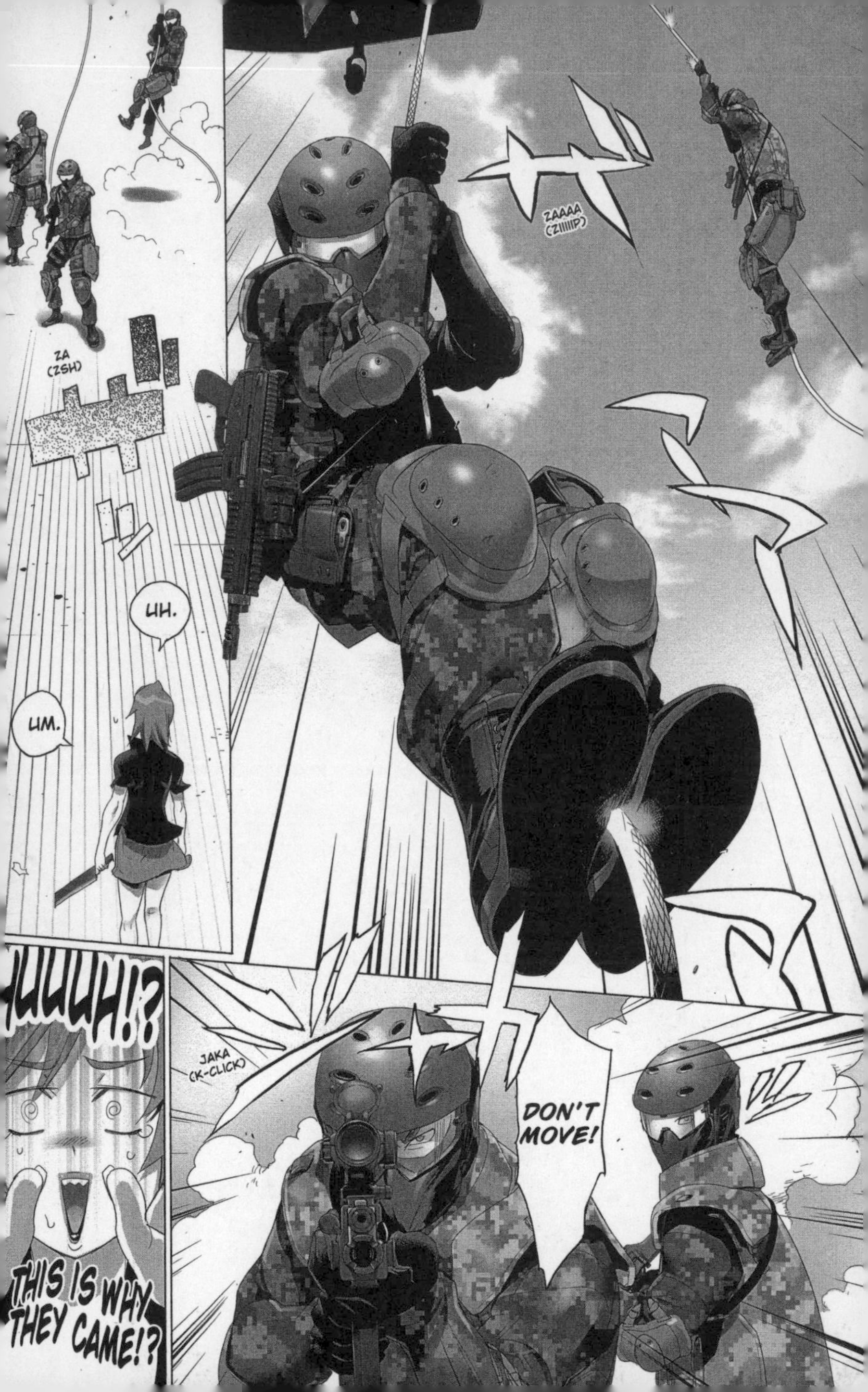
ZAAAA
(ZIIIIIP)
ZA
(ZSH)
UH.
UM.
JAKA
(K-CLICK)
DON'T MOVE!
UUUH!?
THIS IS WHY THEY CAME!?

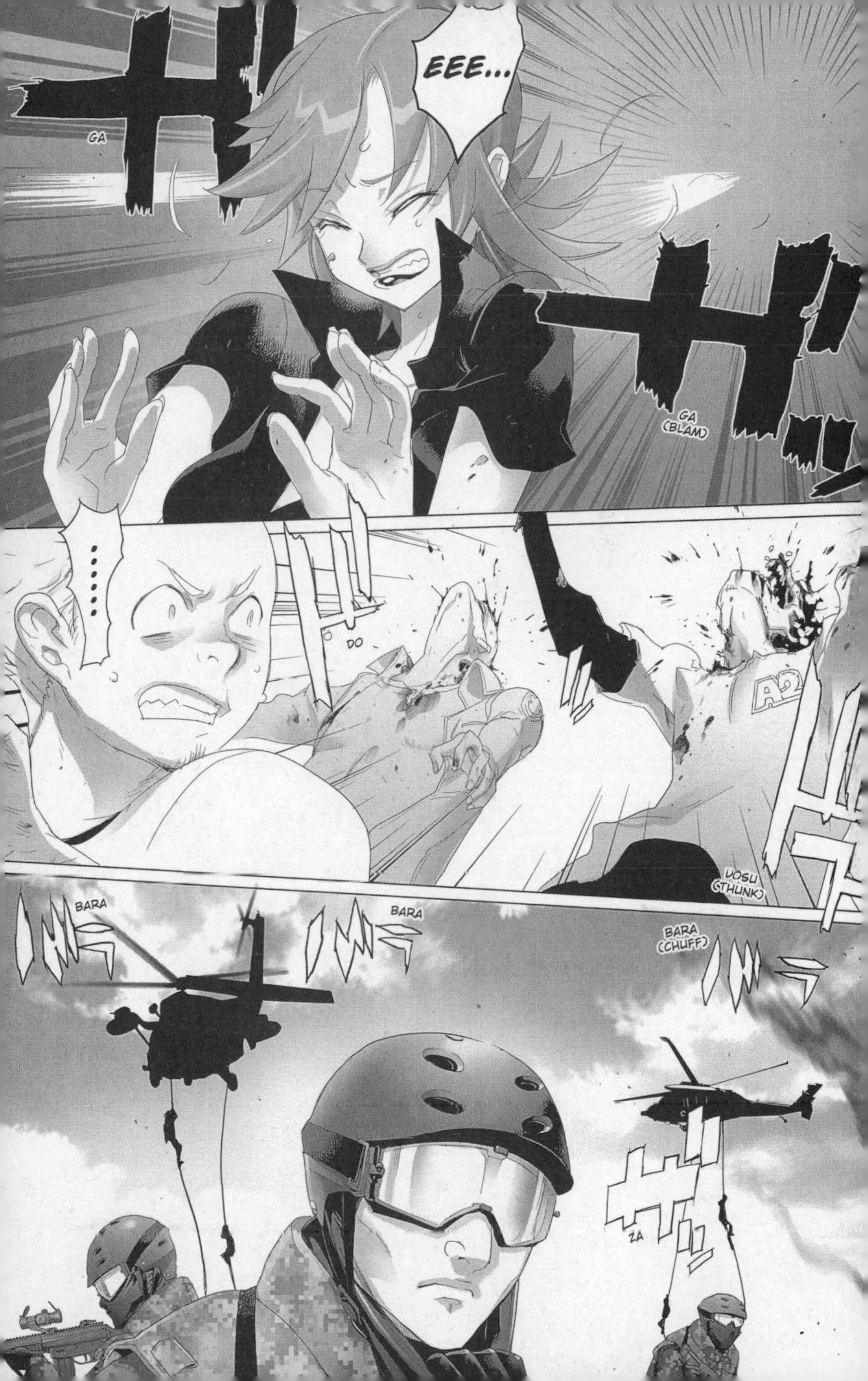
EEE...
GA
GA (BLAM)
......
DO
VOSU (THUNK)
BARA (CHUFF)
BARA
BARA
ZA

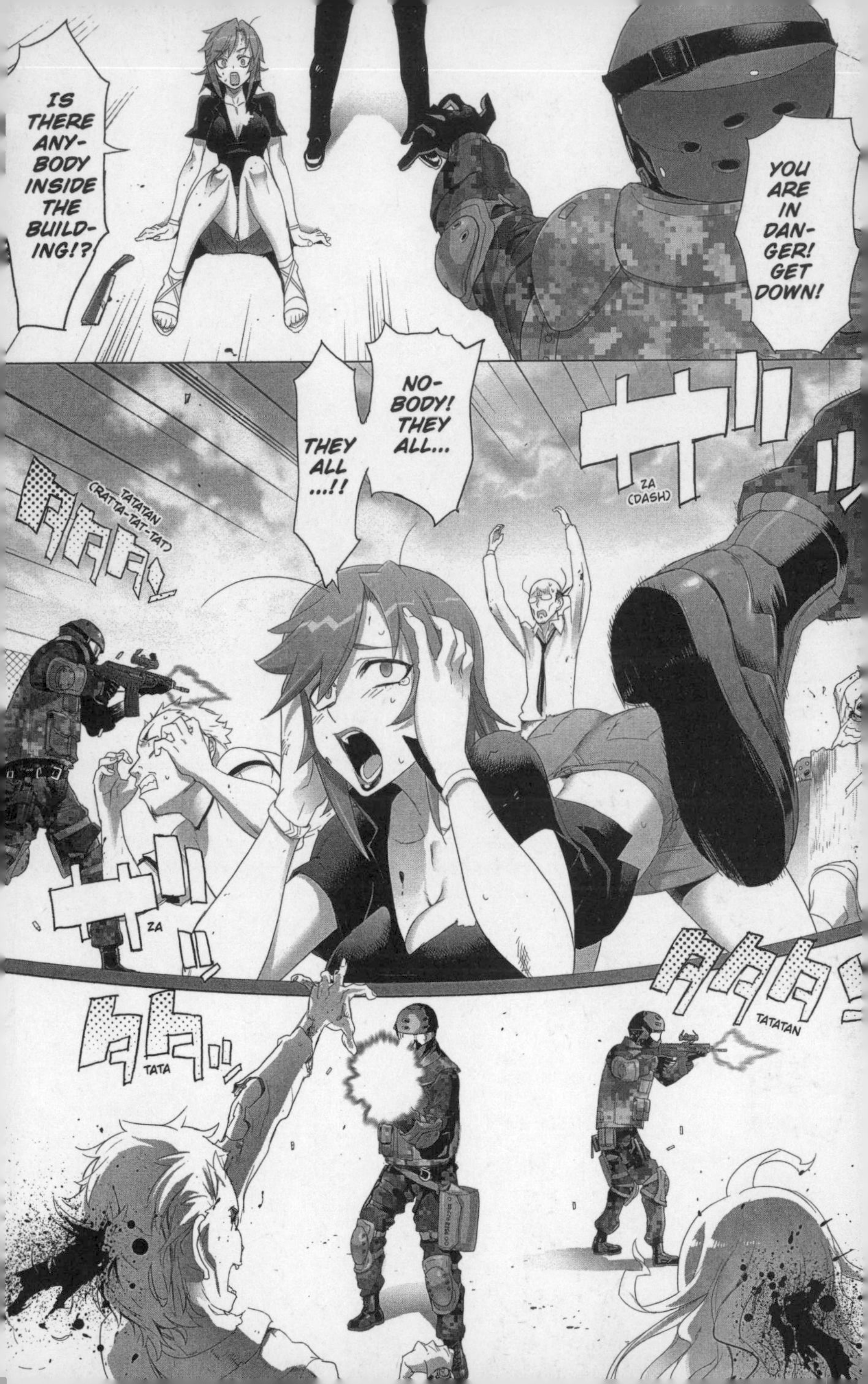
YOU ARE IN DAN-GER! GET DOWN!
IS THERE ANY-BODY INSIDE THE BUILD-ING!?
ZA (DASH)
NO-BODY! THEY ALL...
THEY ALL ...!!
TATATAN (RATTA-TAT-TAT)
ZA
TATATAN
TATA

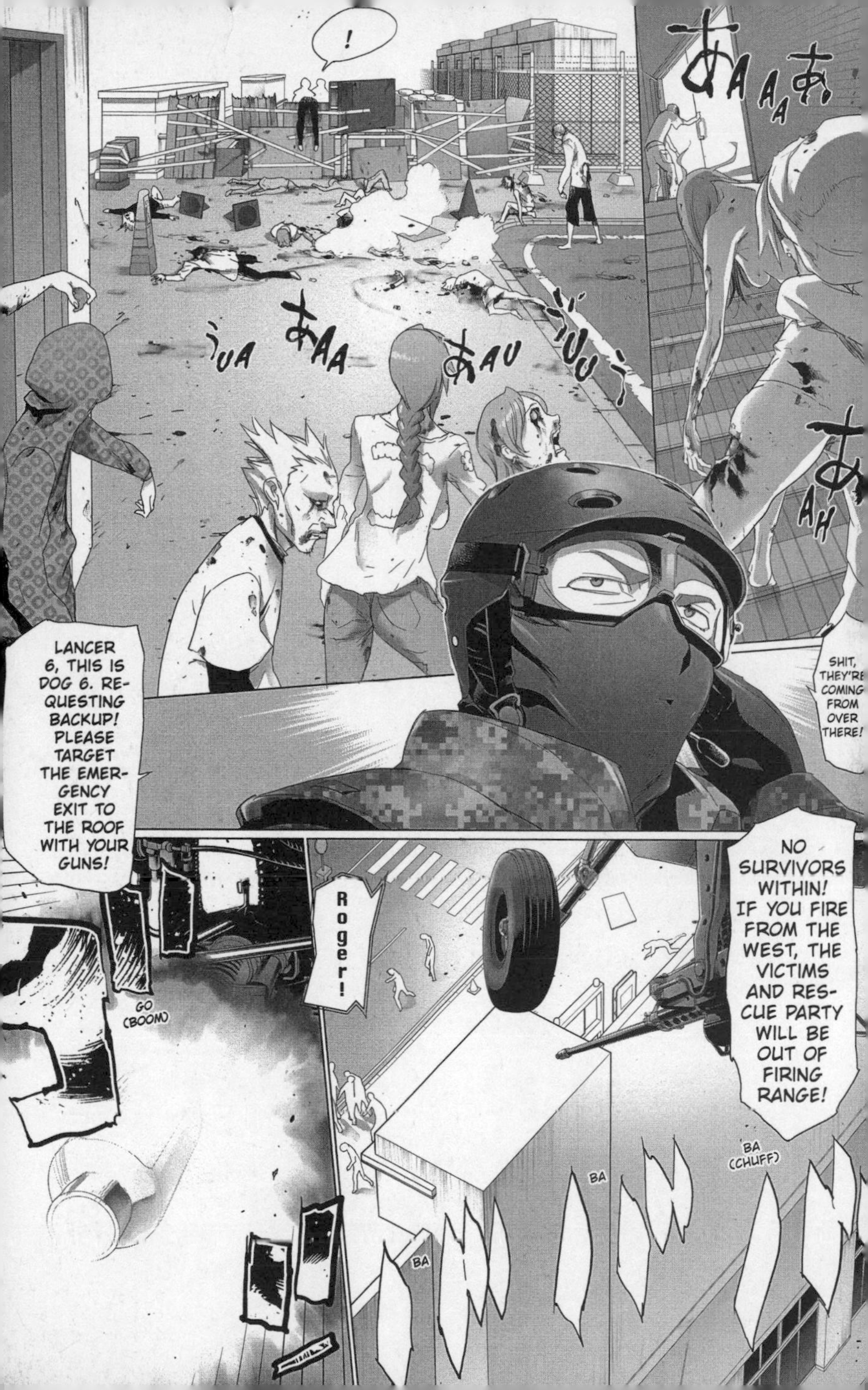
あAAAあ
!
あAH
ジUUう
あAU
あAA
うUA
SHIT, THEY'RE COMING FROM OVER THERE!
LANCER 6, THIS IS DOG 6. REQUESTING BACKUP! PLEASE TARGET THE EMERGENCY EXIT TO THE ROOF WITH YOUR GUNS!
NO SURVIVORS WITHIN! IF YOU FIRE FROM THE WEST, THE VICTIMS AND RESCUE PARTY WILL BE OUT OF FIRING RANGE!
BA (CHUFF)
BA
Roger!
BA
GO (BOOM)

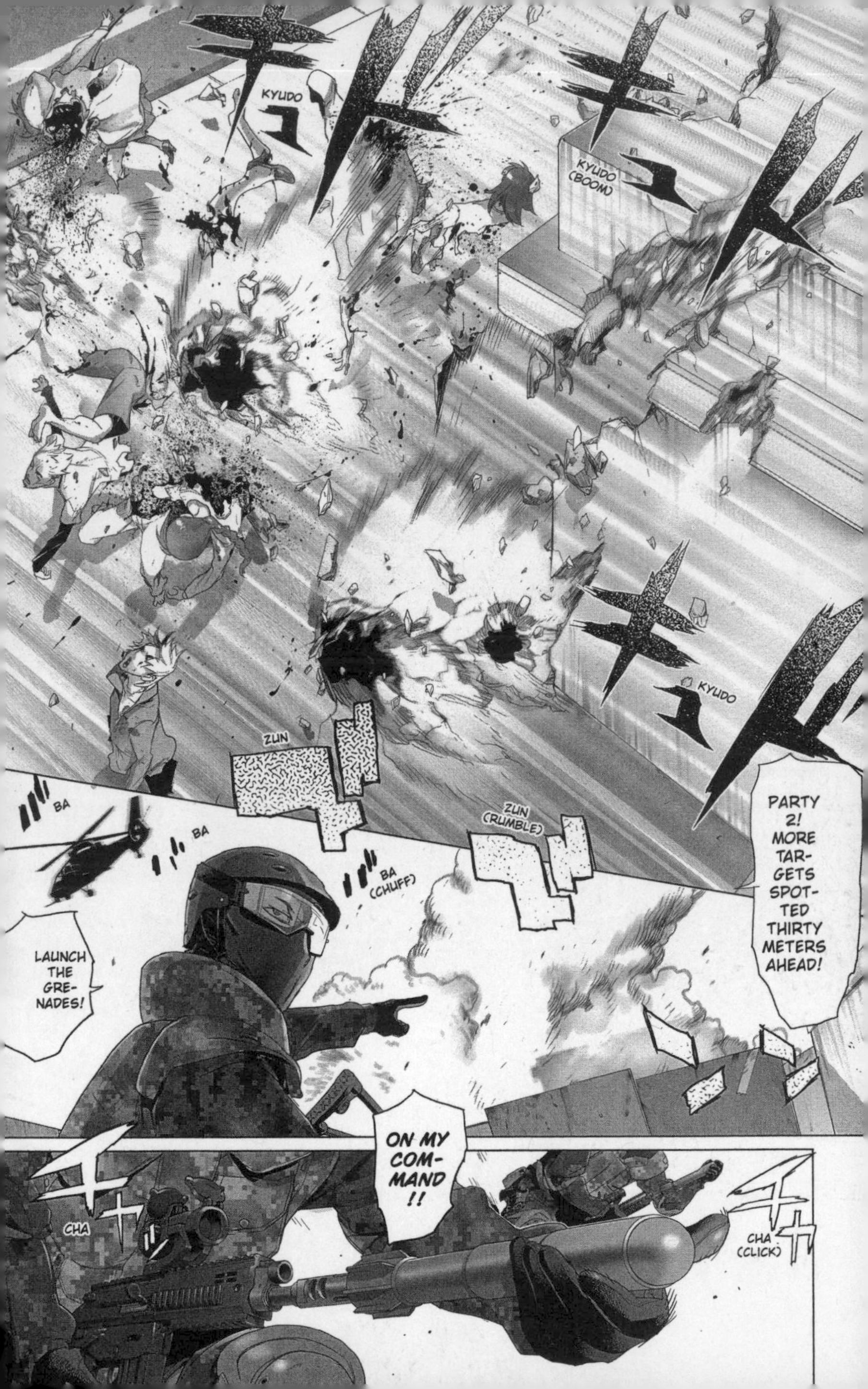

KYUDO
KYUDO (BOOM)
KYUDO
ZUN
PARTY 2! MORE TARGETS SPOTTED THIRTY METERS AHEAD!
ZUN (RUMBLE)
BA (CHUFF)
BA
BA
LAUNCH THE GRENADES!
ON MY COMMAND!!
CHA (CLICK)
CHA

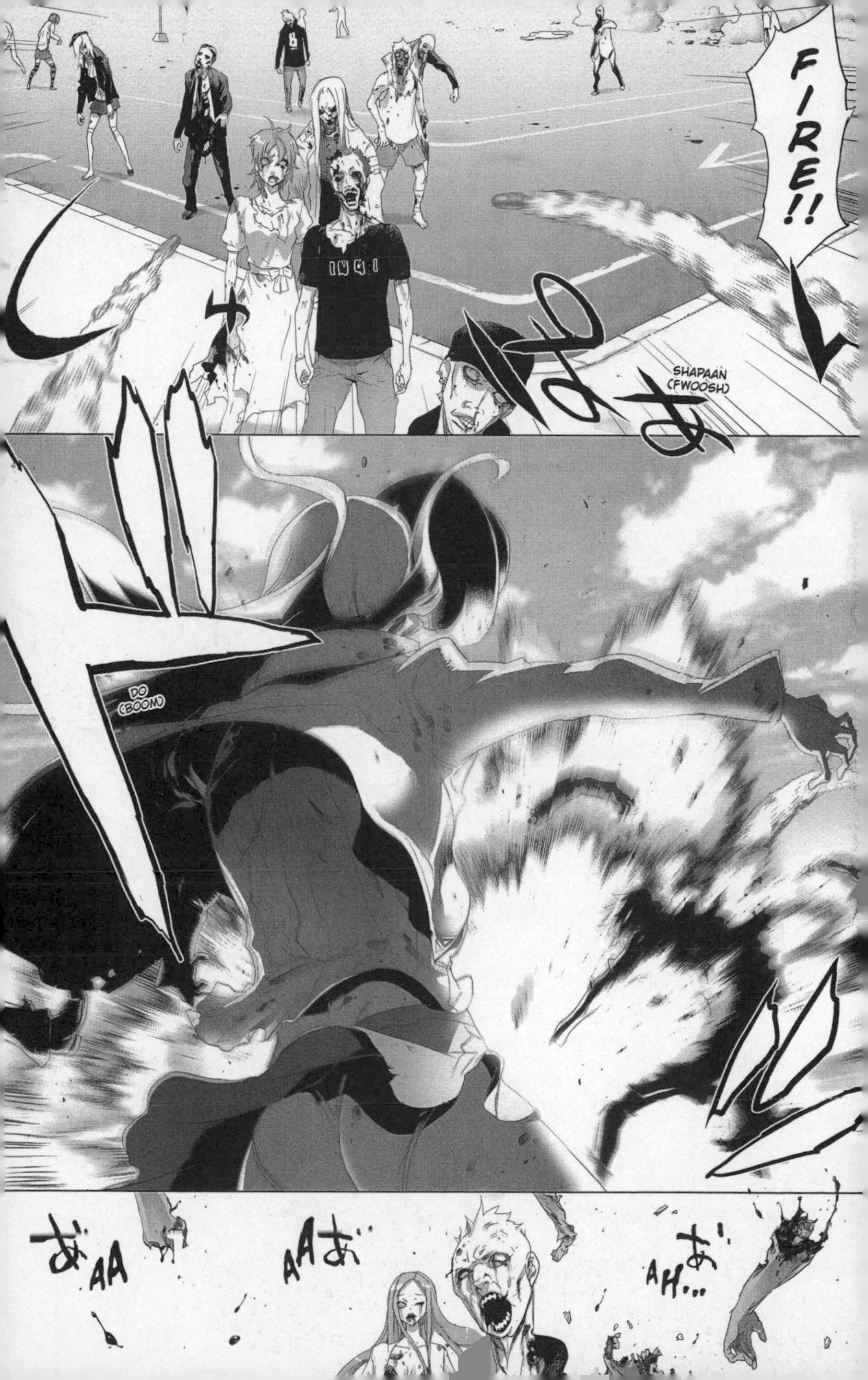
FIRE!!
SHAPAAN (FWOOSH)
DO (BOOM)
AH...
AA
AA

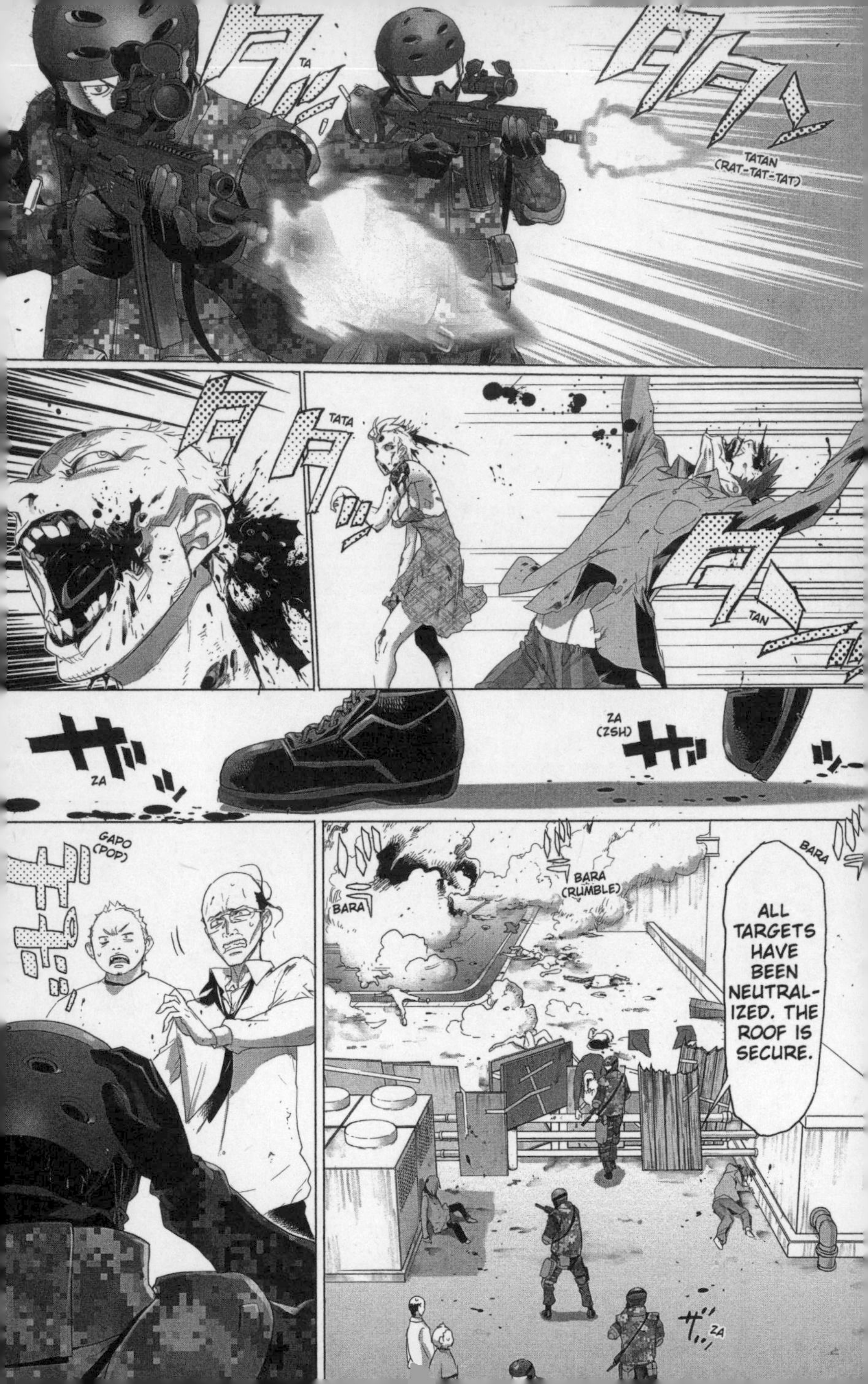
TATAN
(RAT-TAT-TAT)
TA
TAN
TATA
ZA
(ZSH)
ZA
BARA
ALL TARGETS HAVE BEEN NEUTRAL-IZED. THE ROOF IS SECURE.
BARA
(RUMBLE)
BARA
ZA
GAPO
(POP)

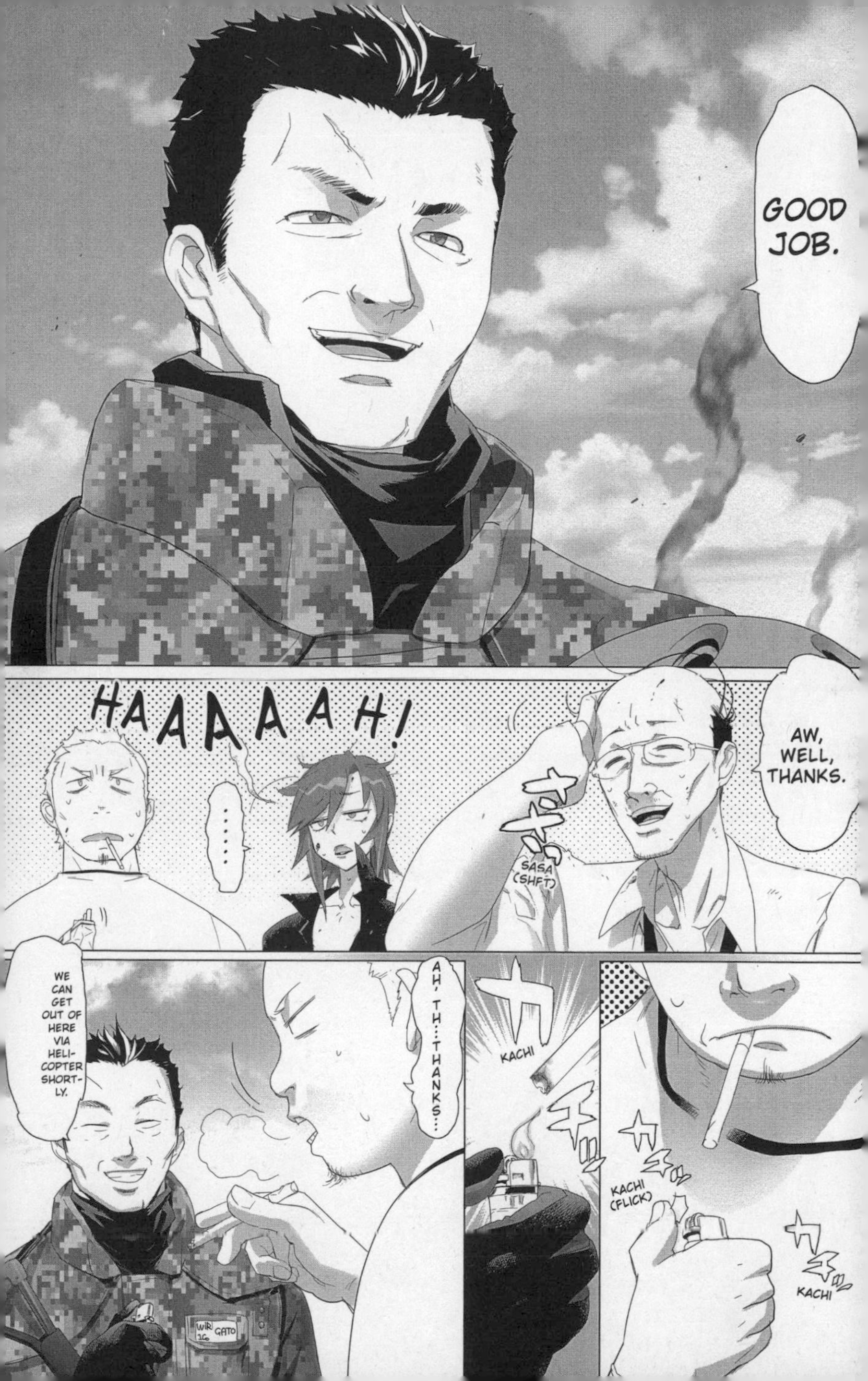
GOOD JOB.
AW, WELL, THANKS.
SASA (SHFT)
HAAAAAH!
......
KACHI (FLICK)
KACHI
KACHI
AH, TH...THANKS...
WE CAN GET OUT OF HERE VIA HELI-COPTER SHORT-LY.
GATO

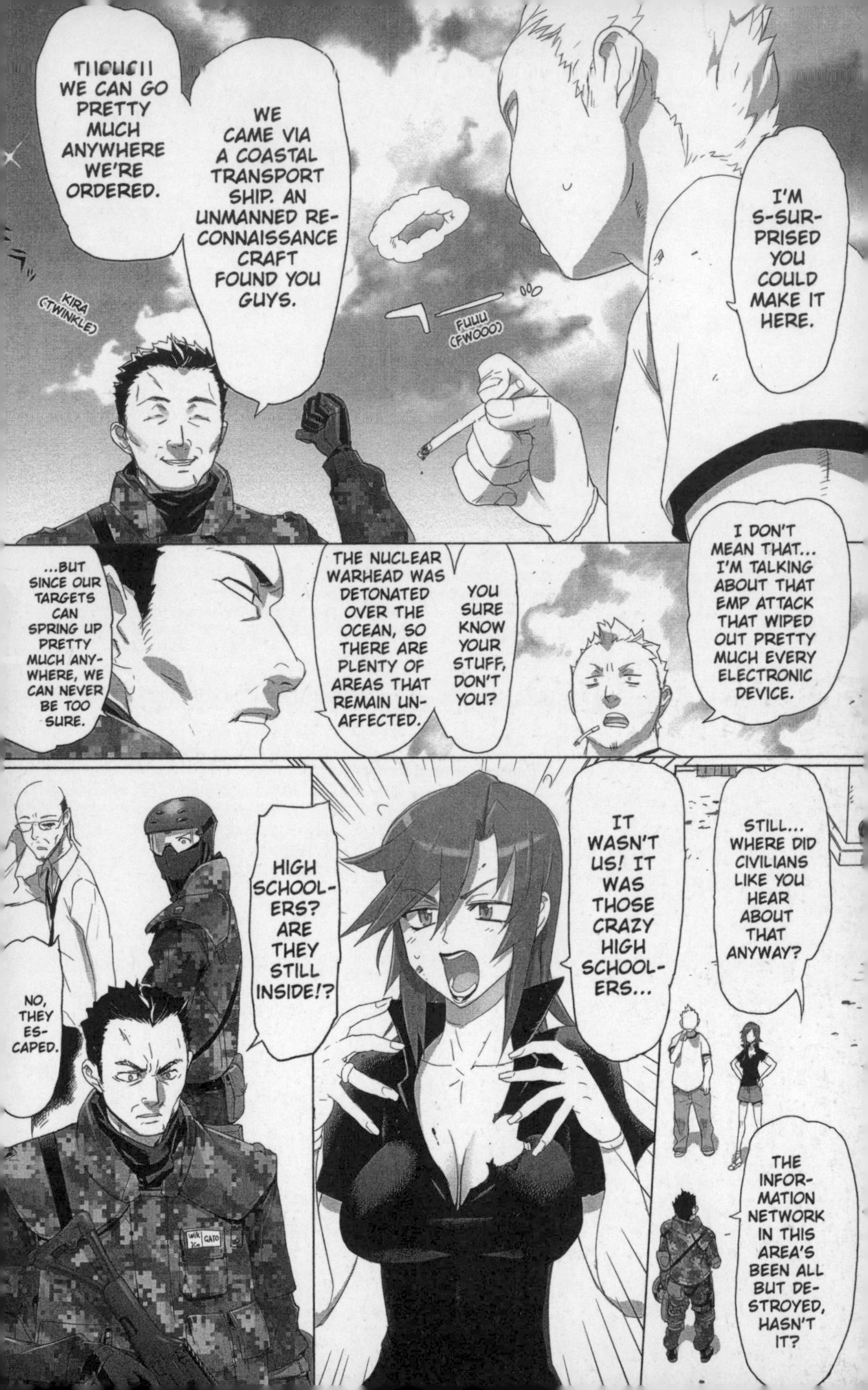
I'M S-SURPRISED YOU COULD MAKE IT HERE.
FUUU (FWOOO)
WE CAME VIA A COASTAL TRANSPORT SHIP. AN UNMANNED RECONNAISSANCE CRAFT FOUND YOU GUYS.
THOUGH WE CAN GO PRETTY MUCH ANYWHERE WE'RE ORDERED.
KIRA (TWINKLE)
I DON'T MEAN THAT... I'M TALKING ABOUT THAT EMP ATTACK THAT WIPED OUT PRETTY MUCH EVERY ELECTRONIC DEVICE.
YOU SURE KNOW YOUR STUFF, DON'T YOU?
THE NUCLEAR WARHEAD WAS DETONATED OVER THE OCEAN, SO THERE ARE PLENTY OF AREAS THAT REMAIN UNAFFECTED.
...BUT SINCE OUR TARGETS CAN SPRING UP PRETTY MUCH ANYWHERE, WE CAN NEVER BE TOO SURE.
STILL... WHERE DID CIVILIANS LIKE YOU HEAR ABOUT THAT ANYWAY?
THE INFORMATION NETWORK IN THIS AREA'S BEEN ALL BUT DESTROYED, HASN'T IT?
IT WASN'T US! IT WAS THOSE CRAZY HIGH SCHOOLERS...
HIGH SCHOOLERS? ARE THEY STILL INSIDE!?
NO, THEY ESCAPED.

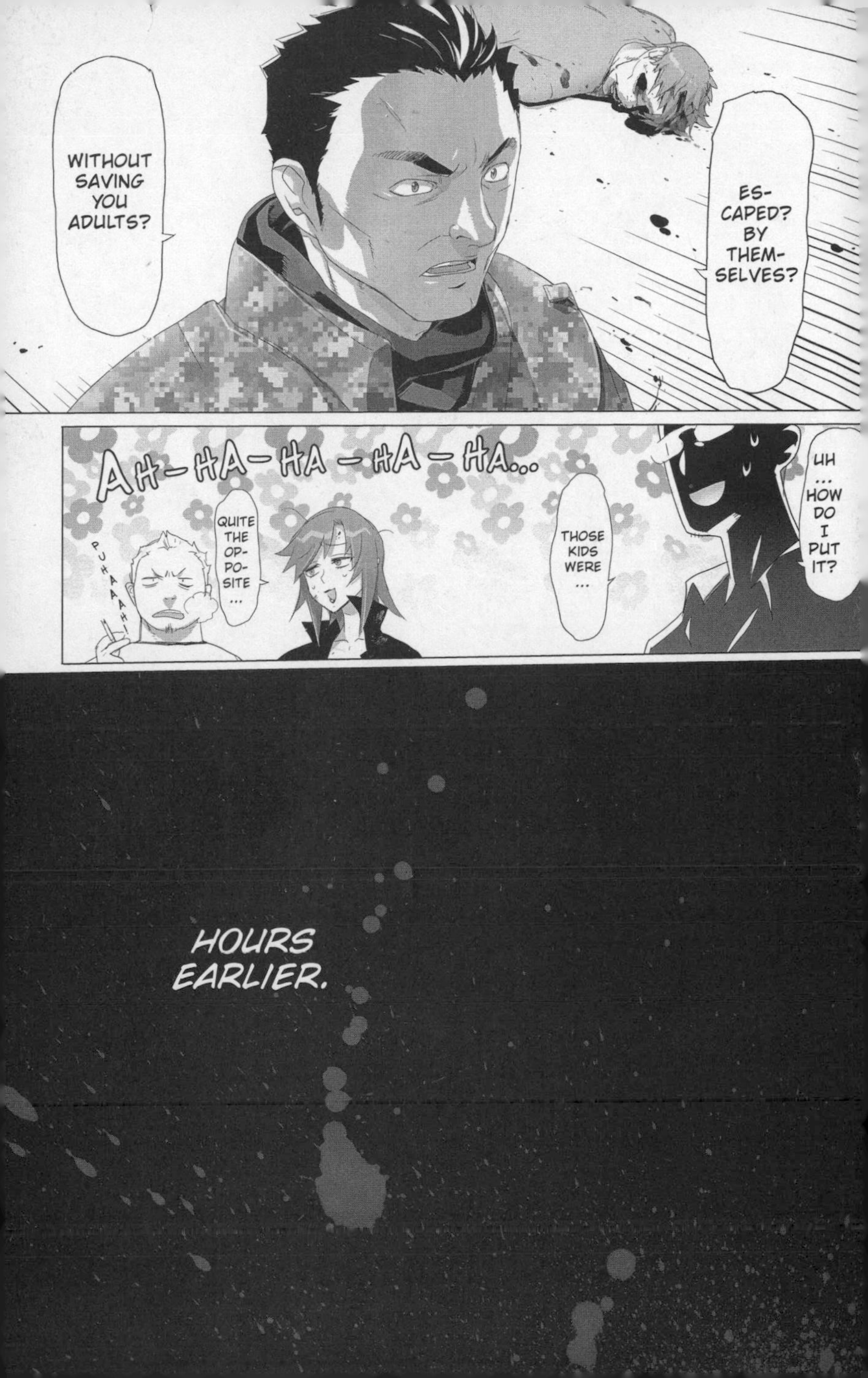
ES-CAPED? BY THEM-SELVES?
WITHOUT SAVING YOU ADULTS?
UH... HOW DO I PUT IT?
THOSE KIDS WERE...
AH-HA-HA-HA-HA...
QUITE THE OP-PO-SITE...
PUHAAAH!
HOURS EARLIER.

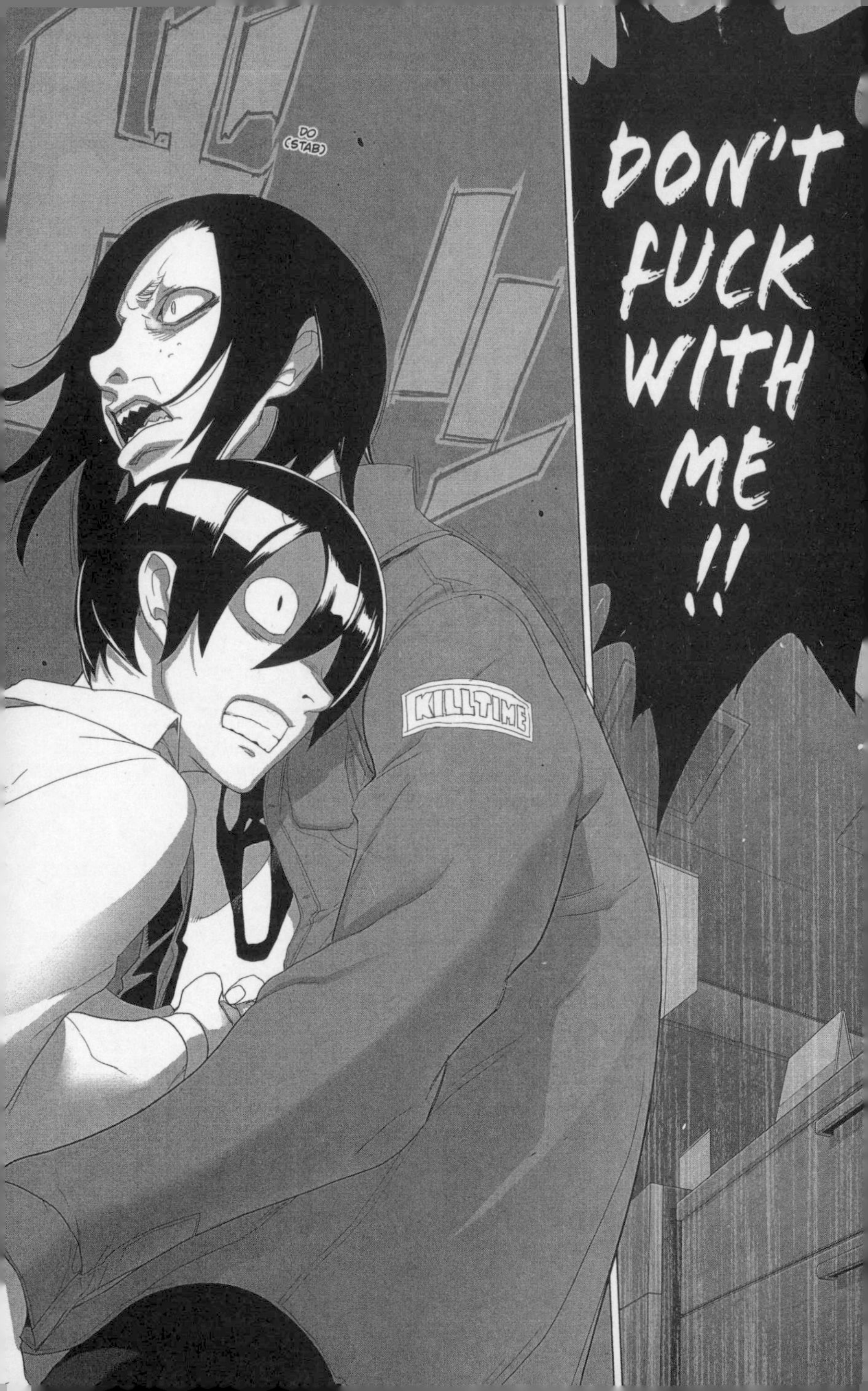
DON'T FUCK WITH ME!!
DO (STAB)
KILLTIME

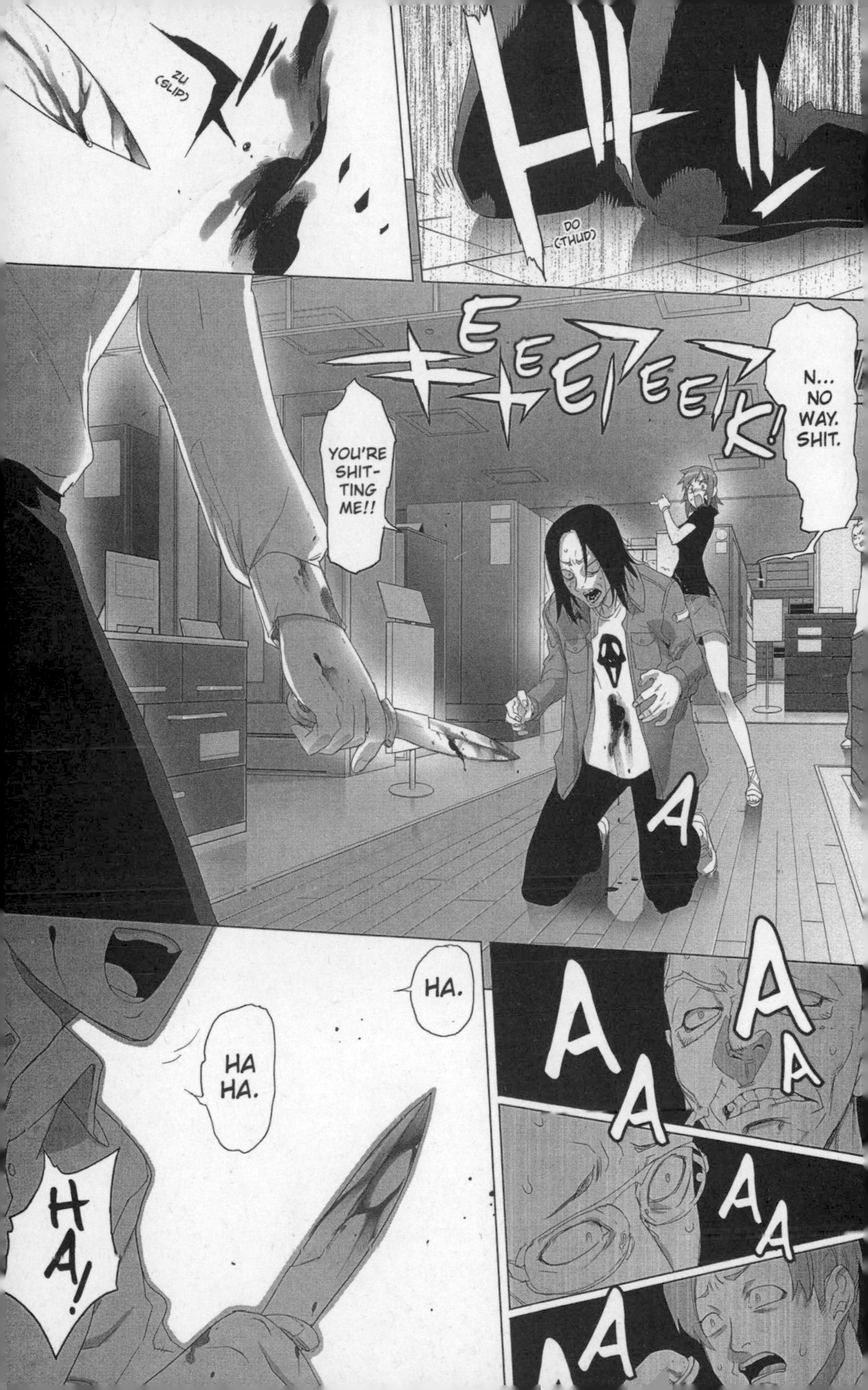
DO
(THUD)
ZU
(SLIP)
N... NO WAY. SHIT.
EEEEEEEK!
YOU'RE SHIT-TING ME!!
A
AAAAAAAAA
HA.
HA HA.
HA HA!

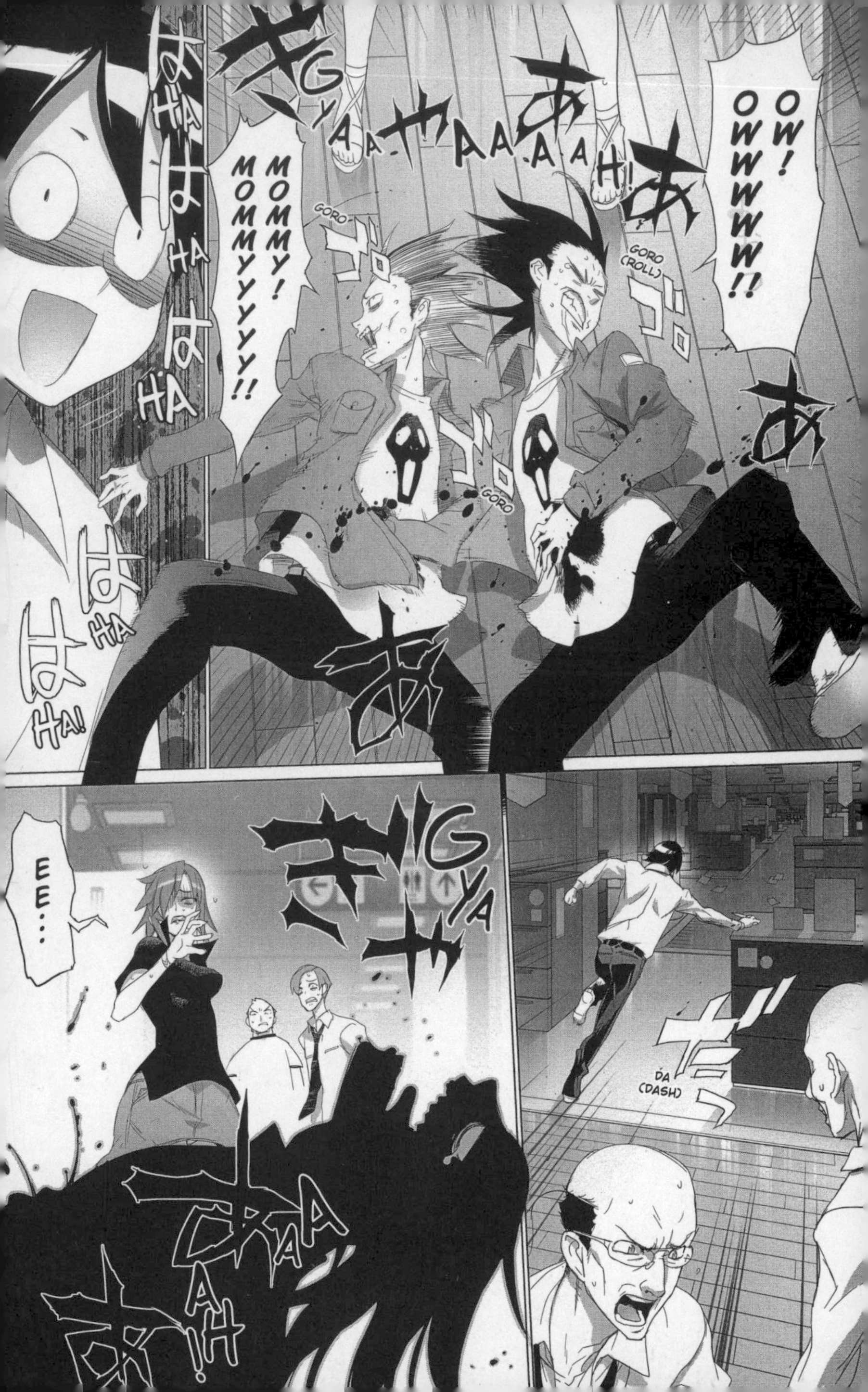
OW! OWWWWWWW!!
GYAAAAAAAH!
GORO (ROLL)
GORO
MOMMY! MOMMYYYYYYY!!
HA HA HA HA
GORO
HA HA!
DA (DASH)
EE...
GYA
GRAAAAH!

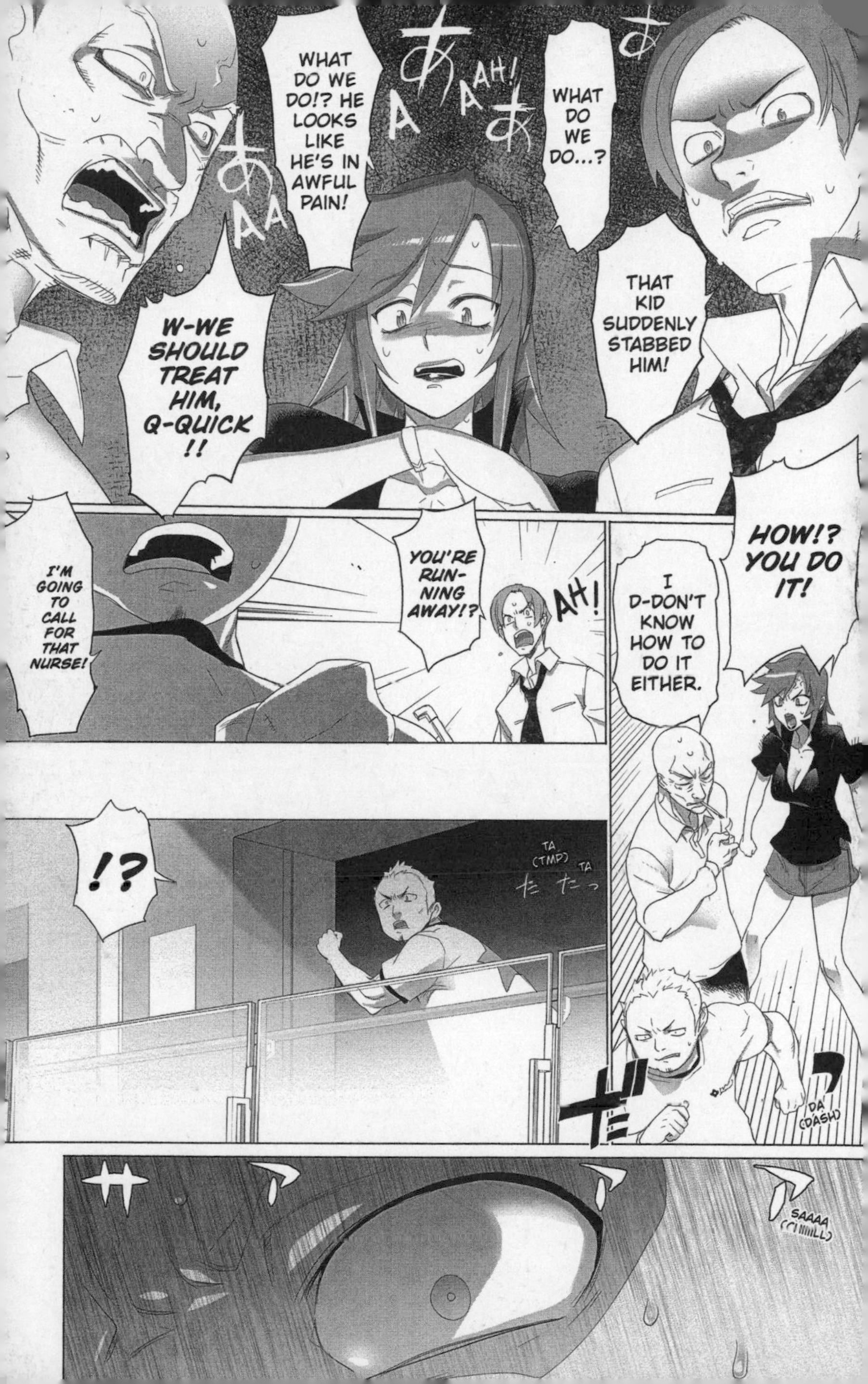
WHAT DO WE DO...?
THAT KID SUDDENLY STABBED HIM!
AAH!
A
A
WHAT DO WE DO!? HE LOOKS LIKE HE'S IN AWFUL PAIN!
AA
W-WE SHOULD TREAT HIM, Q-QUICK!!
HOW!? YOU DO IT!
I D-DON'T KNOW HOW TO DO IT EITHER.
DA (DASH)
YOU'RE RUN-NING AWAY!?
AH!
I'M GOING TO CALL FOR THAT NURSE!
TA (TMP) TA
!?
SAAAA (CHIIIILL)

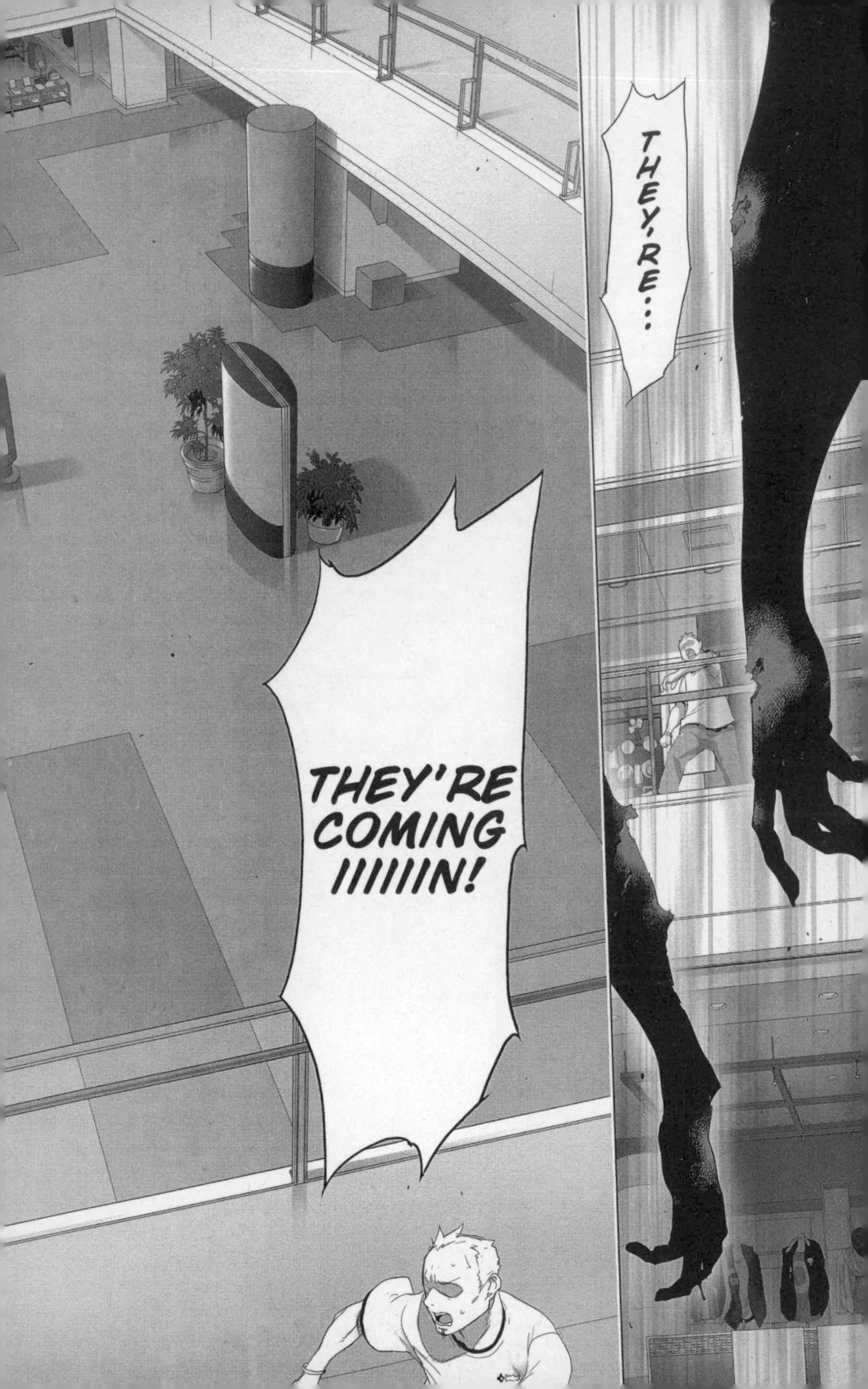
THEY'RE...
THEY'RE COMING IIIIIIN!

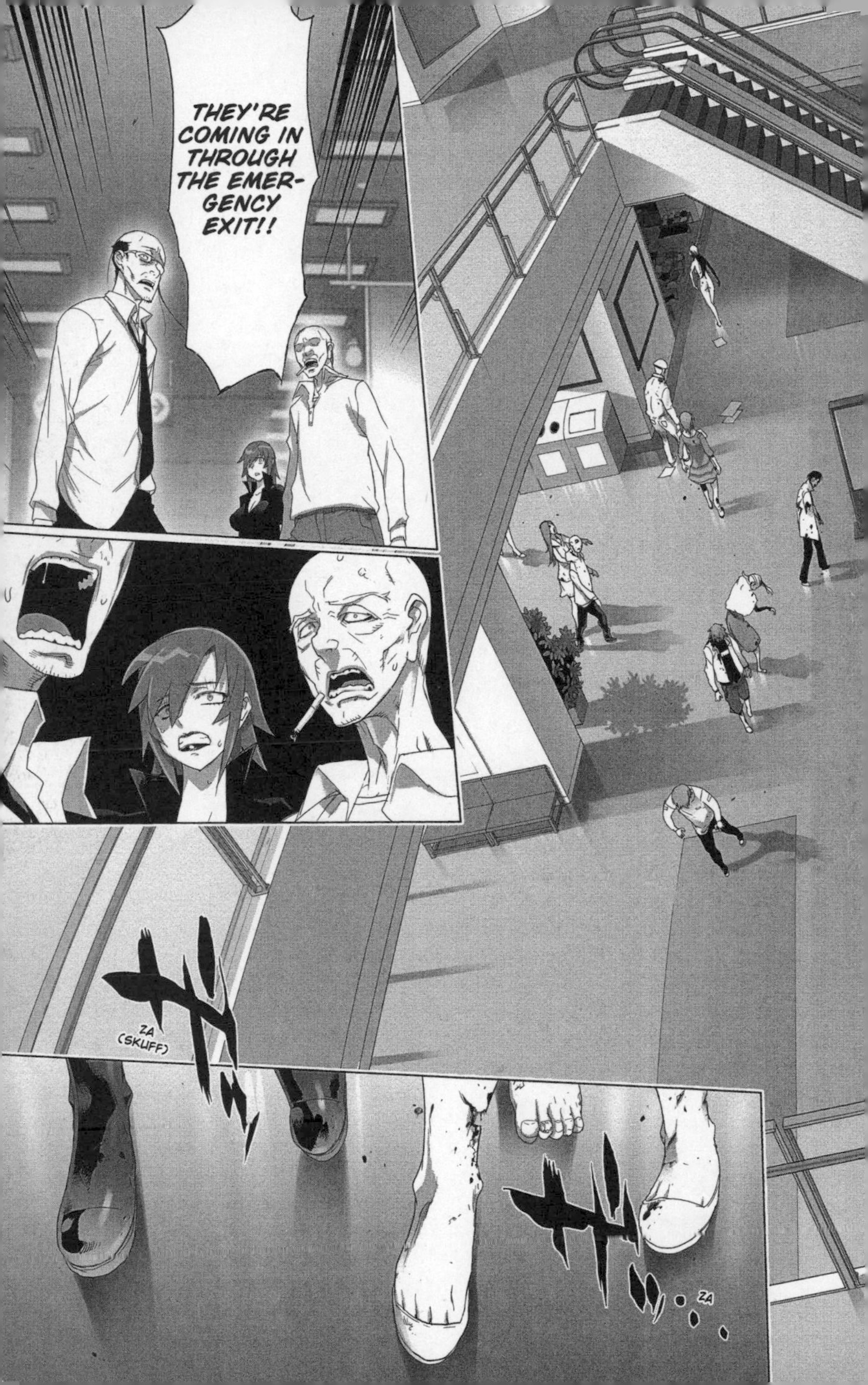
THEY'RE COMING IN THROUGH THE EMERGENCY EXIT!!
ZA (SKUFF)
ZA

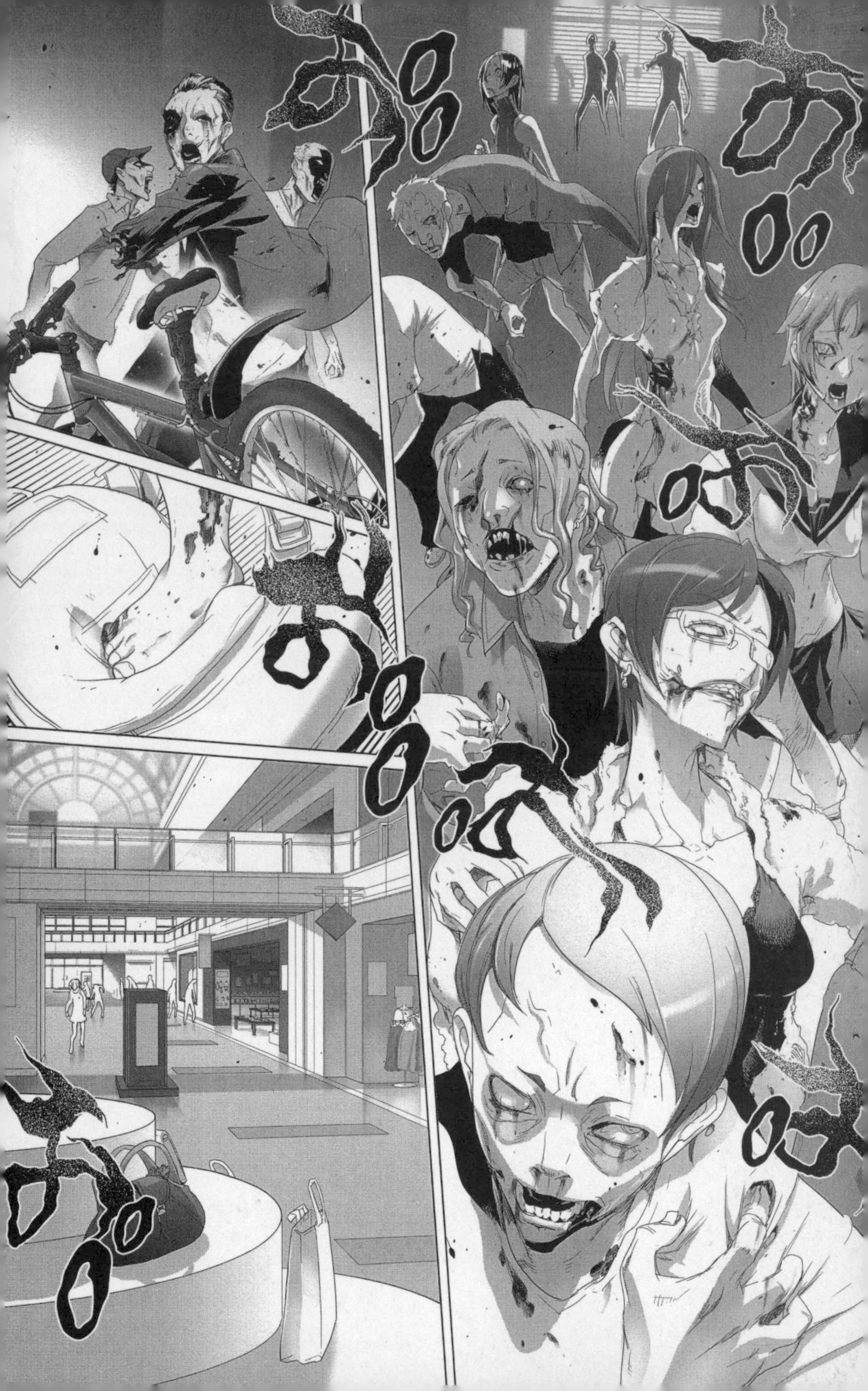

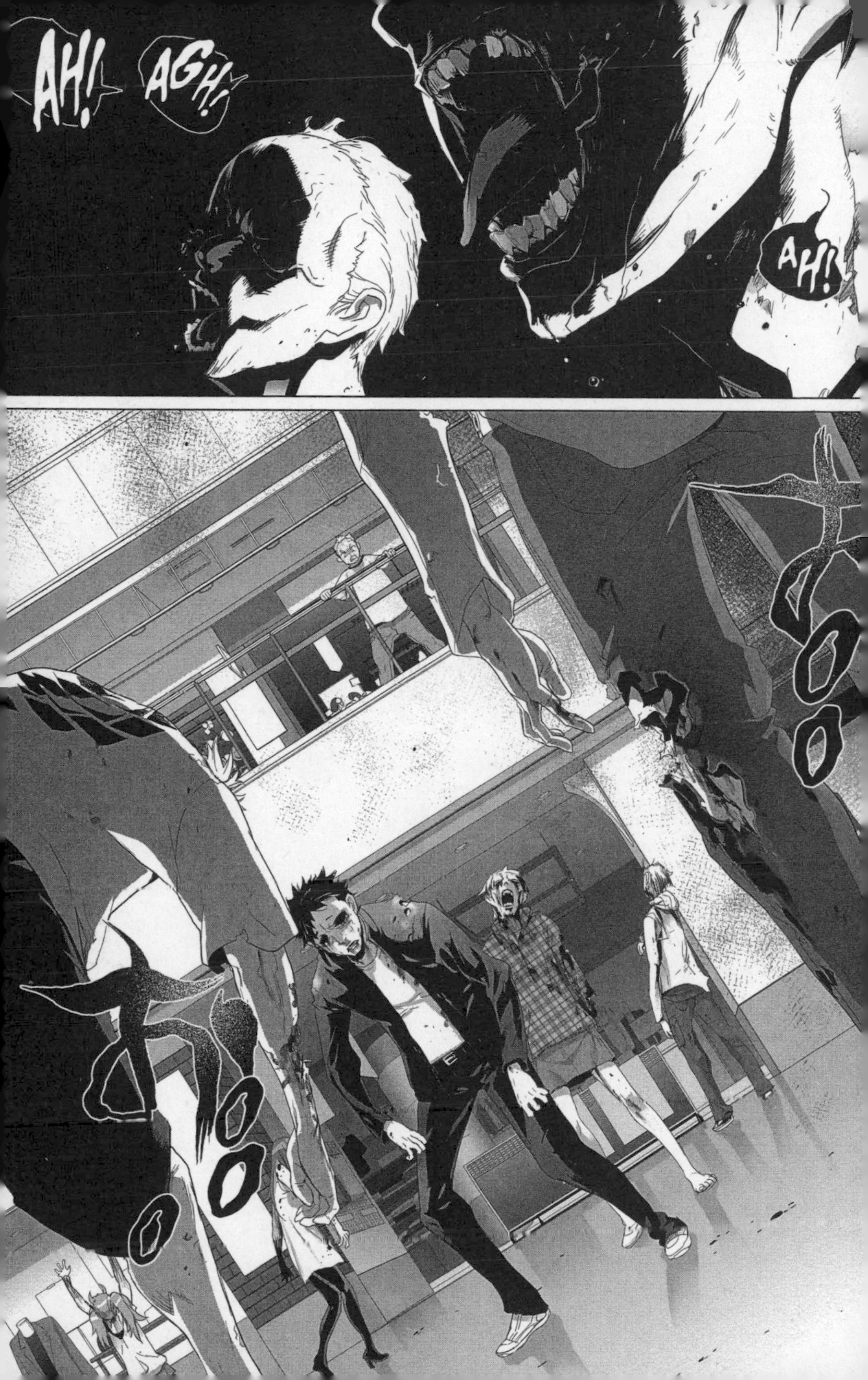
AH!
AGH!
AH!

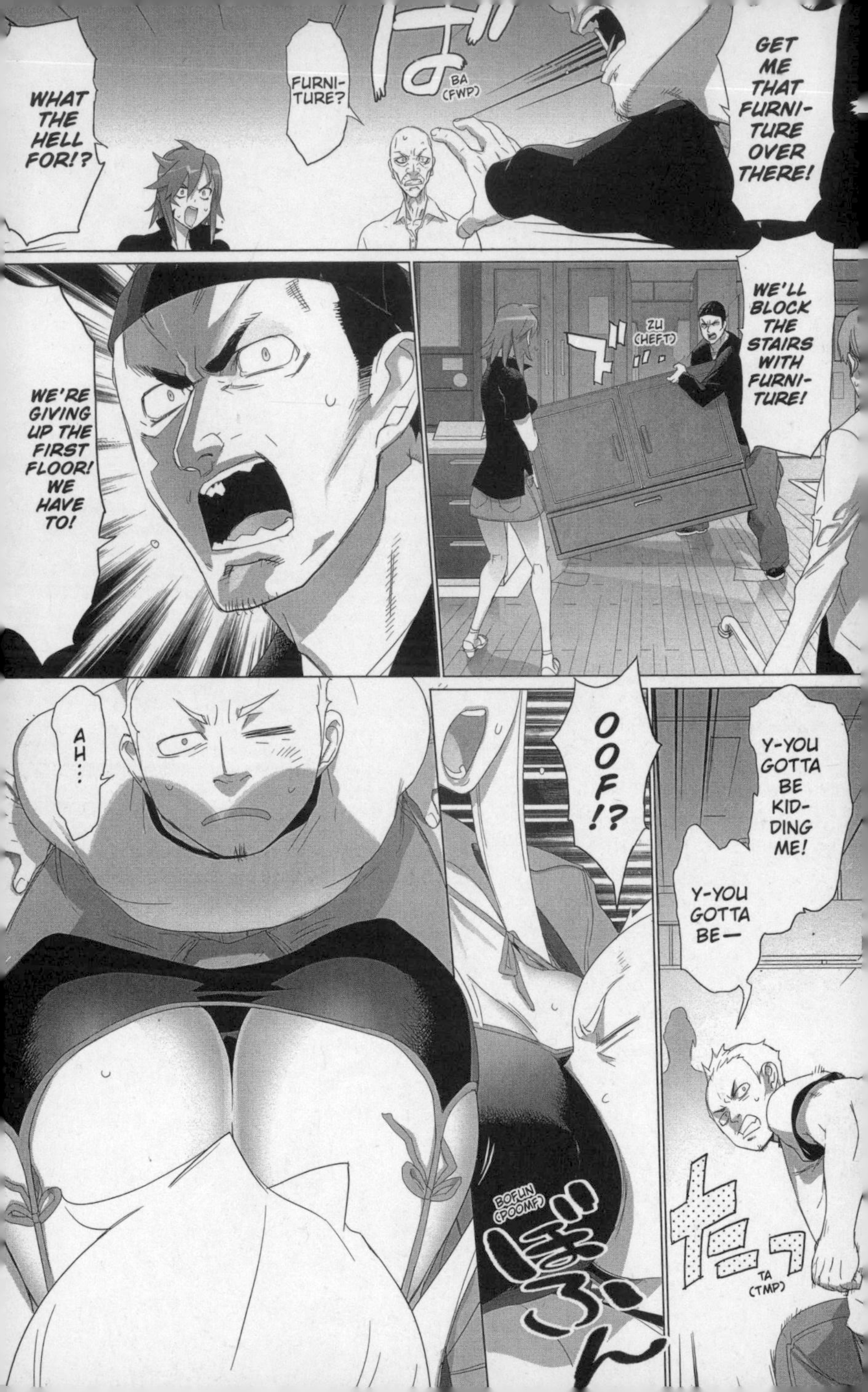
GET ME THAT FURNITURE OVER THERE!
BA (FWP)
FURNITURE?
WHAT THE HELL FOR!?
WE'LL BLOCK THE STAIRS WITH FURNITURE!
ZU (HEFT)
WE'RE GIVING UP THE FIRST FLOOR! WE HAVE TO!
Y-YOU GOTTA BE KIDDING ME!
Y-YOU GOTTA BE—
TA (TMP)
OOF!?
AH…
BOFUN (POOMF)

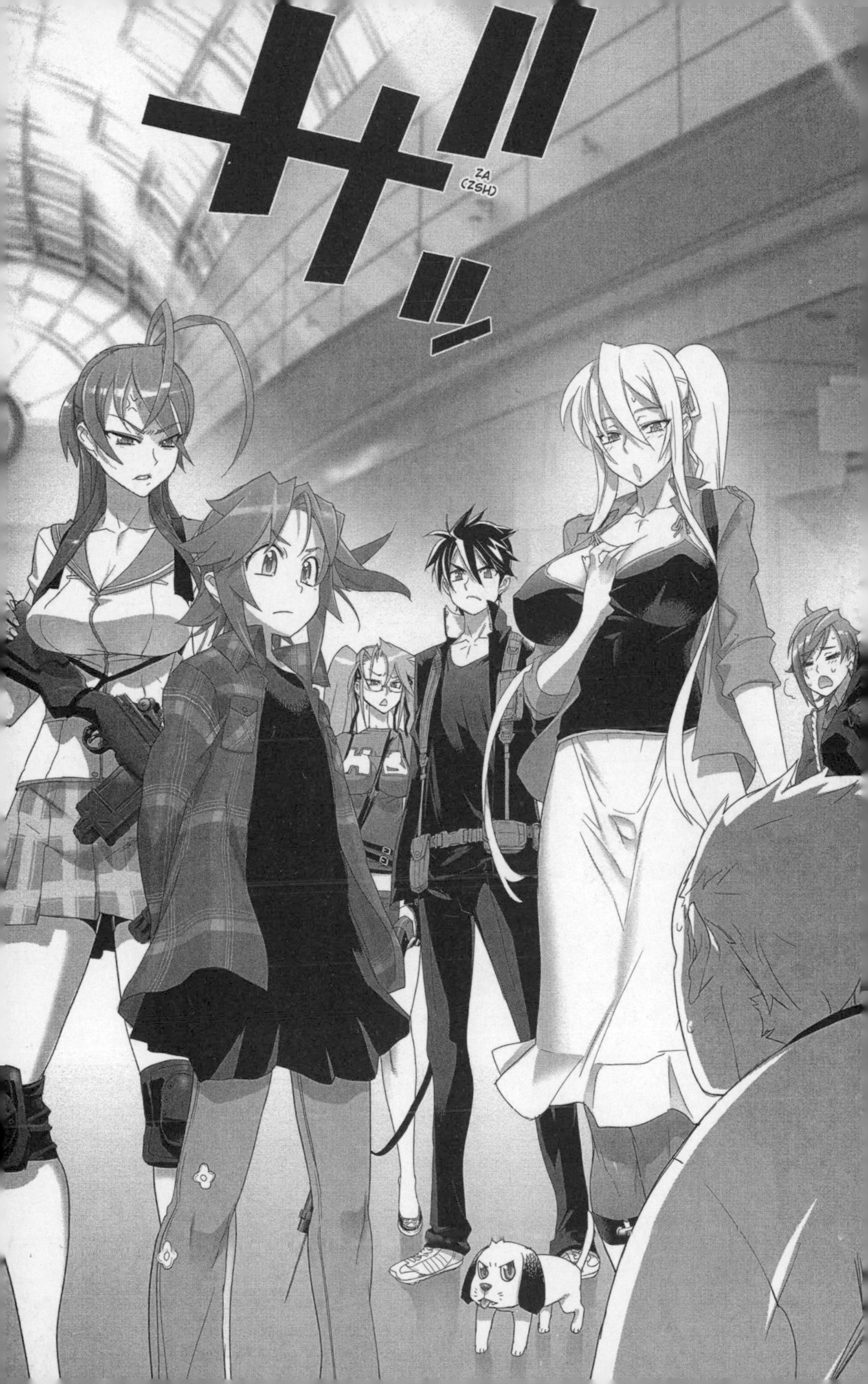
ZA
(ZSH)

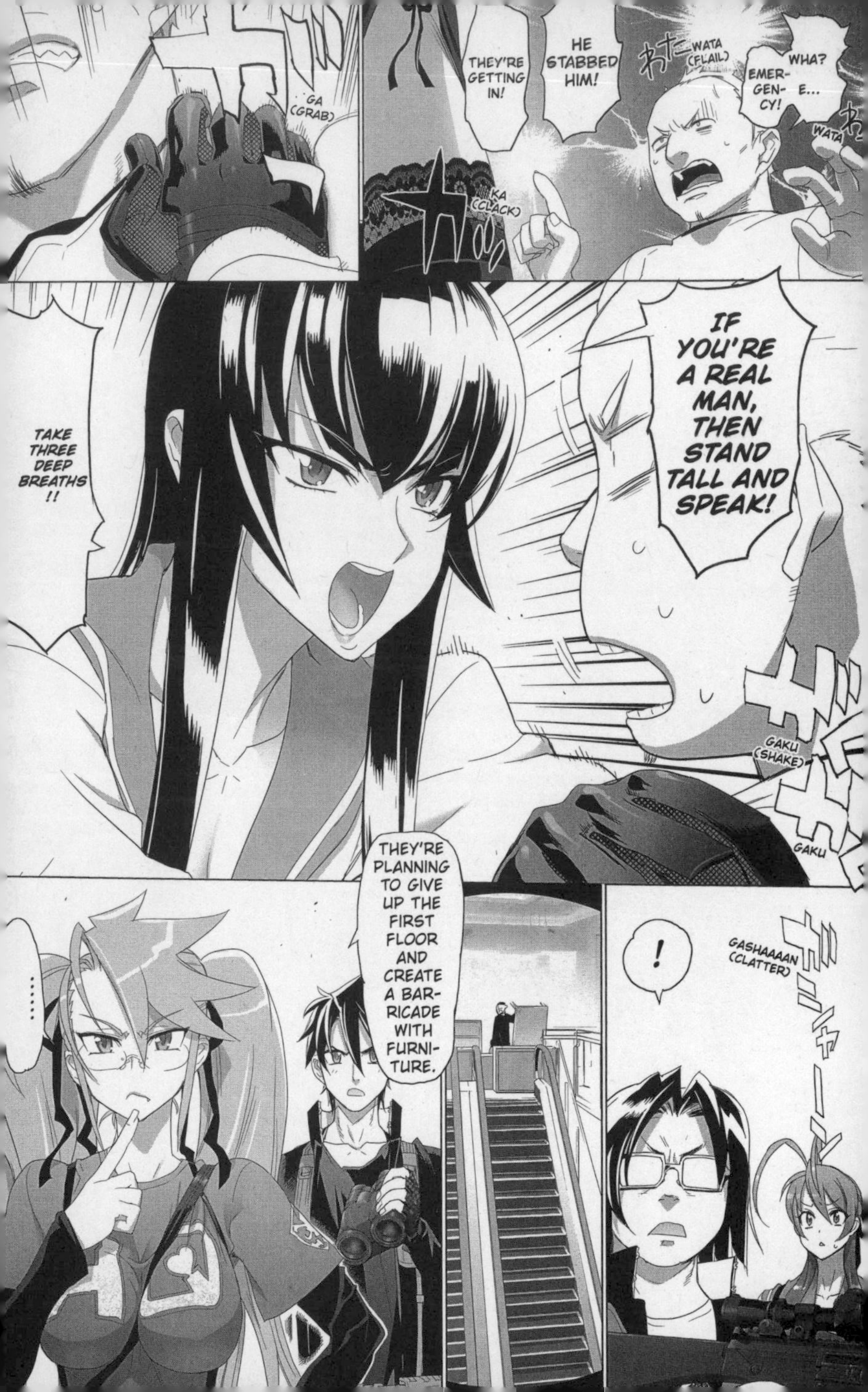

WHA? E...
EMER-GEN-CY!
WATA
わた
WATA (FLAIL)
HE STABBED HIM!
THEY'RE GETTING IN!
KA (CLACK)
GA (GRAB)
IF YOU'RE A REAL MAN, THEN STAND TALL AND SPEAK!
GAKU (SHAKE)
GAKU
TAKE THREE DEEP BREATHS!!
GASHAAAAN (CLATTER)
!
THEY'RE PLANNING TO GIVE UP THE FIRST FLOOR AND CREATE A BARRICADE WITH FURNITURE.
......

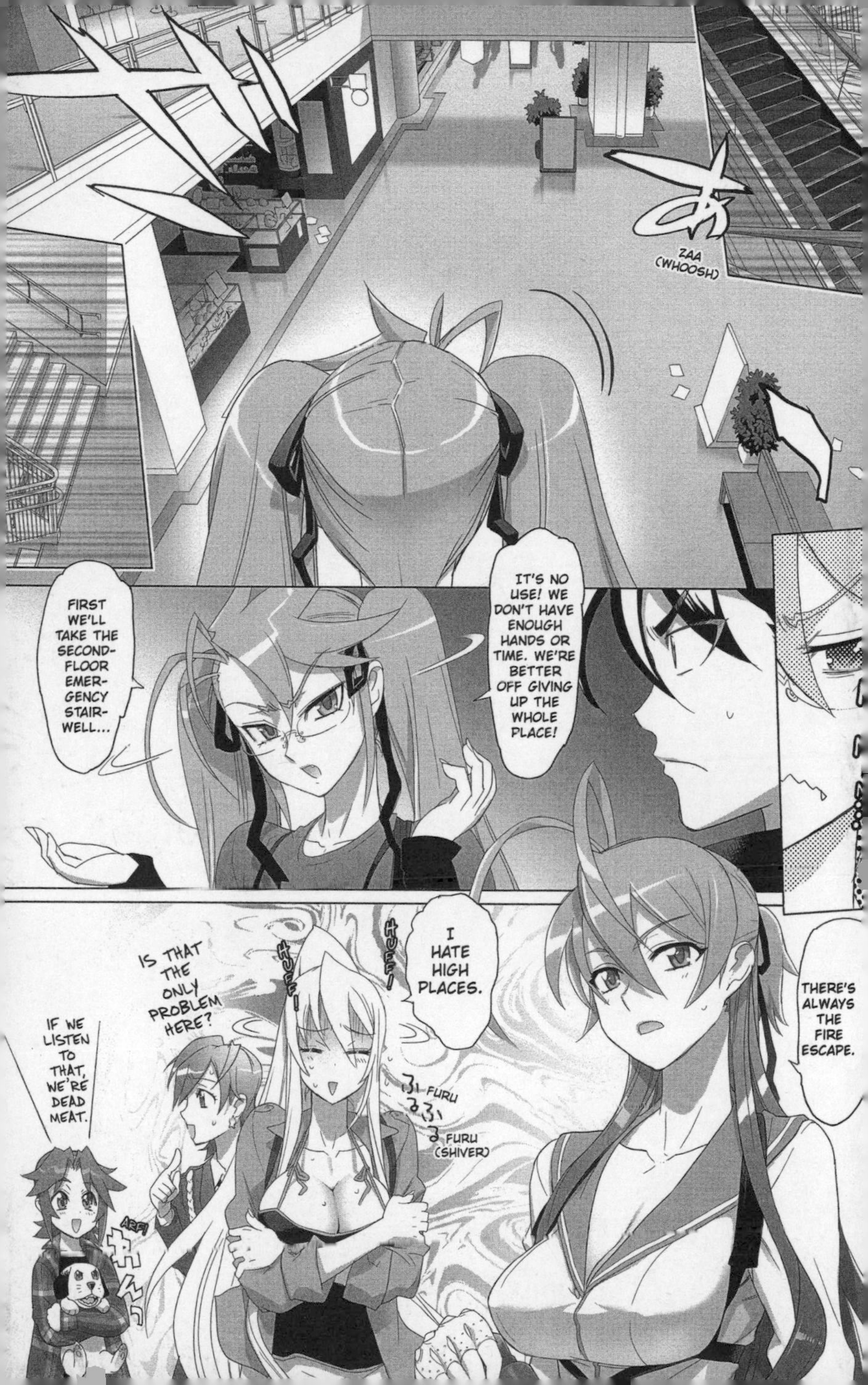
ZAA
(WHOOSH)
IT'S NO USE! WE DON'T HAVE ENOUGH HANDS OR TIME. WE'RE BETTER OFF GIVING UP THE WHOLE PLACE!
FIRST WE'LL TAKE THE SECOND-FLOOR EMERGENCY STAIR-WELL...
THERE'S ALWAYS THE FIRE ESCAPE.
I HATE HIGH PLACES.
HUFF! HUFF!
FURU FURU (SHIVER)
IS THAT THE ONLY PROBLEM HERE?
IF WE LISTEN TO THAT, WE'RE DEAD MEAT.
ARF!

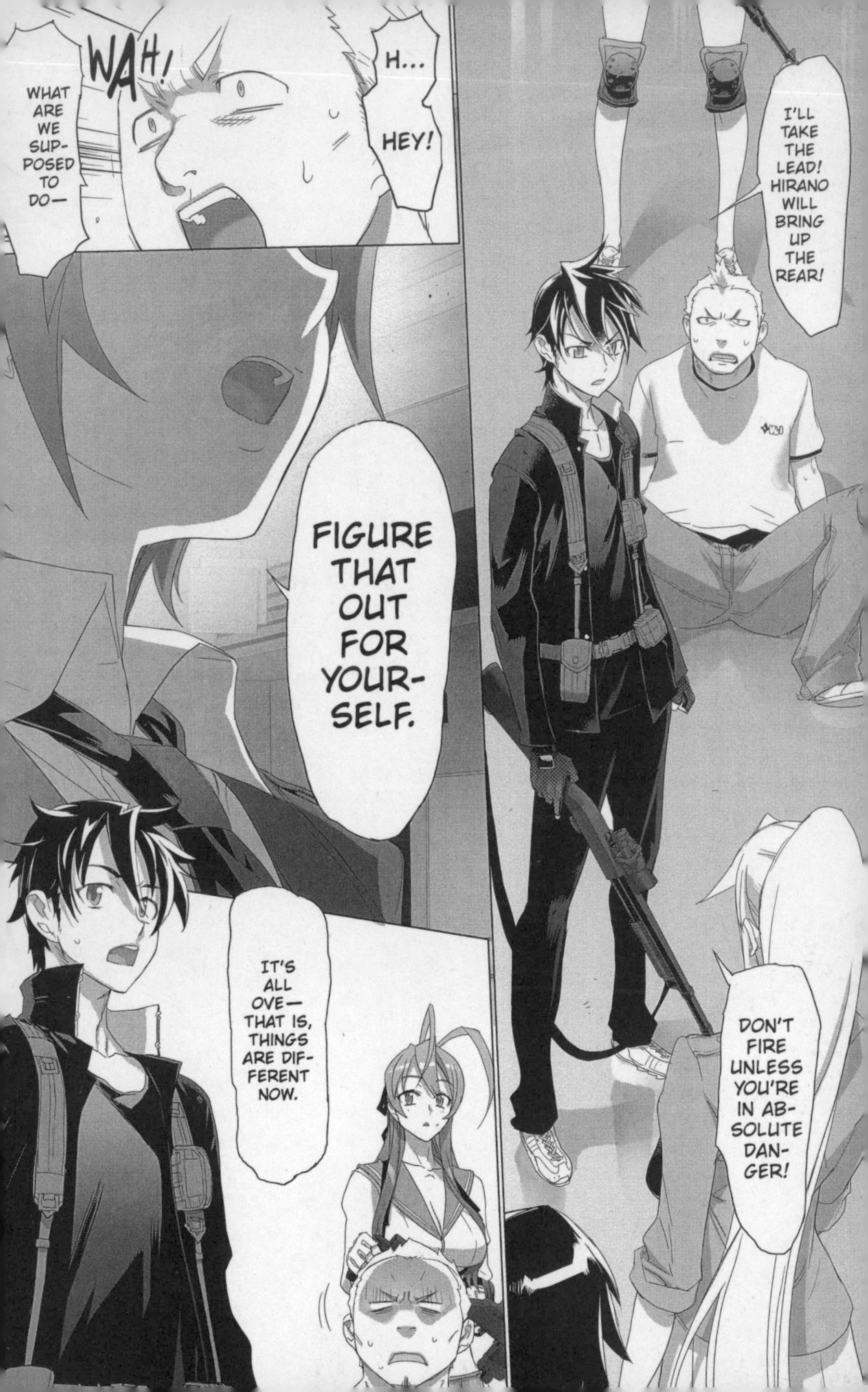
I'LL TAKE THE LEAD! HIRANO WILL BRING UP THE REAR!
DON'T FIRE UNLESS YOU'RE IN ABSOLUTE DANGER!
H... HEY!
WAH!
WHAT ARE WE SUPPOSED TO DO—
FIGURE THAT OUT FOR YOURSELF.
IT'S ALL OVE— THAT IS, THINGS ARE DIFFERENT NOW.

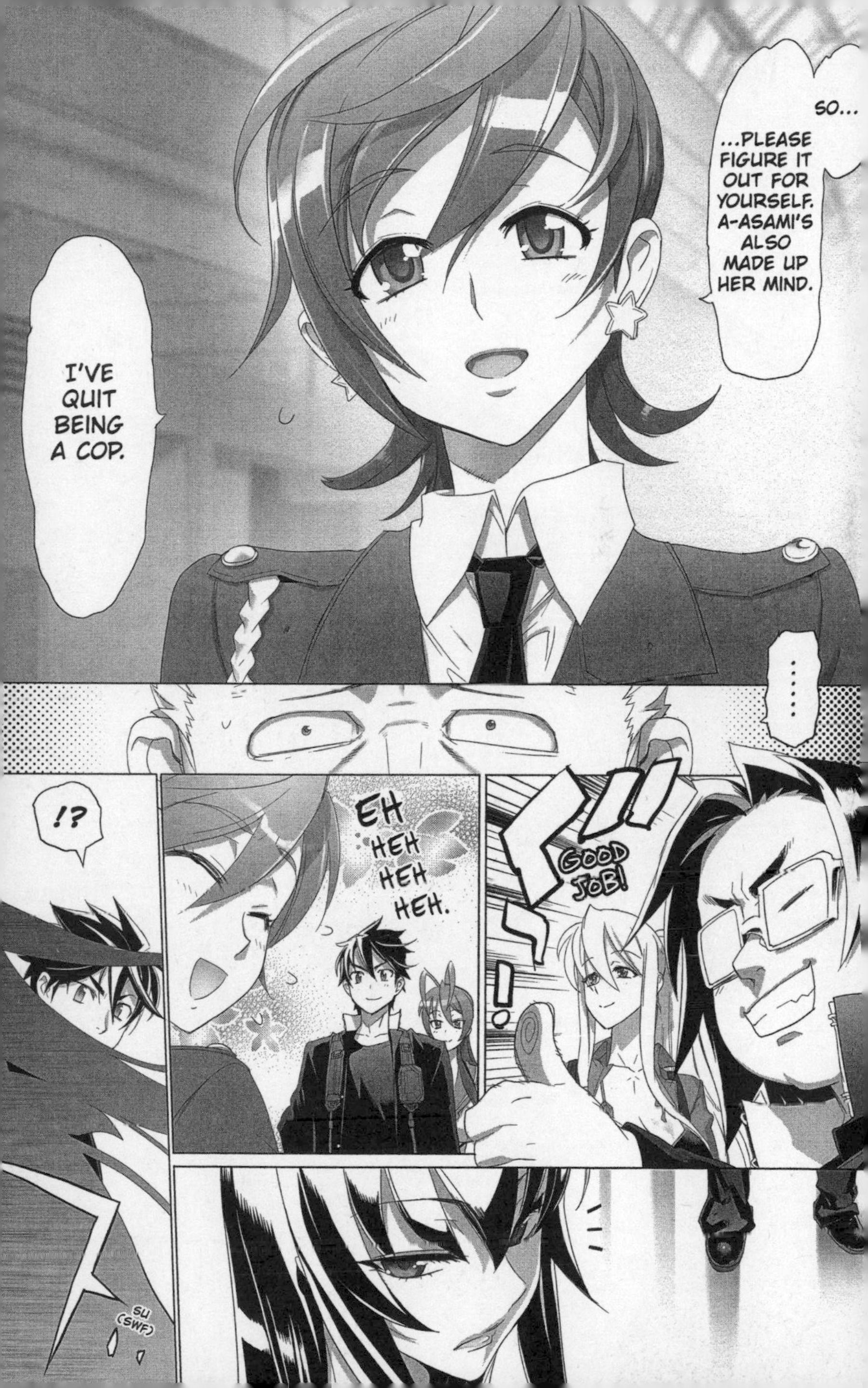
SO...
...PLEASE FIGURE IT OUT FOR YOURSELF. A-ASAMI'S ALSO MADE UP HER MIND.
I'VE QUIT BEING A COP.
......
GOOD JOB!
!
EH HEH HEH HEH.
!?
SU (SWF)

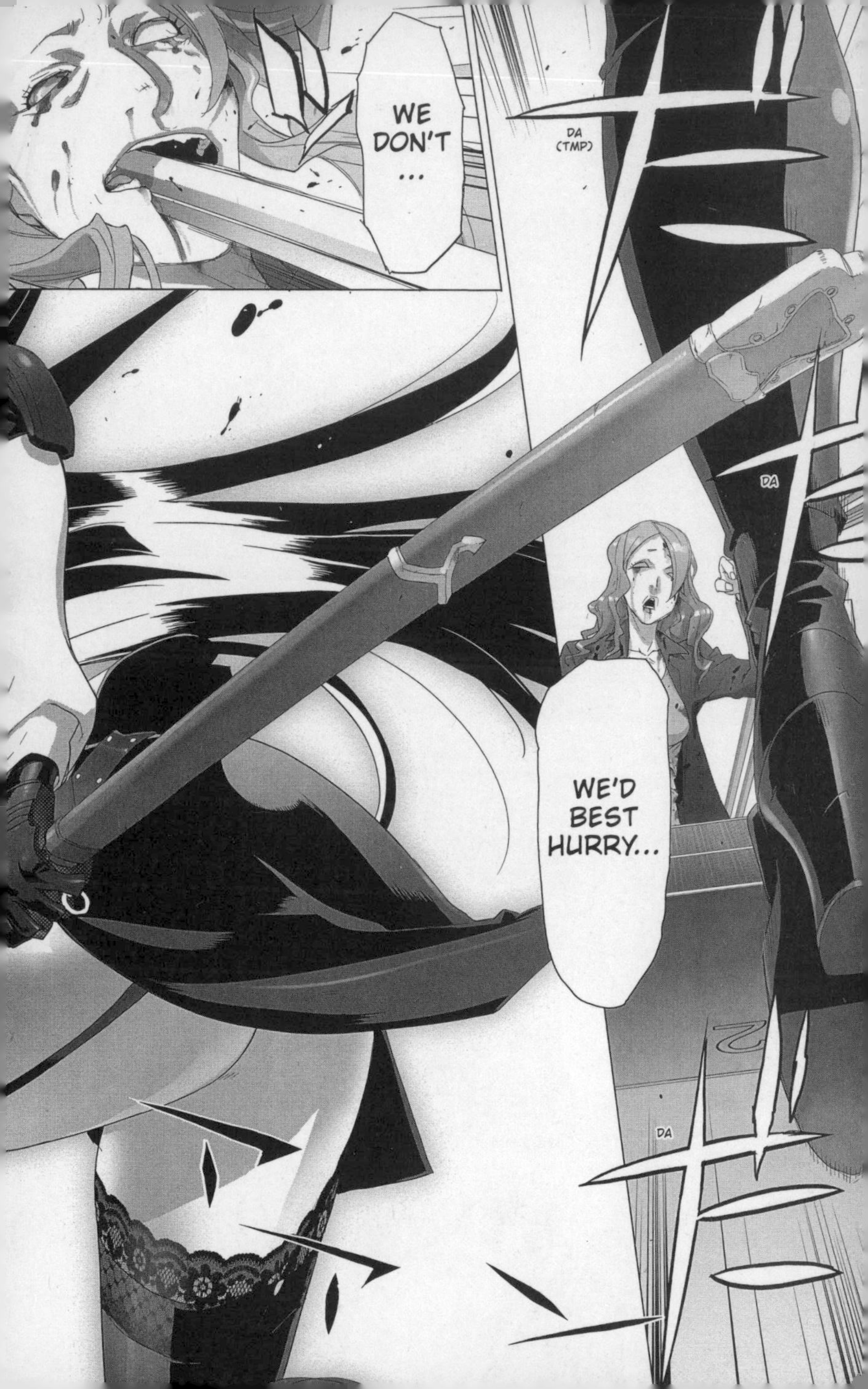
DA (TMP)
WE DON'T ...
DA
WE'D BEST HURRY...
DA

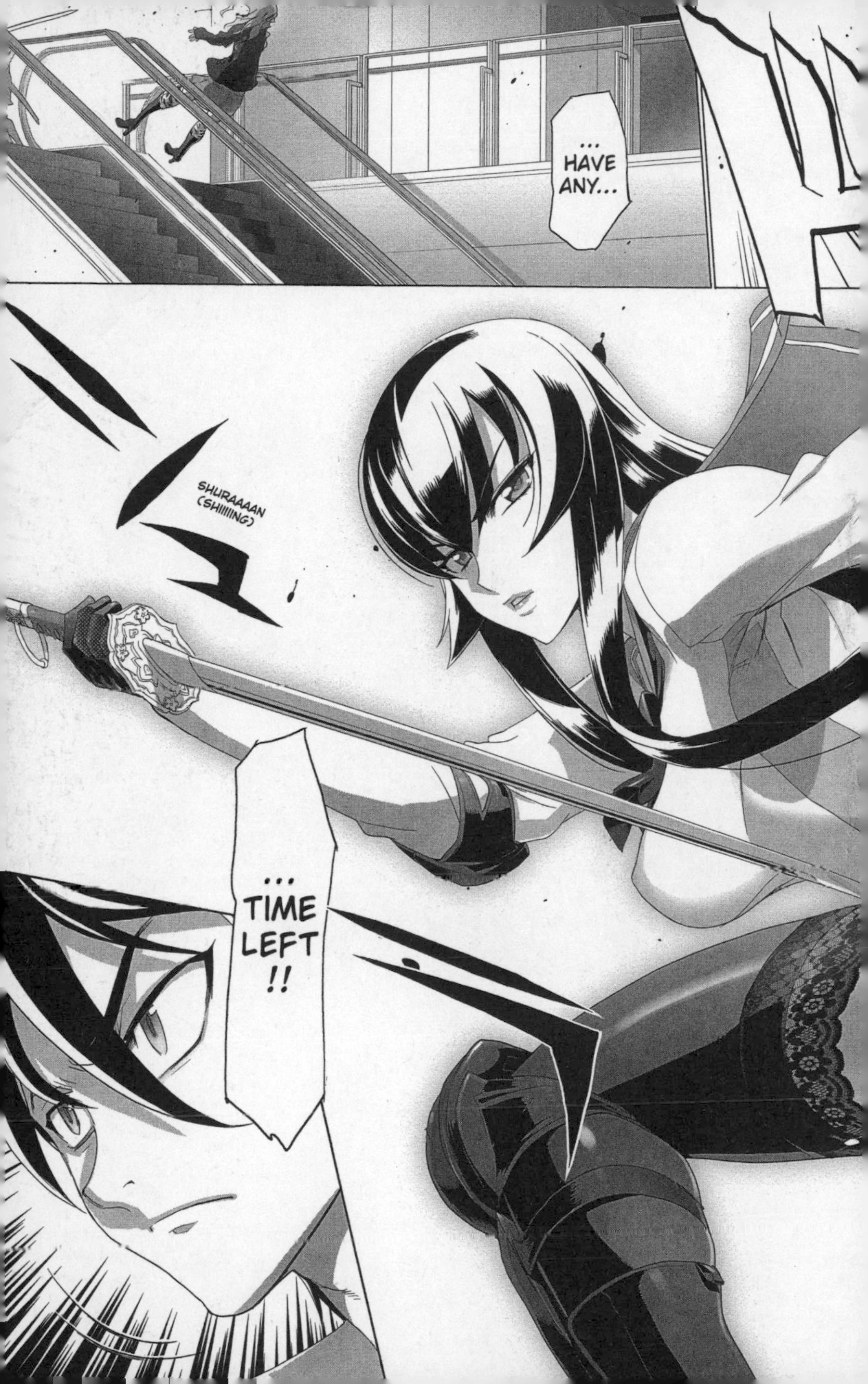
... HAVE ANY...
SHURAAAAN (SHIIIIING)
... TIME LEFT !!

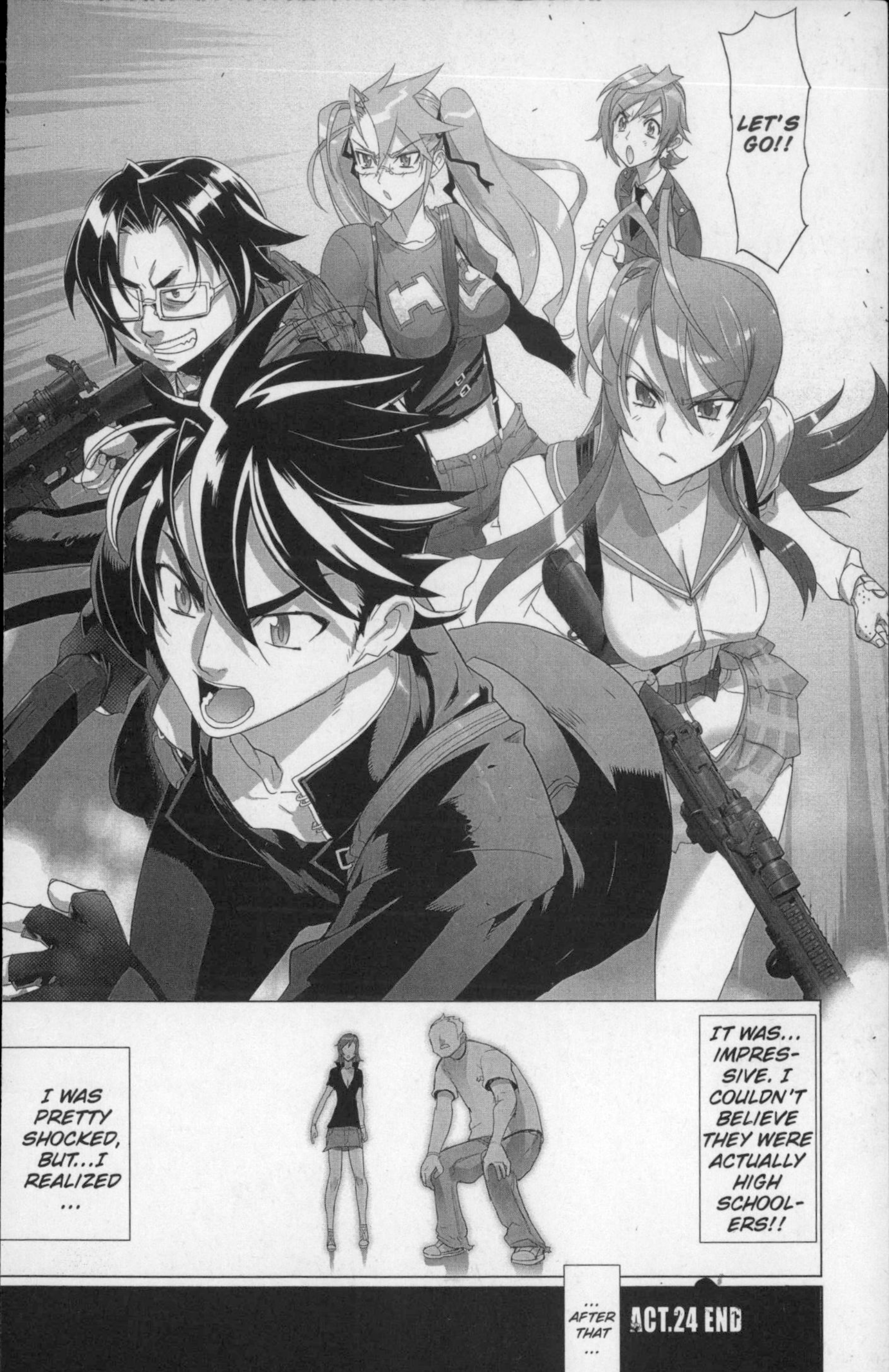
LET'S GO!!
IT WAS... IMPRESSIVE. I COULDN'T BELIEVE THEY WERE ACTUALLY HIGH SCHOOLERS!!
I WAS PRETTY SHOCKED, BUT...I REALIZED ...
... AFTER THAT ...
ACT.24 END

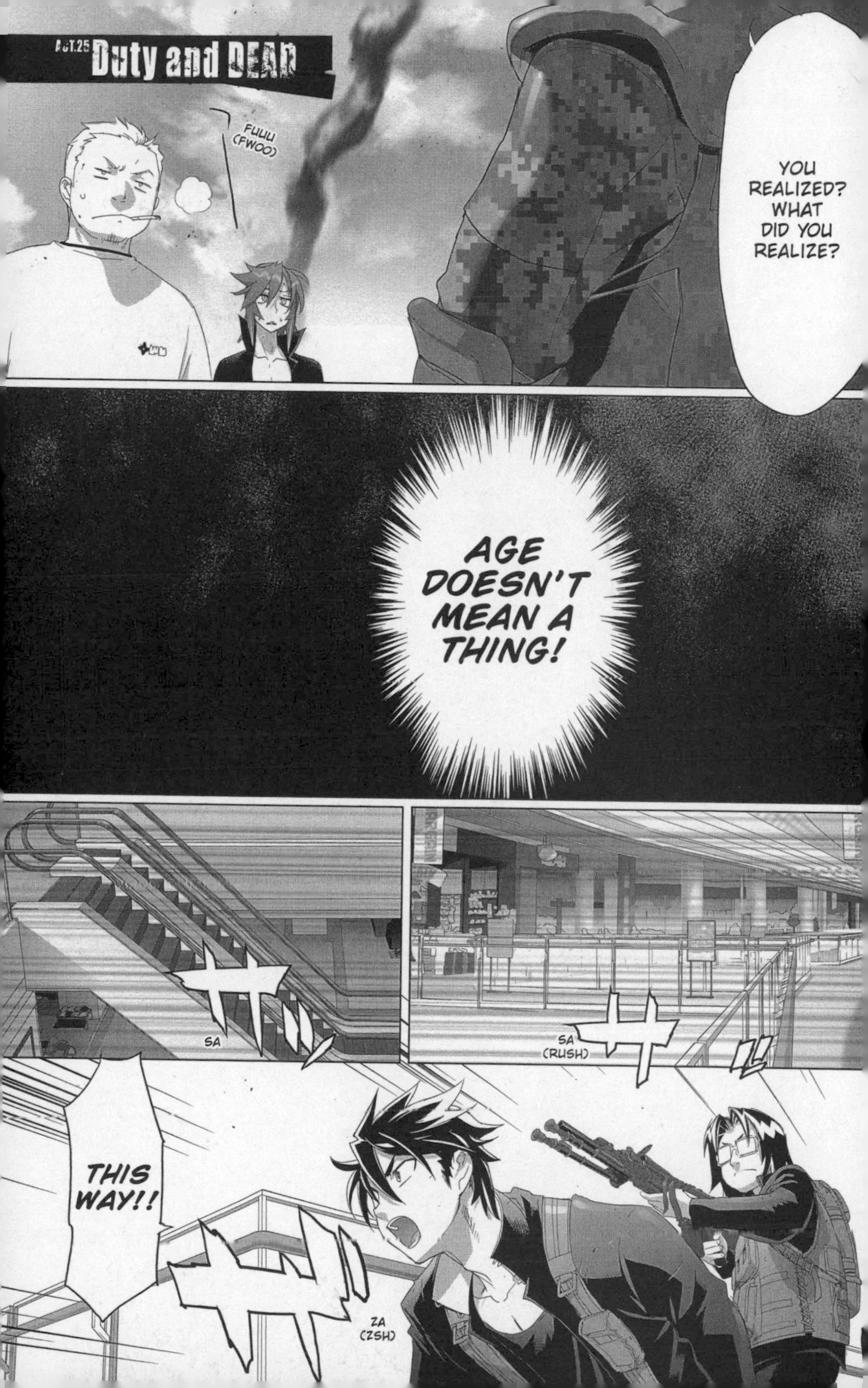
ACT.25 Duty and DEAD
YOU REALIZED? WHAT DID YOU REALIZE?
FUUU (FWOO)
AGE DOESN'T MEAN A THING!
SA (RUSH)
SA
THIS WAY!!
ZA (ZSH)

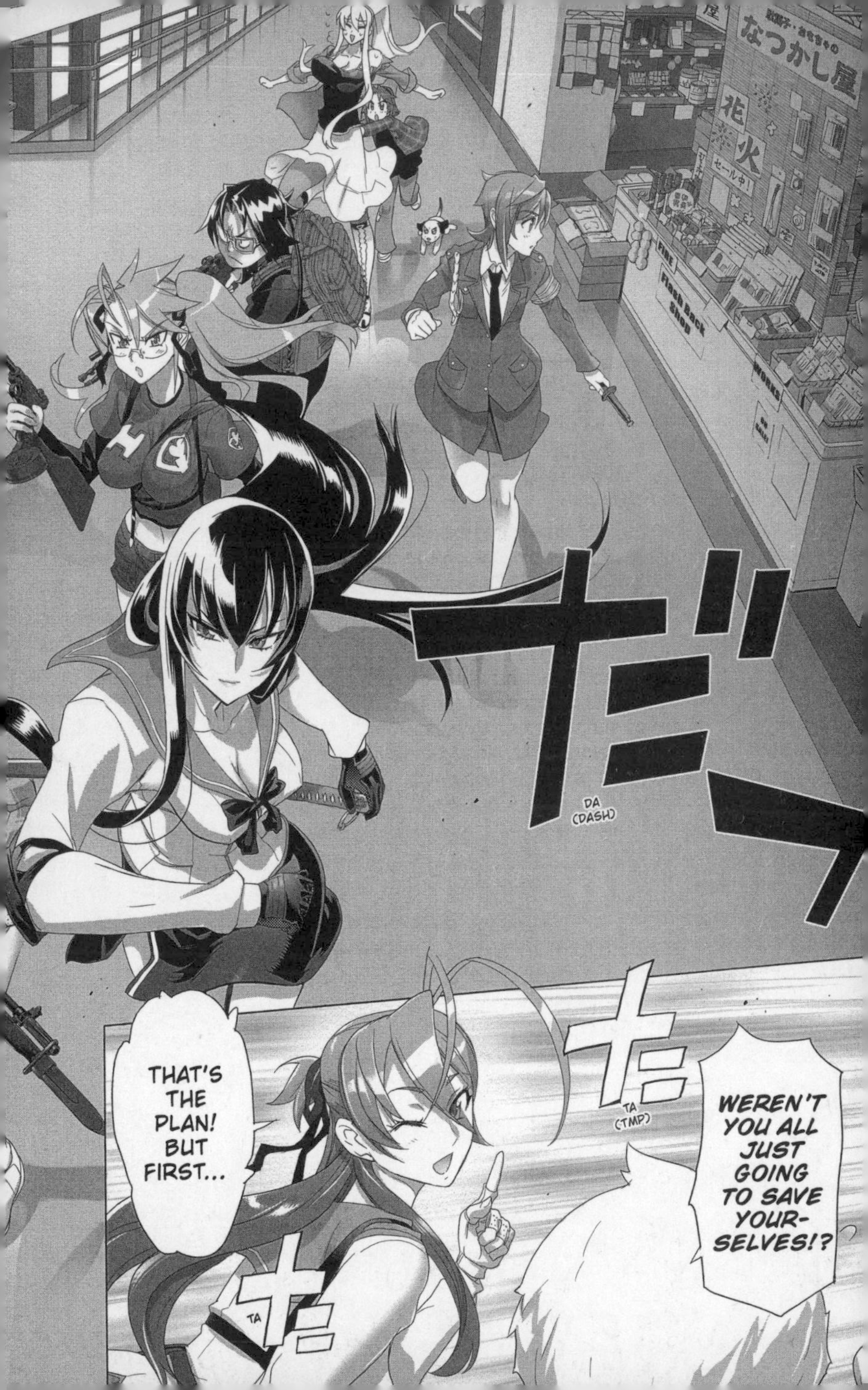
なつかし屋
花火
セール中!
Flash Back Shop
DA
(DASH)
WEREN'T YOU ALL JUST GOING TO SAVE YOUR-SELVES!?
TA
(TMP)
THAT'S THE PLAN! BUT FIRST...
TA

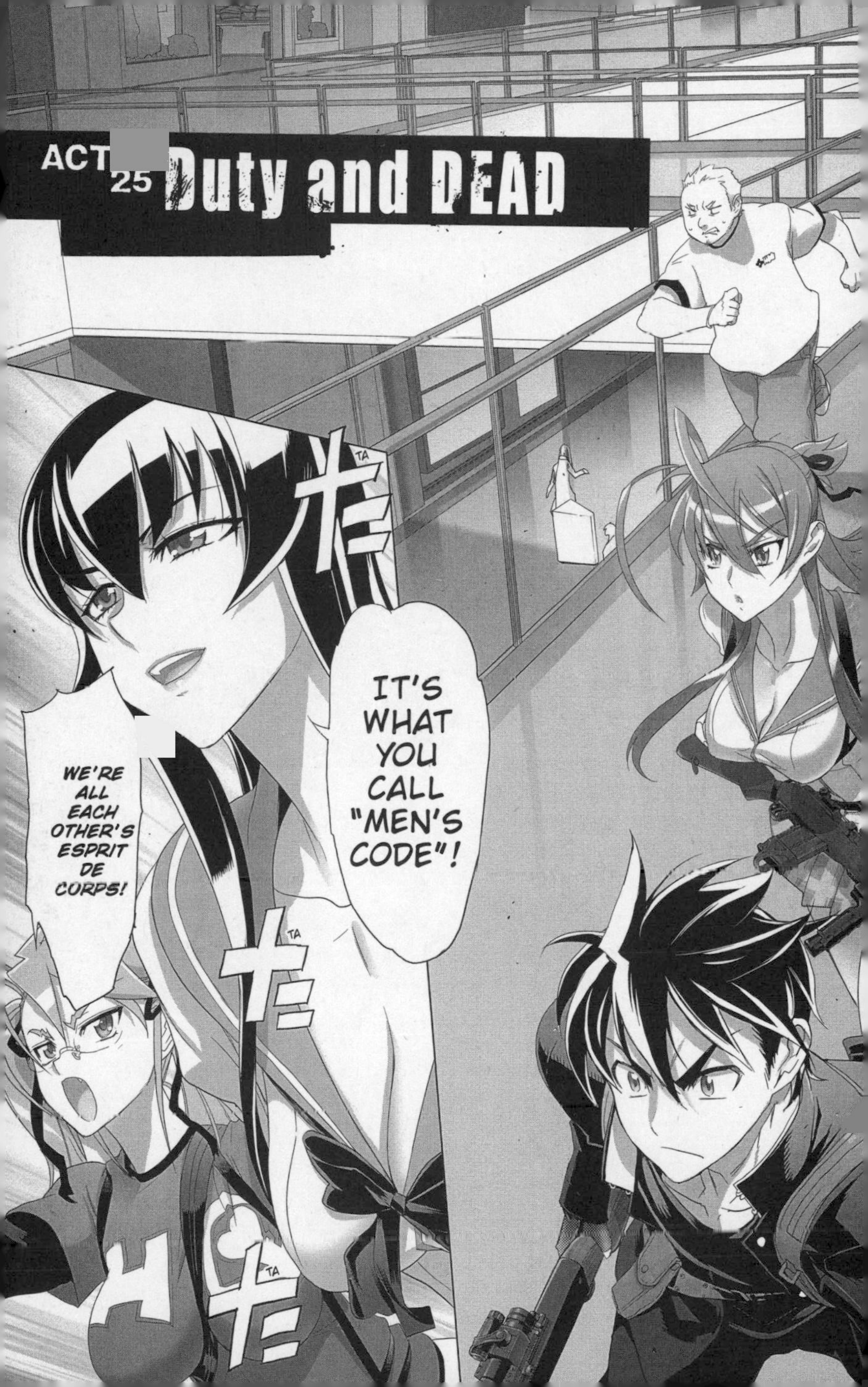
ACT 25 Duty and DEAD
TA
IT'S WHAT YOU CALL "MEN'S CODE"!
WE'RE ALL EACH OTHER'S ESPRIT DE CORPS!
TA
TA

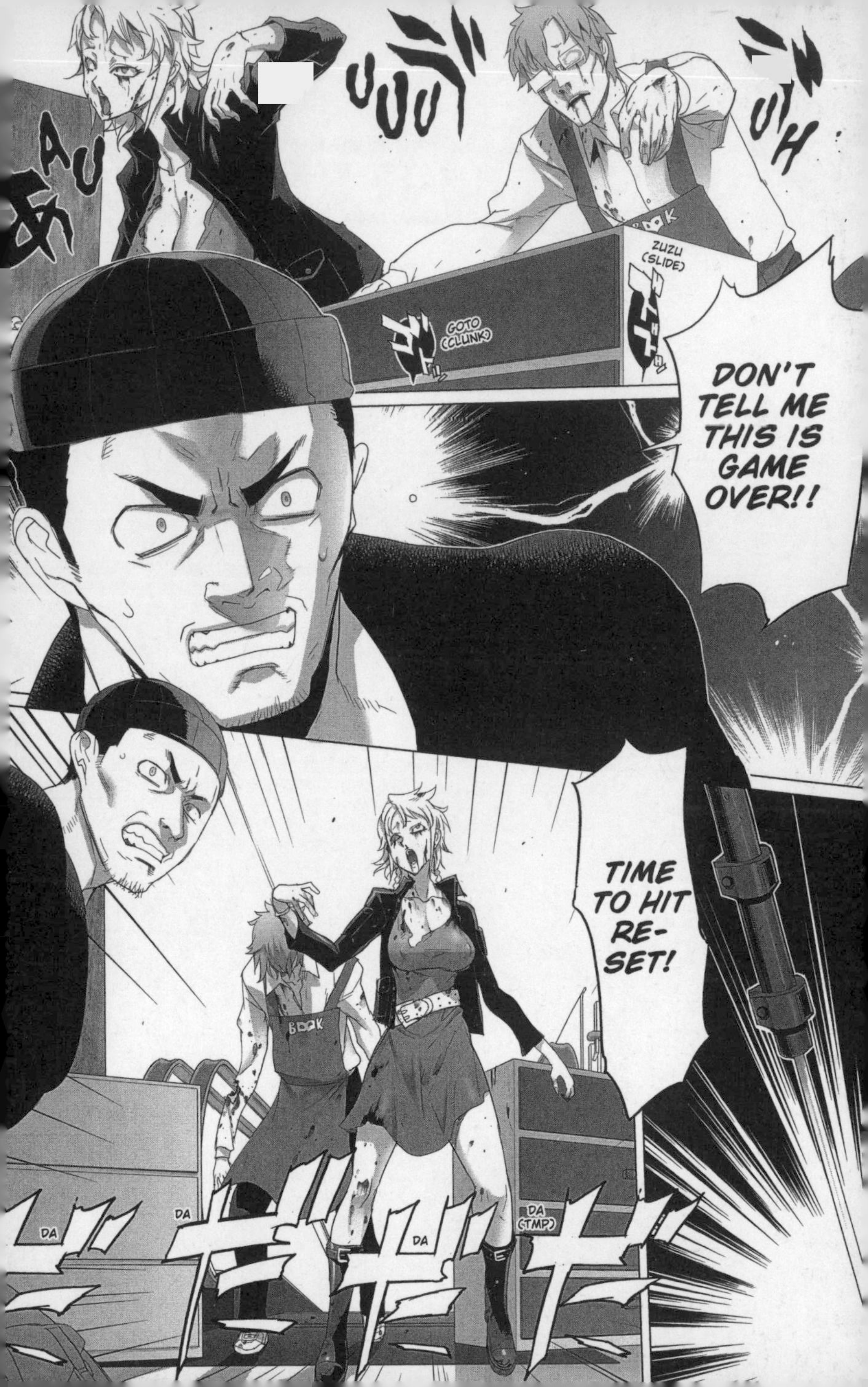
UUH
UUU
AU
ZUZU (SLIDE)
GOTO (CLUNK)
DON'T TELL ME THIS IS GAME OVER!!
TIME TO HIT RE-SET!
DA (TMP)
DA
DA
DA

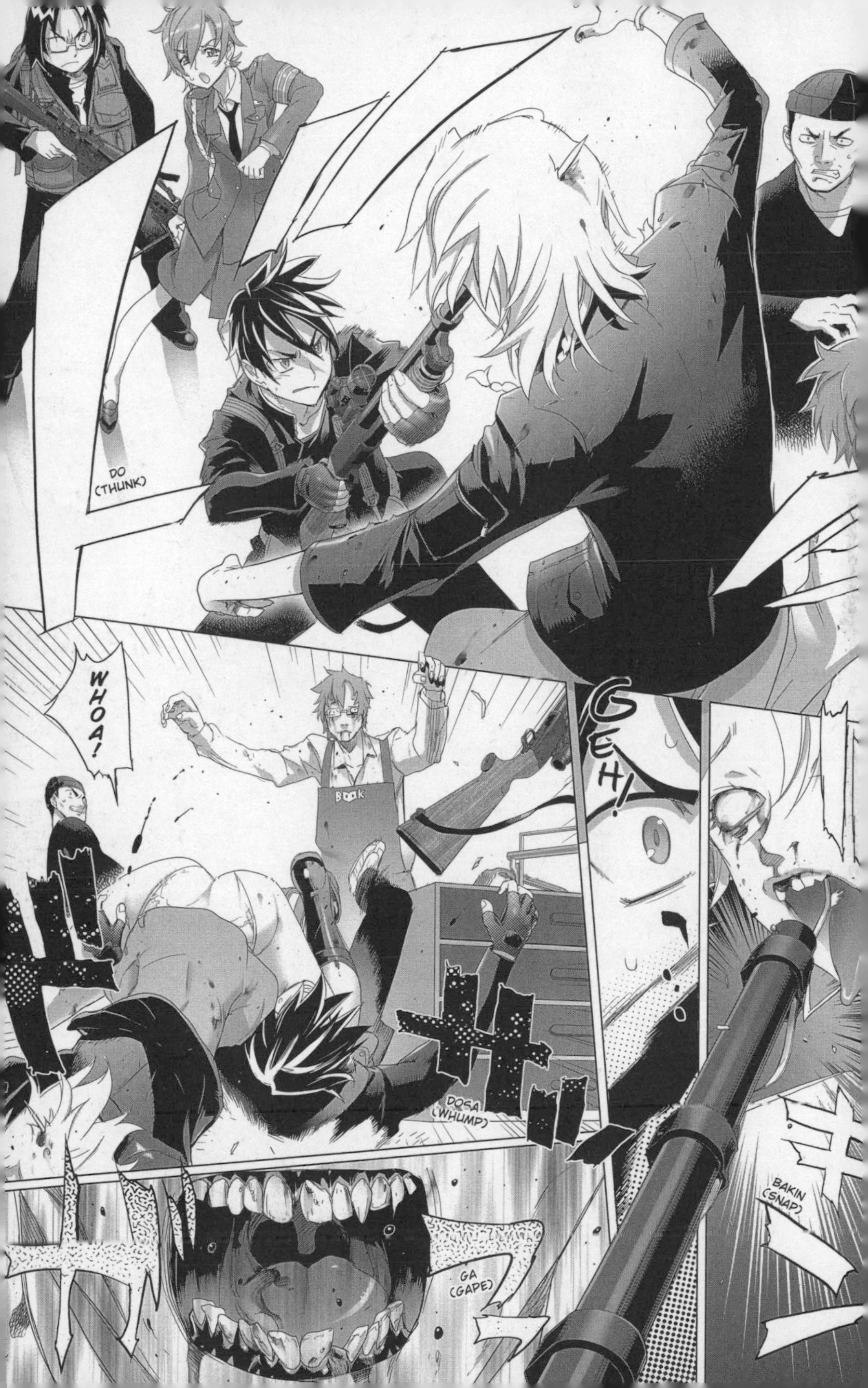
DO (THUNK)
BAKIN (SNAP)
GEH!
WHOA!
DOSA (WHUMP)
GA (GAPE)

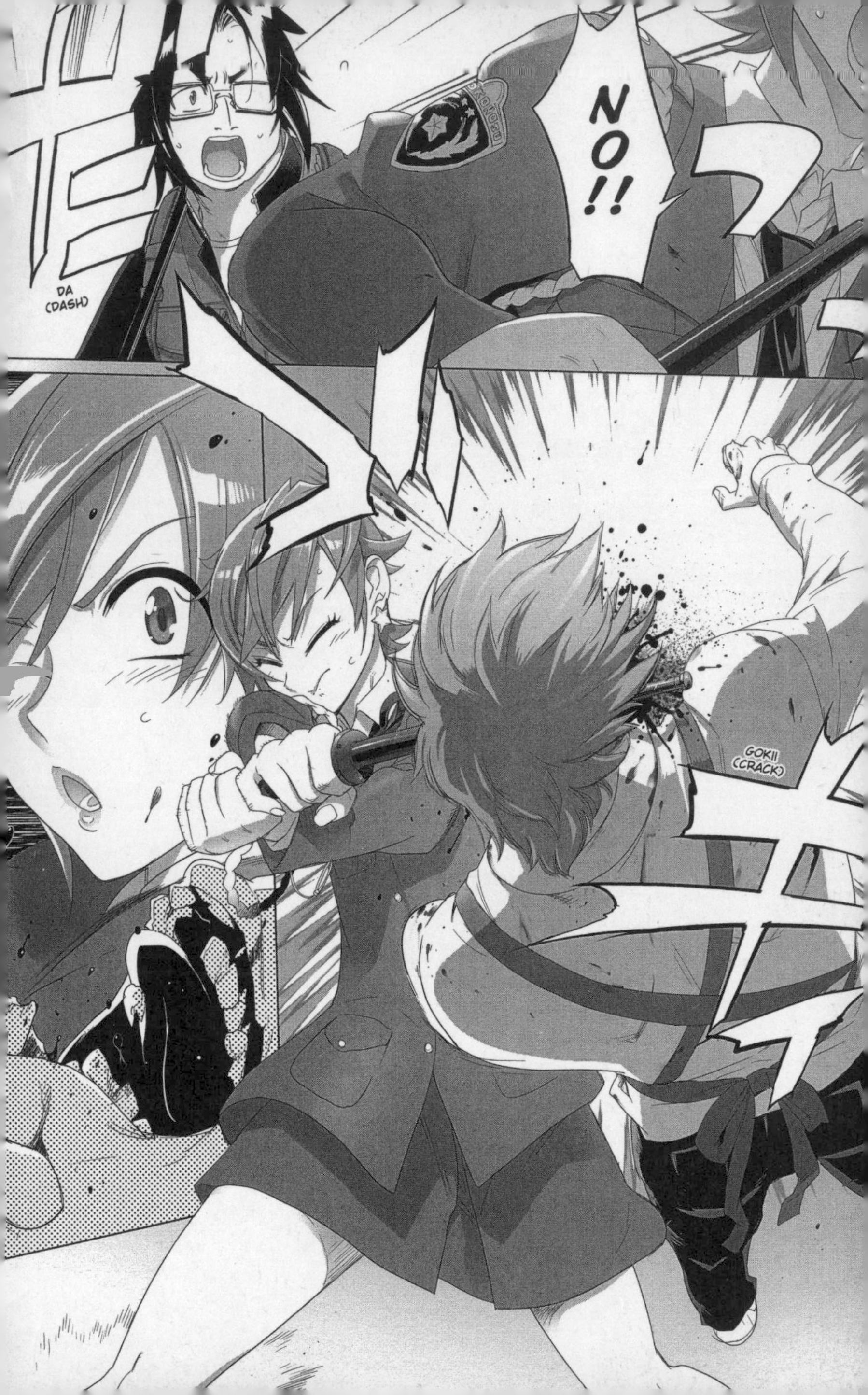
NO!!
DA (DASH)
GOKII (CRACK)

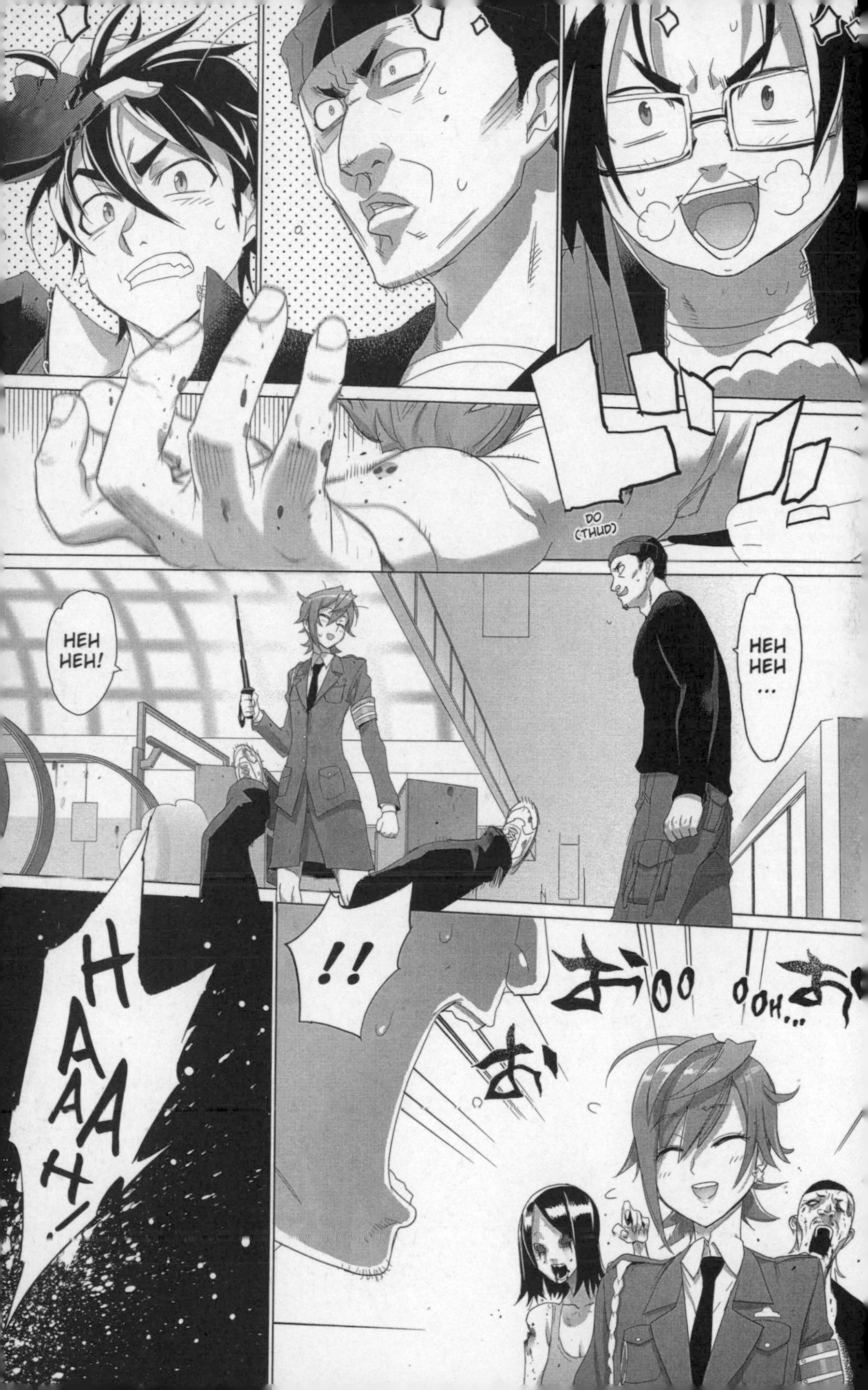
DO
(THUD)
HEH HEH ...
HEH HEH!
おOO
OOH...お
お
!!
HAAAH!

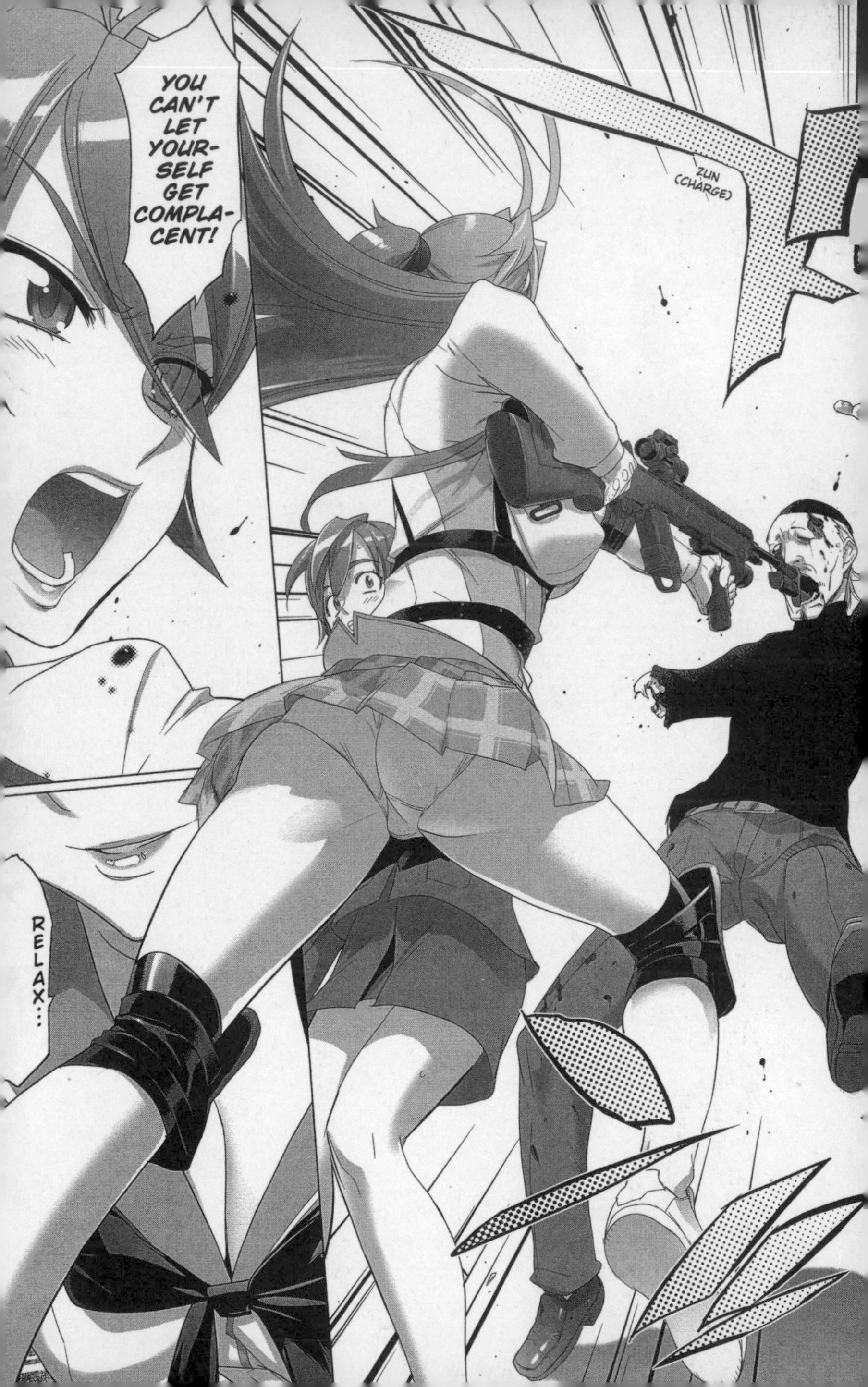
ZUN (CHARGE)
YOU CAN'T LET YOURSELF GET COMPLACENT!
RELAX...

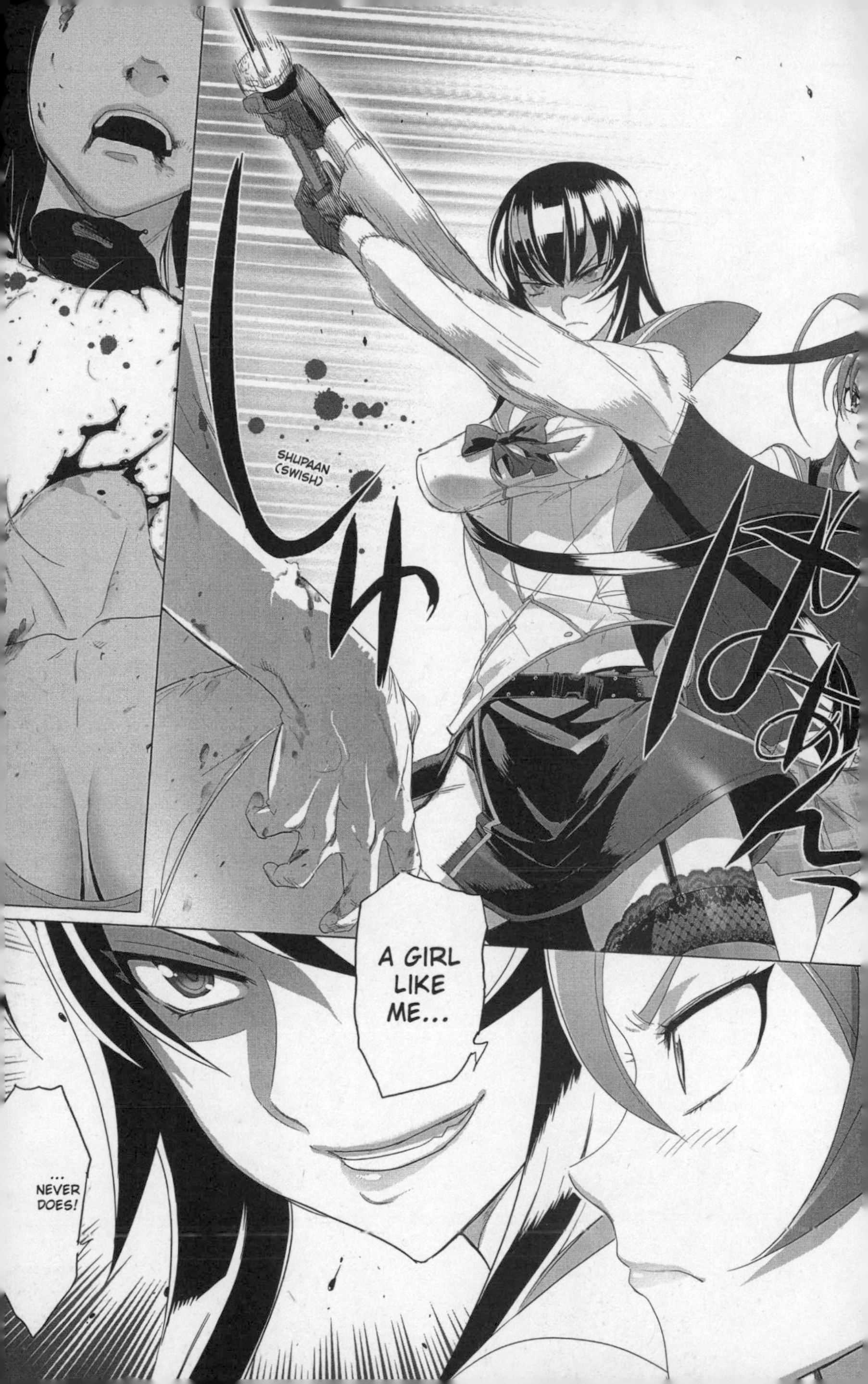
SHUPAAN (SWISH)
A GIRL LIKE ME...
... NEVER DOES!

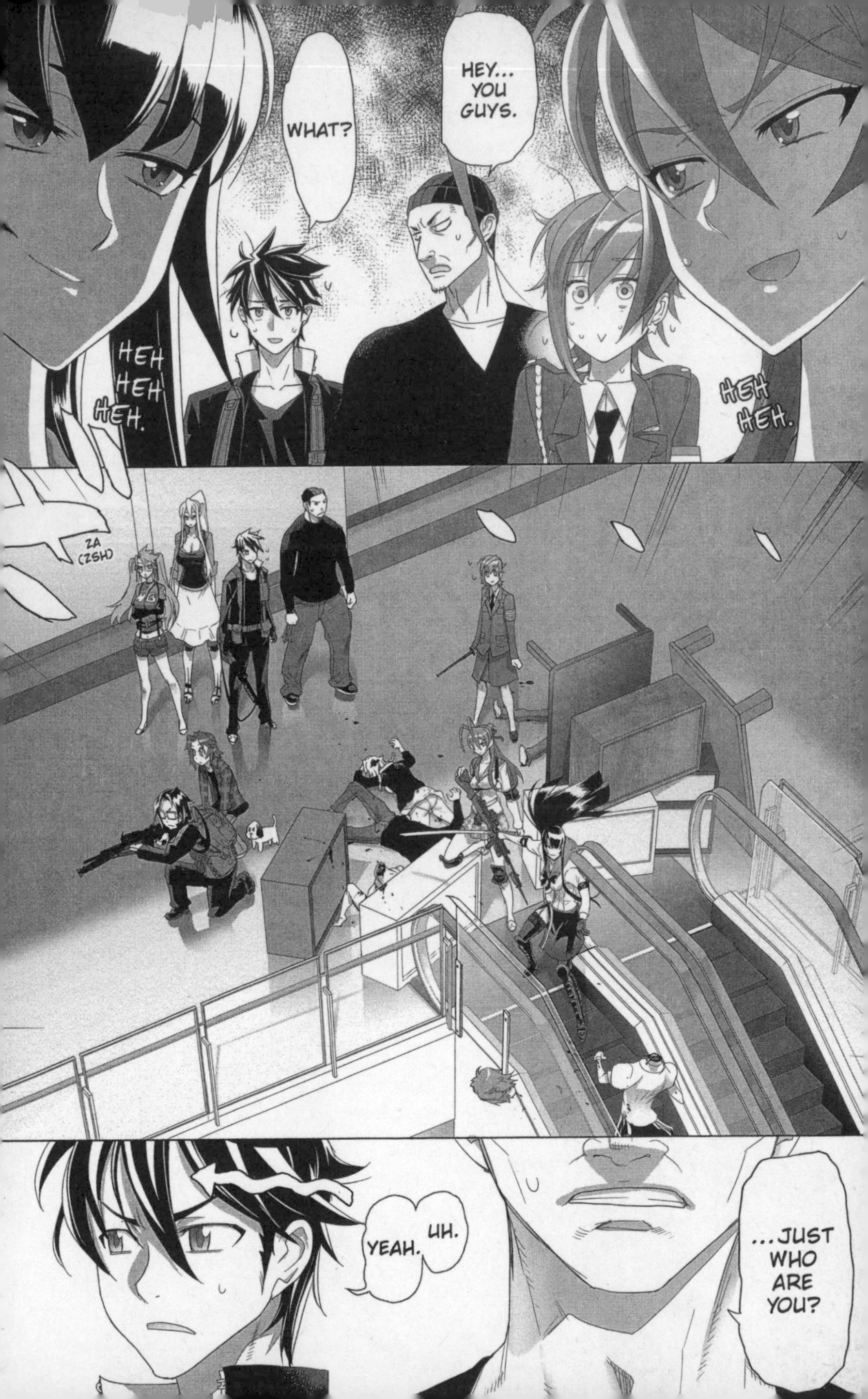
HEY... YOU GUYS.
WHAT?
HEH HEH.
HEH HEH HEH.
ZA (ZSH)
...JUST WHO ARE YOU?
UH.
YEAH.

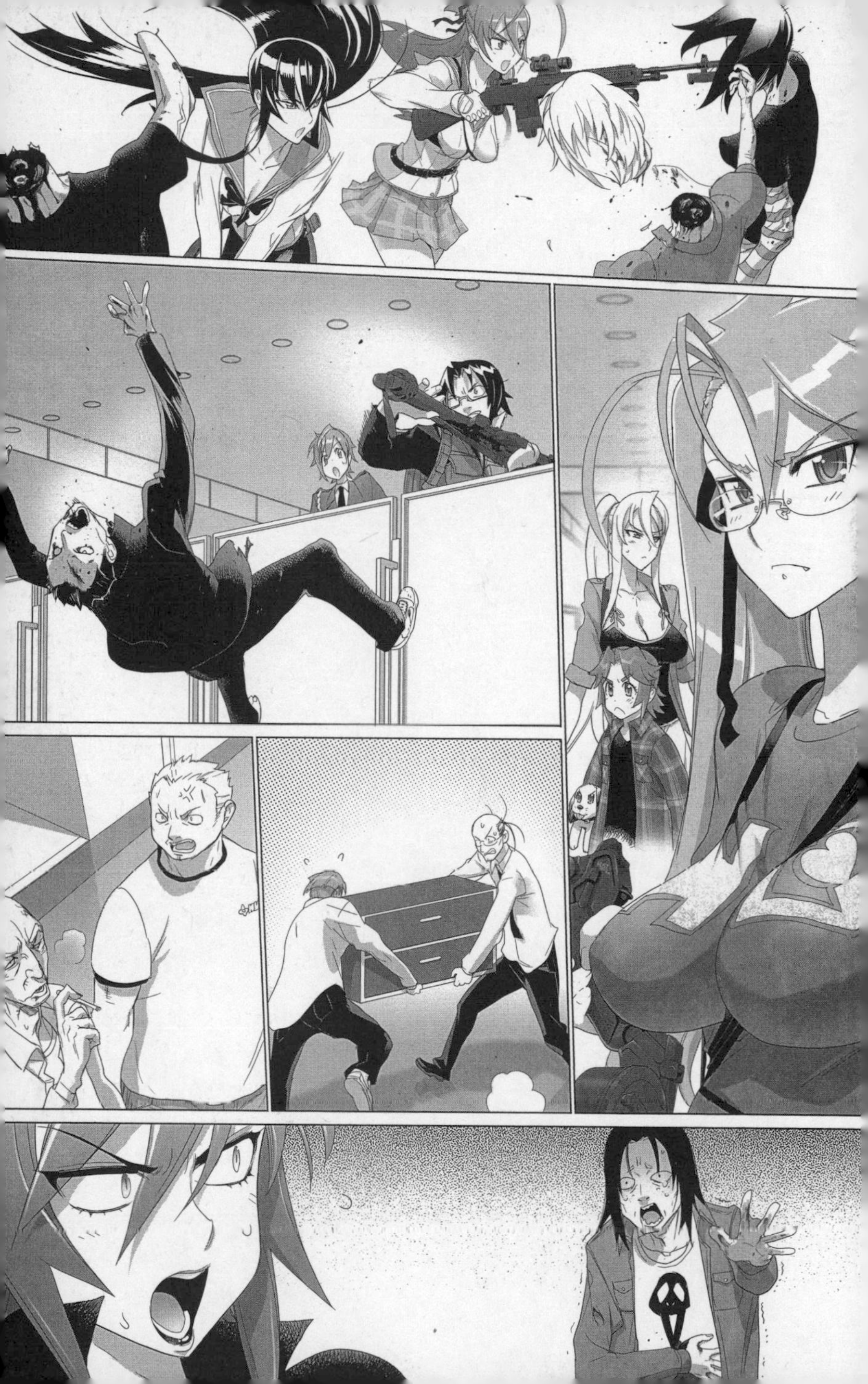

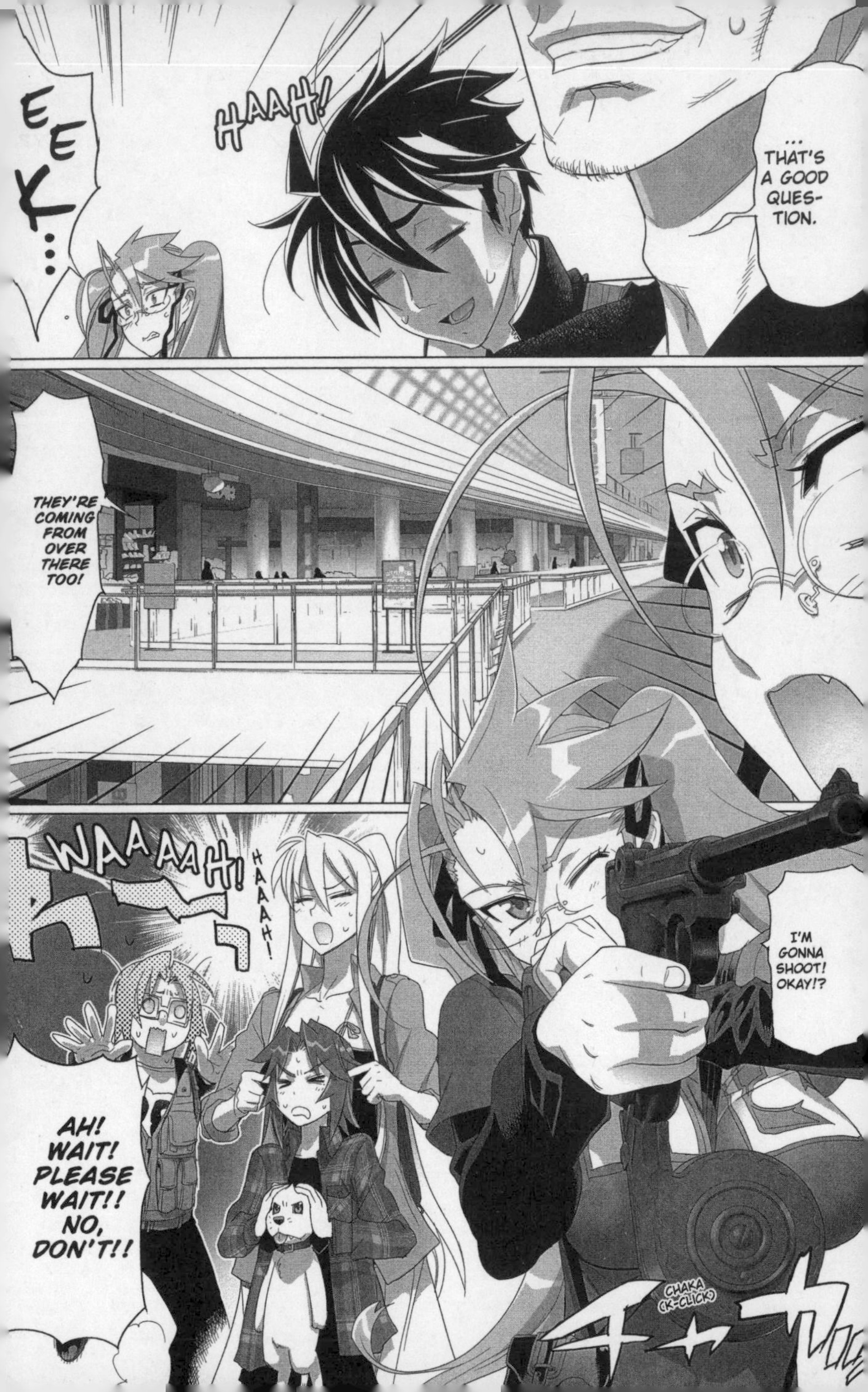
... THAT'S A GOOD QUES-TION.
HAAH!
EEK...
THEY'RE COMING FROM OVER THERE TOO!
I'M GONNA SHOOT! OKAY!?
CHAKA (K-CLICK)
HAAAAH!
WAAAAAH!
AH! WAIT! PLEASE WAIT!! NO, DON'T!!

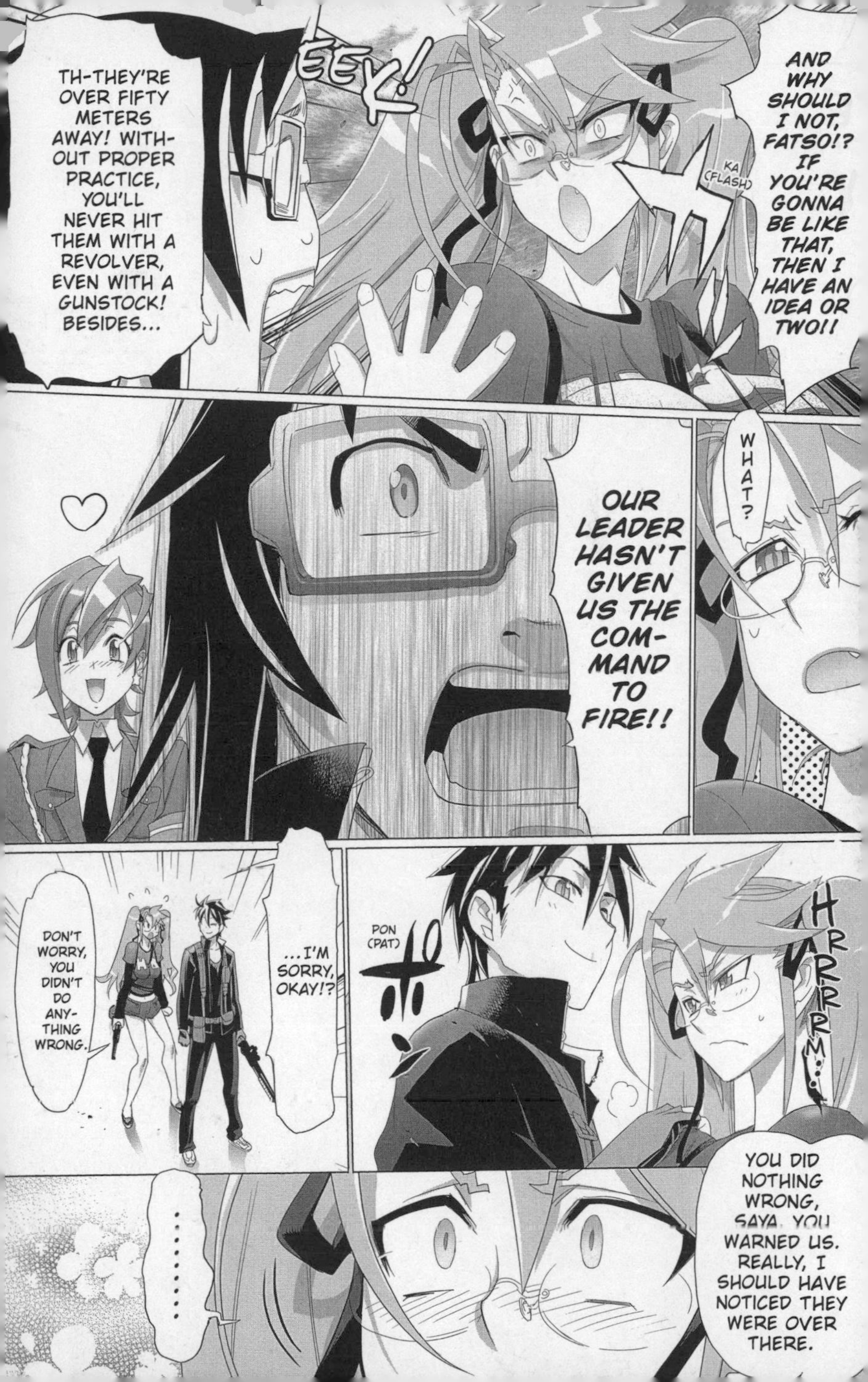
AND WHY SHOULD I NOT, FATSO!? IF YOU'RE GONNA BE LIKE THAT, THEN I HAVE AN IDEA OR TWO!!
KA (FLASH)
EEK!
TH-THEY'RE OVER FIFTY METERS AWAY! WITH-OUT PROPER PRACTICE, YOU'LL NEVER HIT THEM WITH A REVOLVER, EVEN WITH A GUNSTOCK! BESIDES...
WHAT?
OUR LEADER HASN'T GIVEN US THE COM-MAND TO FIRE!!
HRRRRM...
PON (PAT)
...I'M SORRY, OKAY!?
DON'T WORRY, YOU DIDN'T DO ANY-THING WRONG.
YOU DID NOTHING WRONG, SAYA. YOU WARNED US. REALLY, I SHOULD HAVE NOTICED THEY WERE OVER THERE.
......

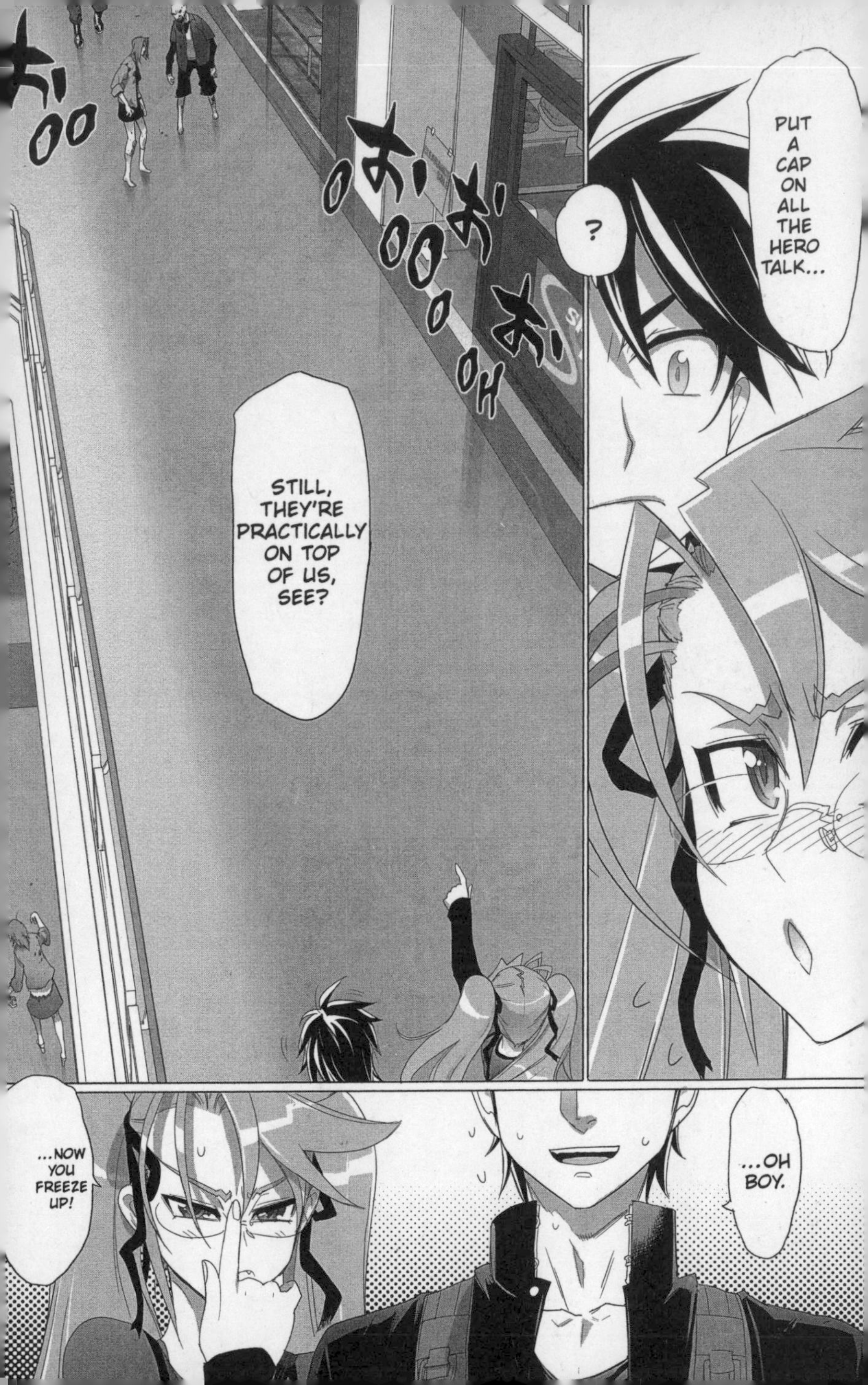
PUT A CAP ON ALL THE HERO TALK...
?
OH
STILL, THEY'RE PRACTICALLY ON TOP OF US, SEE?
...OH BOY.
...NOW YOU FREEZE UP!

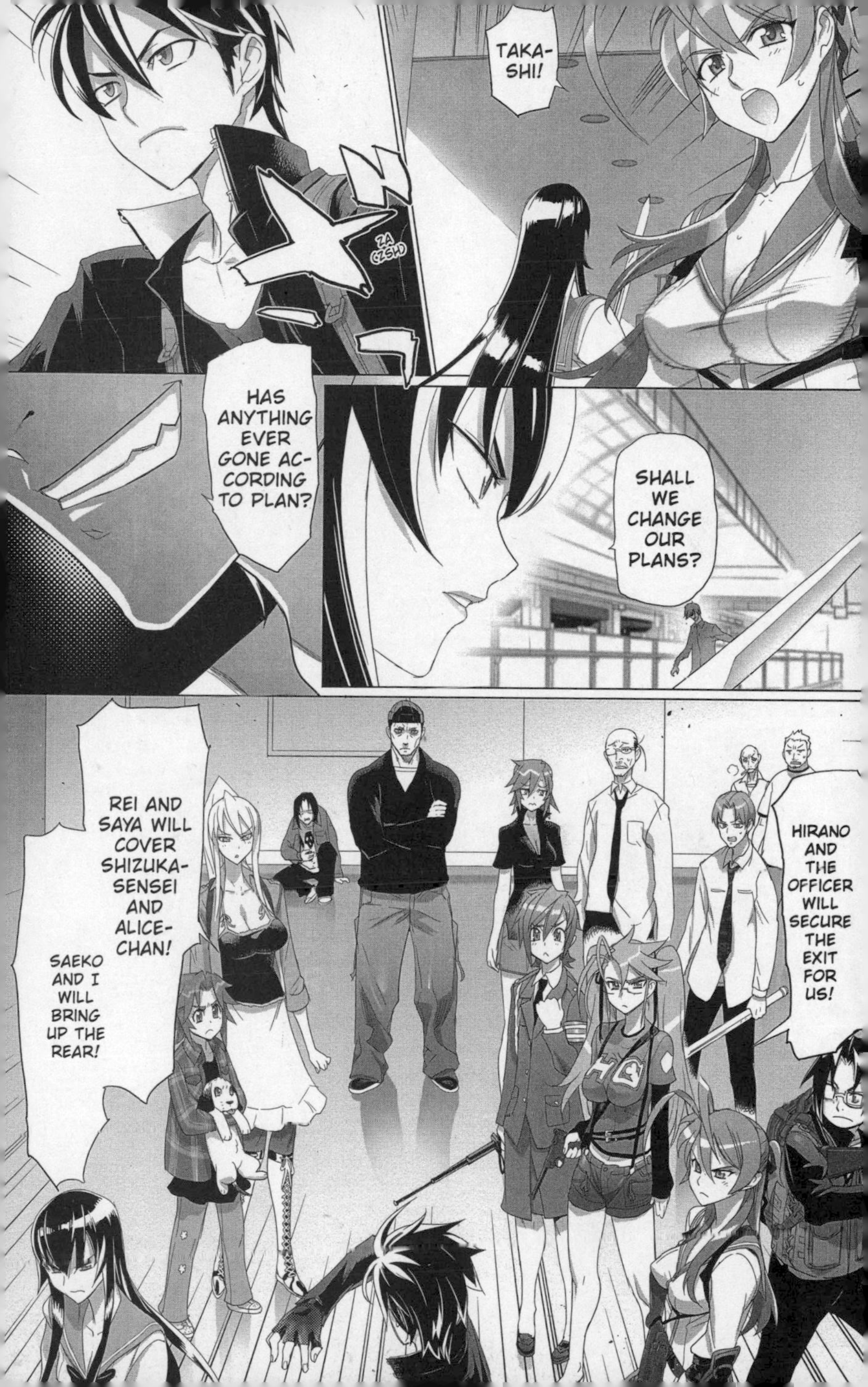
TAKA-SHI!
ZA (ZSH)
SHALL WE CHANGE OUR PLANS?
HAS ANYTHING EVER GONE AC-CORDING TO PLAN?
HIRANO AND THE OFFICER WILL SECURE THE EXIT FOR US!
REI AND SAYA WILL COVER SHIZUKA-SENSEI AND ALICE-CHAN!
SAEKO AND I WILL BRING UP THE REAR!

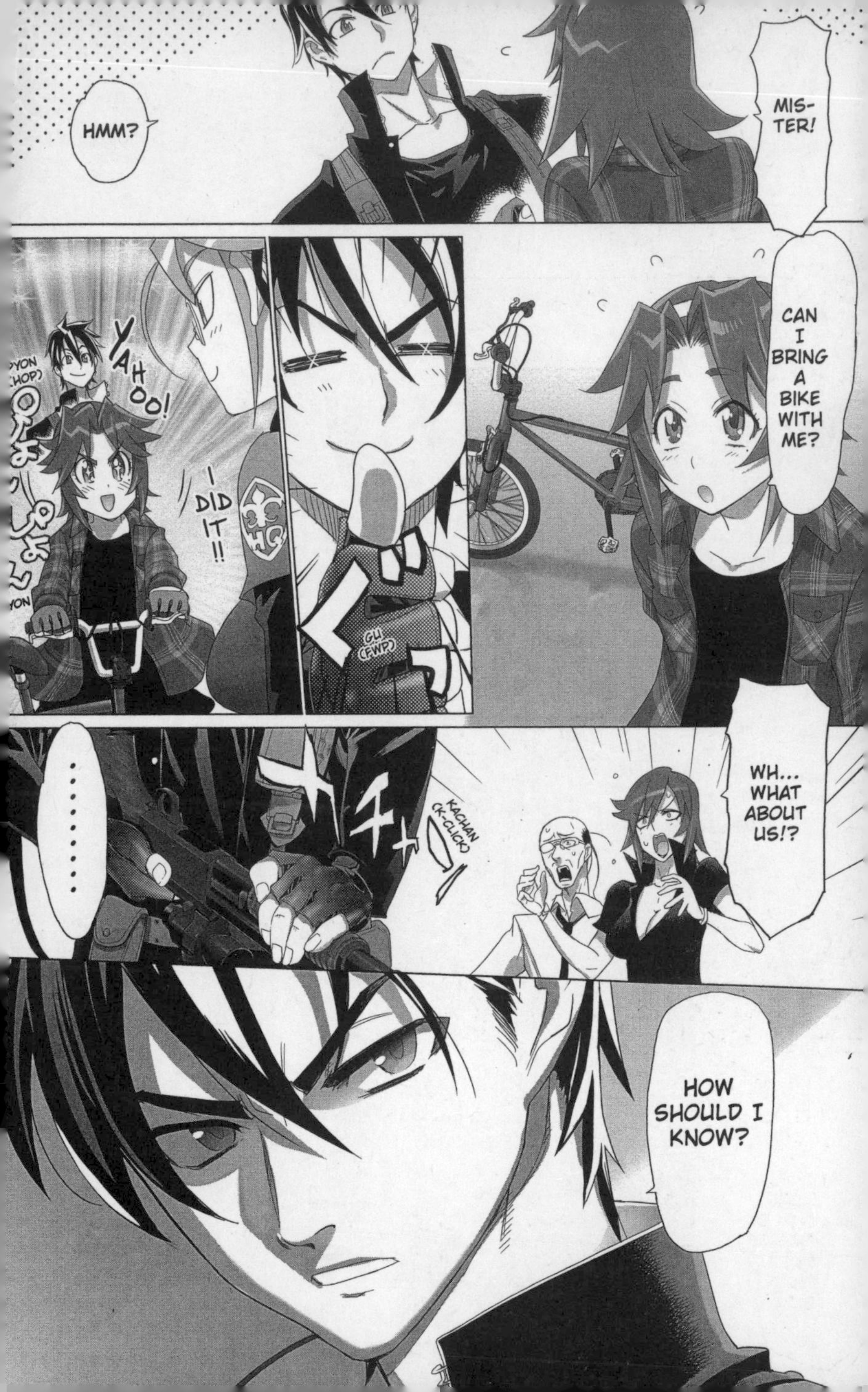
MIS-TER!
HMM?
CAN I BRING A BIKE WITH ME?
GU (FWP)
YAHOO!
I DID IT!!
PYON (HOP)
WH... WHAT ABOUT US!?
KACHAN (K-CLICK)
......
HOW SHOULD I KNOW?

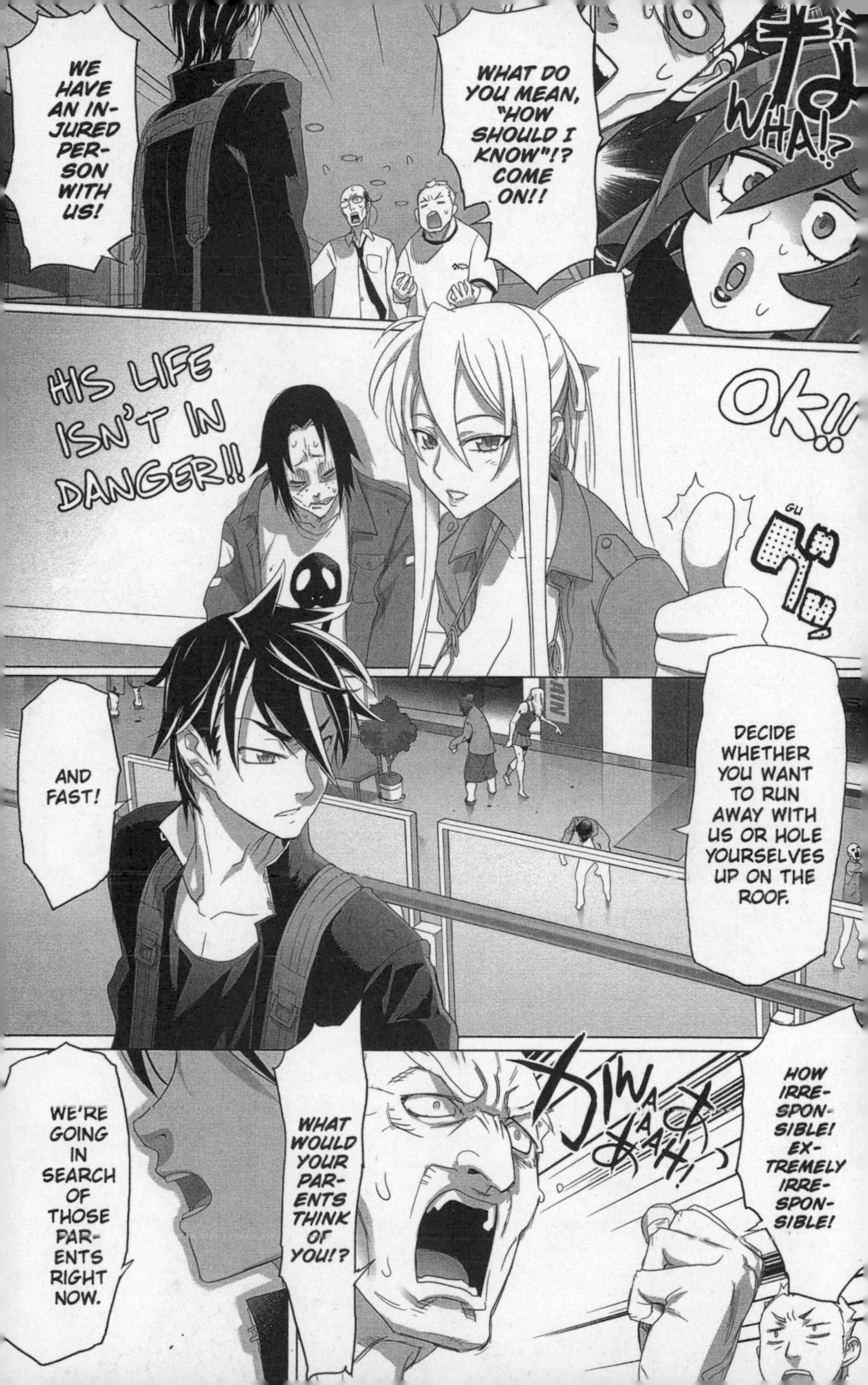
WHA!?
WHAT DO YOU MEAN, "HOW SHOULD I KNOW"!? COME ON!!
WE HAVE AN INJURED PERSON WITH US!
OK!!
GU
HIS LIFE ISN'T IN DANGER!!
DECIDE WHETHER YOU WANT TO RUN AWAY WITH US OR HOLE YOURSELVES UP ON THE ROOF.
AND FAST!
HOW IRRESPONSIBLE! EXTREMELY IRRESPONSIBLE!
WAAAAH!
WHAT WOULD YOUR PARENTS THINK OF YOU!?
WE'RE GOING IN SEARCH OF THOSE PARENTS RIGHT NOW.

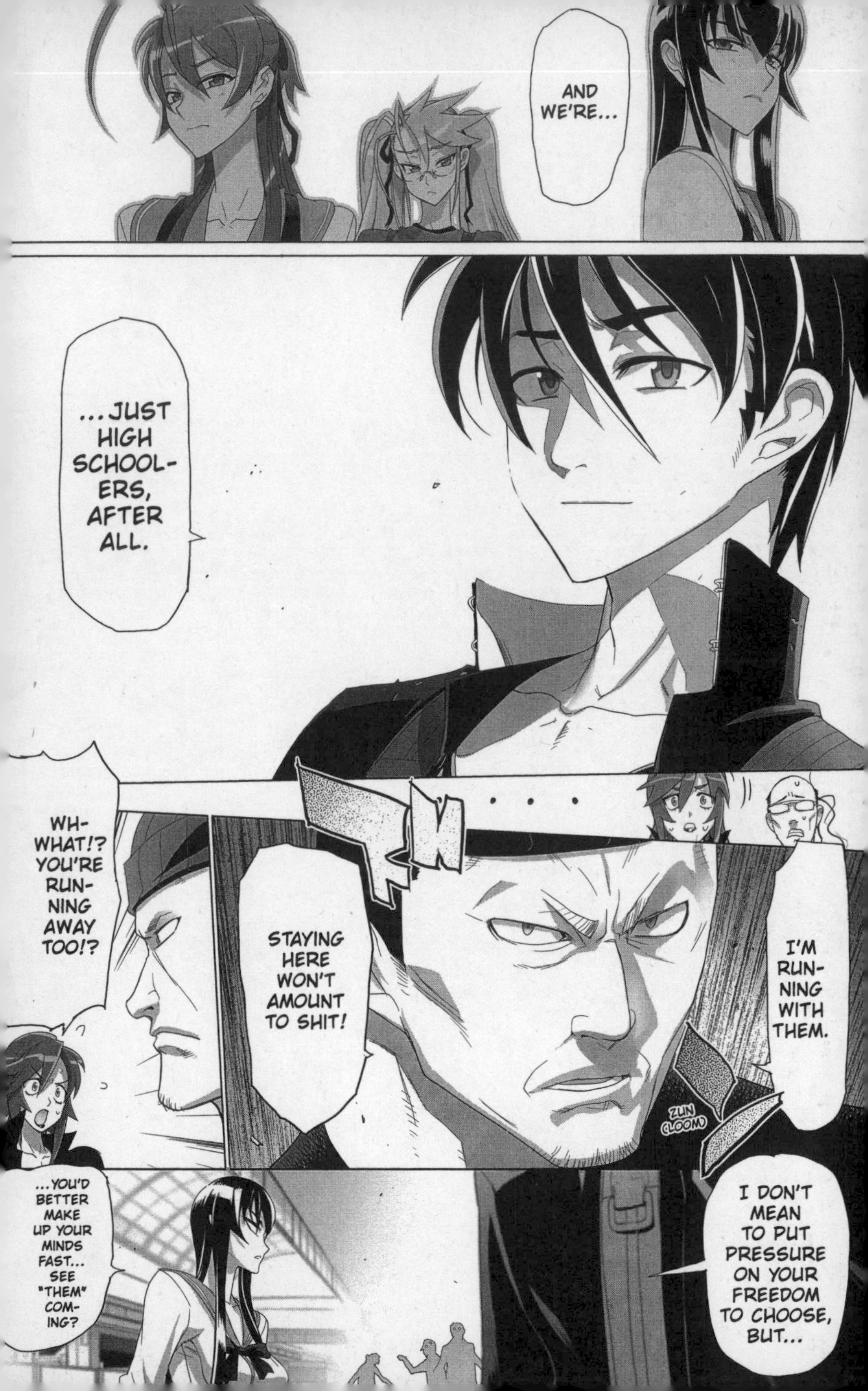
AND WE'RE...
...JUST HIGH SCHOOLERS, AFTER ALL.
. . .
I'M RUNNING WITH THEM.
ZUN (LOOM)
STAYING HERE WON'T AMOUNT TO SHIT!
WH-WHAT!? YOU'RE RUNNING AWAY TOO!?
I DON'T MEAN TO PUT PRESSURE ON YOUR FREEDOM TO CHOOSE, BUT...
...YOU'D BETTER MAKE UP YOUR MINDS FAST... SEE "THEM" COMING?

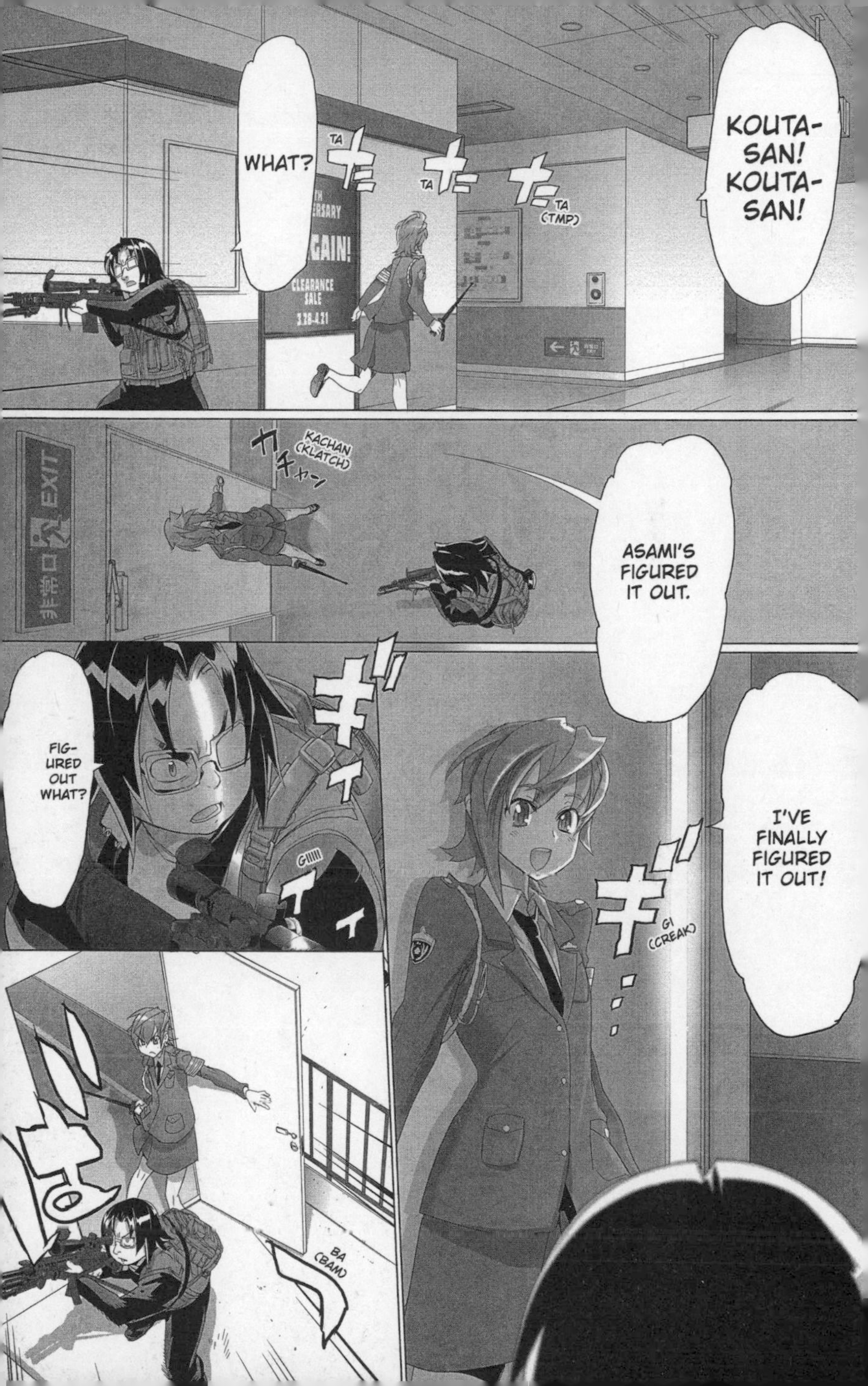
KOUTA-SAN! KOUTA-SAN!
TA
TA
TA (TMP)
WHAT?
CLEARANCE SALE
KACHAN (KLATCH)
EXIT
非常口
ASAMI'S FIGURED IT OUT.
I'VE FINALLY FIGURED IT OUT!
GI (CREAK)
FIG-URED OUT WHAT?
GI!!!!
BA (BAM)

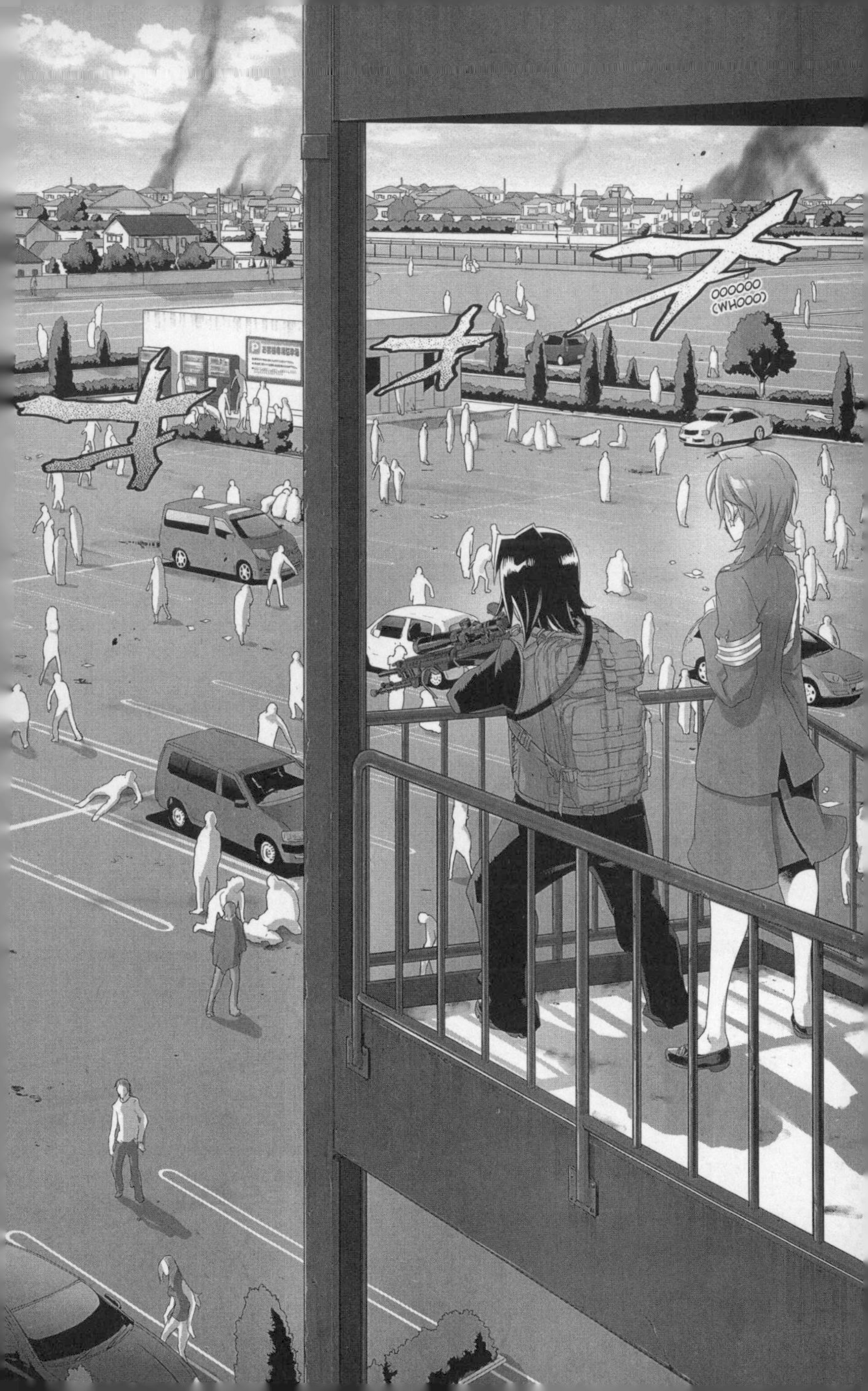
OOOOOO
(WHOOO)

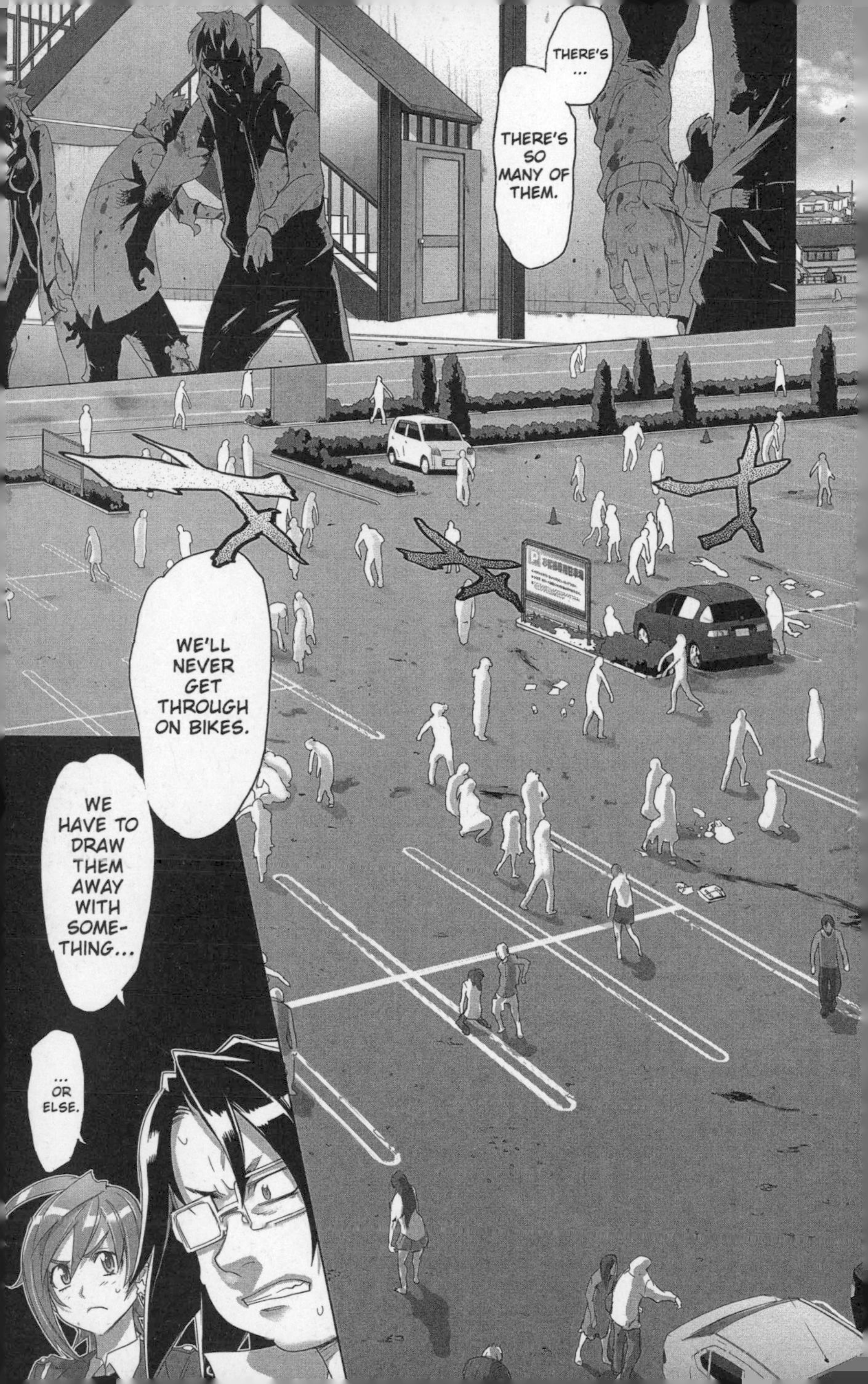
THERE'S ...
THERE'S SO MANY OF THEM.
WE'LL NEVER GET THROUGH ON BIKES.
WE HAVE TO DRAW THEM AWAY WITH SOME-THING...
... OR ELSE.

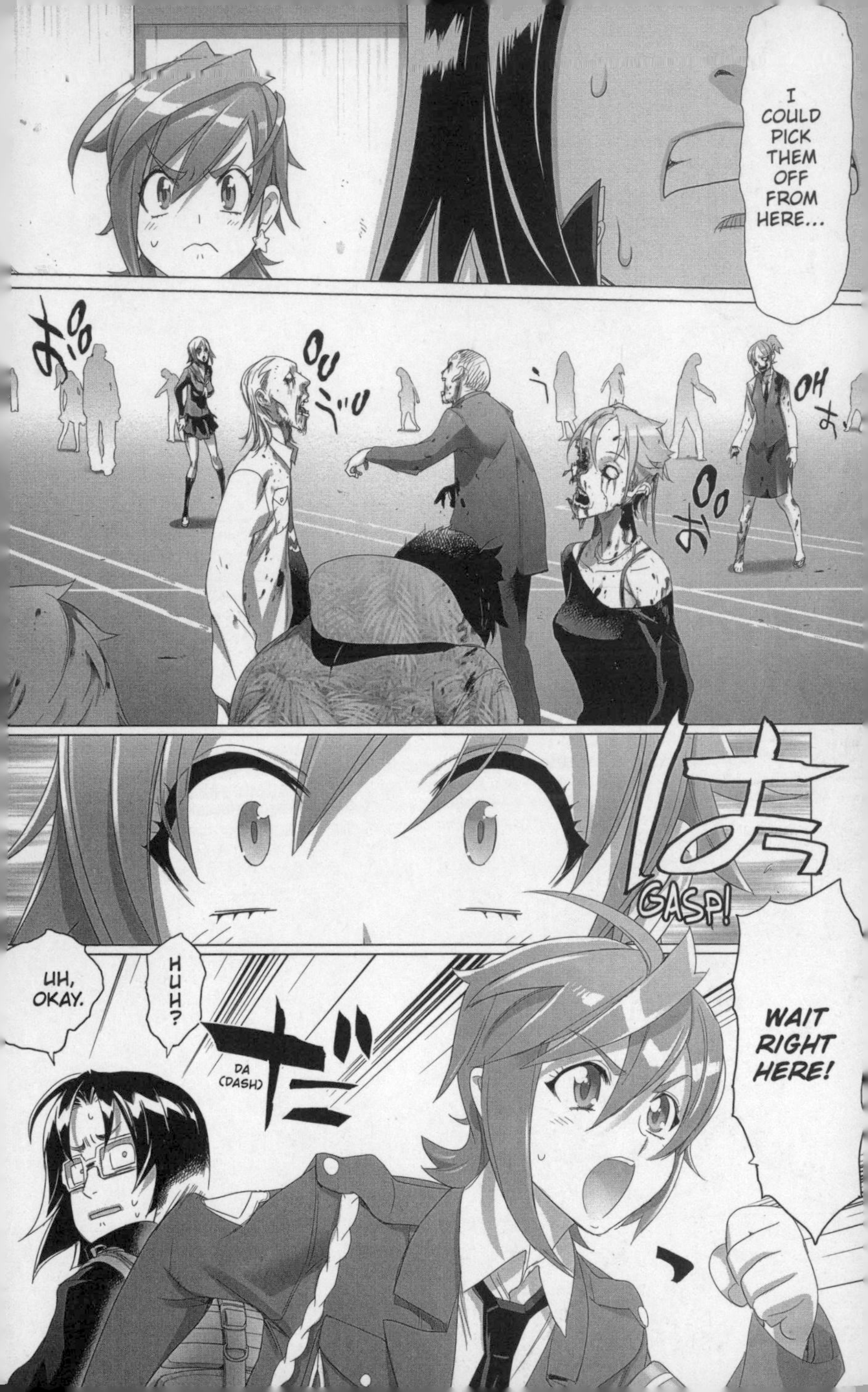
I COULD PICK THEM OFF FROM HERE...
OH
OO
OU
OO
GASP!
WAIT RIGHT HERE!
DA (DASH)
HUH?
UH, OKAY.

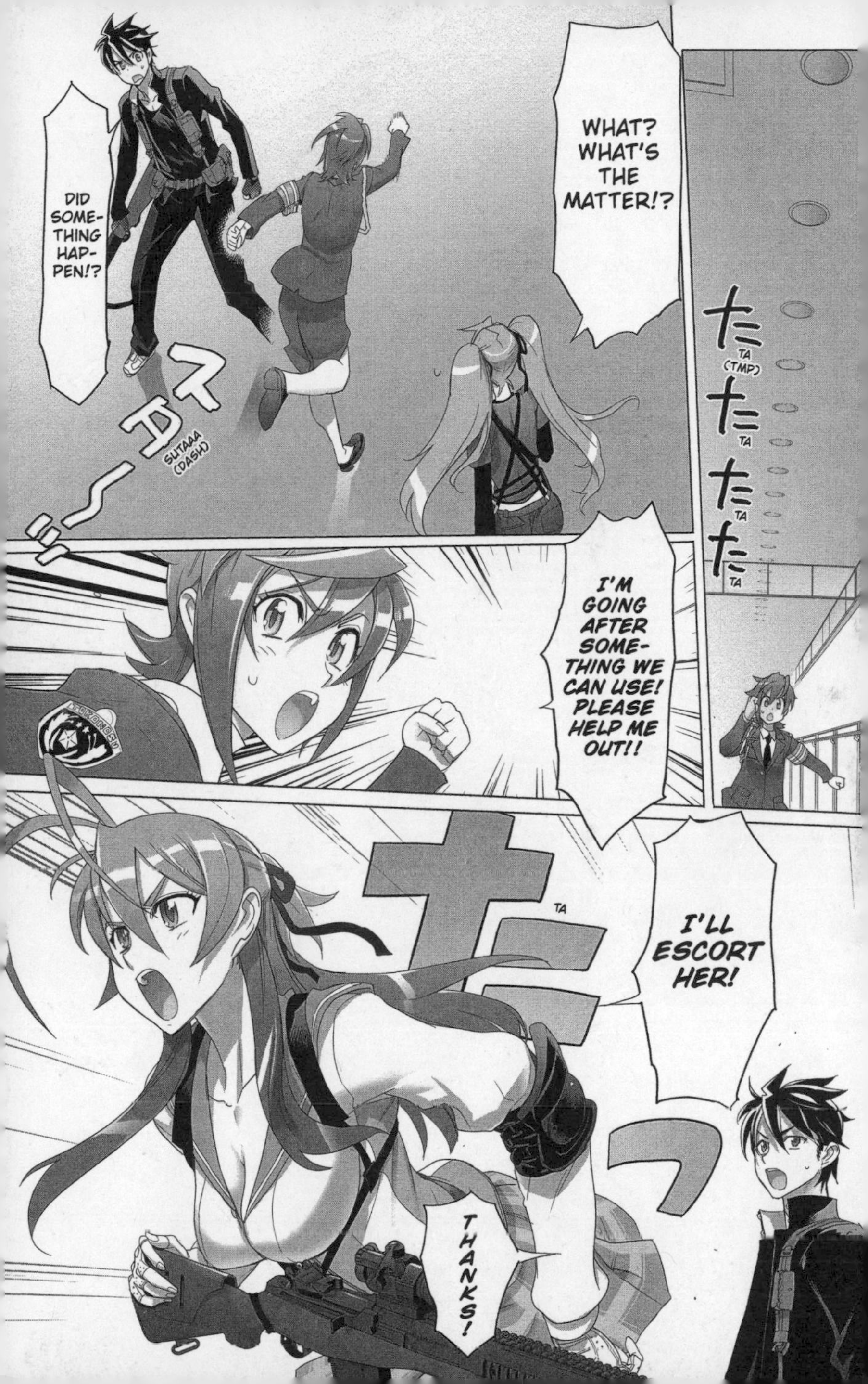
TA (TMP)
TA
TA
TA
WHAT? WHAT'S THE MATTER!?
DID SOMETHING HAPPEN!?
SUTAAA (DASH)
I'M GOING AFTER SOMETHING WE CAN USE! PLEASE HELP ME OUT!!
I'LL ESCORT HER!
TA
THANKS!

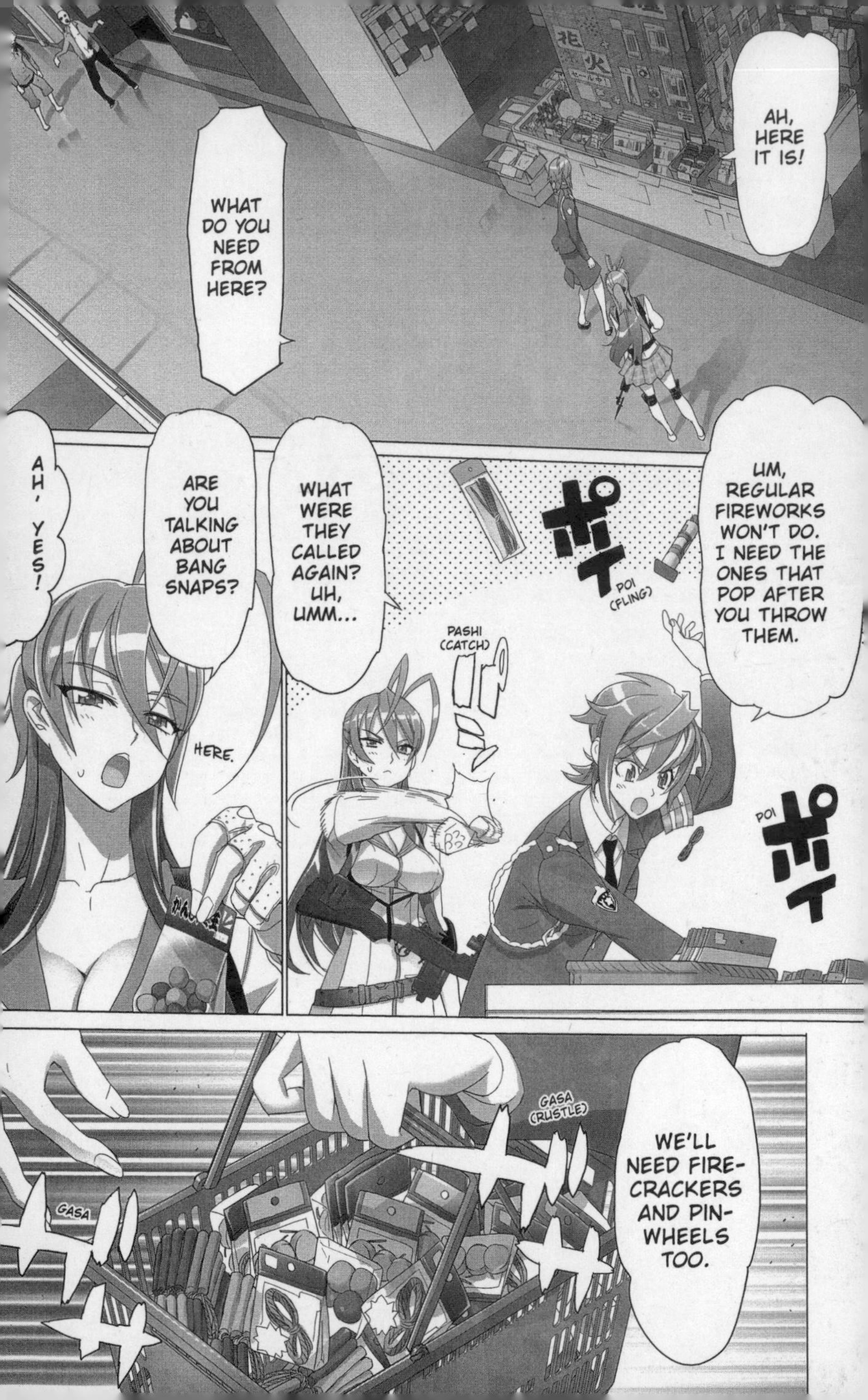
AH, HERE IT IS!
WHAT DO YOU NEED FROM HERE?
UM, REGULAR FIREWORKS WON'T DO. I NEED THE ONES THAT POP AFTER YOU THROW THEM.
ポイ
POI
ポイ
POI (FLING)
PASHI (CATCH)
WHAT WERE THEY CALLED AGAIN? UH, UMM...
ARE YOU TALKING ABOUT BANG SNAPS?
AH, YES!
HERE.
GASA (RUSTLE)
WE'LL NEED FIRE-CRACKERS AND PIN-WHEELS TOO.
GASA

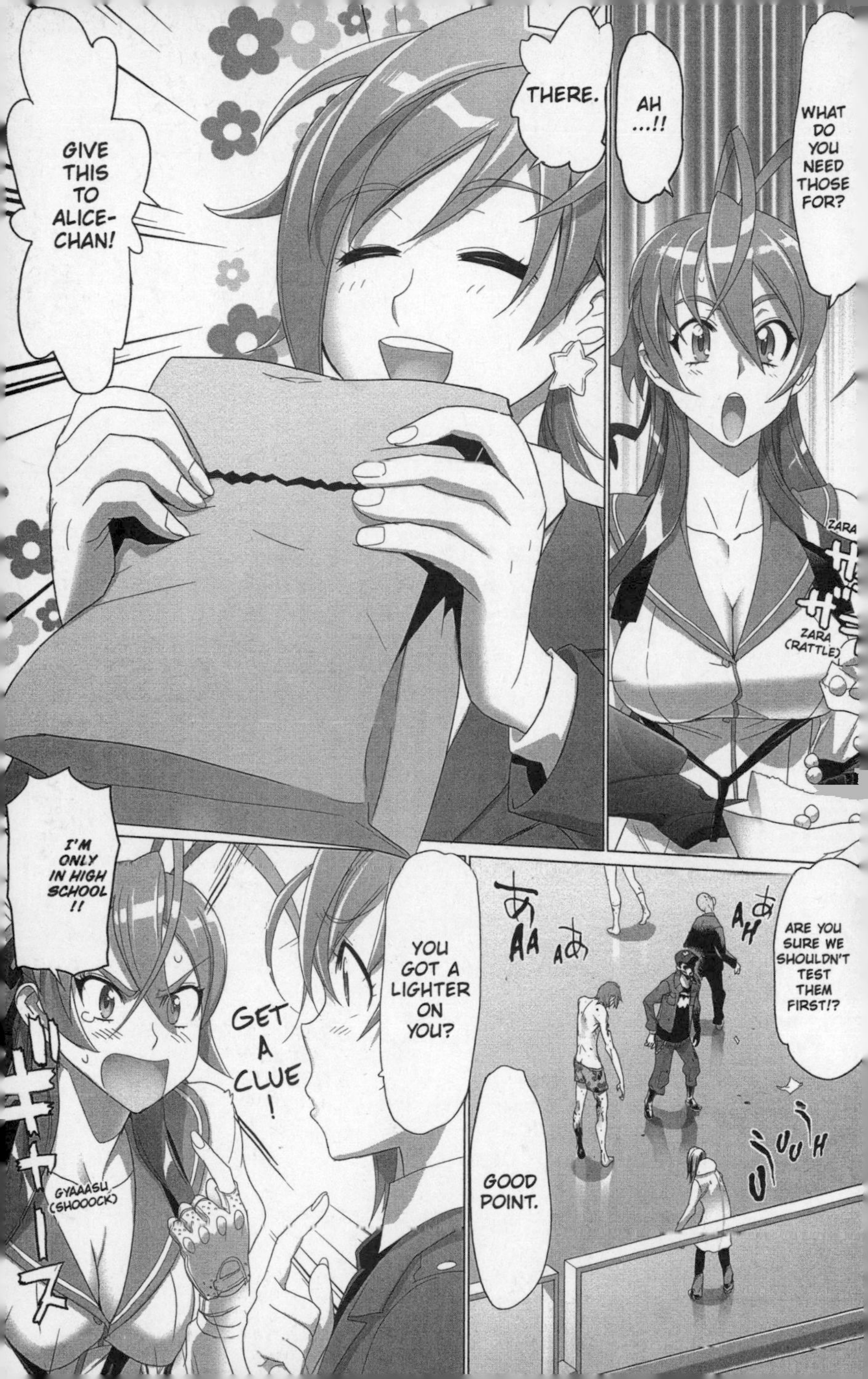
WHAT DO YOU NEED THOSE FOR?
AH ...!!
ZARA
ZARA (RATTLE)
THERE.
GIVE THIS TO ALICE-CHAN!
ARE YOU SURE WE SHOULDN'T TEST THEM FIRST!?
AH
AA
A
GOOD POINT.
UUUH
YOU GOT A LIGHTER ON YOU?
GET A CLUE!
I'M ONLY IN HIGH SCHOOL!!
GYAASU (SHOOOCK)

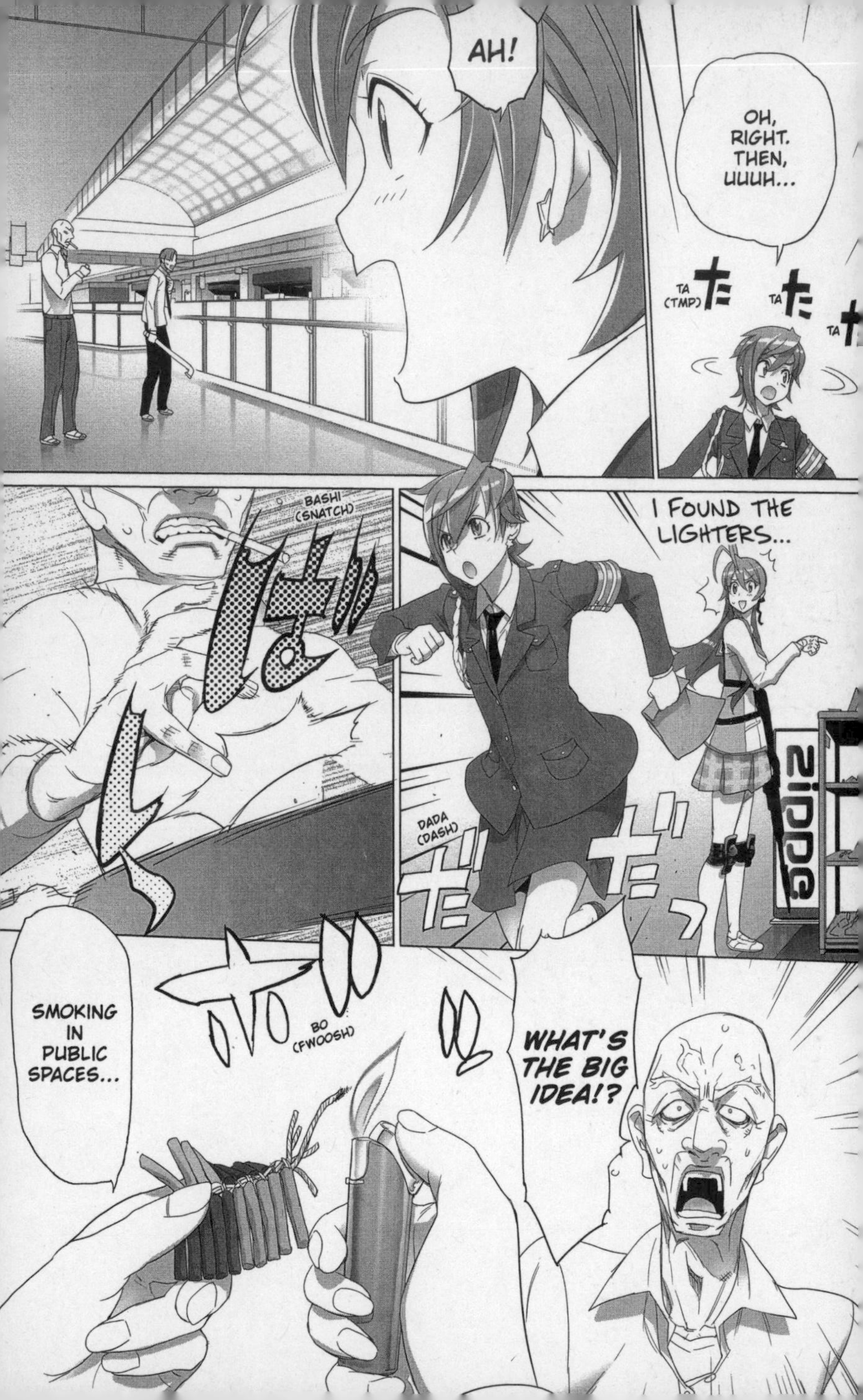
OH, RIGHT. THEN, UUUH...
TA (TMP)
TA
TA
AH!
I FOUND THE LIGHTERS...
DADA (DASH)
BASHI (SNATCH)
WHAT'S THE BIG IDEA!?
BO (FWOOSH)
SMOKING IN PUBLIC SPACES...

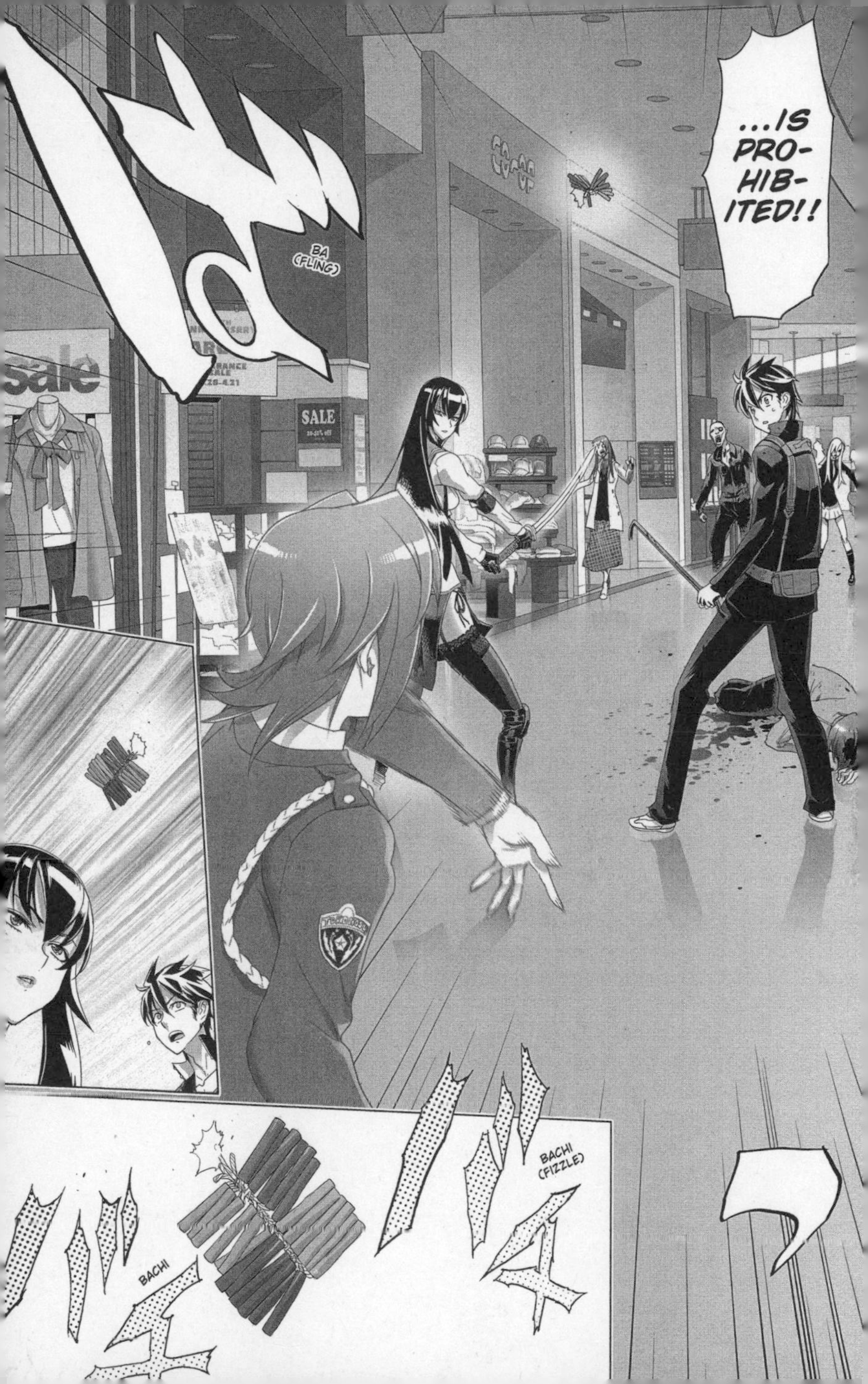
...IS PRO-HIB-ITED!!
BA (FLING)
sale
SALE
BACHI (FIZZLE)
BACHI

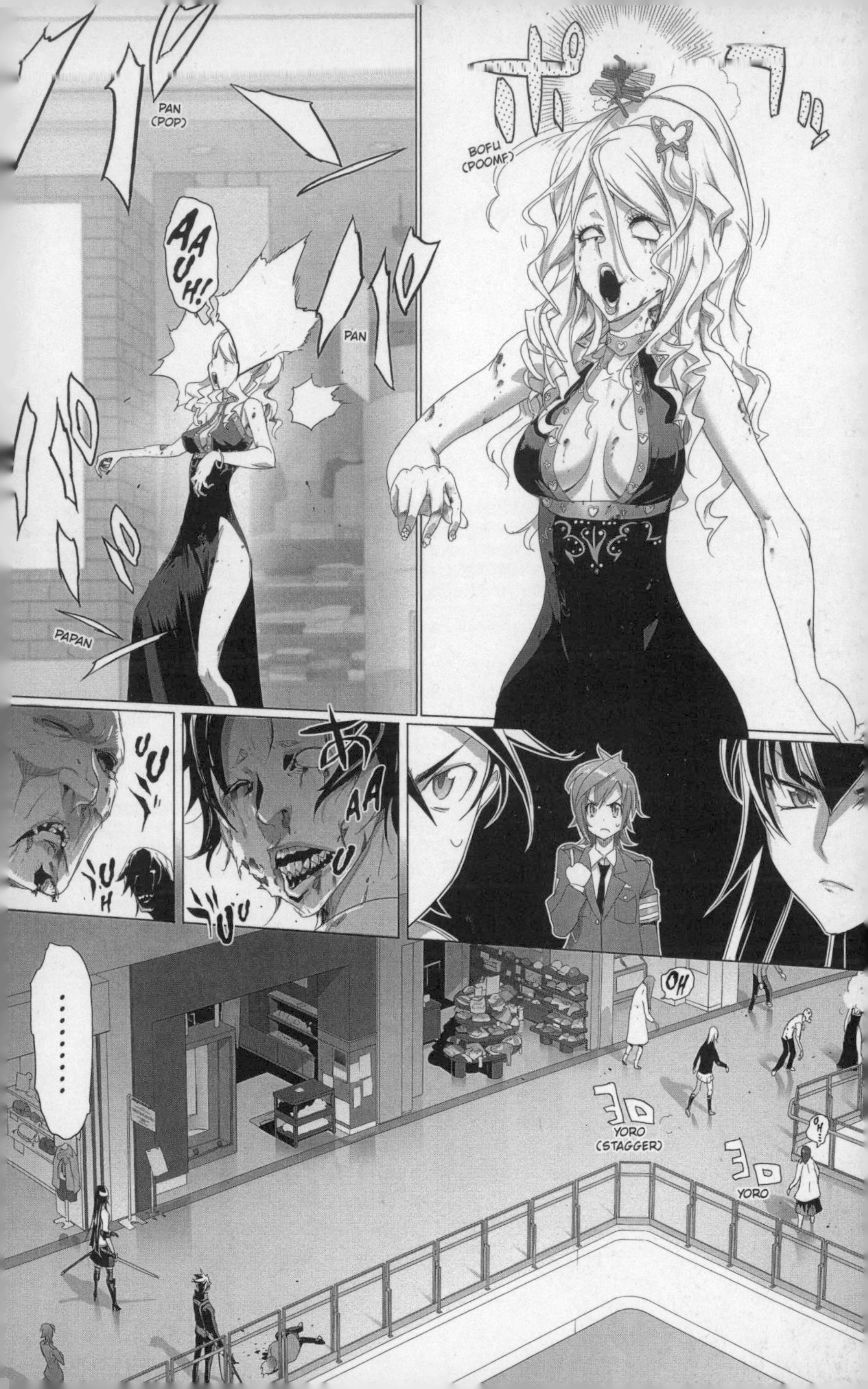

BOFU
(POOMF)
PAN
(POP)
AAUH!
PAN
PAPAN
AAU
UU
UU
UH
OH
YORO
(STAGGER)
OH...
YORO
......

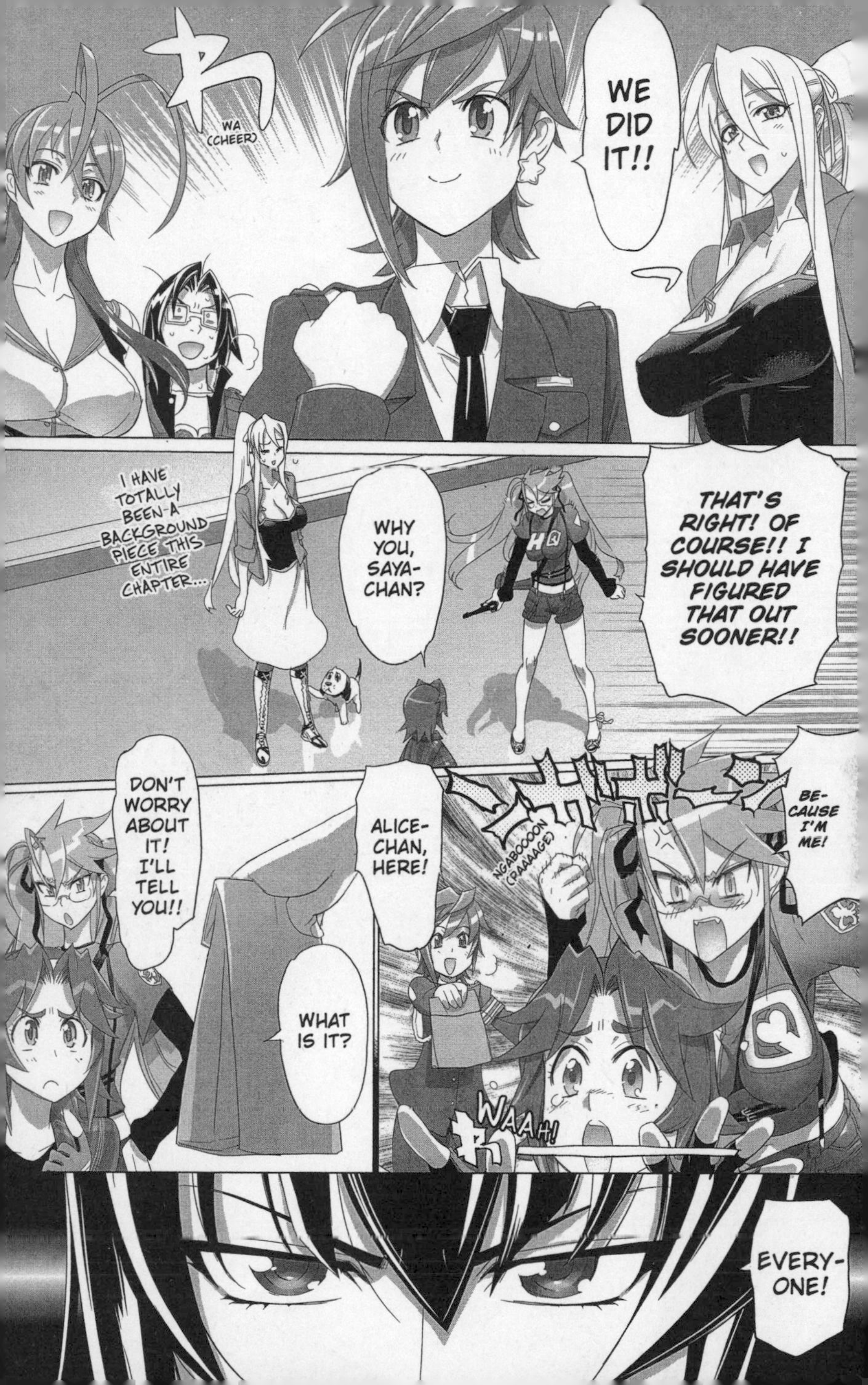
WE DID IT!!
WA (CHEER)
THAT'S RIGHT! OF COURSE!! I SHOULD HAVE FIGURED THAT OUT SOONER!!
WHY YOU, SAYA-CHAN?
I HAVE TOTALLY BEEN-A BACKGROUND PIECE THIS ENTIRE CHAPTER...
BE-CAUSE I'M ME!
NGABOOOON (PAAAAGE)
WAAAH!
ALICE-CHAN, HERE!
DON'T WORRY ABOUT IT! I'LL TELL YOU!!
WHAT IS IT?
EVERY-ONE!

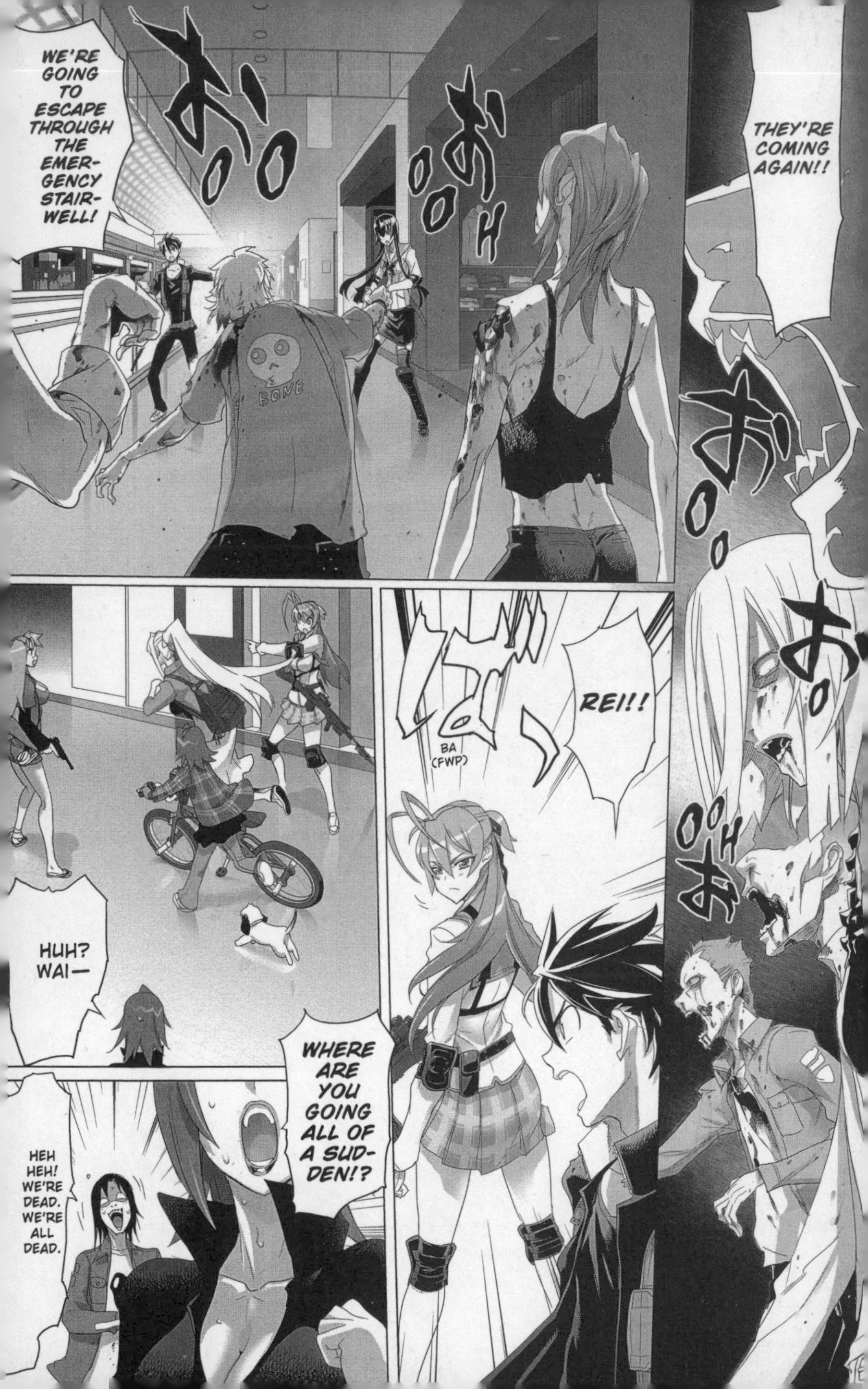
THEY'RE COMING AGAIN!!
おおお
OOH
WE'RE GOING TO ESCAPE THROUGH THE EMERGENCY STAIRWELL!
おお
OOH
REI!!
BA (FWP)
WHERE ARE YOU GOING ALL OF A SUDDEN!?
HUH? WAI—
HEH HEH! WE'RE DEAD. WE'RE ALL DEAD.

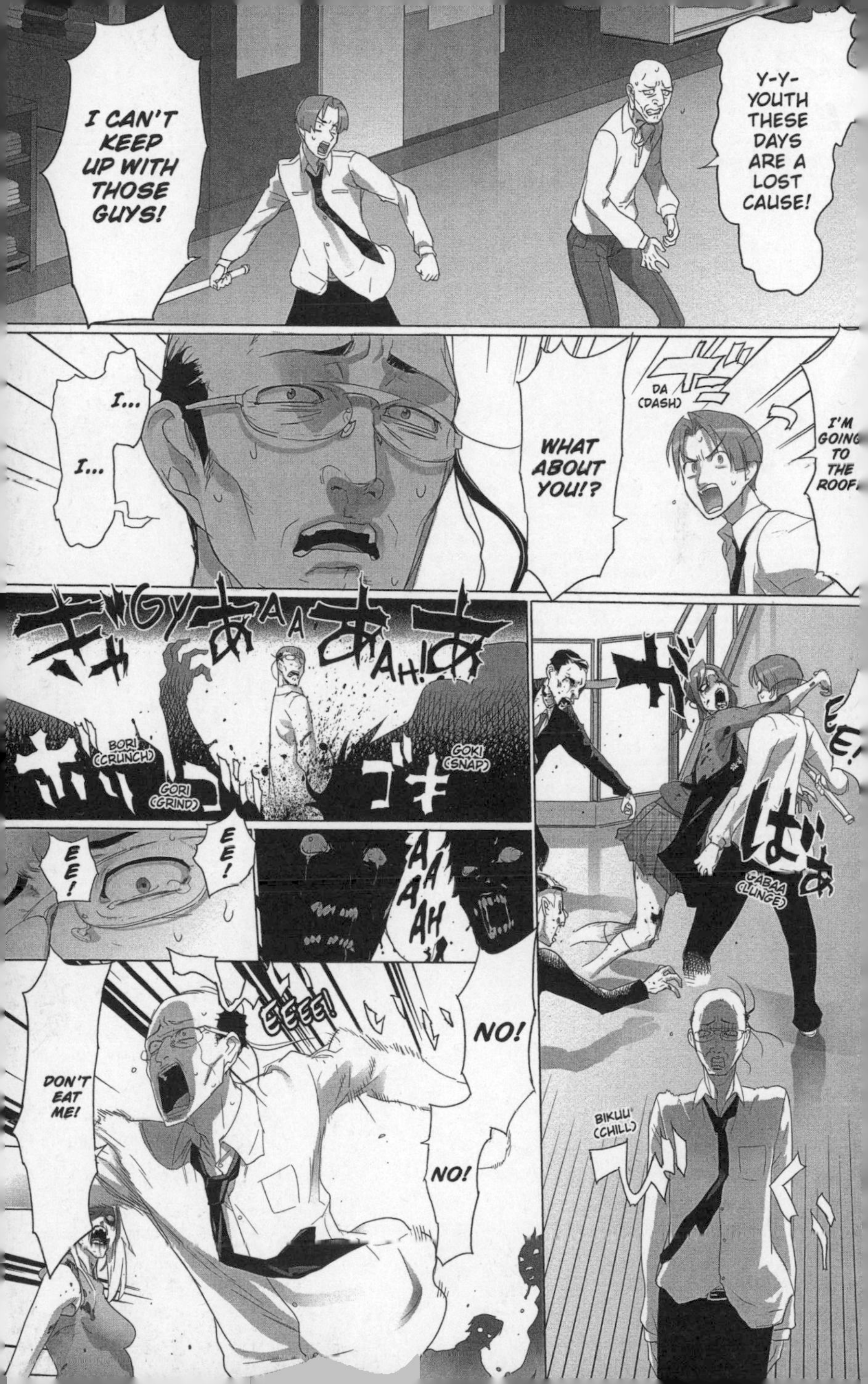

Y-Y-YOUTH THESE DAYS ARE A LOST CAUSE!
I CAN'T KEEP UP WITH THOSE GUYS!
DA (DASH)
I'M GOING TO THE ROOF!
WHAT ABOUT YOU!?
I...
I...
EE!
GABAA (LUNGE)
BIKUU (CHILL)
GYAAAH!
BORI (CRUNCH)
GORI (GRIND)
GOKI (SNAP)
AAAAH
EE!
EE!
EEEE!
NO!
NO!
DON'T EAT ME!

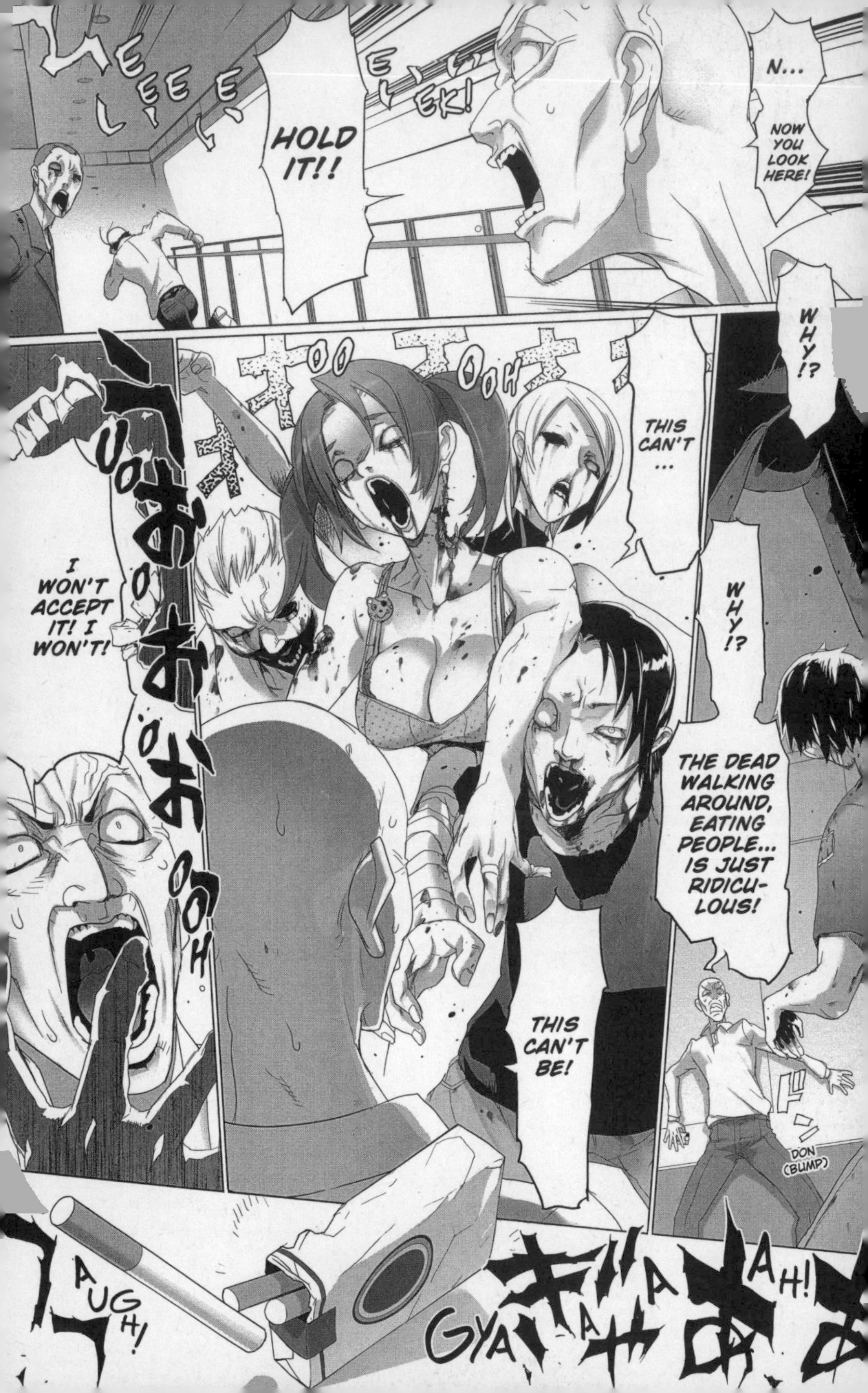

N...
NOW YOU LOOK HERE!
EEEK!
HOLD IT!!
LEEEE
WHY!?
THIS CAN'T ...
WHY!?
THE DEAD WALKING AROUND, EATING PEOPLE... IS JUST RIDICULOUS!
DON (BUMP)
THIS CAN'T BE!
OOOH
I WON'T ACCEPT IT! I WON'T!
OOOOOH
GYAAAAH!
AUGH!

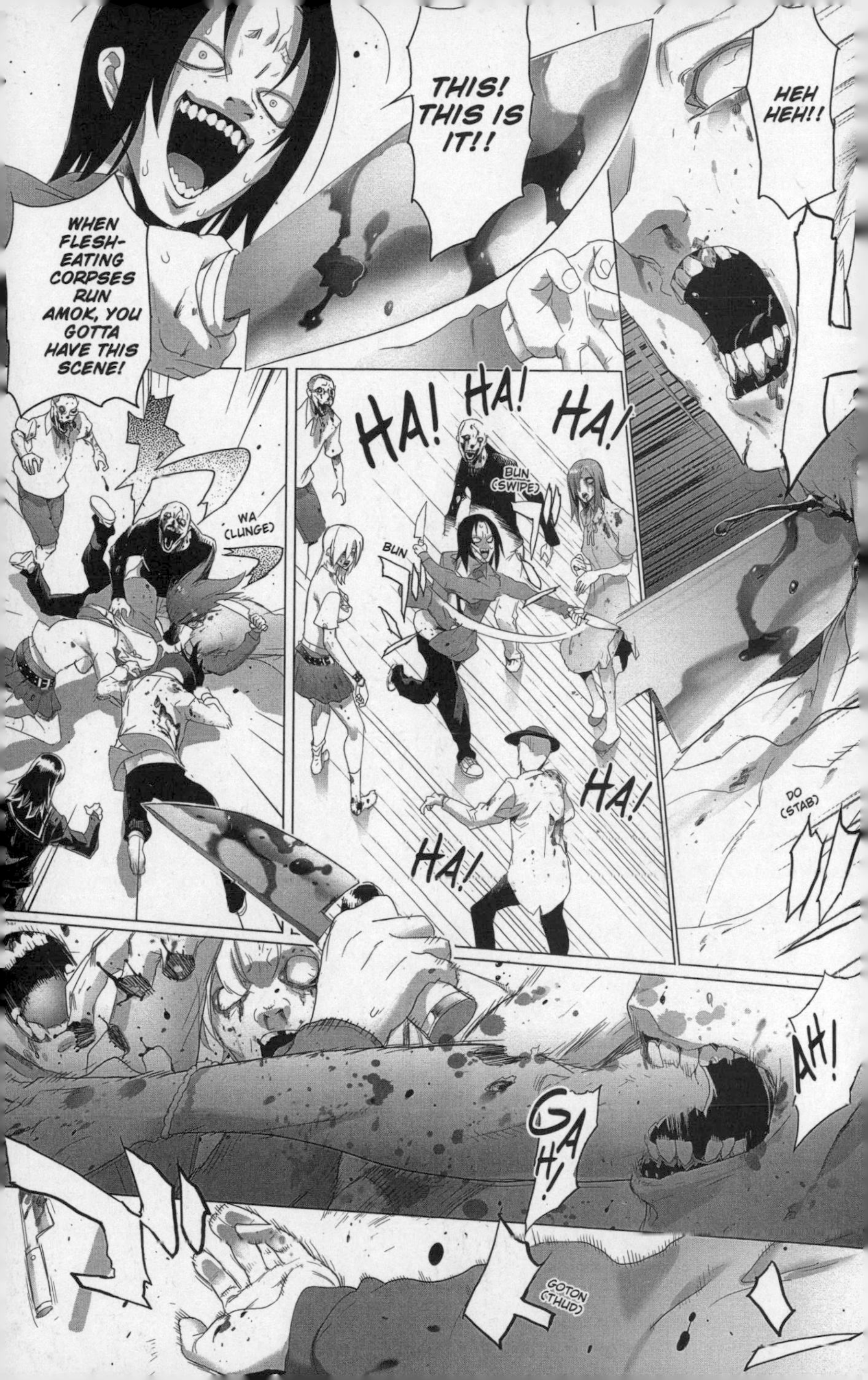
HEH HEH!!
DO (STAB)
THIS! THIS IS IT!!
WHEN FLESH-EATING CORPSES RUN AMOK, YOU GOTTA HAVE THIS SCENE!
HA! HA! HA!
BUN (SWIPE)
BUN
HA!
HA!
WA (LUNGE)
AH!
GAH!
GOTON (THUD)

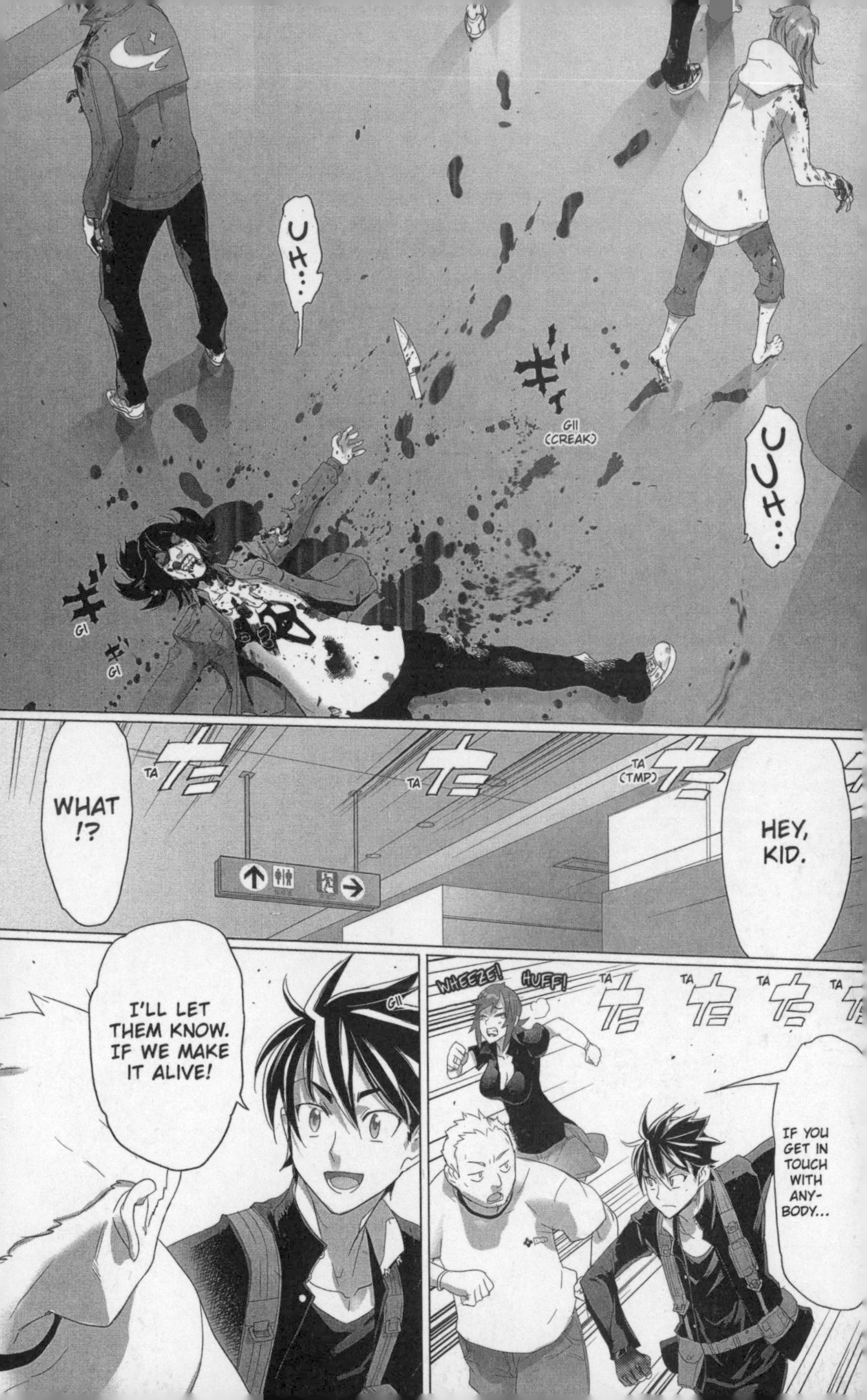
UUH...
GII (CREAK)
UH...
GI
GI
HEY, KID.
TA (TMP)
TA
TA
WHAT !?
TA
TA
TA
TA
IF YOU GET IN TOUCH WITH ANY-BODY...
HUFF!
WHEEZE!
GII
I'LL LET THEM KNOW. IF WE MAKE IT ALIVE!

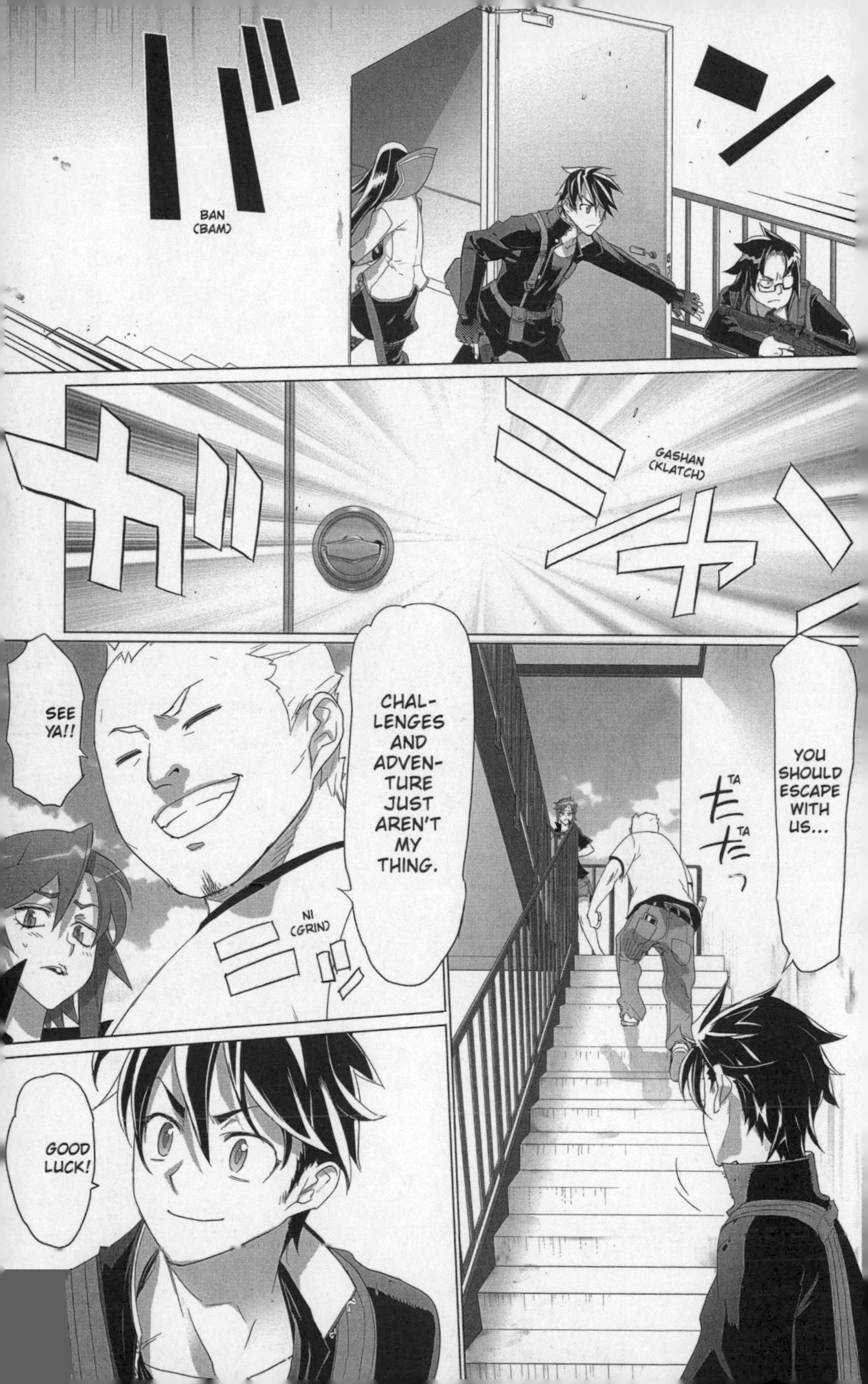
BAN (BAM)
GASHAN (KLATCH)
YOU SHOULD ESCAPE WITH US...
TA TA
CHAL-LENGES AND ADVEN-TURE JUST AREN'T MY THING.
SEE YA!!
NI (GRIN)
GOOD LUCK!

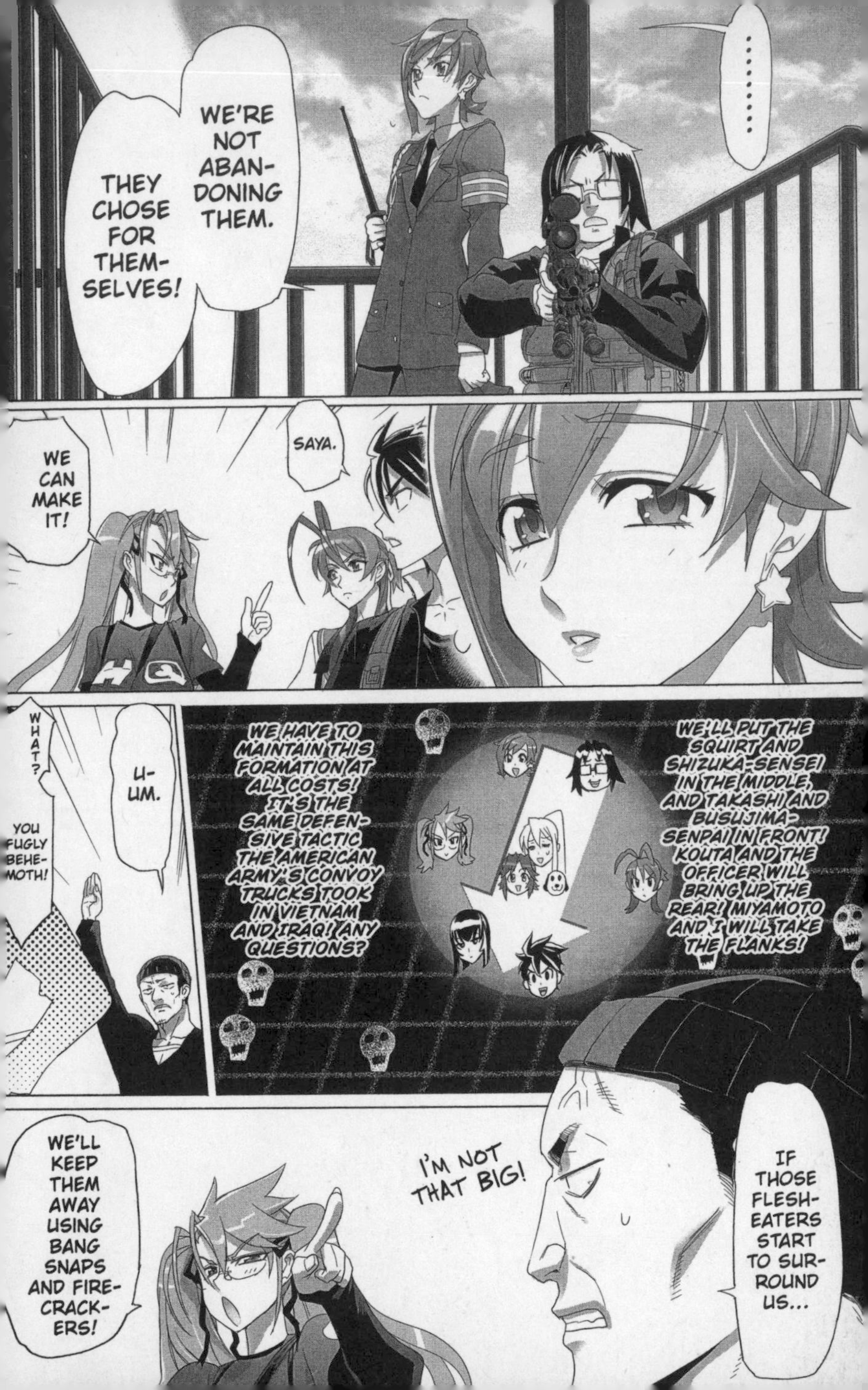

......
WE'RE NOT ABANDONING THEM.
THEY CHOSE FOR THEMSELVES!
SAYA.
WE CAN MAKE IT!
WE'LL PUT THE SQUIRT AND SHIZUKA-SENSEI IN THE MIDDLE, AND TAKASHI AND BUSUJIMA-SENPAI IN FRONT! KOUTA AND THE OFFICER WILL BRING UP THE REAR! MIYAMOTO AND I WILL TAKE THE FLANKS!
WE HAVE TO MAINTAIN THIS FORMATION AT ALL COSTS! IT'S THE SAME DEFENSIVE TACTIC THE AMERICAN ARMY'S CONVOY TRUCKS TOOK IN VIETNAM AND IRAQ! ANY QUESTIONS?
U-UM.
WHAT?
YOU FUGLY BEHEMOTH!
IF THOSE FLESH-EATERS START TO SURROUND US...
I'M NOT THAT BIG!
WE'LL KEEP THEM AWAY USING BANG SNAPS AND FIRECRACKERS!

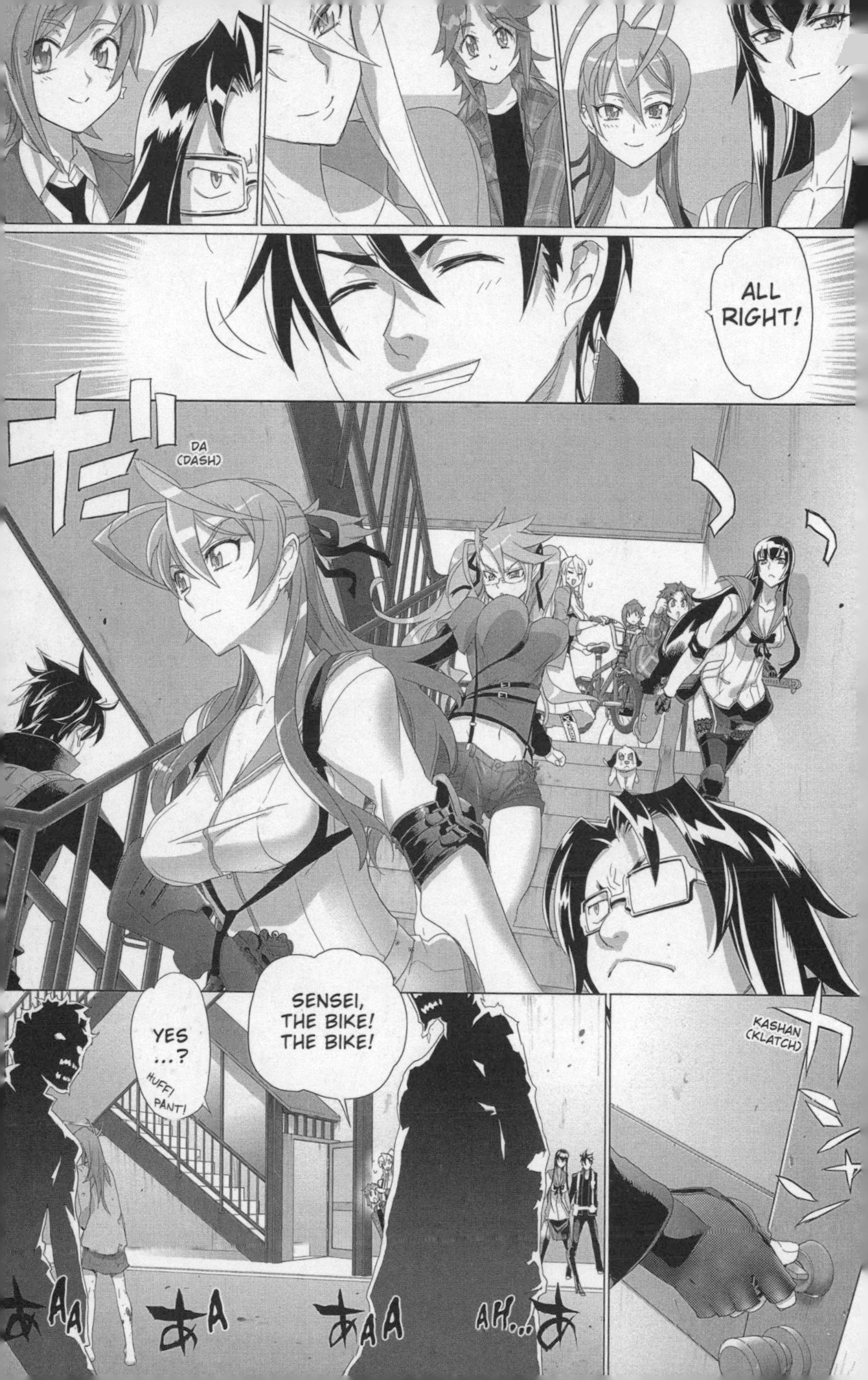
ALL RIGHT!
DA (DASH)
KASHAN (KLATCH)
SENSEI, THE BIKE! THE BIKE!
YES ...?
HUFF! PANT!
AH...
AA
A
AA

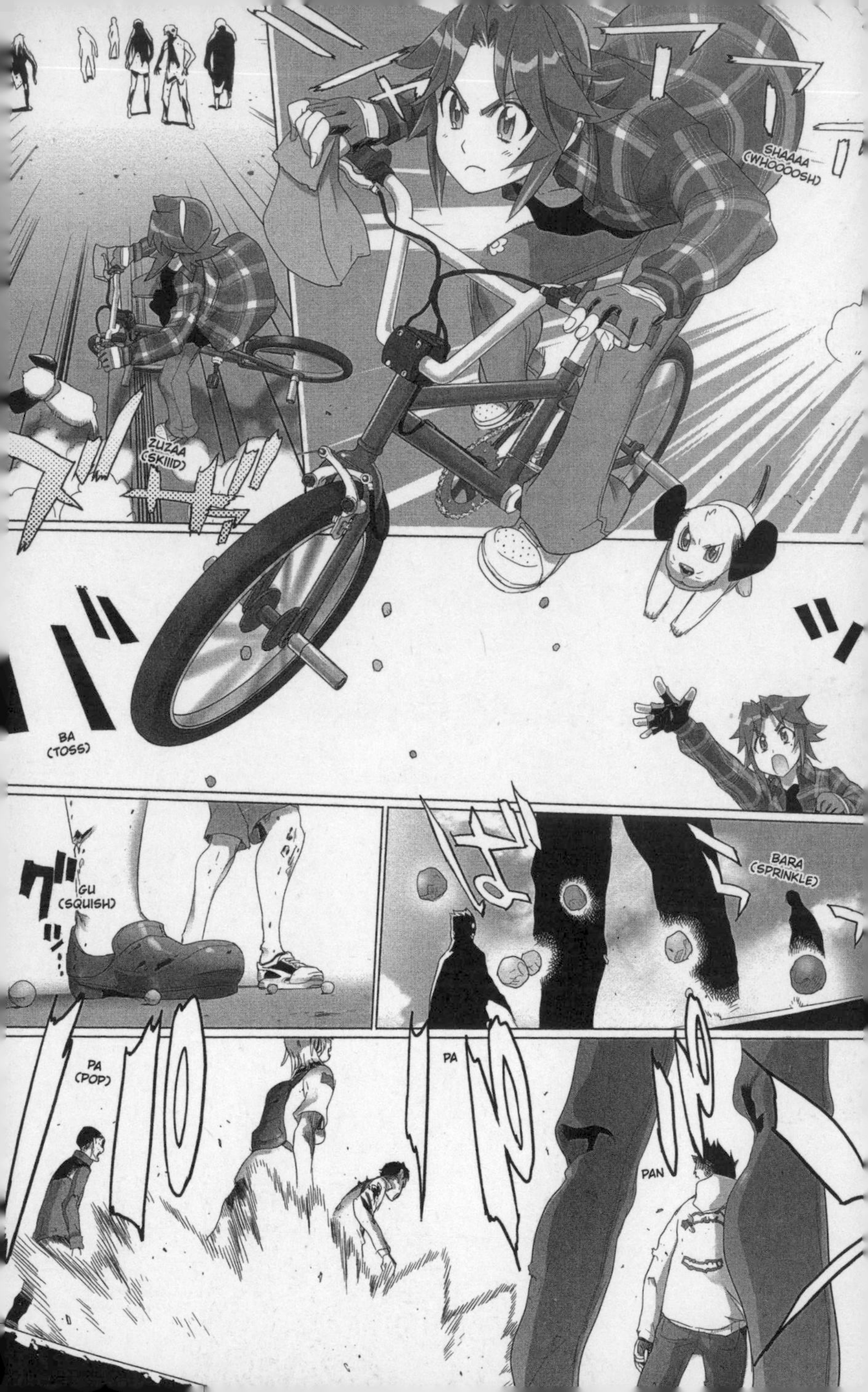
SHAAAA (WHOOOOSH)
ZUZAA (SKIIID)
BA (TOSS)
BARA (SPRINKLE)
GU (SQUISH)
PAN
PA
PA (POP)

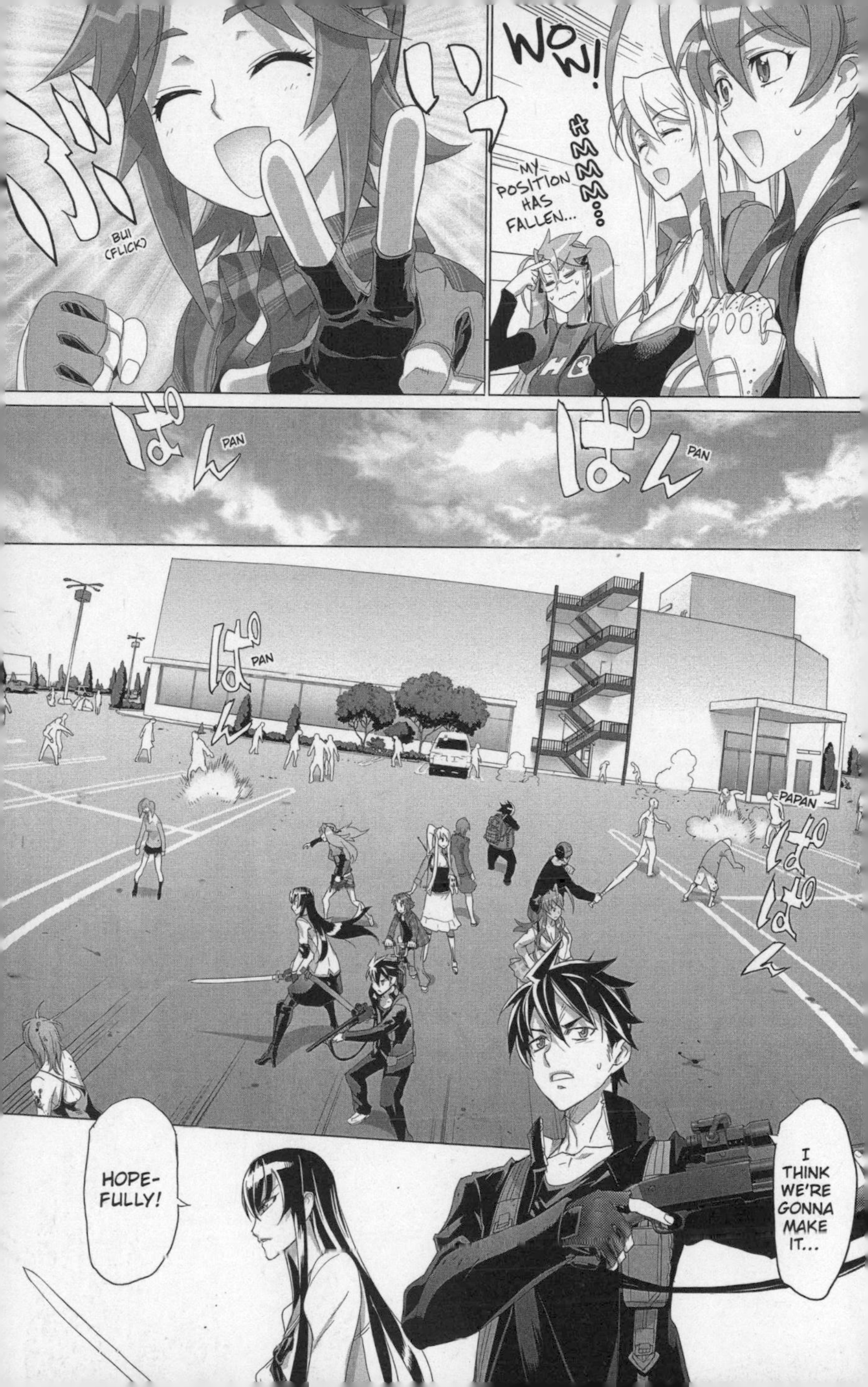
WOW!
HMMM...
MY POSITION HAS FALLEN...
BUI (FLICK)
PAN
PAN
PAPAN
PAN
I THINK WE'RE GONNA MAKE IT...
HOPE-FULLY!

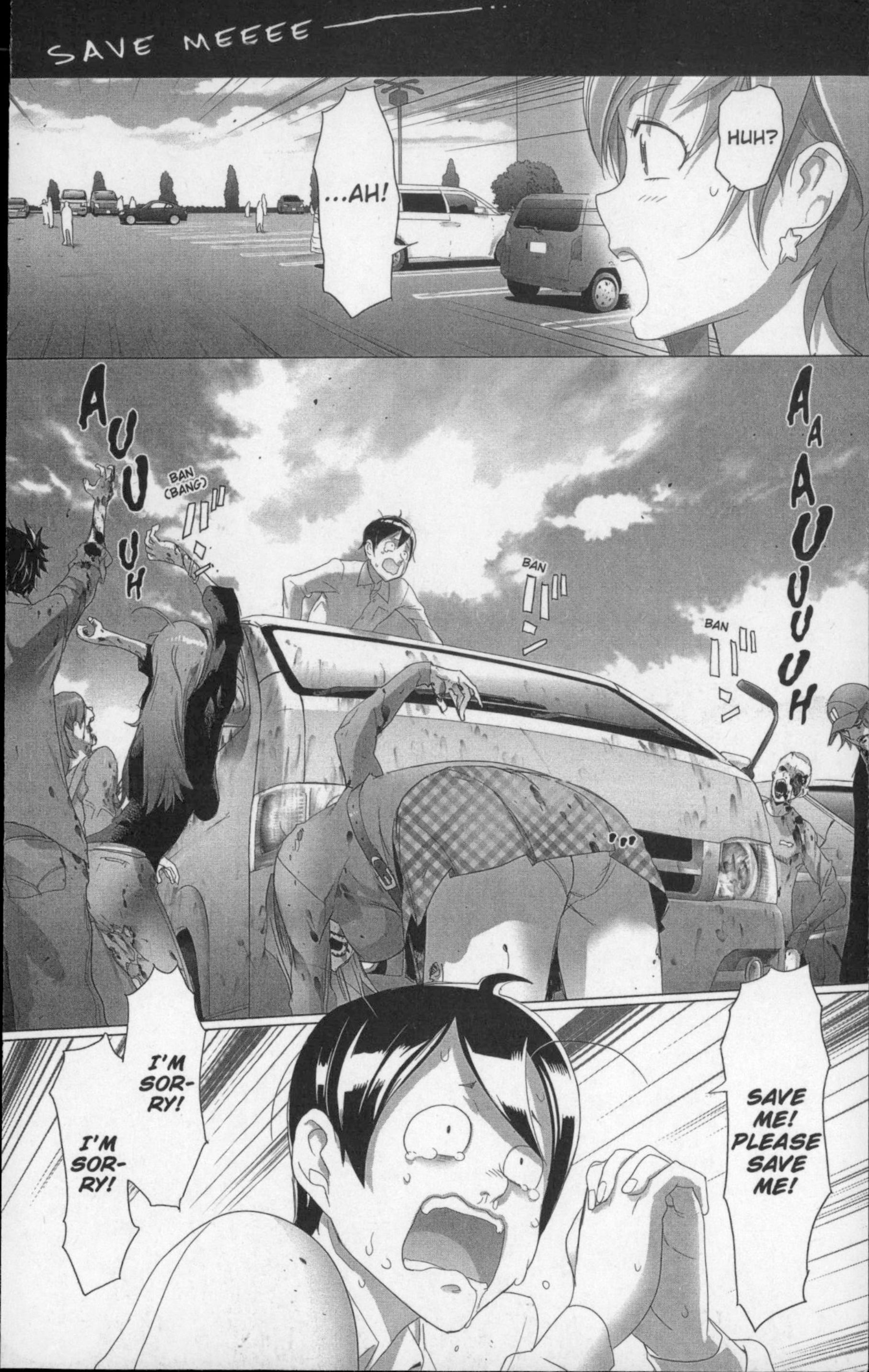
SAVE MEEEE
HUH?
...AH!
AAAUUUUUH
BAN
BAN
BAN (BANG)
AUUUH
SAVE ME! PLEASE SAVE ME!
I'M SORRY! I'M SORRY!

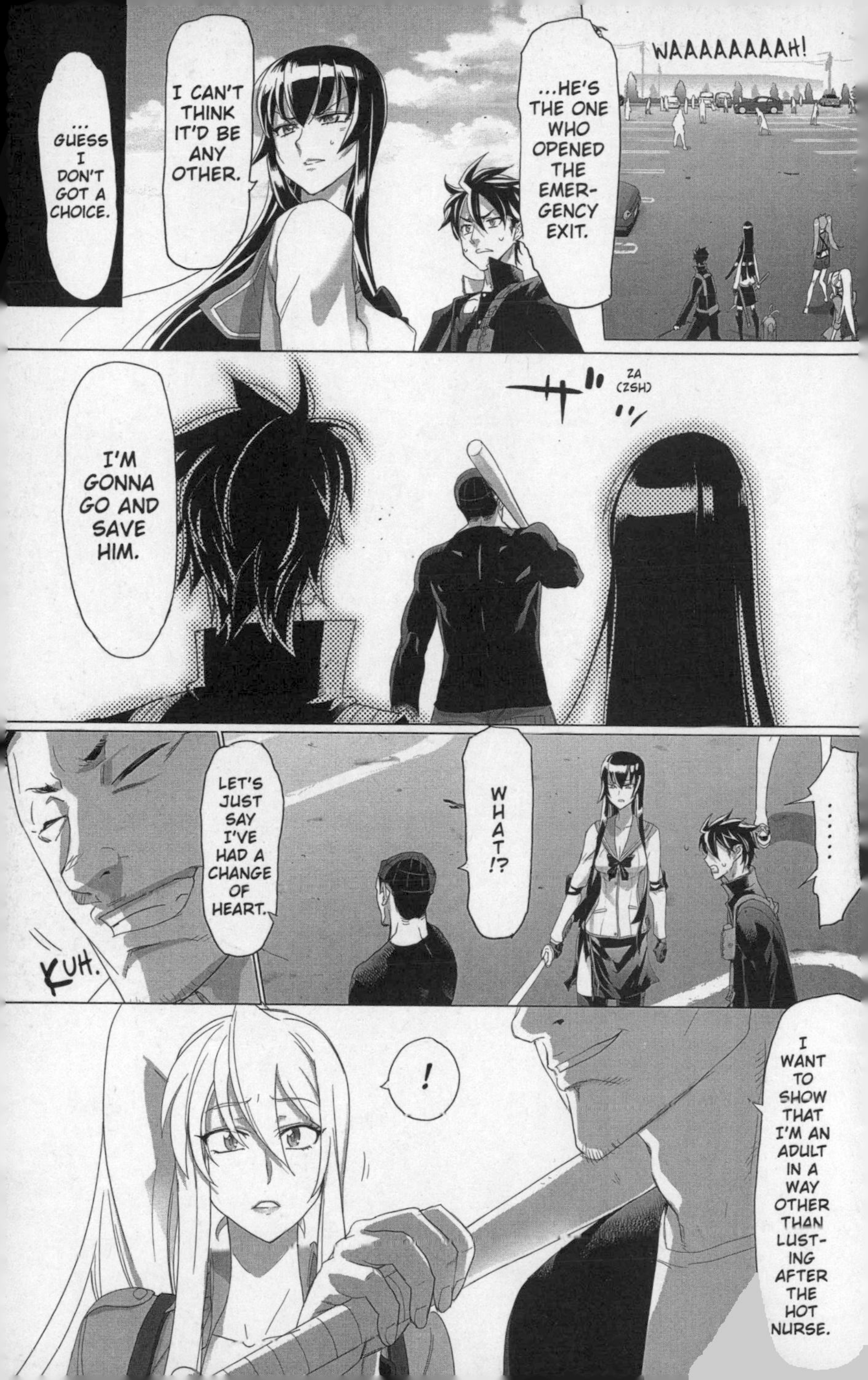
WAAAAAAAAH!
...HE'S THE ONE WHO OPENED THE EMERGENCY EXIT.
I CAN'T THINK IT'D BE ANY OTHER.
... GUESS I DON'T GOT A CHOICE.
ZA (ZSH)
I'M GONNA GO AND SAVE HIM.
......
WHAT!?
LET'S JUST SAY I'VE HAD A CHANGE OF HEART.
KUH.
I WANT TO SHOW THAT I'M AN ADULT IN A WAY OTHER THAN LUSTING AFTER THE HOT NURSE.
!

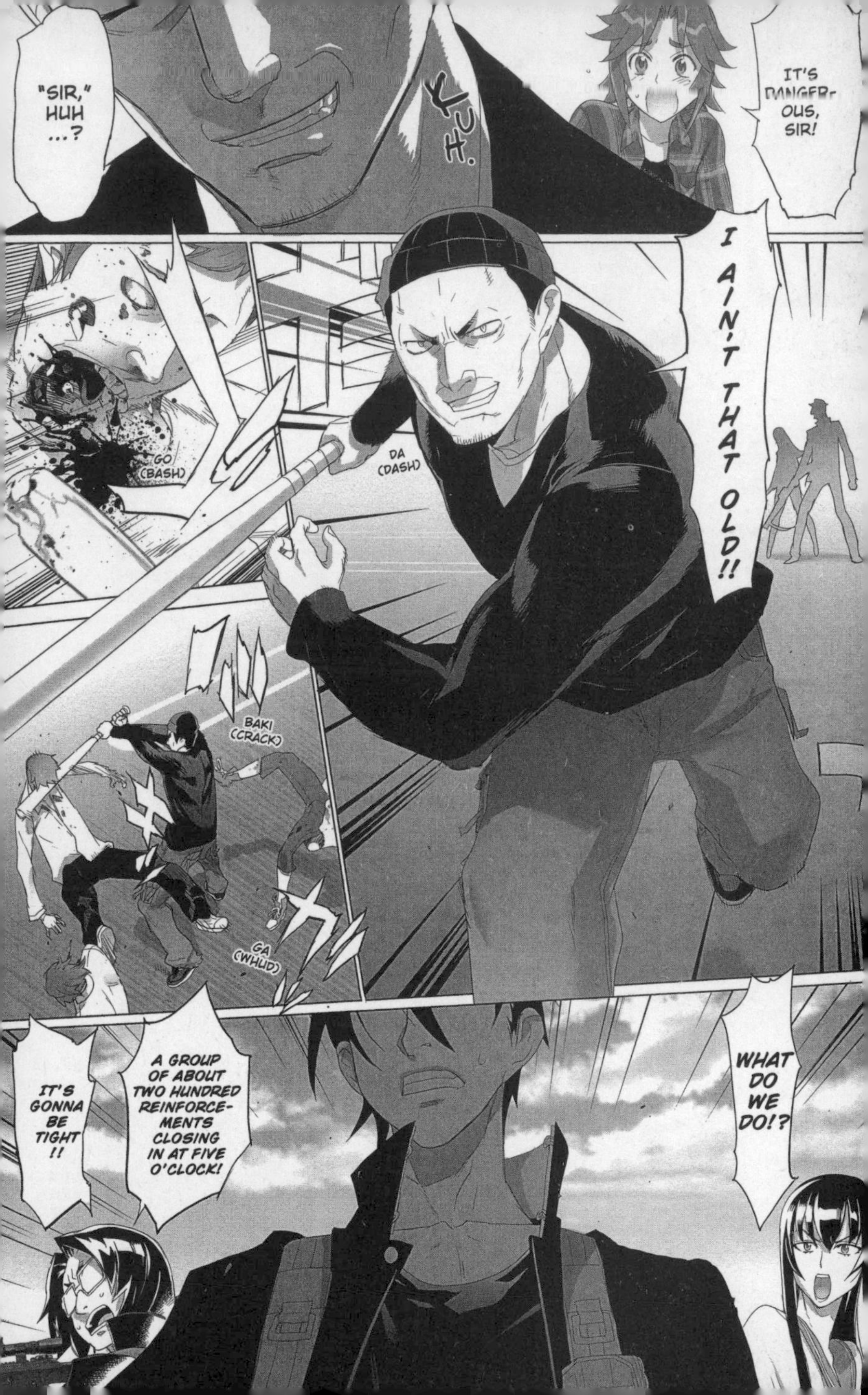
IT'S DANGER-OUS, SIR!
KUH.
"SIR," HUH ...?
I AIN'T THAT OLD!!
DA (DASH)
GO (BASH)
BAKI (CRACK)
GA (WHUD)
WHAT DO WE DO!?
A GROUP OF ABOUT TWO HUNDRED REINFORCE-MENTS CLOSING IN AT FIVE O'CLOCK!
IT'S GONNA BE TIGHT !!

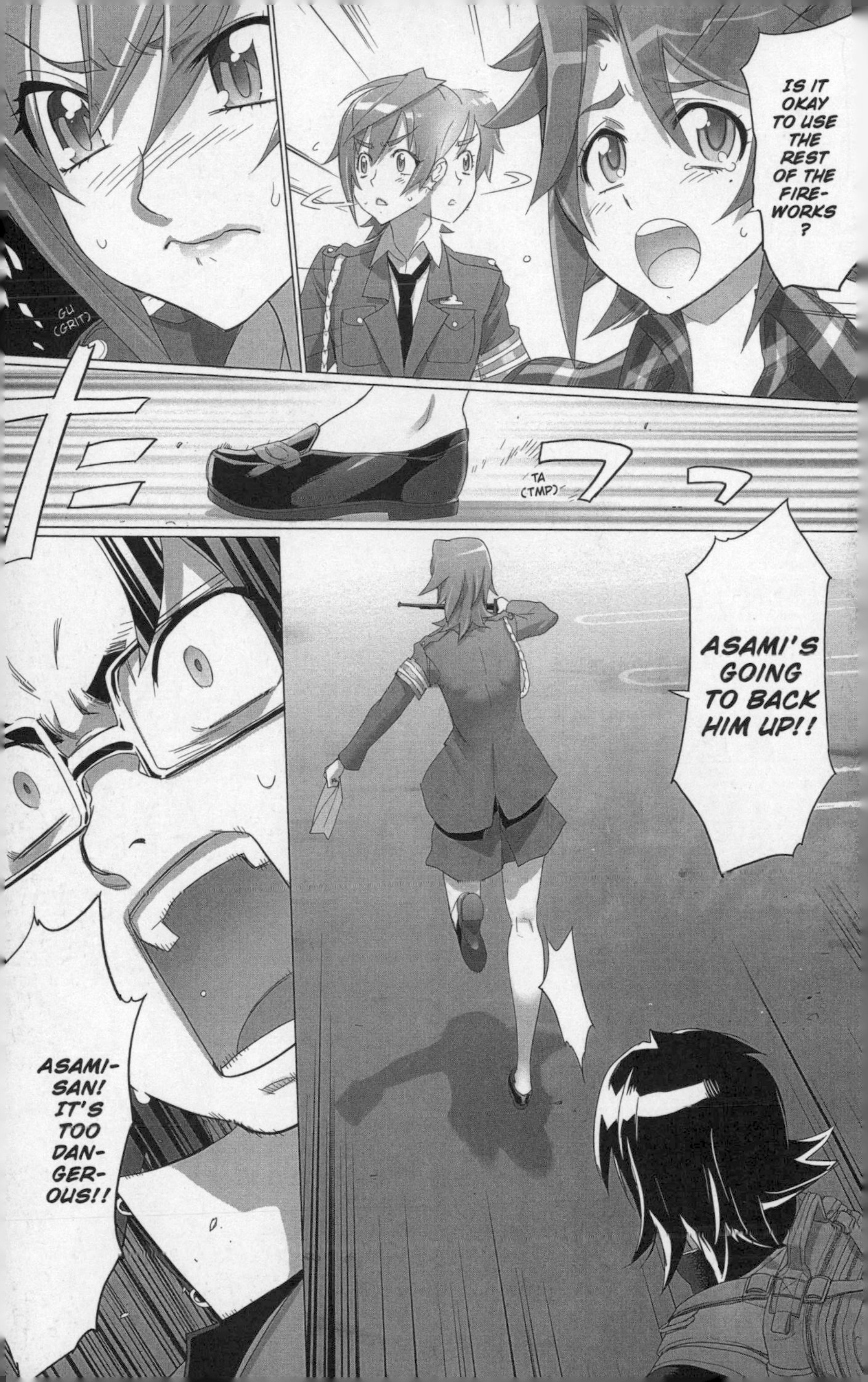
IS IT OKAY TO USE THE REST OF THE FIRE-WORKS?
GU (GRIT)
TA (TMP)
ASAMI'S GOING TO BACK HIM UP!!
ASAMI-SAN! IT'S TOO DAN-GER-OUS!!

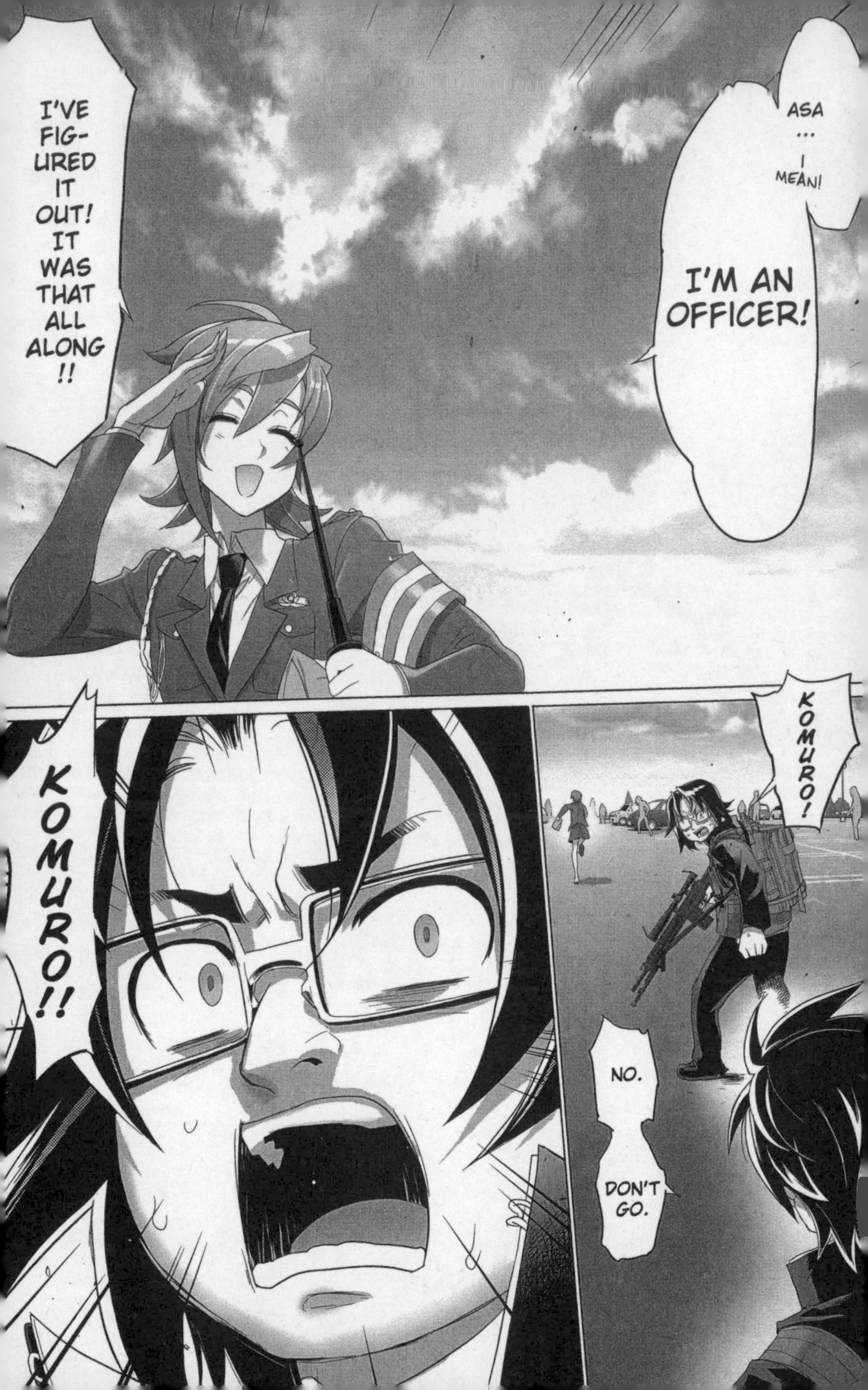
ASA... I MEAN!
I'M AN OFFICER!
I'VE FIG-URED IT OUT! IT WAS THAT ALL ALONG!!
KOMURO!
NO.
DON'T GO.
KOMURO!!

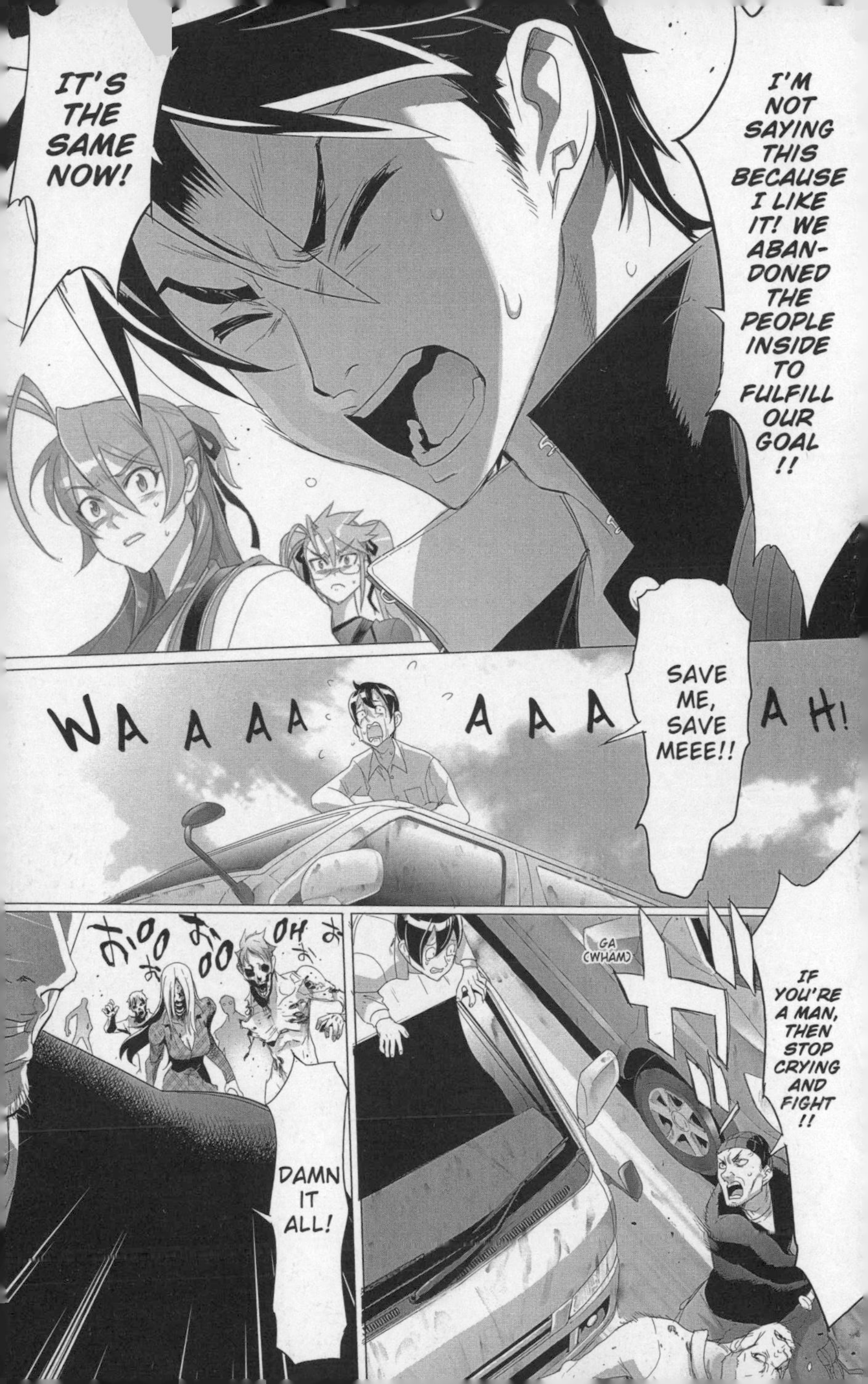
I'M NOT SAYING THIS BECAUSE I LIKE IT! WE ABAN-DONED THE PEOPLE INSIDE TO FULFILL OUR GOAL!!
IT'S THE SAME NOW!
SAVE ME, SAVE MEEE!!
WAAAAAAAH!
IF YOU'RE A MAN, THEN STOP CRYING AND FIGHT!!
GA (WHAM)
OH
DAMN IT ALL!

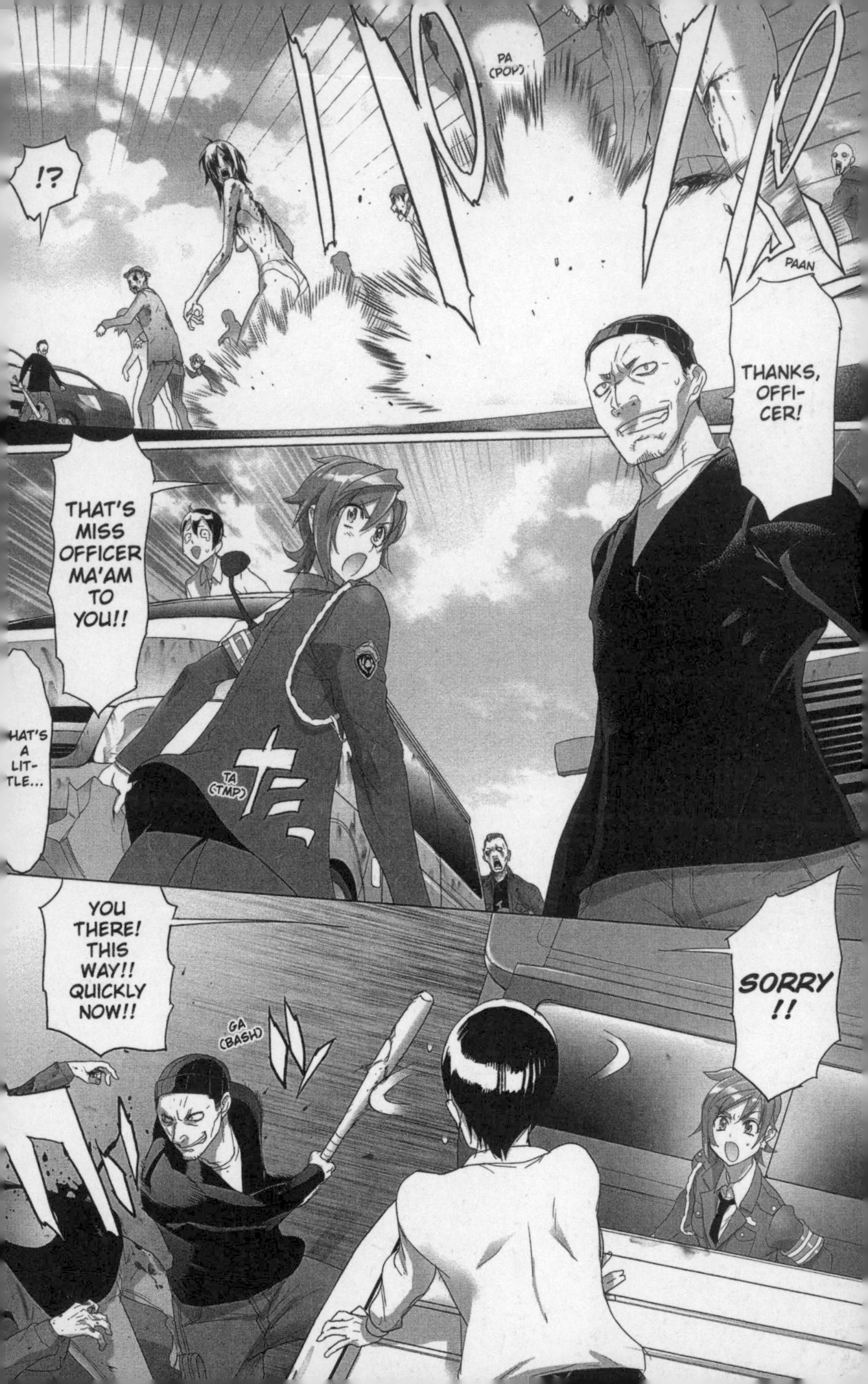
PAAN
PA (POW)
!?
THANKS, OFFICER!
THAT'S MISS OFFICER MA'AM TO YOU!!
TA (TMP)
HAT'S A LITTLE...
SORRY!!
GA (BASH)
YOU THERE! THIS WAY!! QUICKLY NOW!!

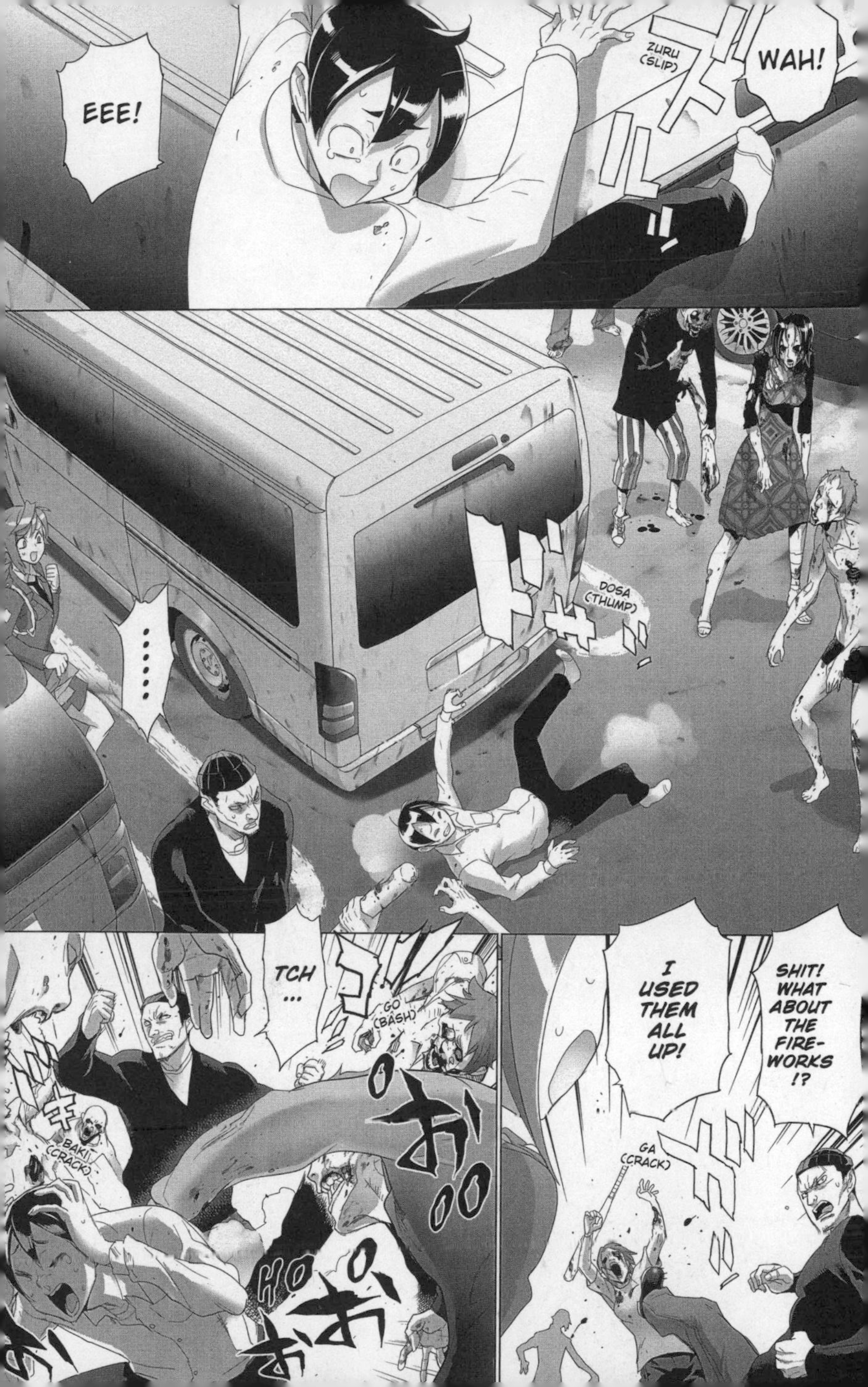
WAH!
ZURU (SLIP)
EEE!
DOSA (THUMP)
......
SHIT! WHAT ABOUT THE FIRE-WORKS!?
I USED THEM ALL UP!
GA (CRACK)
TCH ...
GO (BASH)
BAKI (CRACK)
HO

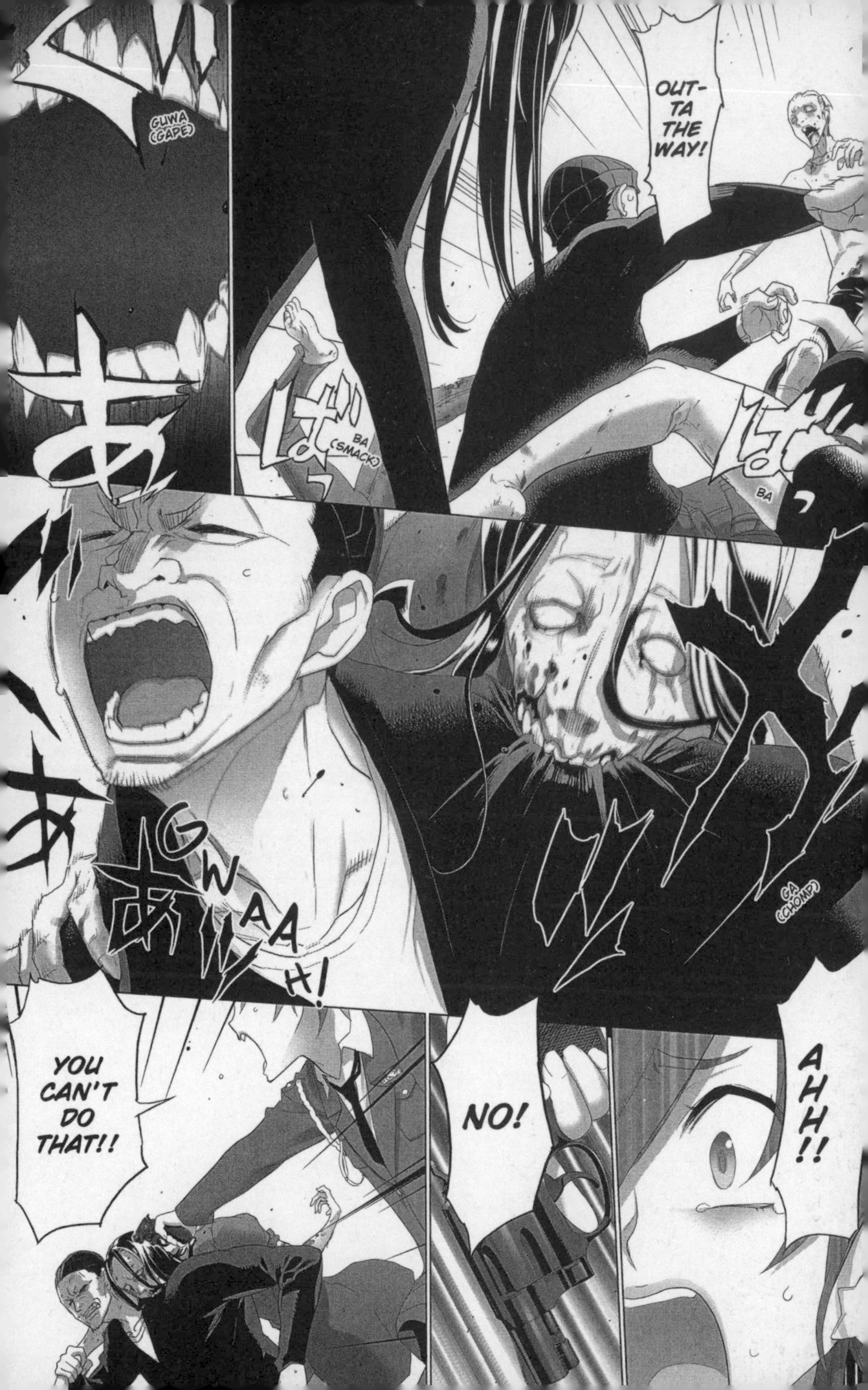
OUT-TA THE WAY!
BA
BA (SMACK)
GUWA (GAPE)
GA (CHOMP)
GWAAAH!
AHH!!
NO!
YOU CAN'T DO THAT!!

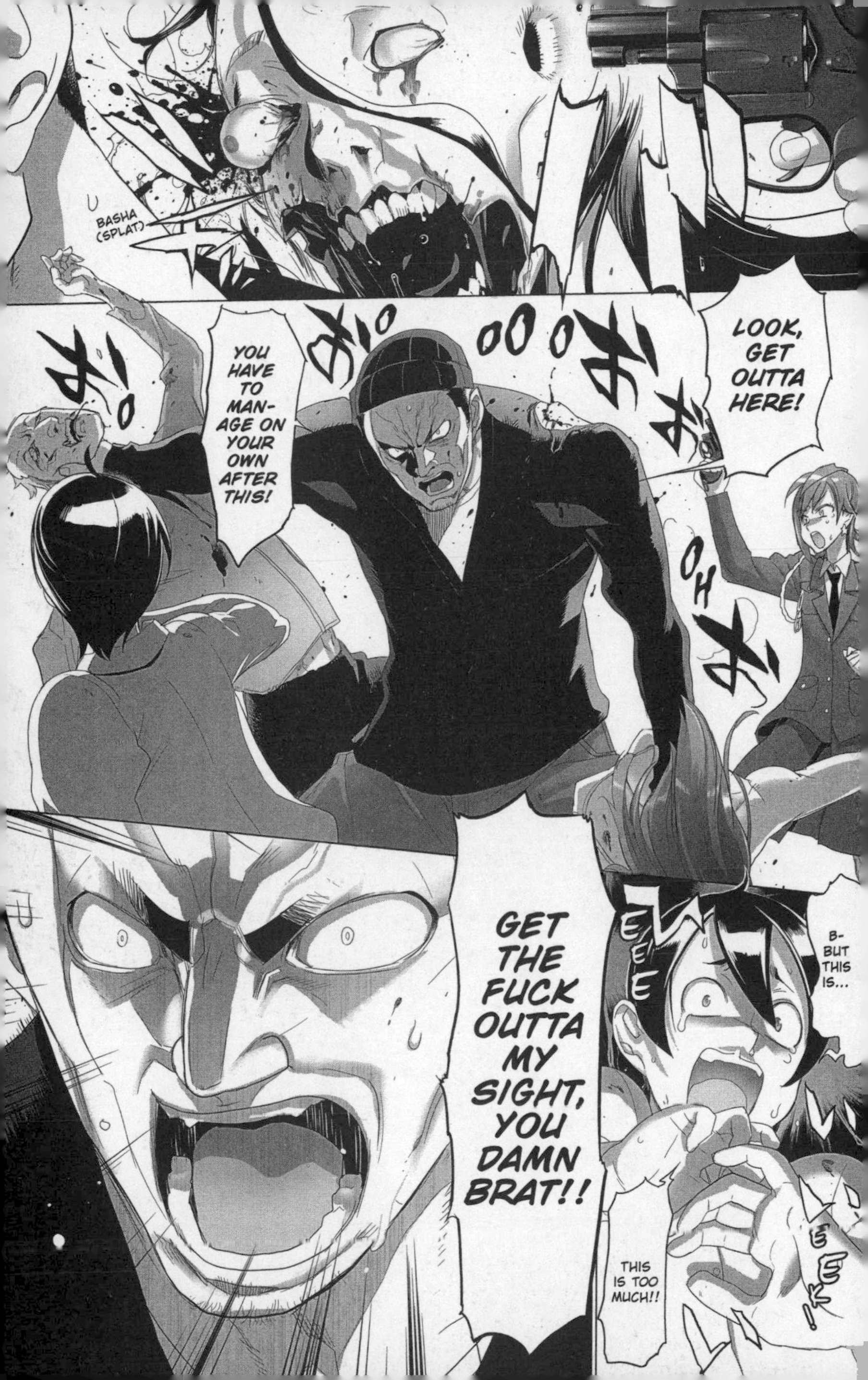

BASHA (SPLAT)
LOOK, GET OUTTA HERE!
OH
OOO
YOU HAVE TO MAN-AGE ON YOUR OWN AFTER THIS!
B-BUT THIS IS...
THIS IS TOO MUCH!!
GET THE FUCK OUTTA MY SIGHT, YOU DAMN BRAT!!

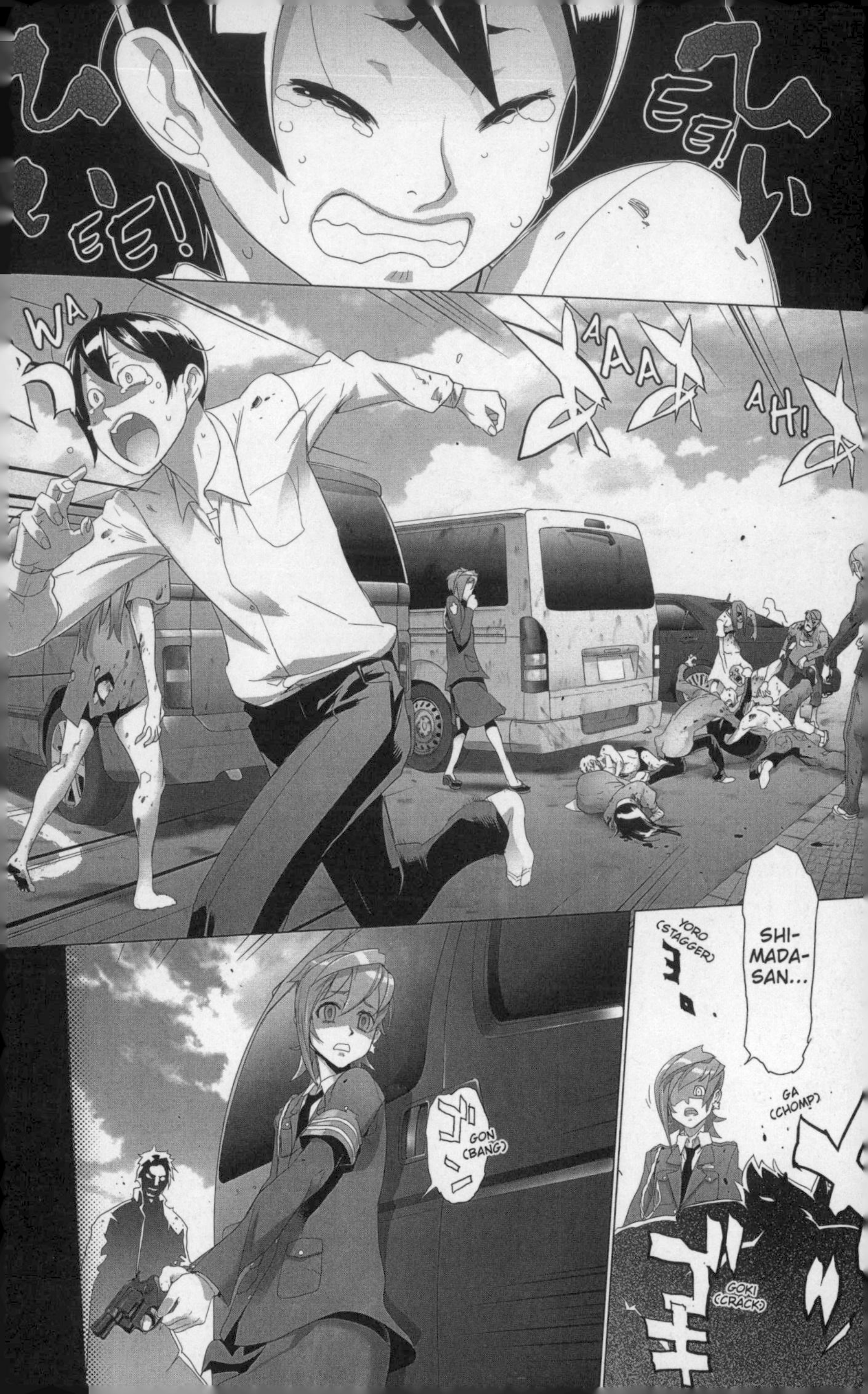
EE!
EE!
AH!
AAA
WA
SHI-MADA-SAN...
YORO (STAGGER)
GA (CHOMP)
GOKI (CRACK)
GON (BANG)

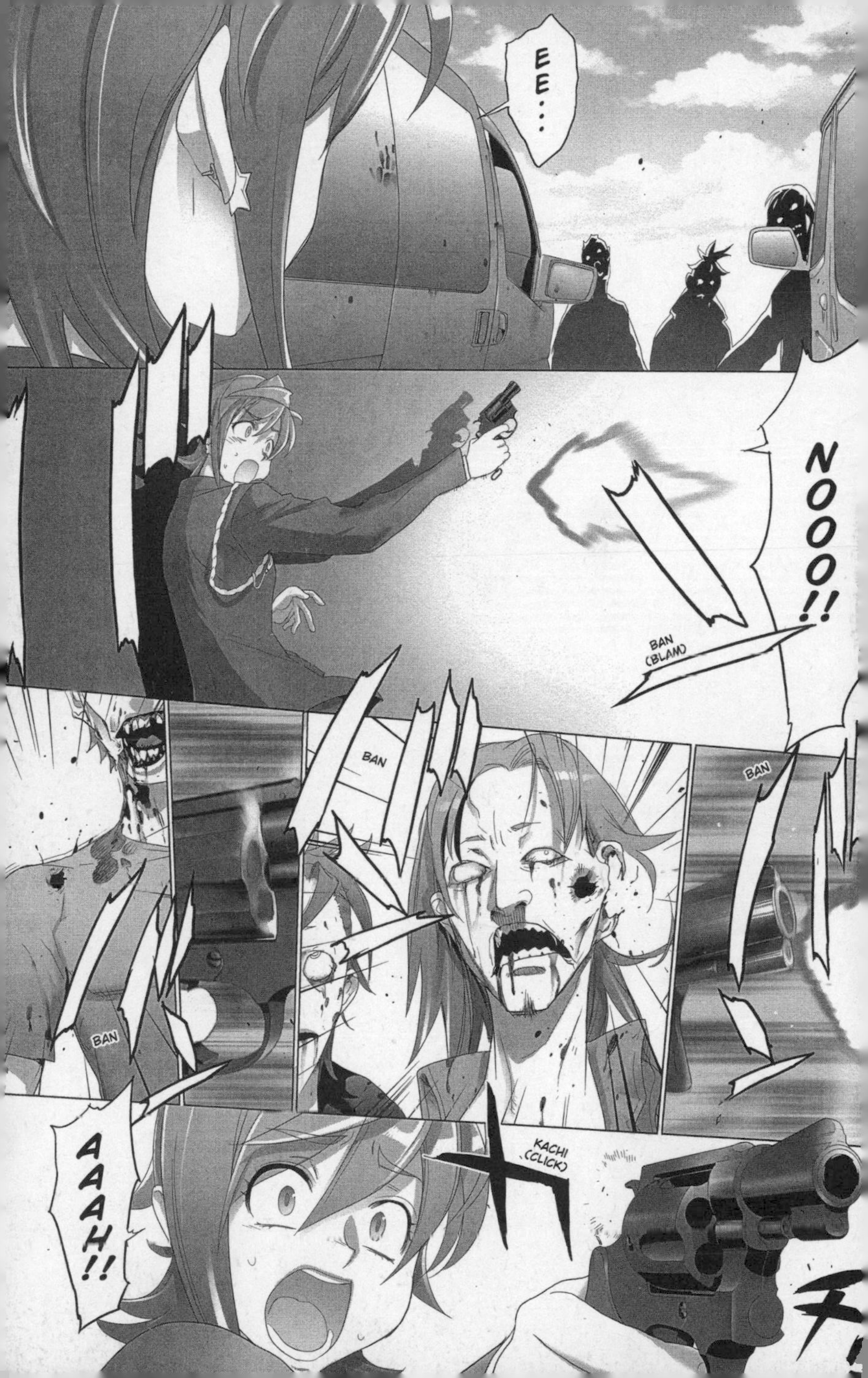
EE...
NOOOO!!
BAN (BLAM)
BAN
BAN
BAN
KACHI (CLICK)
AAAH!!

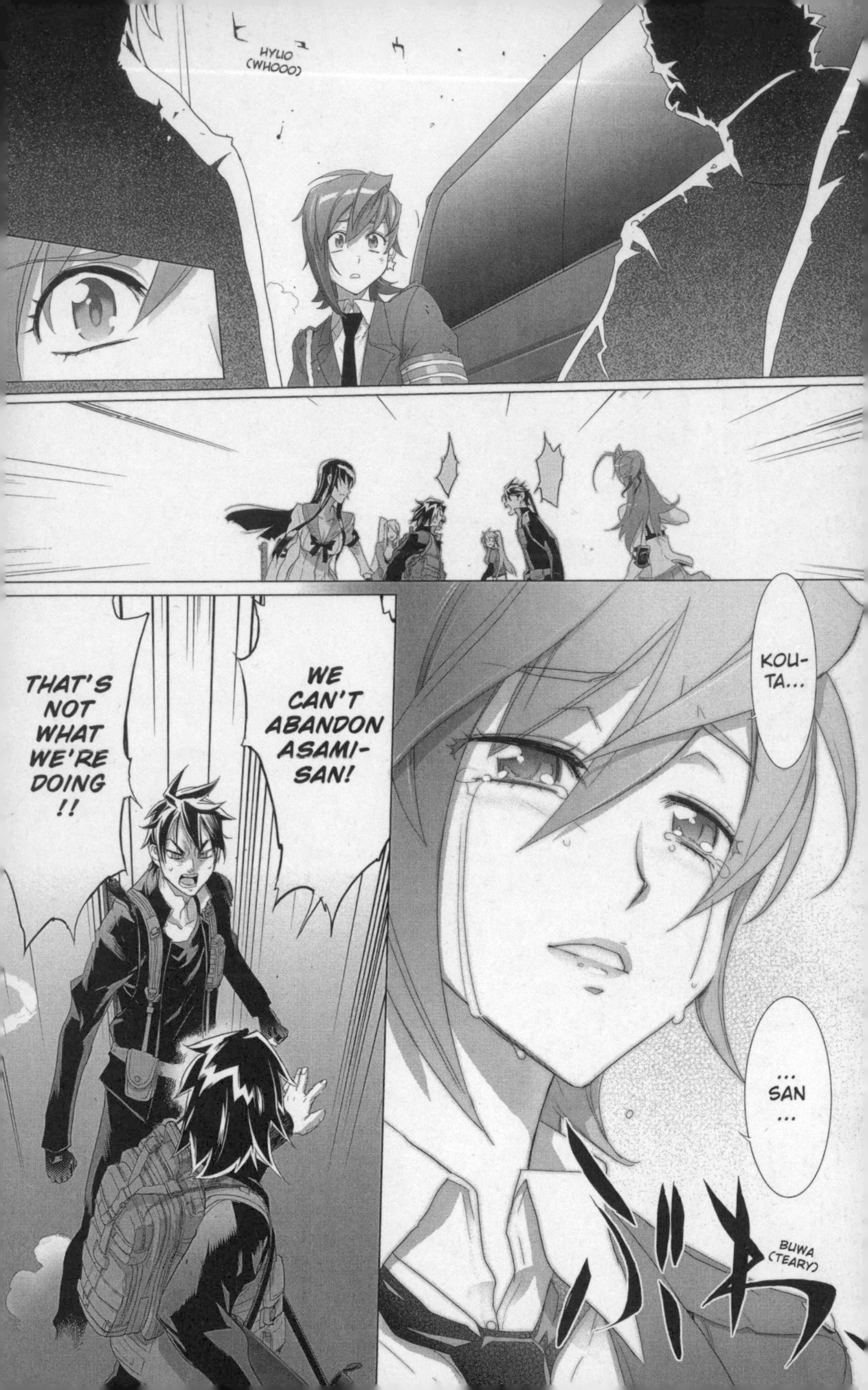
HYUO (WHOOO)
KOU-TA...
...SAN...
BUWA (TEARY)
WE CAN'T ABANDON ASAMI-SAN!
THAT'S NOT WHAT WE'RE DOING!!

KOU-
TA-
SAAA-
AAAN
!!

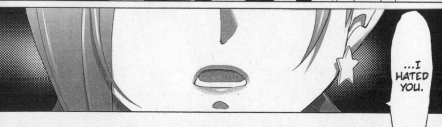

...I
HATED
YOU.

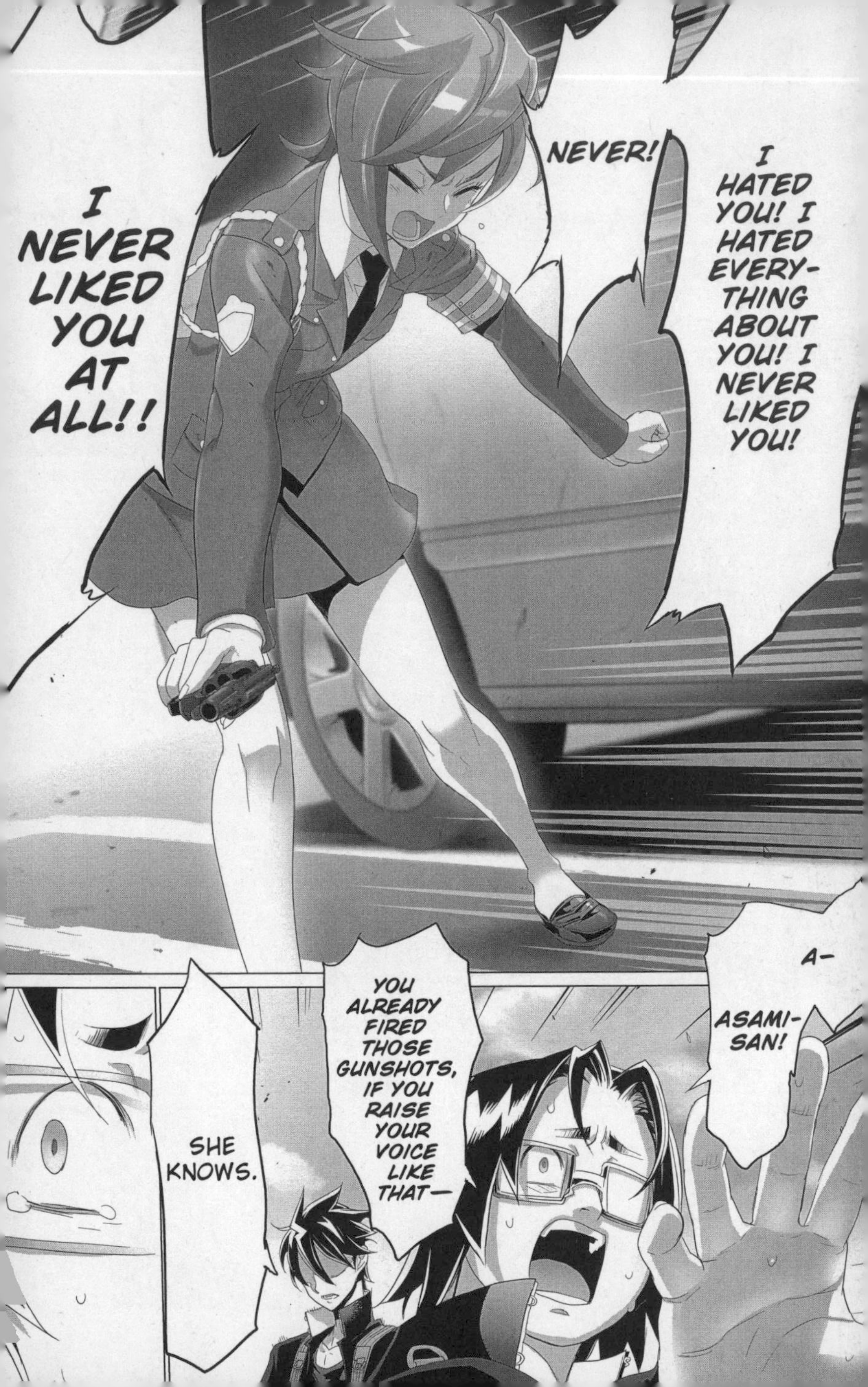
I HATED YOU! I HATED EVERY-THING ABOUT YOU! I NEVER LIKED YOU!
NEVER!
I NEVER LIKED YOU AT ALL!!
A-
ASAMI-SAN!
YOU ALREADY FIRED THOSE GUNSHOTS, IF YOU RAISE YOUR VOICE LIKE THAT—
SHE KNOWS.

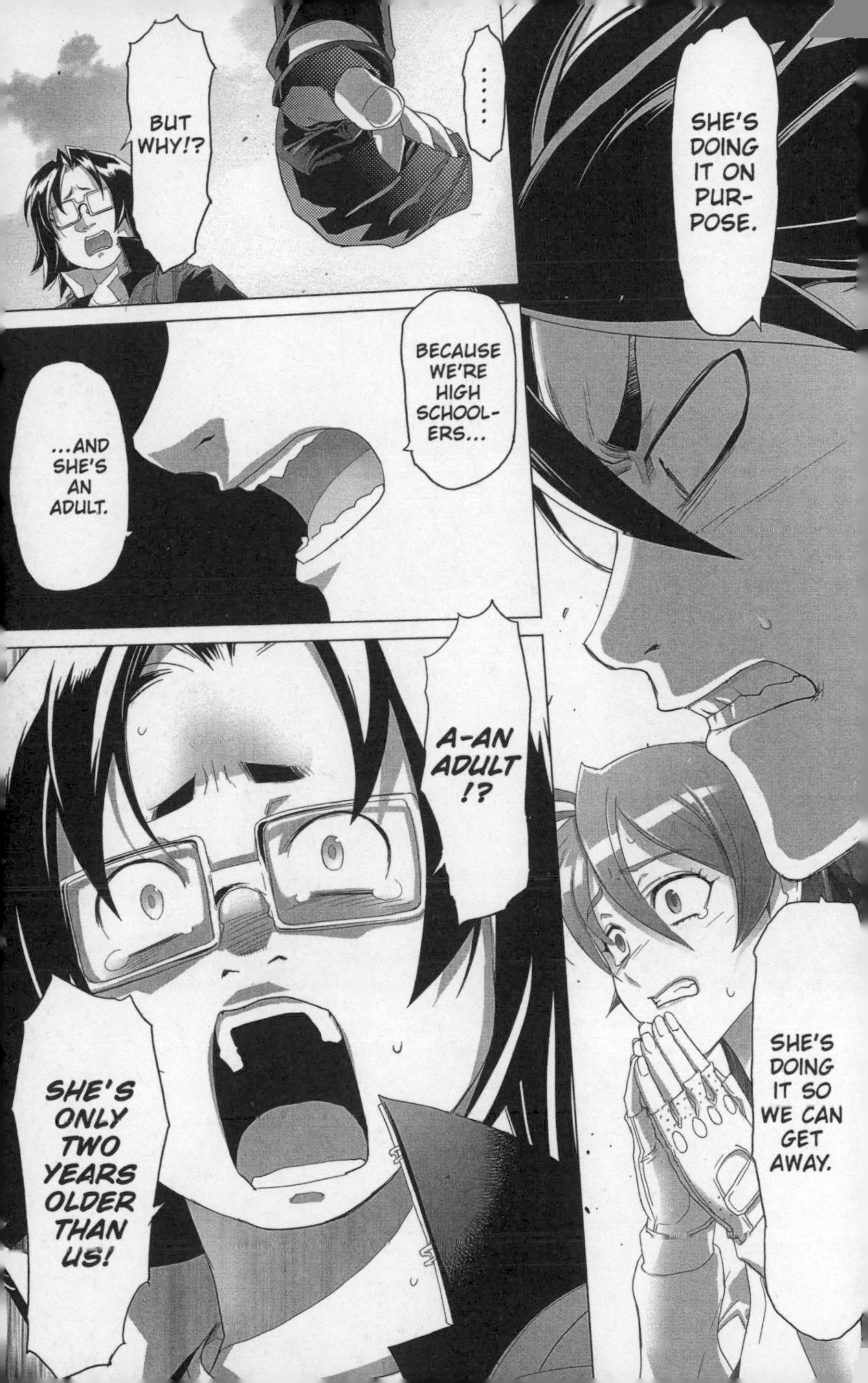
SHE'S DOING IT ON PUR-POSE.
......
BUT WHY!?
BECAUSE WE'RE HIGH SCHOOL-ERS...
...AND SHE'S AN ADULT.
SHE'S DOING IT SO WE CAN GET AWAY.
A-AN ADULT!?
SHE'S ONLY TWO YEARS OLDER THAN US!

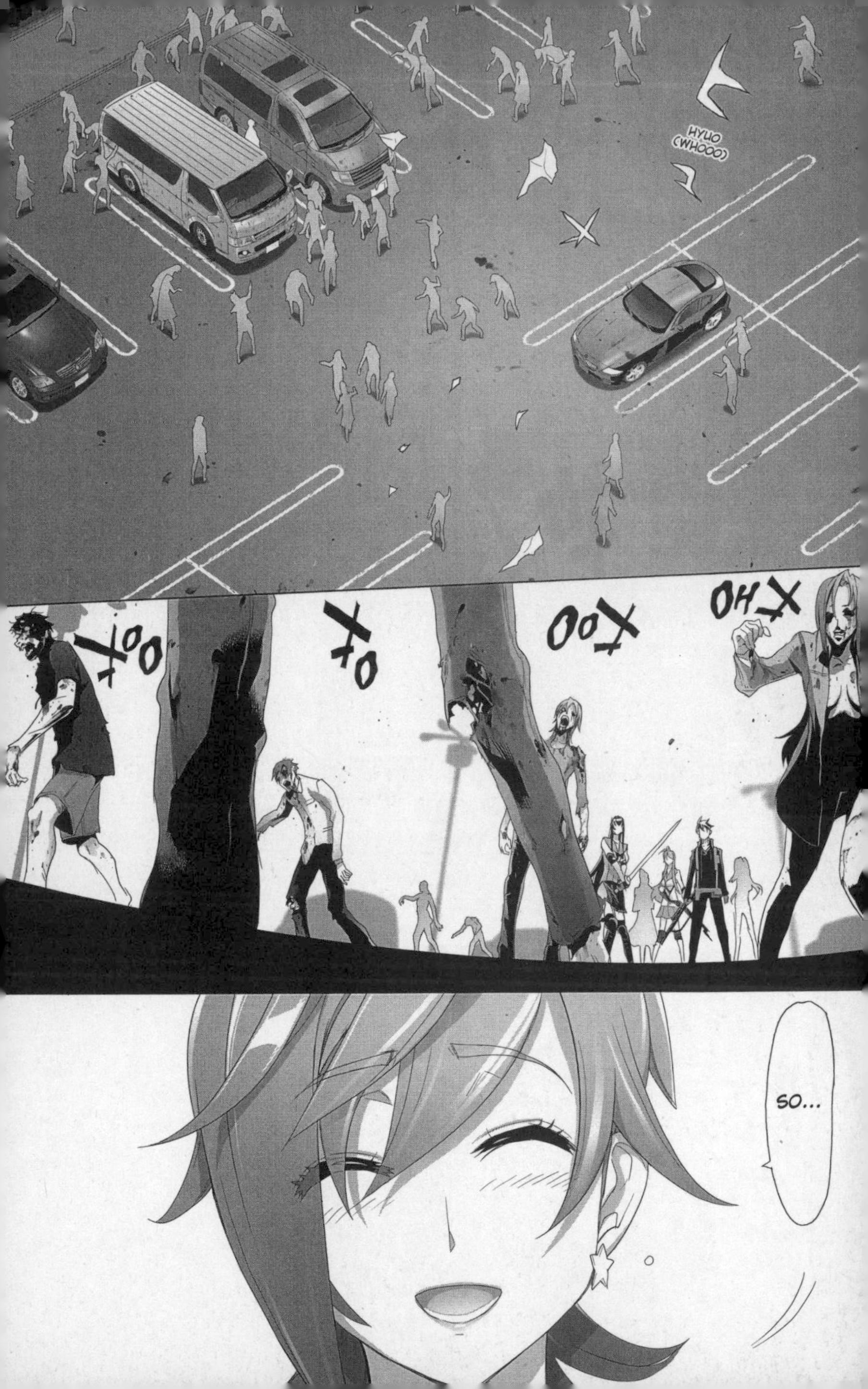
HYUO
(WHOOO)
OH
OO
O
OO
SO...

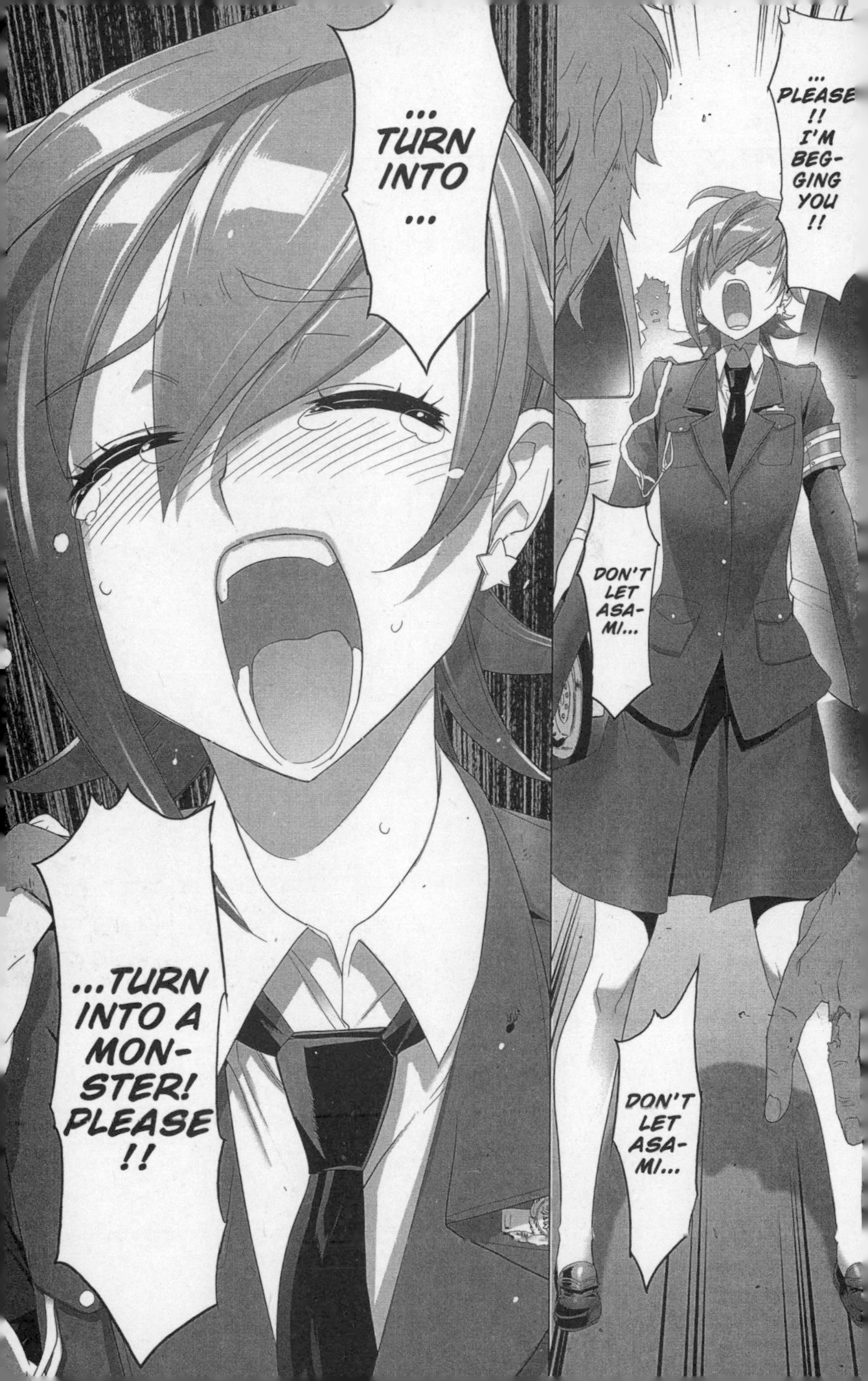
...PLEASE!! I'M BEGGING YOU!!
DON'T LET ASAMI...
DON'T LET ASAMI...
...TURN INTO...
...TURN INTO A MONSTER! PLEASE!!

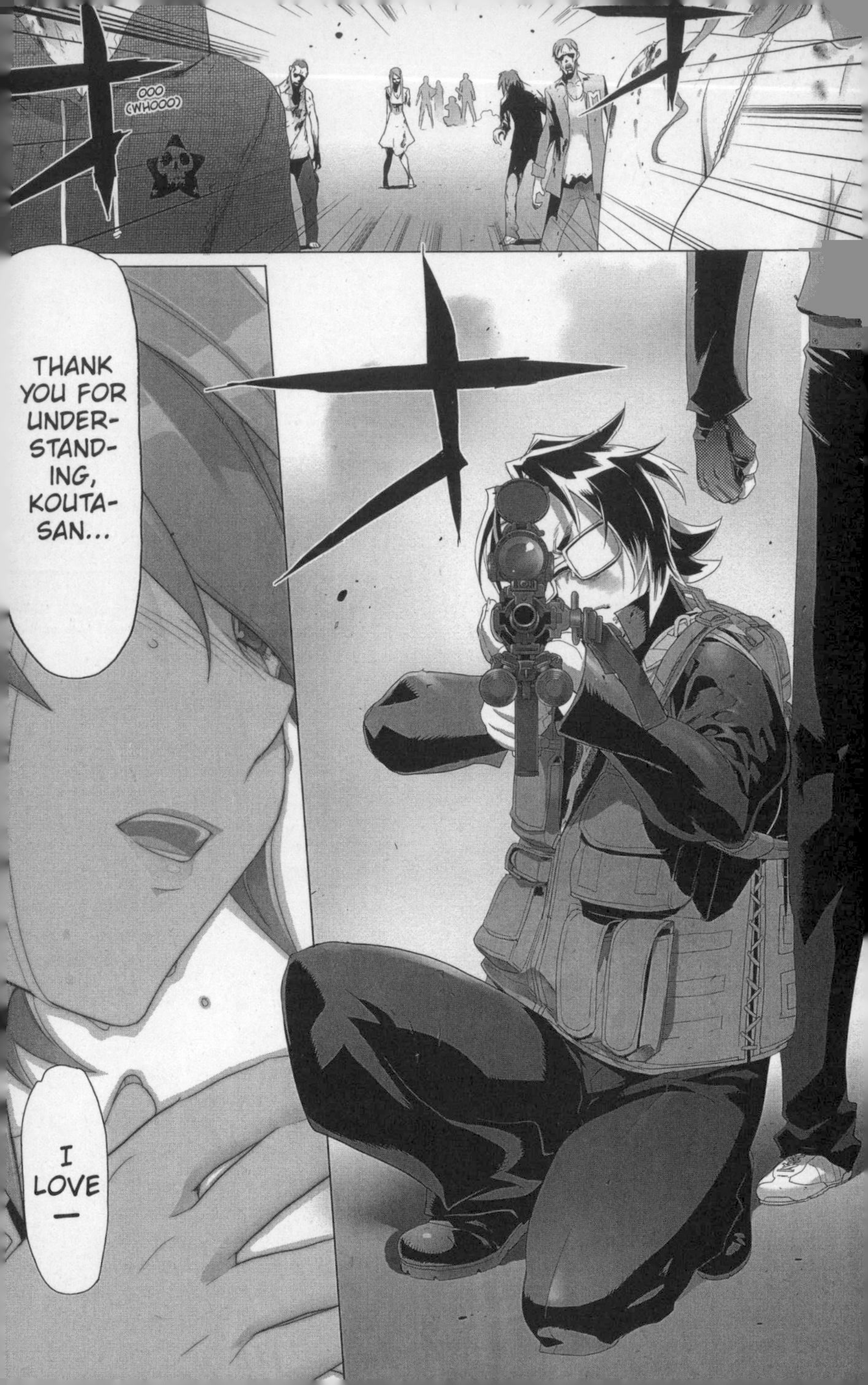
OOO
(WHOOO)
THANK YOU FOR UNDER-STANDING, KOUTA-SAN...
I LOVE —

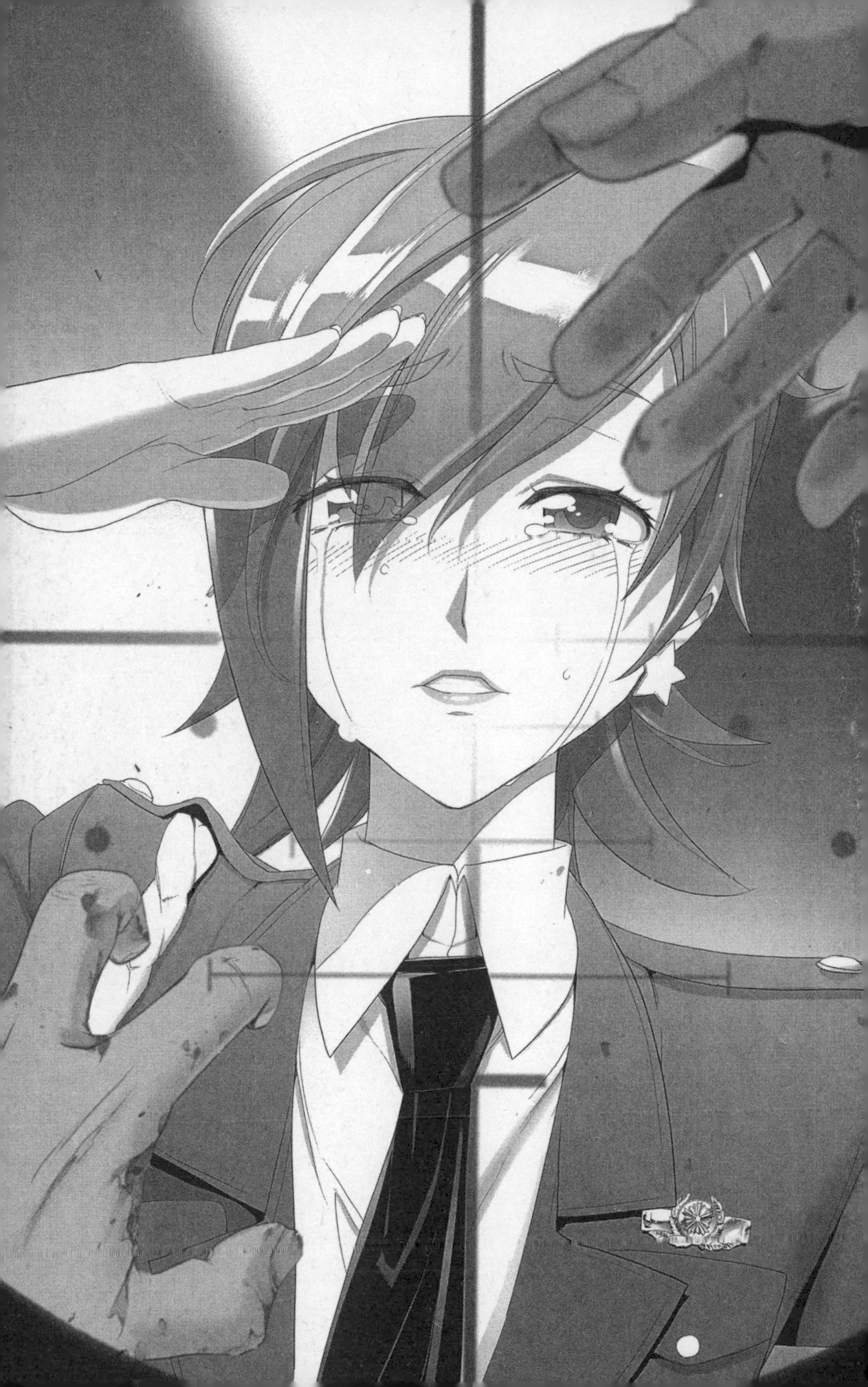

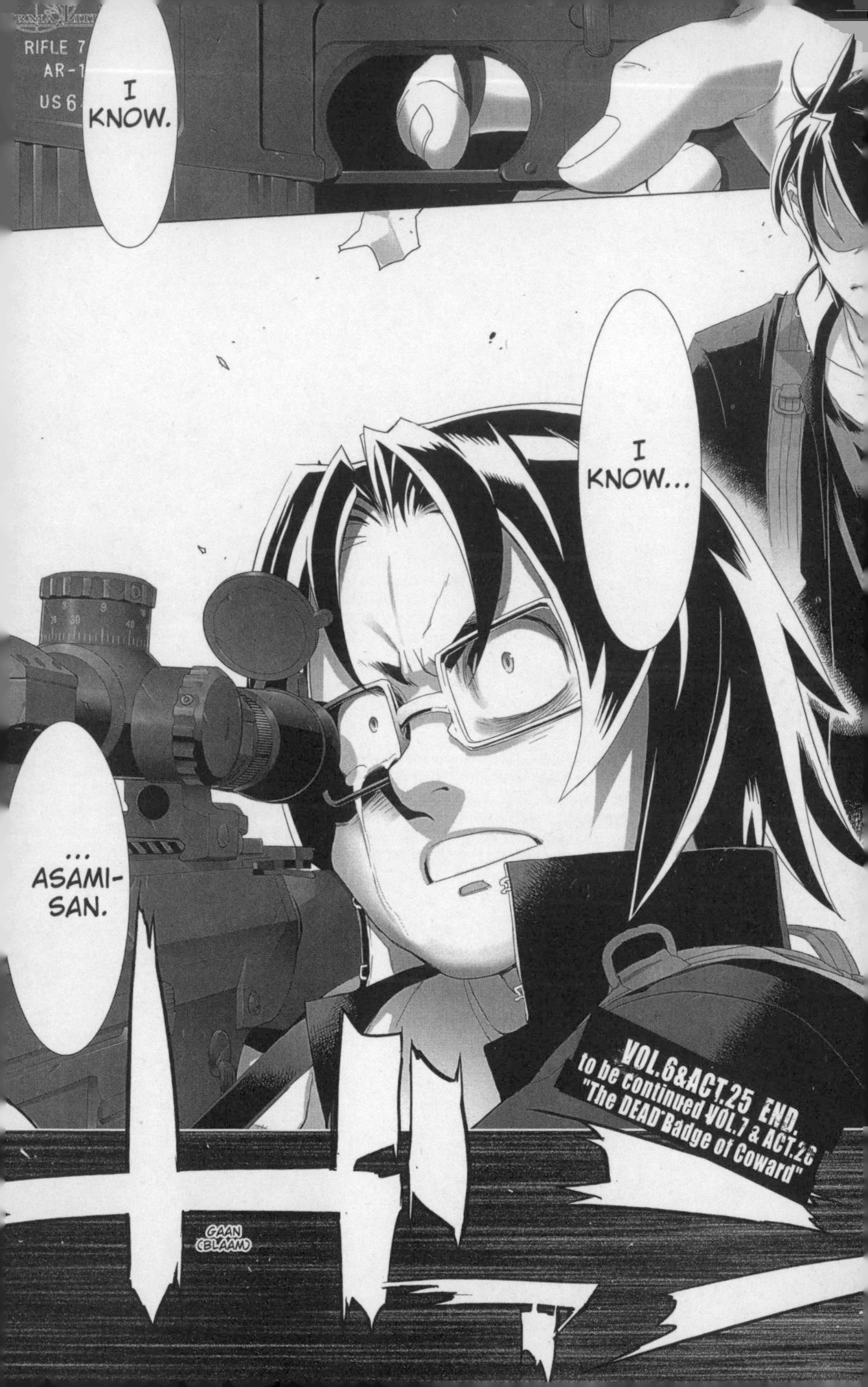
I KNOW.
I KNOW...
... ASAMI-SAN.
VOL.6&ACT.25 END.
to be continued VOL.7 & ACT.26
"The DEAD Badge of Coward"
GAAN (BLAAM)

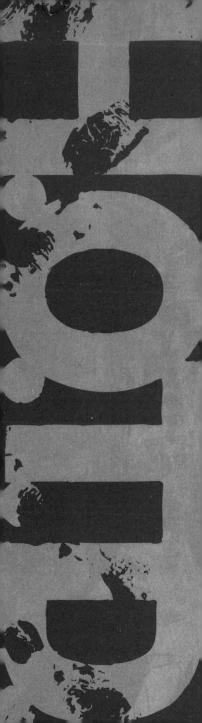

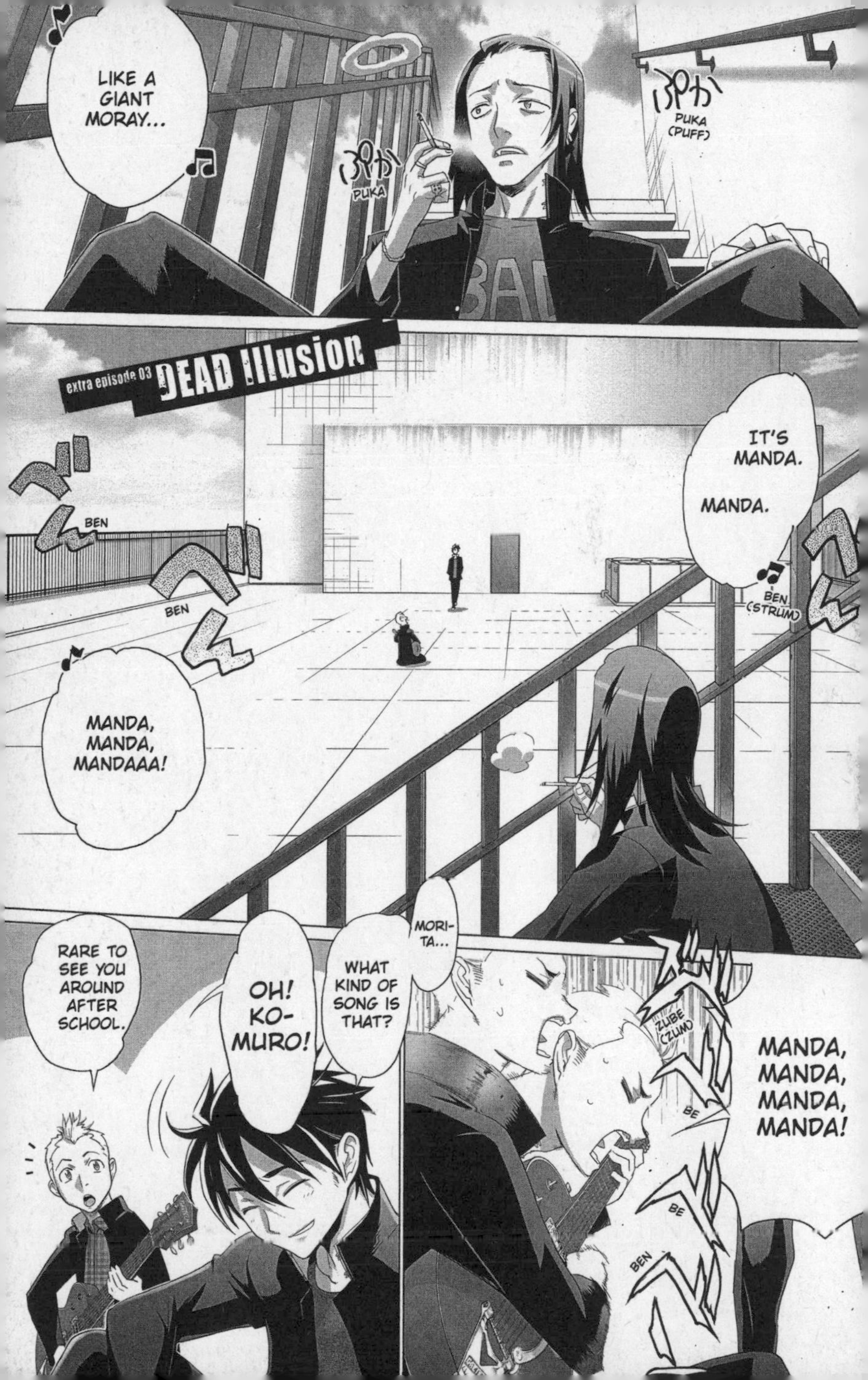
PUKA (PUFF)
PUKA
LIKE A GIANT MORAY...
extra episode 03 DEAD Illusion
IT'S MANDA.
MANDA.
BEN (STRUM)
BEN
BEN
MANDA, MANDA, MANDAAA!
MANDA, MANDA, MANDA, MANDA!
ZUBE (ZUM)
BE
BE
BEN
MORI-TA...
WHAT KIND OF SONG IS THAT?
OH! KO-MURO!
RARE TO SEE YOU AROUND AFTER SCHOOL.

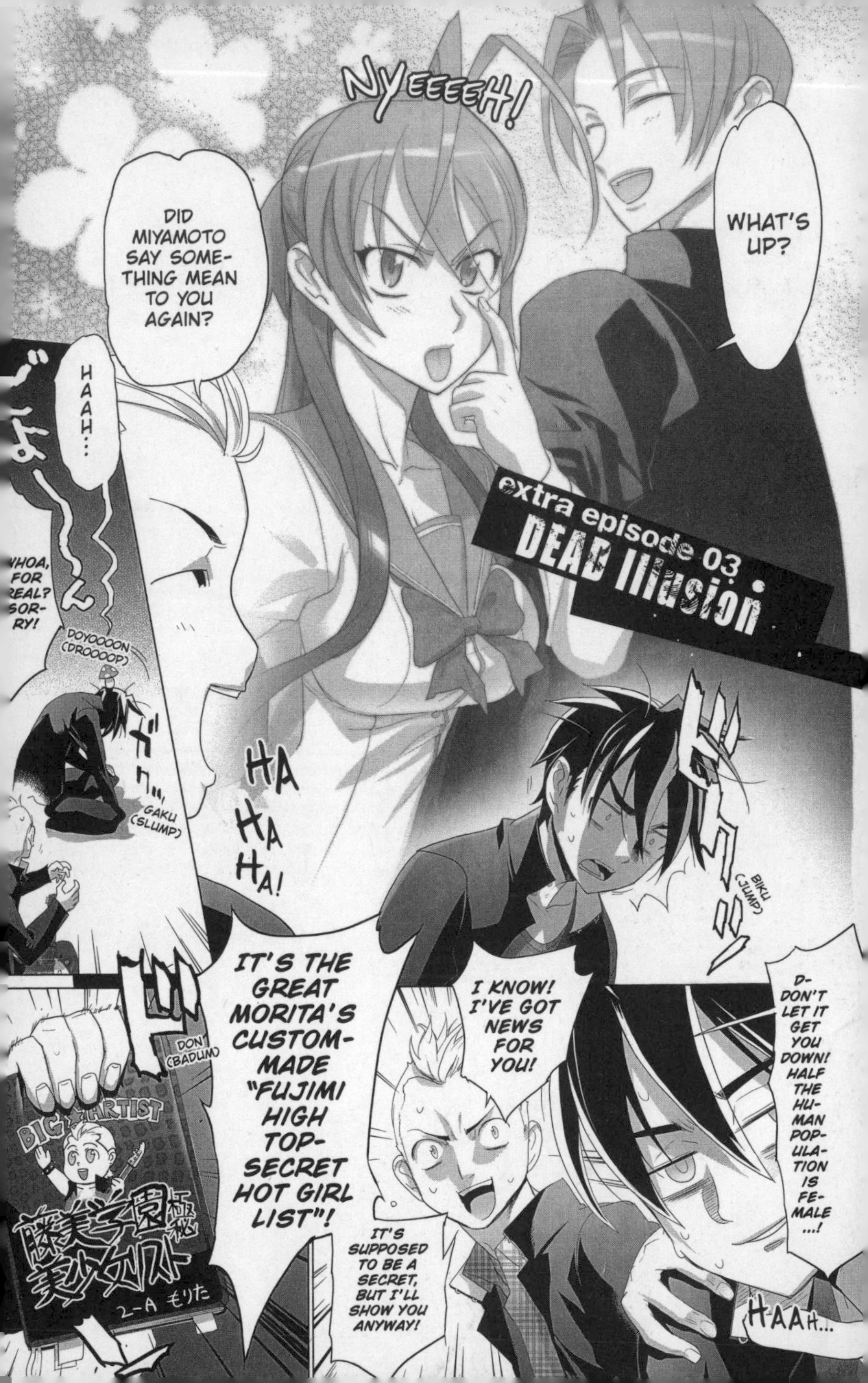

extra episode 03
DEAD Illusion
NYEEEEH!
WHAT'S UP?
DID MIYAMOTO SAY SOMETHING MEAN TO YOU AGAIN?
HAAAH...
WHOA, FOR REAL? SORRY!
DOYOOOON (DROOOOP)
GAKU (SLUMP)
HA HA HA!
BIKU (SLUMP)
D-DON'T LET IT GET YOU DOWN! HALF THE HUMAN POPULATION IS FEMALE...!
HAAH...
I KNOW! I'VE GOT NEWS FOR YOU!
IT'S SUPPOSED TO BE A SECRET, BUT I'LL SHOW YOU ANYWAY!
IT'S THE GREAT MORITA'S CUSTOM-MADE "FUJIMI HIGH TOP-SECRET HOT GIRL LIST"!
DON (BADUM)
BIG☆ARTIST
藤美学園 極秘 美少女リスト
2-A もりた

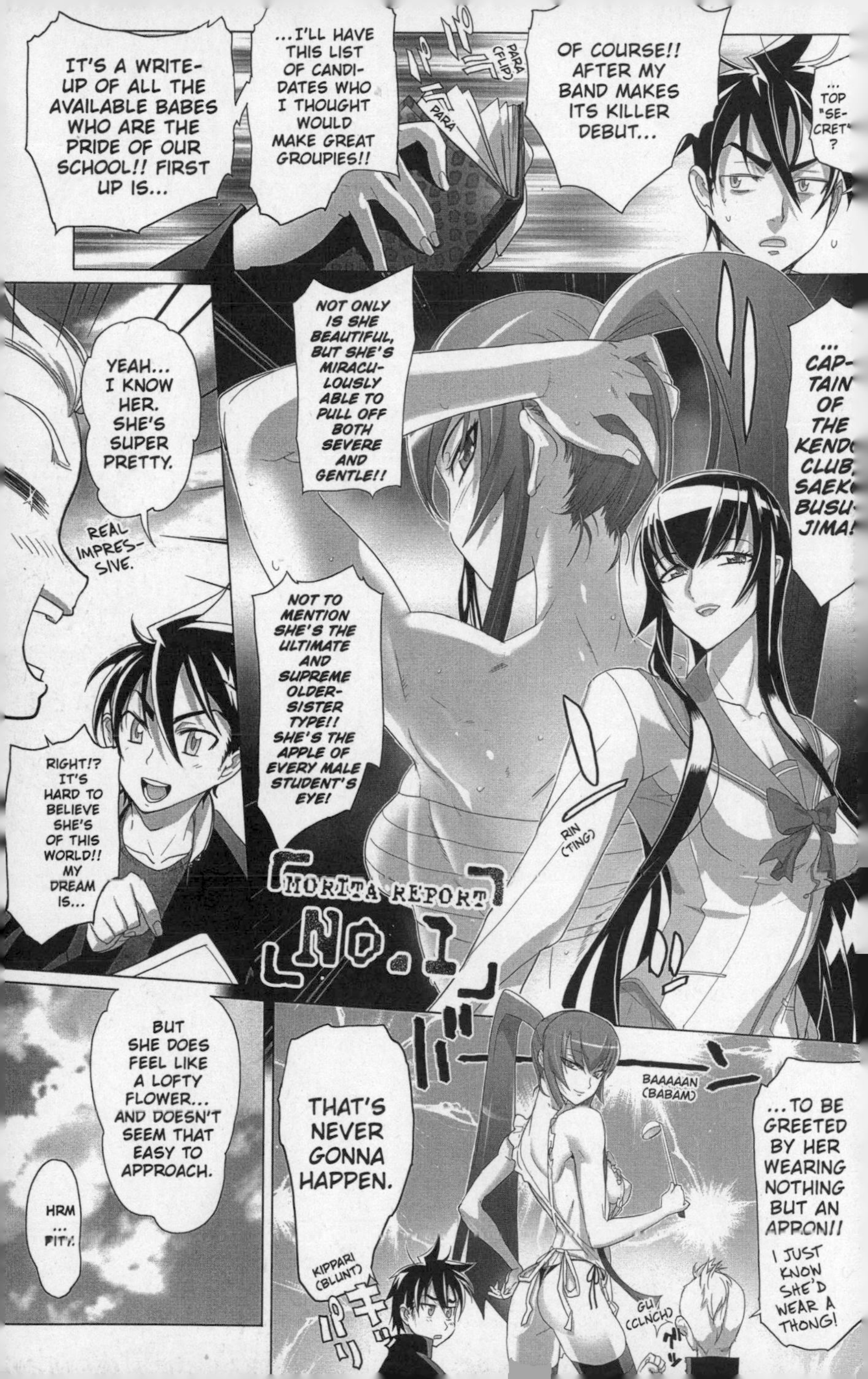
...TOP "SE-CRET"?
OF COURSE!! AFTER MY BAND MAKES ITS KILLER DEBUT...
PARA (FLIP)
PARA
...I'LL HAVE THIS LIST OF CANDI-DATES WHO I THOUGHT WOULD MAKE GREAT GROUPIES!!
IT'S A WRITE-UP OF ALL THE AVAILABLE BABES WHO ARE THE PRIDE OF OUR SCHOOL!! FIRST UP IS...
...CAP-TAIN OF THE KEND CLUB, SAEK BUSU-JIMA!
NOT ONLY IS SHE BEAUTIFUL, BUT SHE'S MIRACU-LOUSLY ABLE TO PULL OFF BOTH SEVERE AND GENTLE!!
NOT TO MENTION SHE'S THE ULTIMATE AND SUPREME OLDER-SISTER TYPE!! SHE'S THE APPLE OF EVERY MALE STUDENT'S EYE!
RIN (TING)
MORITA REPORT NO. 1
YEAH... I KNOW HER. SHE'S SUPER PRETTY.
REAL IMPRES-SIVE.
RIGHT!? IT'S HARD TO BELIEVE SHE'S OF THIS WORLD!! MY DREAM IS...
...TO BE GREETED BY HER WEARING NOTHING BUT AN APRON!!
I JUST KNOW SHE'D WEAR A THONG!
BAAAAAN (BABAM)
THAT'S NEVER GONNA HAPPEN.
KIPPARI (BLUNT)
GU (CLNCH)
BUT SHE DOES FEEL LIKE A LOFTY FLOWER... AND DOESN'T SEEM THAT EASY TO APPROACH.
HRM... PITY.

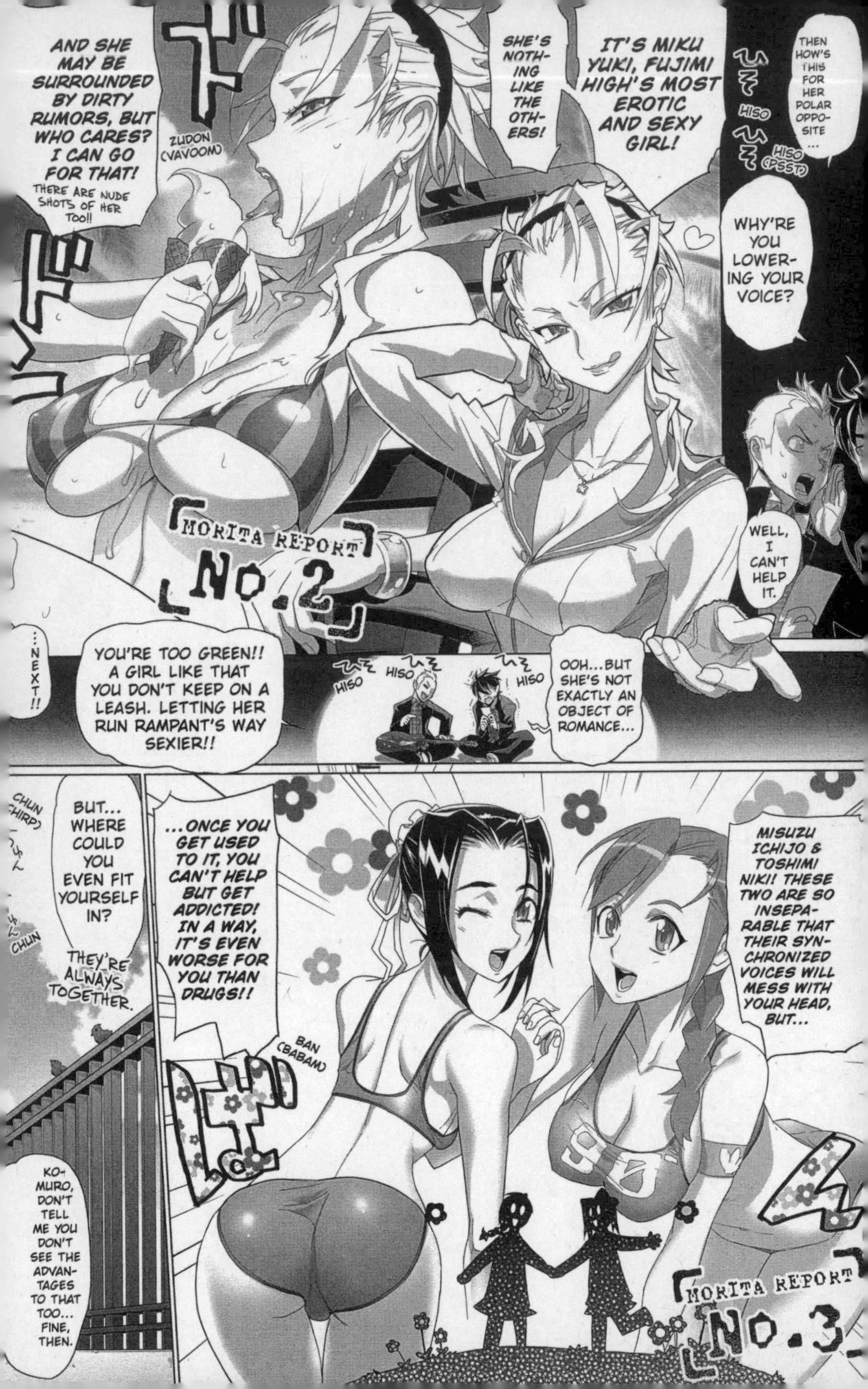
THEN HOW'S THIS FOR HER POLAR OPPOSITE...
HISO HISO (PSST)
WHY'RE YOU LOWERING YOUR VOICE?
WELL, I CAN'T HELP IT.
IT'S MIKU YUKI, FUJIMI HIGH'S MOST EROTIC AND SEXY GIRL!
SHE'S NOTHING LIKE THE OTHERS!
AND SHE MAY BE SURROUNDED BY DIRTY RUMORS, BUT WHO CARES? I CAN GO FOR THAT!
ZUDON (VAVOOM)
THERE ARE NUDE SHOTS OF HER TOO!!
MORITA REPORT NO. 2
OOH...BUT SHE'S NOT EXACTLY AN OBJECT OF ROMANCE...
HISO
HISO
HISO
YOU'RE TOO GREEN!! A GIRL LIKE THAT YOU DON'T KEEP ON A LEASH. LETTING HER RUN RAMPANT'S WAY SEXIER!!
...NEXT!!
MISUZU ICHIJO & TOSHIMI NIKI! THESE TWO ARE SO INSEPARABLE THAT THEIR SYNCHRONIZED VOICES WILL MESS WITH YOUR HEAD, BUT...
...ONCE YOU GET USED TO IT, YOU CAN'T HELP BUT GET ADDICTED! IN A WAY, IT'S EVEN WORSE FOR YOU THAN DRUGS!!
BUT... WHERE COULD YOU EVEN FIT YOURSELF IN?
THEY'RE ALWAYS TOGETHER.
CHUN (CHIRP)
CHUN
BAN (BABAM)
KOMURO, DON'T TELL ME YOU DON'T SEE THE ADVANTAGES TO THAT TOO... FINE, THEN.
MORITA REPORT NO. 3

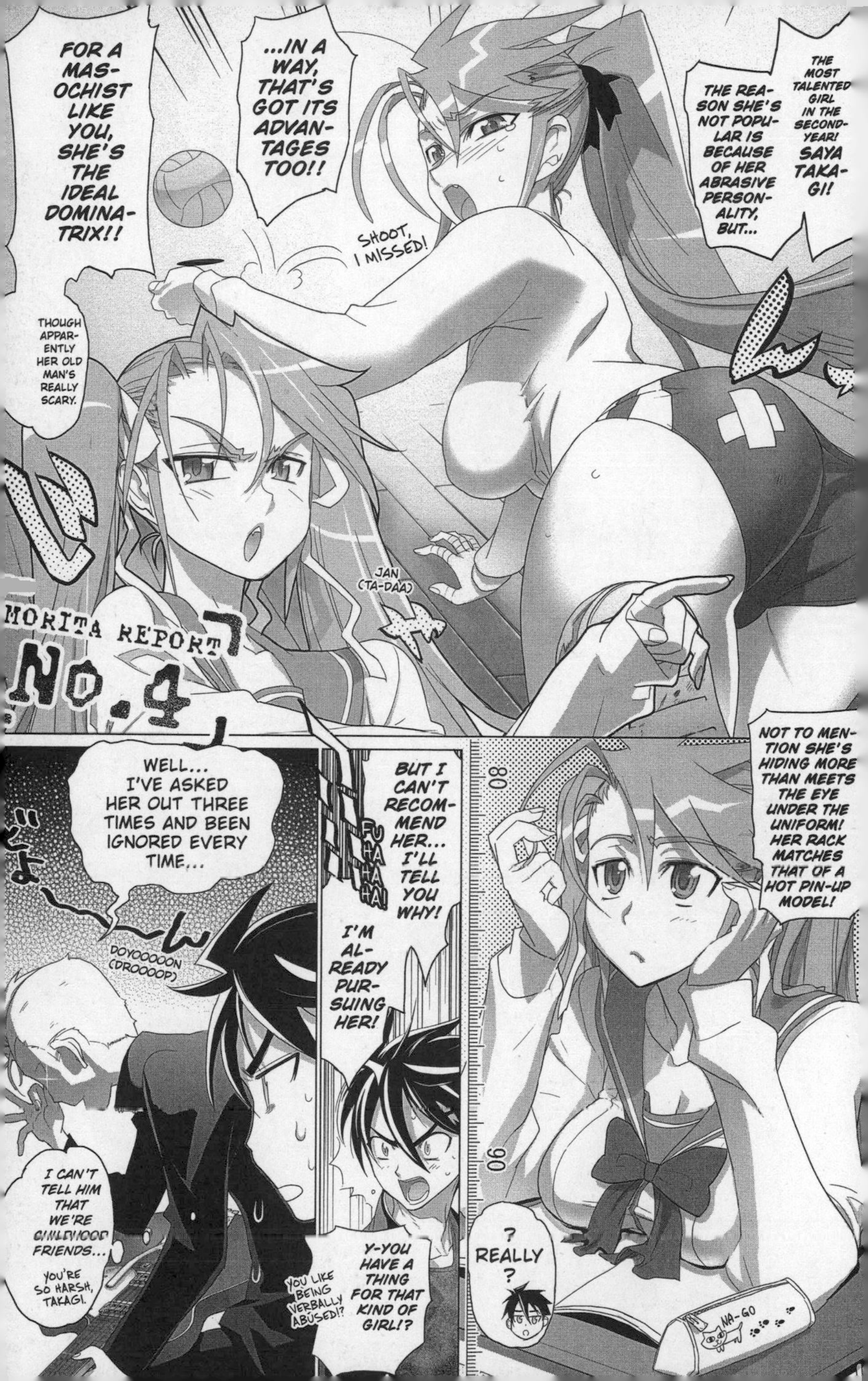
THE MOST TALENTED GIRL IN THE SECOND-YEAR! SAYA TAKAGI!
THE REASON SHE'S NOT POPULAR IS BECAUSE OF HER ABRASIVE PERSONALITY, BUT...
SHOOT, I MISSED!
...IN A WAY, THAT'S GOT ITS ADVANTAGES TOO!!
FOR A MASOCHIST LIKE YOU, SHE'S THE IDEAL DOMINATRIX!!
THOUGH APPARENTLY HER OLD MAN'S REALLY SCARY.
JAN (TA-DAA)
MORITA REPORT NO. 4
NOT TO MENTION SHE'S HIDING MORE THAN MEETS THE EYE UNDER THE UNIFORM! HER RACK MATCHES THAT OF A HOT PIN-UP MODEL!
80
90
? REALLY ?
NA-GO
BUT I CAN'T RECOMMEND HER... I'LL TELL YOU WHY!
FU HA HA HA!
I'M ALREADY PURSUING HER!
Y-YOU HAVE A THING FOR THAT KIND OF GIRL!?
YOU LIKE BEING VERBALLY ABUSED!?
WELL... I'VE ASKED HER OUT THREE TIMES AND BEEN IGNORED EVERY TIME...
DOYOOOOON (DROOOOP)
I CAN'T TELL HIM THAT WE'RE CHILDHOOD FRIENDS...
YOU'RE SO HARSH, TAKAGI.

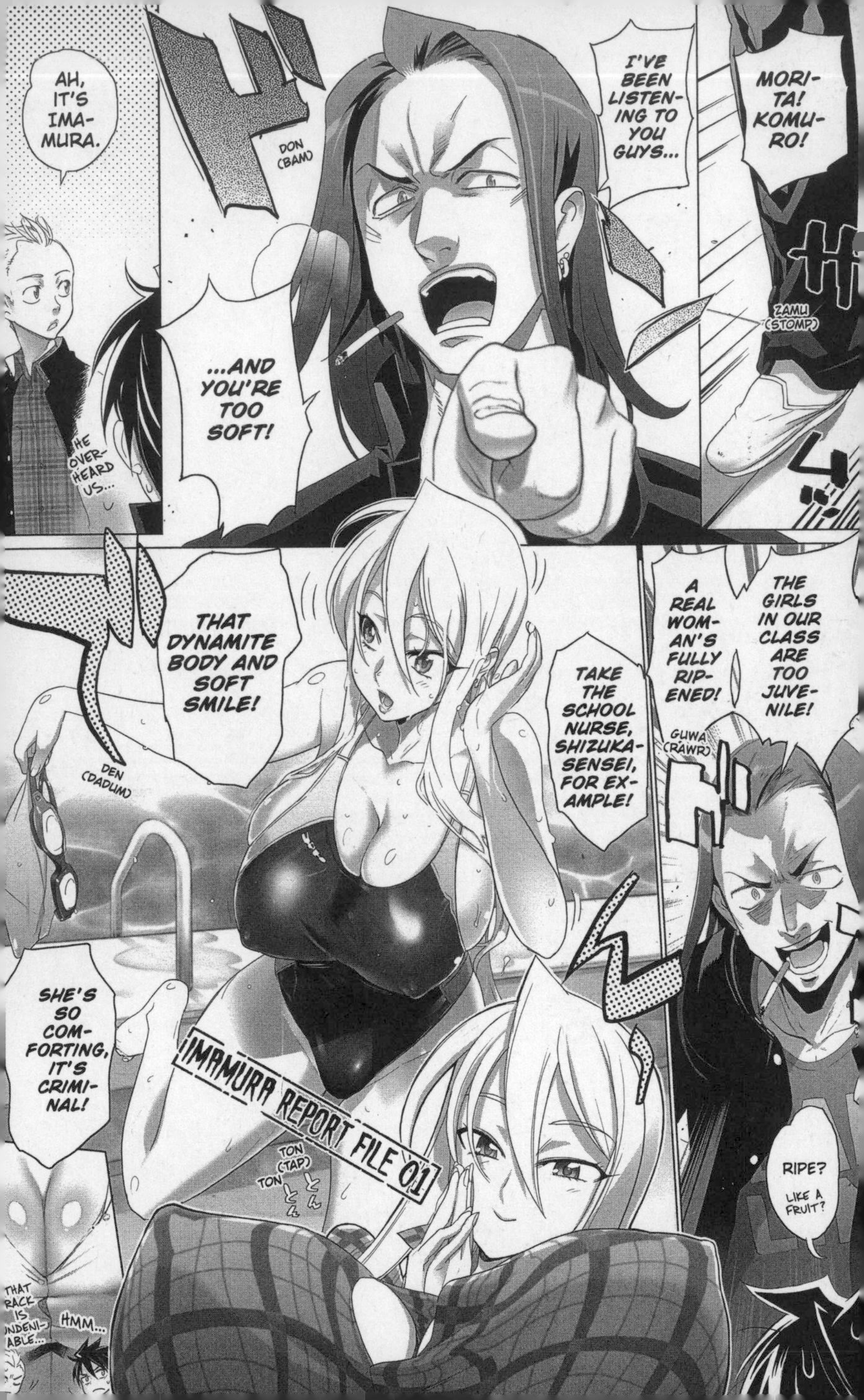
MORITA! KOMURO!
ZAMU (STOMP)
I'VE BEEN LISTENING TO YOU GUYS...
DON (BAM)
...AND YOU'RE TOO SOFT!
AH, IT'S IMAMURA.
HE OVERHEARD US...
THE GIRLS IN OUR CLASS ARE TOO JUVENILE!
A REAL WOMAN'S FULLY RIPENED!
GUWA (RAWR)
TAKE THE SCHOOL NURSE, SHIZUKA-SENSEI, FOR EXAMPLE!
THAT DYNAMITE BODY AND SOFT SMILE!
DEN (DADUM)
SHE'S SO COMFORTING, IT'S CRIMINAL!
IMAMURA REPORT FILE 01
TON (TAP) TON
RIPE? LIKE A FRUIT?
HMM...
THAT RACK IS UNDENIABLE...

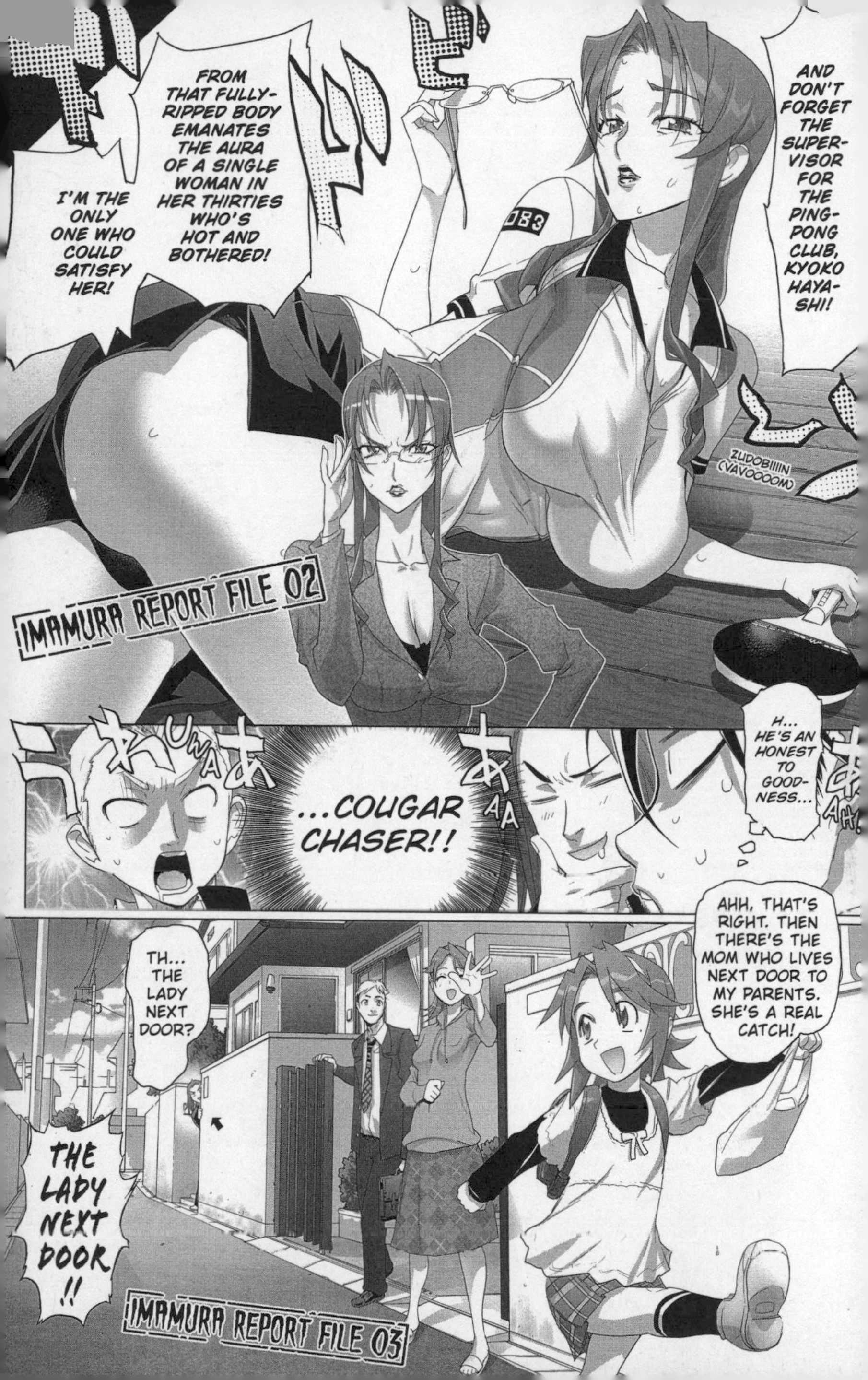
AND DON'T FORGET THE SUPERVISOR FOR THE PING-PONG CLUB, KYOKO HAYASHI!
ZUDOBIIIIN (VAVOOOOM)
FROM THAT FULLY-RIPPED BODY EMANATES THE AURA OF A SINGLE WOMAN IN HER THIRTIES WHO'S HOT AND BOTHERED!
I'M THE ONLY ONE WHO COULD SATISFY HER!
IMAMURA REPORT FILE 02
H... HE'S AN HONEST TO GOODNESS...
AH!
AA
...COUGAR CHASER!!
UWA
AHH, THAT'S RIGHT. THEN THERE'S THE MOM WHO LIVES NEXT DOOR TO MY PARENTS. SHE'S A REAL CATCH!
TH... THE LADY NEXT DOOR?
THE LADY NEXT DOOR!!
IMAMURA REPORT FILE 03

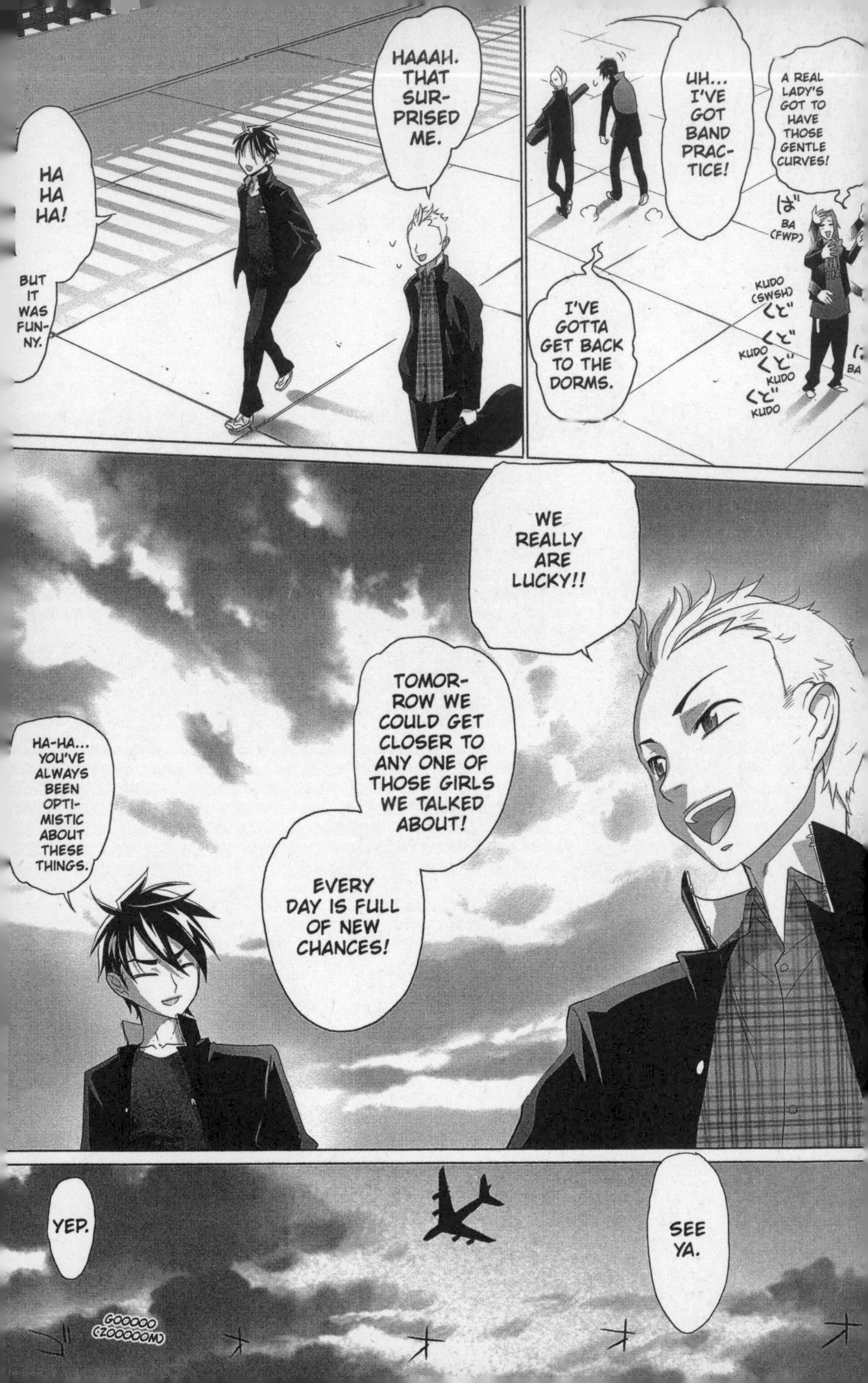
A REAL LADY'S GOT TO HAVE THOSE GENTLE CURVES!
UH... I'VE GOT BAND PRACTICE!
ば BA (F.WP)
くど KUDO (SWSH)
くど KUDO
くど KUDO
くど KUDO
I'VE GOTTA GET BACK TO THE DORMS.
HAAAH. THAT SURPRISED ME.
HA HA HA!
BUT IT WAS FUNNY.
WE REALLY ARE LUCKY!!
TOMORROW WE COULD GET CLOSER TO ANY ONE OF THOSE GIRLS WE TALKED ABOUT!
EVERY DAY IS FULL OF NEW CHANCES!
HA-HA... YOU'VE ALWAYS BEEN OPTIMISTIC ABOUT THESE THINGS.
SEE YA.
YEP.
GOOOOO (ZOOOOOM)

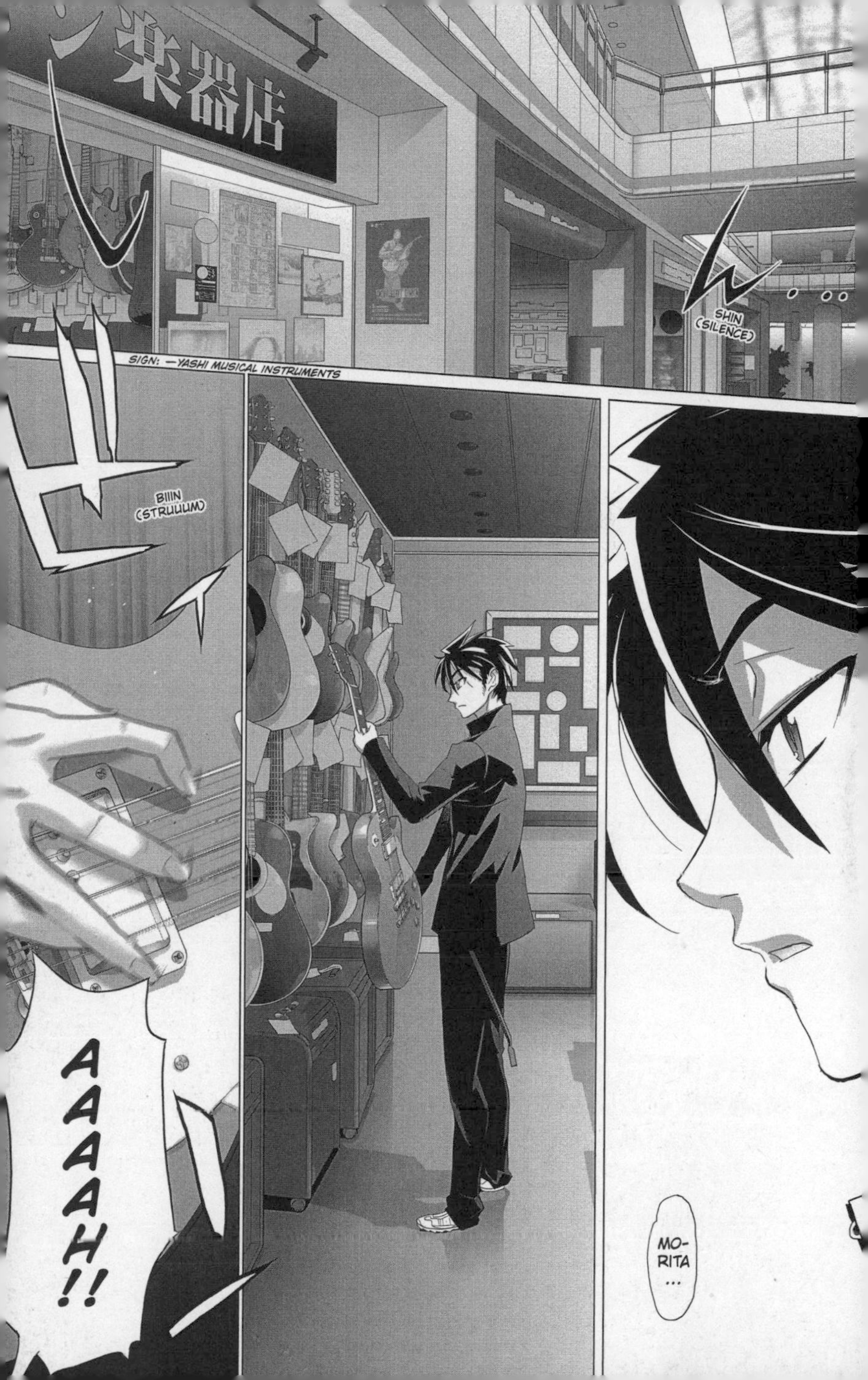
SHIN (SILENCE)
ン楽器店
SIGN: —YASHI MUSICAL INSTRUMENTS
MO-RITA ...
BIIN (STRUUUM)
AAAAAH!!

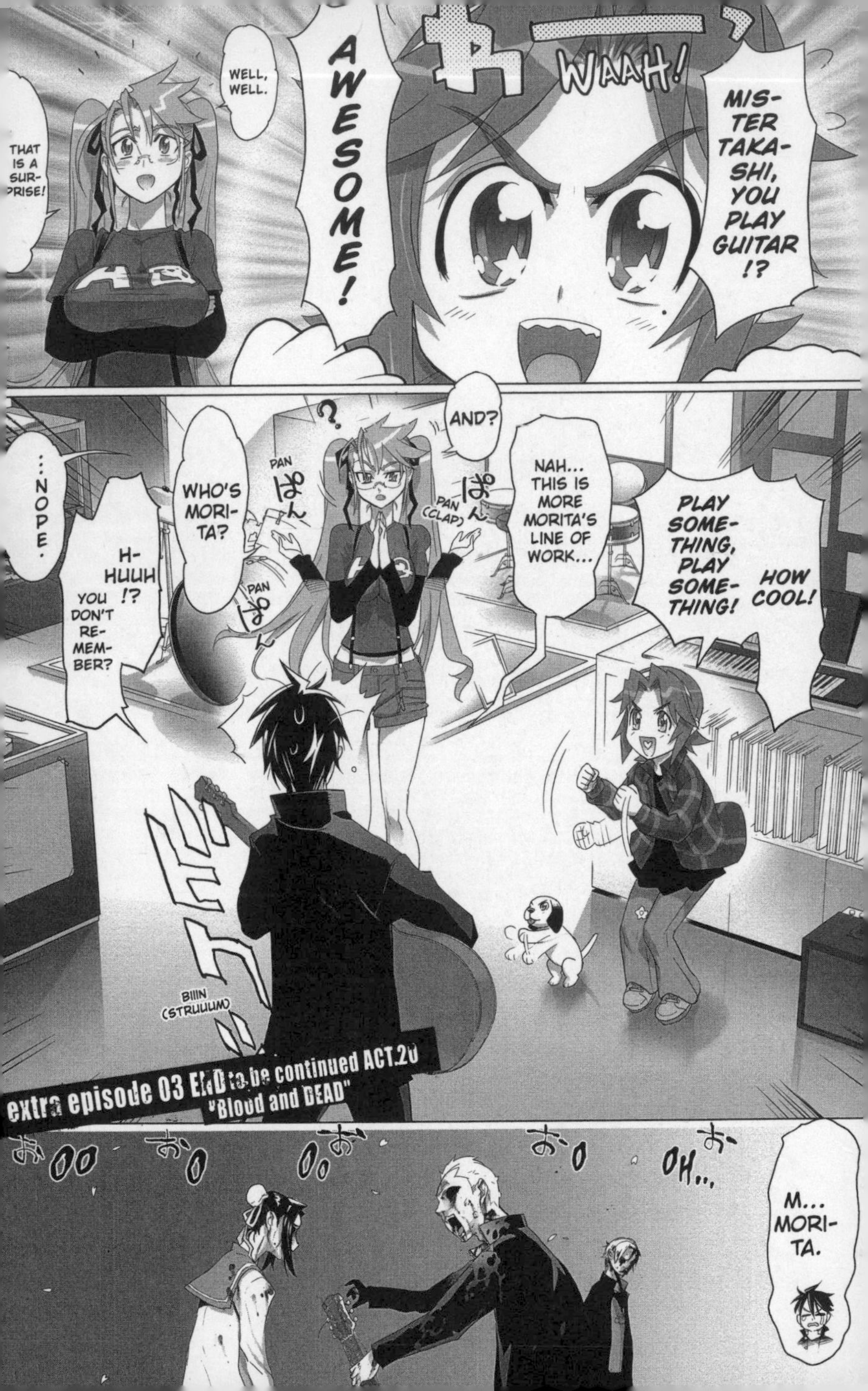
WAAH!
MISTER TAKASHI, YOU PLAY GUITAR!?
AWESOME!
WELL, WELL.
THAT IS A SURPRISE!
HOW COOL!
PLAY SOMETHING, PLAY SOMETHING!
NAH... THIS IS MORE MORITA'S LINE OF WORK...
AND?
PAN (CLAP)
PAN
WHO'S MORITA?
PAN
H-HUUH!? YOU DON'T REMEMBER?
...NOPE.
BIIIN (STRUUUM)
extra episode 03 END to be continued ACT.20 "Blood and DEAD"
M... MORITA.
OH...

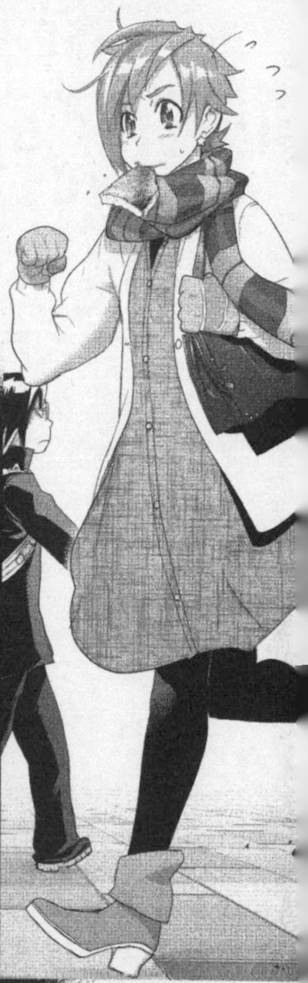

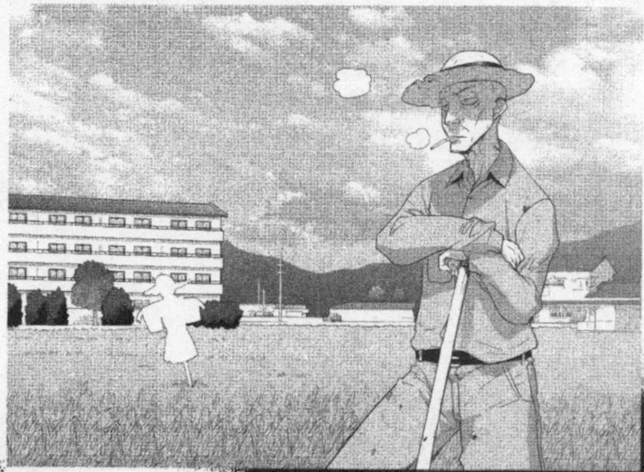

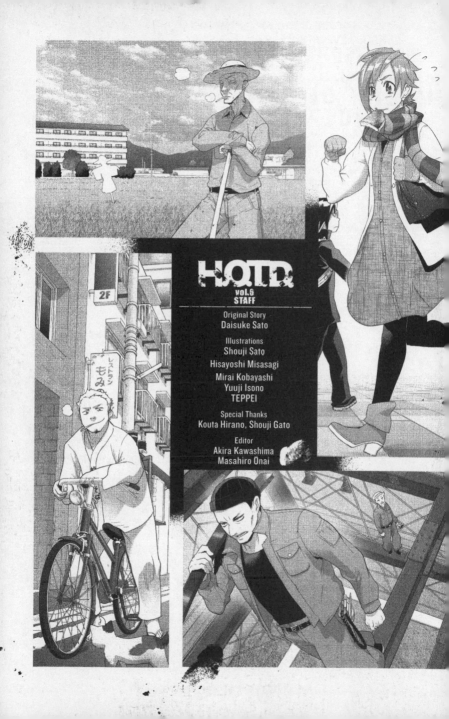

HOTD

vol.6 STAFF

Original Story
Daisuke Sato

Illustrations
Shouji Sato
Hisayoshi Misasagi
Mirai Kobayashi
Yuuji Isono
TEPPEI

Special Thanks
Kouta Hirano, Shouji Gato

Editor
Akira Kawashima
Masahiro Onai

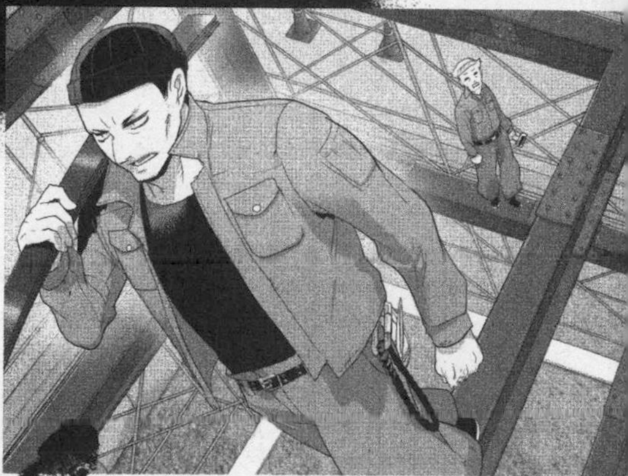

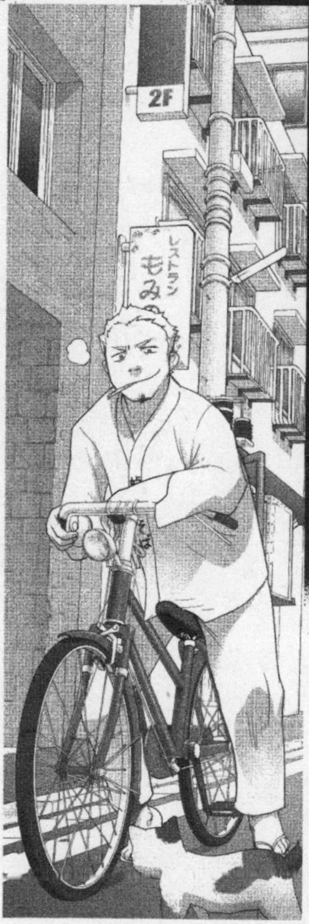
2F
レストラン

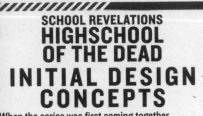

SCHOOL REVELATIONS HIGHSCHOOL OF THE DEAD

INITIAL DESIGN CONCEPTS

When the series was first coming together, Shouji Sato-sensei drew a huge number of visual concepts. Daisuke Sato-sensei's memos on the setting of the story and notes on character concepts were the springboard for the layouts, each character's conception, background materials, and more. Here we present to you the pick-of-the-litter of his early sketched concepts along with the two Sato-senseis' comments.

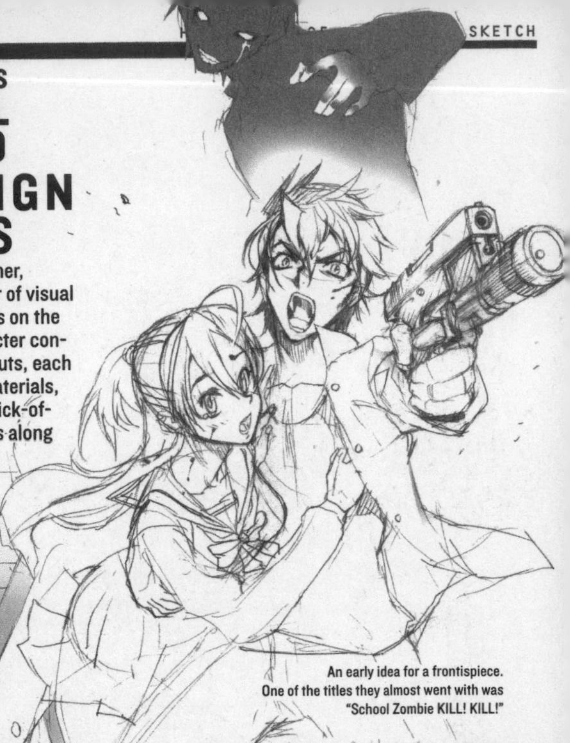

An early idea for a frontispiece. One of the titles they almost went with was "School Zombie KILL! KILL!"

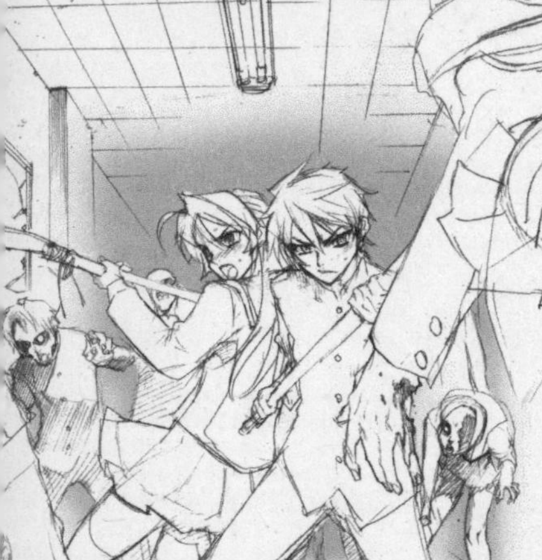

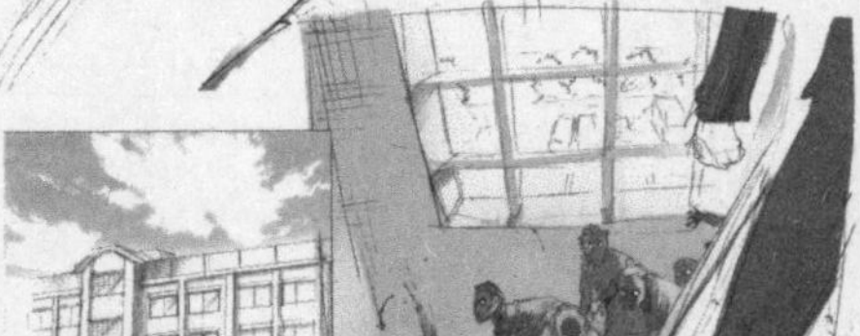

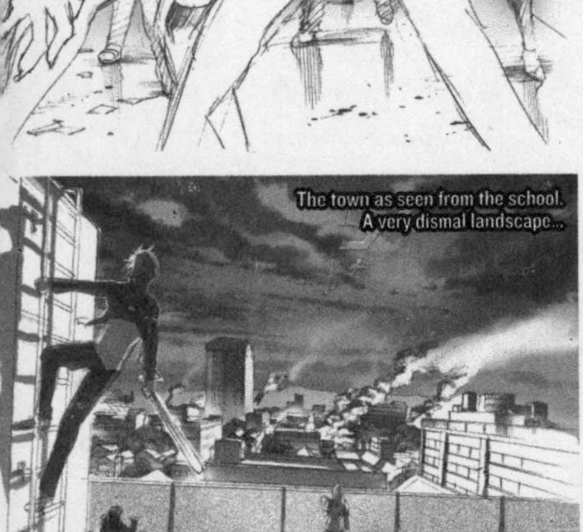

The town as seen from the school. A very dismal landscape...

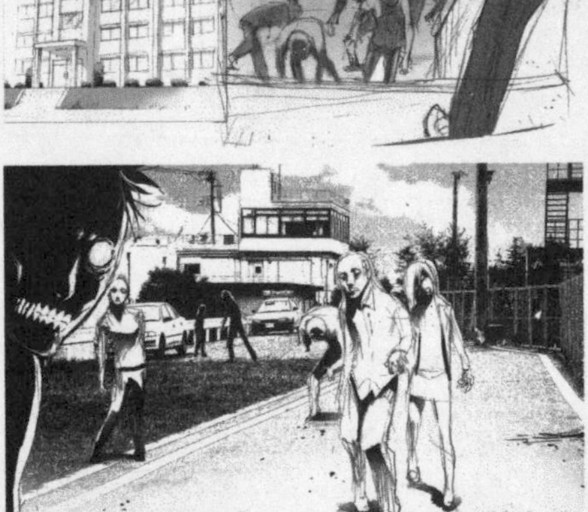

"Them" prowling the town. The houses and stores lining the streets are based off Shouji Sato's hometown!

NAME TAKASHI KOMU

AGE 17 / HEIGHT 5'8" / WEIGHT 128

● The hero of the story, a second-year at the priv school Fujimi High. After his childhood friend R started going out with his best friend, he began to feel like everything was just a pain in the butt and spent his days apathetically. But now he has turned into a guy who takes the initiative on even the most troublesome tasks (heh).

Different facial expressions. Different circumstances demand different behavior out of him.

RO

His hair is always disheveled, and he's of average height and build. The kind of high schooler you'd find anywhere.

PSST PSST

With Hisashi back in the good old days (sniffle).

JUST WOKE UP.

Expected appearance in the near future. We plan on making him a brawny young man (heh).

COMMENTS

SHOUJI SATO

He has unmanageable hair and small pupils. But despite these early designs, I was told to make him not really stand out too much, and in the end, he really was quite plain. Sorry about that. But I tried to depict him in a way where he'd be able to move fast when under attack and still have strength even when his heart isn't in it.

DAISUKE SATO

Man, his original designs make him look so much more like a hero. Which makes sense, since the current Takashi was revised to be almost lacking in hero qualities. He gives off the air of being a high schooler barely holding it together.

HI KO

NAME HISASHI IGOU

AGE 17 / HEIGHT 5'10" / WEIGHT 141 LBS

Takashi's best friend and classmate, he's also Rei's boyfriend. He's the unfortunate character who we decided very early on to kill and turn into one of "them" in Chapter I.

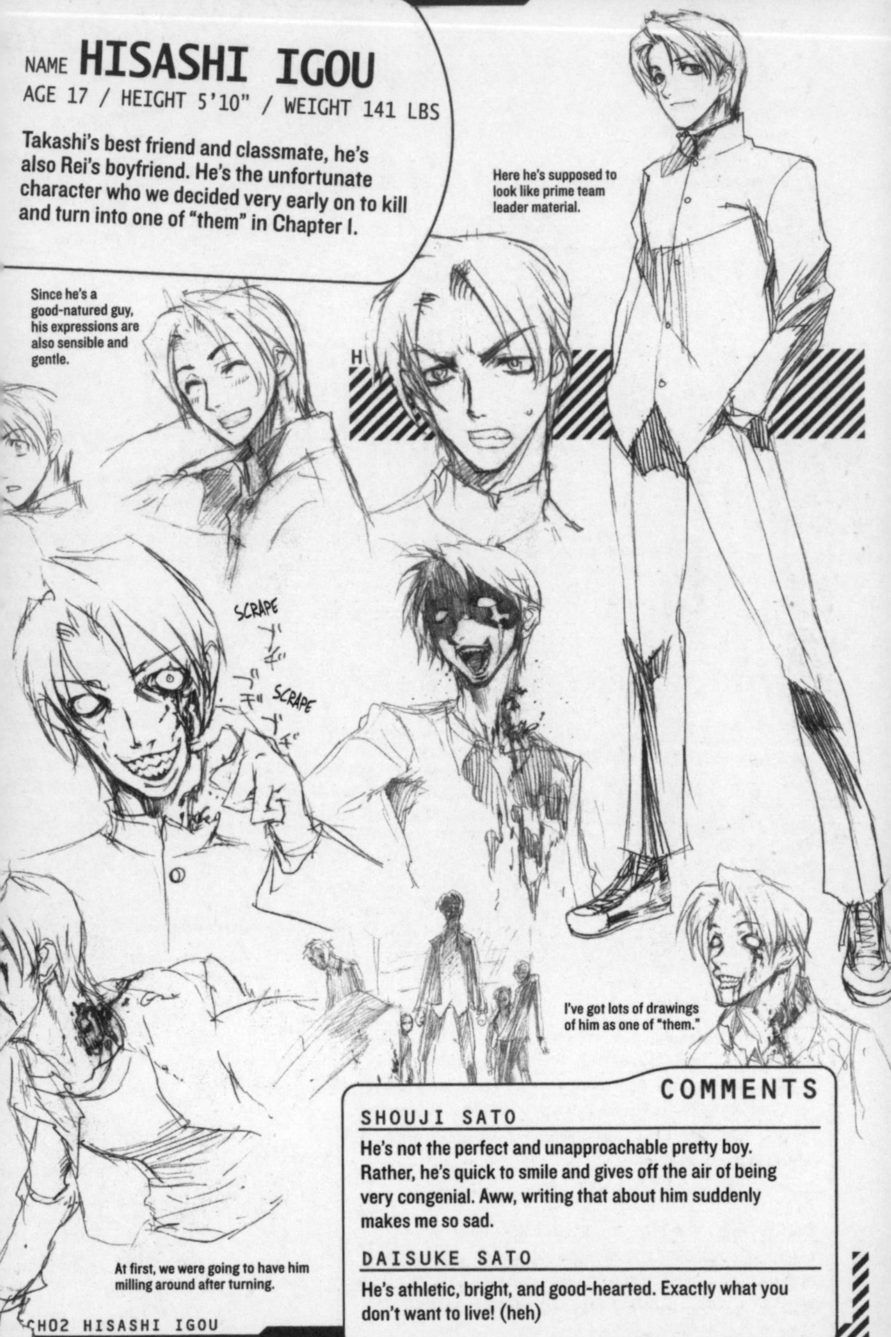
SCRAPE
SCRAPE

Here he's supposed to look like prime team leader material.

Since he's a good-natured guy, his expressions are also sensible and gentle.

I've got lots of drawings of him as one of "them."

At first, we were going to have him milling around after turning.

COMMENTS

SHOUJI SATO

He's not the perfect and unapproachable pretty boy. Rather, he's quick to smile and gives off the air of being very congenial. Aww, writing that about him suddenly makes me so sad.

DAISUKE SATO

He's athletic, bright, and good-hearted. Exactly what you don't want to live! (heh)

NAME **REI MIYAMOTO**

AGE 17 / HEIGHT 5'5" / WEIGHT 110 LBS

B34in(DD) W22in H35in

A caring person and Takashi's childhood friend. By the end of the first day of the attack, the distance between her and Takashi closes considerably. She was in the spear club at Fujimi High.

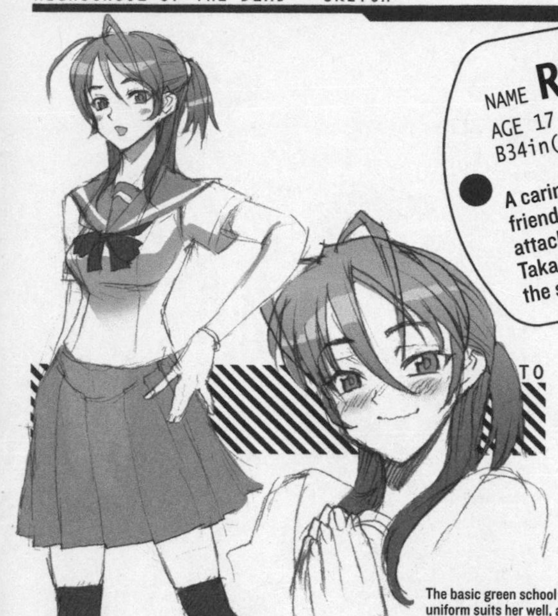

The basic green school uniform suits her well, and her thigh-high socks only add to her image.

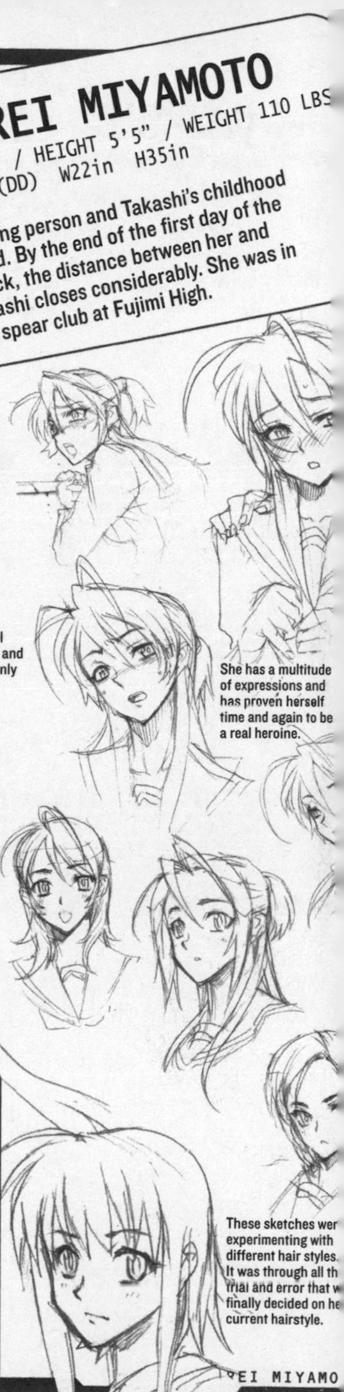

She has a multitude of expressions and has proven herself time and again to be a real heroine.

These sketches wer experimenting with different hair styles. It was through all th trial and error that w finally decided on he current hairstyle.

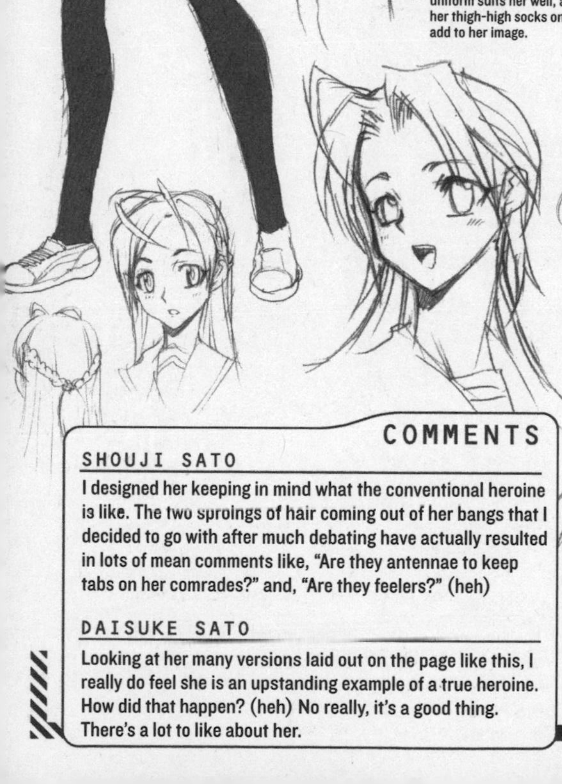

COMMENTS

SHOUJI SATO

I designed her keeping in mind what the conventional heroine is like. The two sproings of hair coming out of her bangs that I decided to go with after much debating have actually resulted in lots of mean comments like, "Are they antennae to keep tabs on her comrades?" and, "Are they feelers?" (heh)

DAISUKE SATO

Looking at her many versions laid out on the page like this, I really do feel she is an upstanding example of a true heroine. How did that happen? (heh) No really, it's a good thing. There's a lot to like about her.

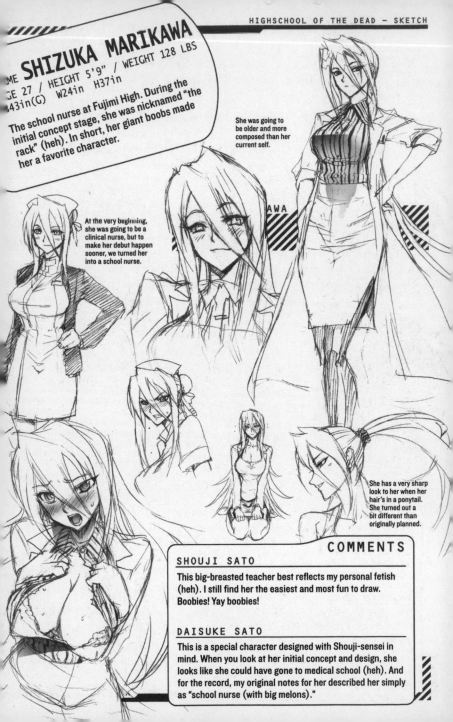

NAME SHIZUKA MARIKAWA

AGE 27 / HEIGHT 5'9" / WEIGHT 128 LBS

B43in(G) W24in H37in

The school nurse at Fujimi High. During the initial concept stage, she was nicknamed "the rack" (heh). In short, her giant boobs made her a favorite character.

She was going to be older and more composed than her current self.

At the very beginning, she was going to be a clinical nurse, but to make her debut happen sooner, we turned her into a school nurse.

She has a very sharp look to her when her hair's in a ponytail. She turned out a bit different than originally planned.

COMMENTS

SHOUJI SATO

This big-breasted teacher best reflects my personal fetish (heh). I still find her the easiest and most fun to draw. Boobies! Yay boobies!

DAISUKE SATO

This is a special character designed with Shouji-sensei in mind. When you look at her initial concept and design, she looks like she could have gone to medical school (heh). And for the record, my original notes for her described her simply as "school nurse (with big melons)."

NAME **SAEKO BUSUJIMA**

AGE 17 / HEIGHT 5'9" / WEIGHT 123

B33in(DD) W22in H34in

Captain of the Kendo Club and the winner of last year's national tournament. In short, in two years' time, she's become the nation's best, and that is a clear sign of her skill. On certain sites abroad, she's even listed as the most popular character (hee)!

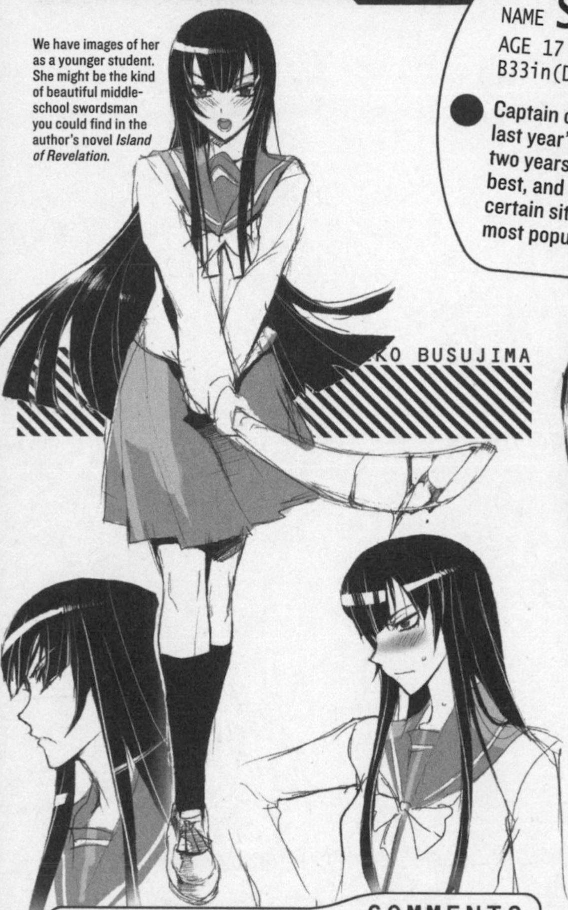
KO BUSUJIMA

We have images of her as a younger student. She might be the kind of beautiful middle-school swordsman you could find in the author's novel *Island of Revelation*.

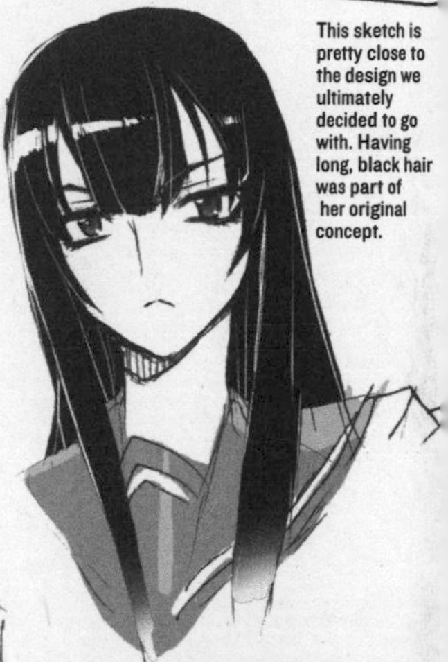

This sketch is pretty close to the design we ultimately decided to go with. Having long, black hair was part of her original concept.

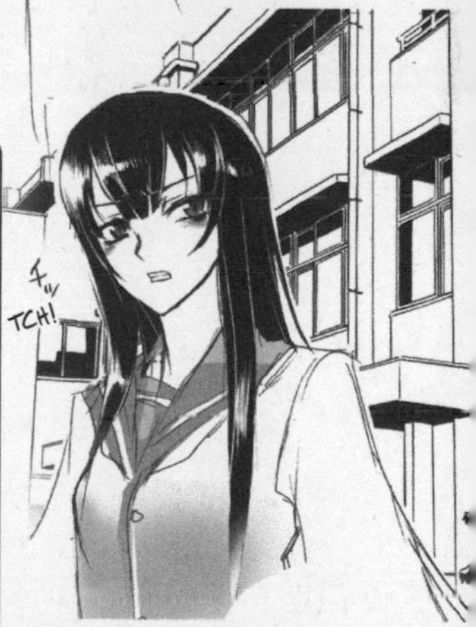
TCH!

Here she is with the school in the background and without her scarf.

COMMENTS

SHOUJI SATO

Looking at our sketches of her now, she was so much more childish. She was the kind of character I'd never had to draw before (I'd never even done black-haired characters), so I remember that at first it was very difficult to draw her. But now I find it fun doing her hair shine. Assuming I have the time for it (heh).

DAISUKE SATO

Compared to the character she turned out to be, she used to have a more childish air about her, so my first instruction was to make her look like Gogo Yubari. After countless revisions, the Busujima-senpai we all know today was born. And she ended up not looking that much like Gogo Yubari in the end (heh). Also, "Busujima" is a traditional family name used in Japanese tough-guy novels.

NAME **KOUTA HIRANO**

AGE 16 / HEIGHT 5'2" / WEIGHT 196 LBS

Like Marikawa-sensei, his original nicknames led to his decided appearance (see the writer's comments). The short hairstyle version found in the bottom left received such comments from Shouji-sensei as "a passionate fatty."

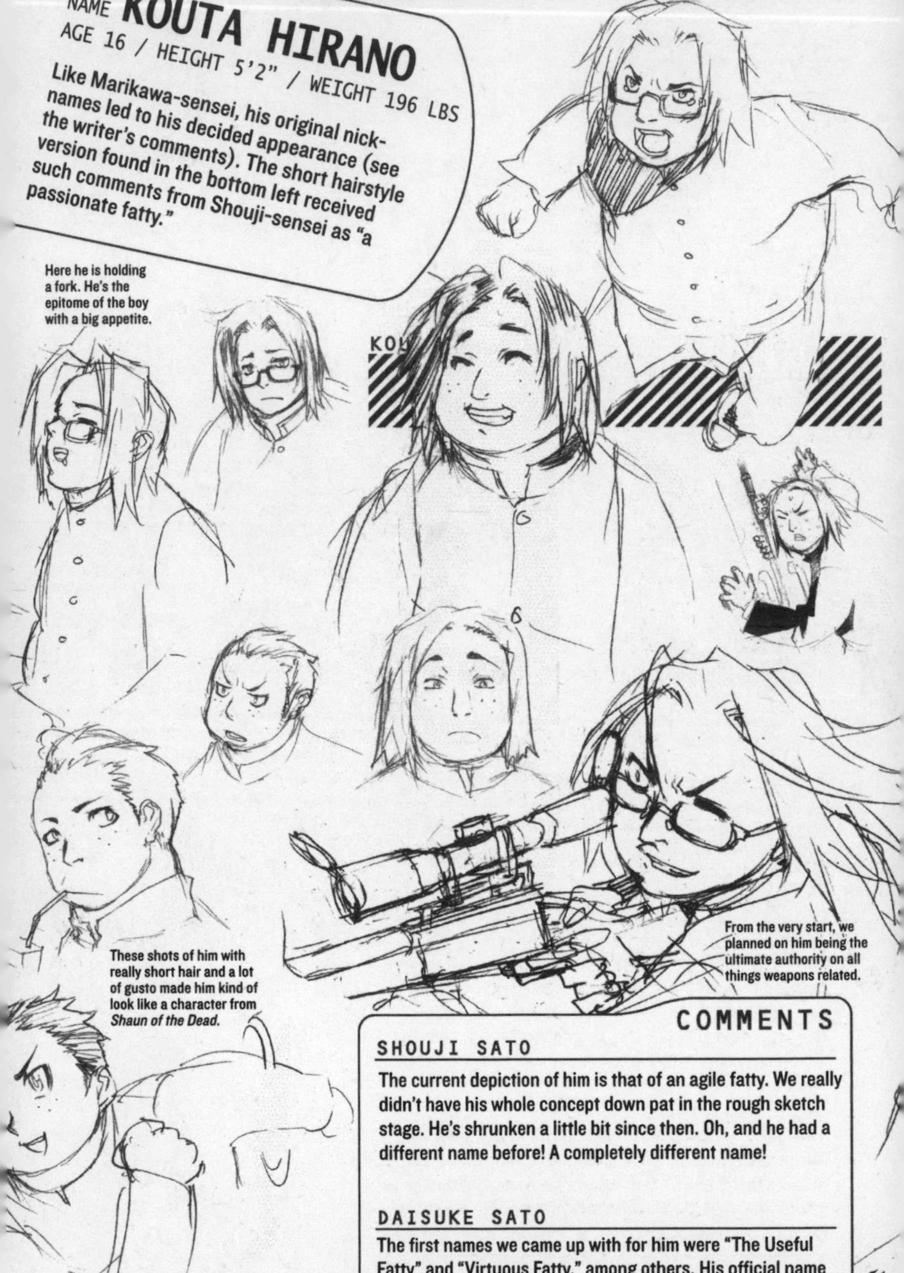

Here he is holding a fork. He's the epitome of the boy with a big appetite.

These shots of him with really short hair and a lot of gusto made him kind of look like a character from *Shaun of the Dead*.

From the very start, we planned on him being the ultimate authority on all things weapons related.

COMMENTS

SHOUJI SATO

The current depiction of him is that of an agile fatty. We really didn't have his whole concept down pat in the rough sketch stage. He's shrunken a little bit since then. Oh, and he had a different name before! A completely different name!

DAISUKE SATO

The first names we came up with for him were "The Useful Fatty" and "Virtuous Fatty," among others. His official name was going to be "Nagumo," but since it wasn't interesting enough, we changed it to his current name. Sorry.

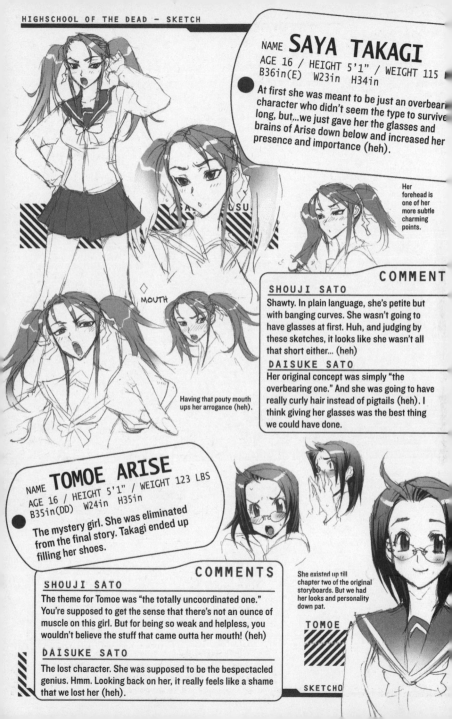

NAME SAYA TAKAGI

AGE 16 / HEIGHT 5'1" / WEIGHT 115
B36in(E) W23in H34in

At first she was meant to be just an overbeari character who didn't seem the type to survive long, but...we just gave her the glasses and brains of Arise down below and increased her presence and importance (heh).

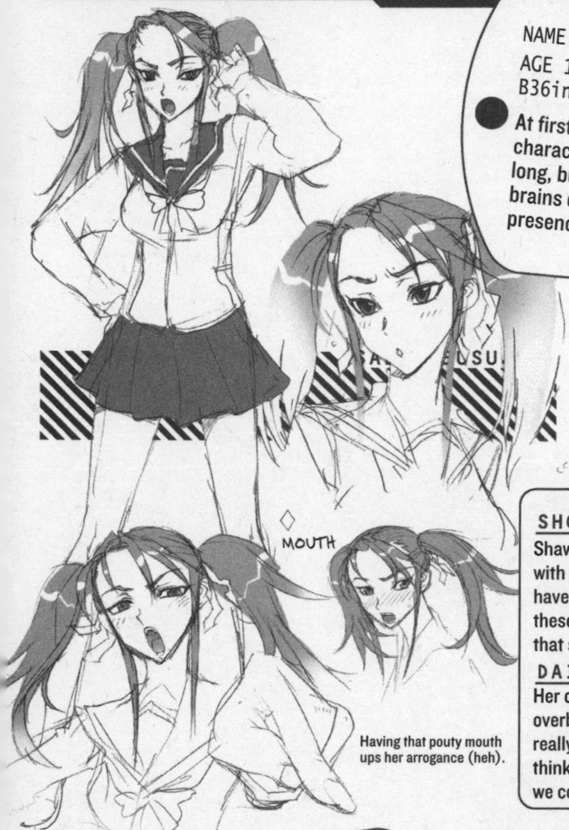
MOUTH

Having that pouty mouth ups her arrogance (heh).

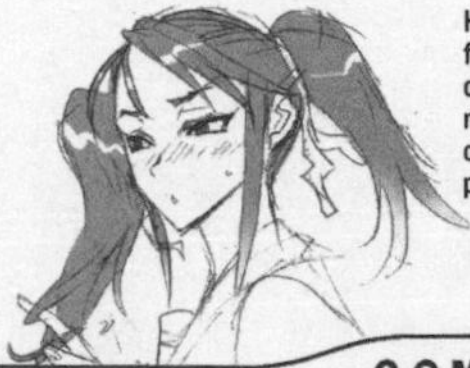

Her forehead is one of her more subtle charming points.

COMMENT

SHOUJI SATO

Shawty. In plain language, she's petite but with banging curves. She wasn't going to have glasses at first. Huh, and judging by these sketches, it looks like she wasn't all that short either... (heh)

DAISUKE SATO

Her original concept was simply "the overbearing one." And she was going to have really curly hair instead of pigtails (heh). I think giving her glasses was the best thing we could have done.

NAME TOMOE ARISE

AGE 16 / HEIGHT 5'1" / WEIGHT 123 LBS
B35in(DD) W24in H35in

The mystery girl. She was eliminated from the final story. Takagi ended up filling her shoes.

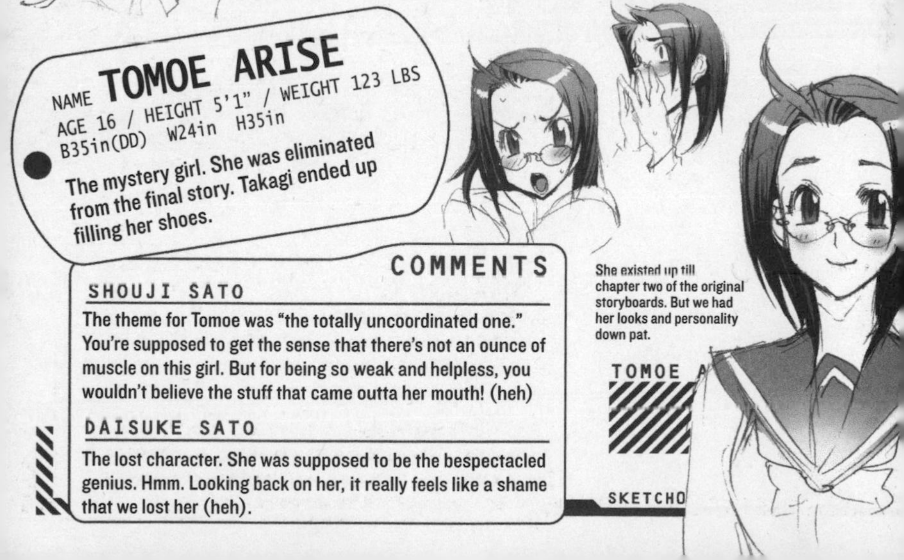

She existed up till chapter two of the original storyboards. But we had her looks and personality down pat.

COMMENTS

SHOUJI SATO

The theme for Tomoe was "the totally uncoordinated one." You're supposed to get the sense that there's not an ounce of muscle on this girl. But for being so weak and helpless, you wouldn't believe the stuff that came outta her mouth! (heh)

DAISUKE SATO

The lost character. She was supposed to be the bespectacled genius. Hmm. Looking back on her, it really feels like a shame that we lost her (heh).

"THEM" AND OTHERS

These make up the rest of the main characters of our story. There's an enormous amount of these kinds of sketches. They're everything from depictions of Takashi's parents, to characters that will be appearing, and different costumes.

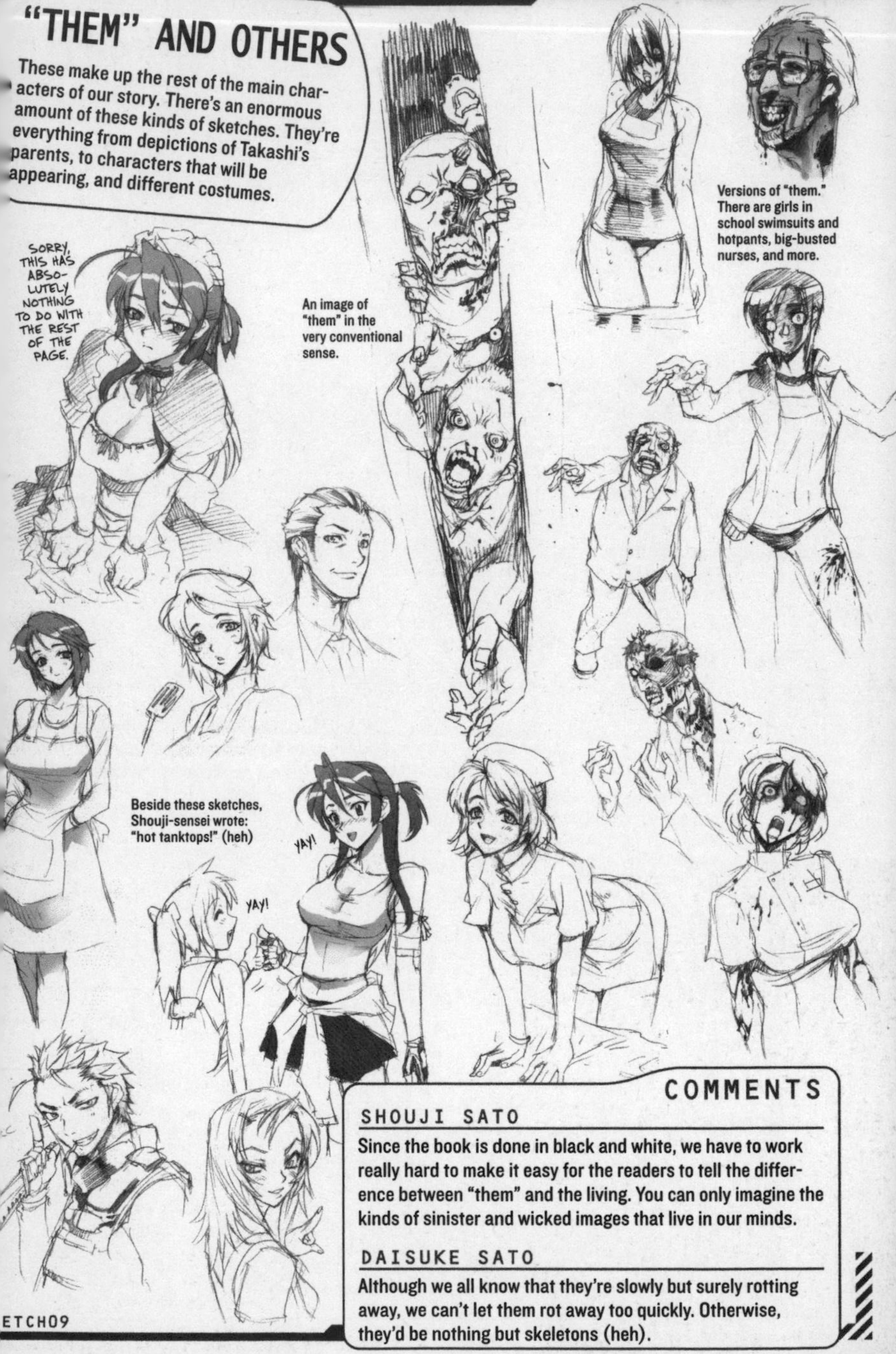
SORRY, THIS HAS ABSOLUTELY NOTHING TO DO WITH THE REST OF THE PAGE.
YAY!
YAY!

An image of "them" in the very conventional sense.

Versions of "them." There are girls in school swimsuits and hotpants, big-busted nurses, and more.

Beside these sketches, Shouji-sensei wrote: "hot tanktops!" (heh)

COMMENTS

SHOUJI SATO

Since the book is done in black and white, we have to work really hard to make it easy for the readers to tell the difference between "them" and the living. You can only imagine the kinds of sinister and wicked images that live in our minds.

DAISUKE SATO

Although we all know that they're slowly but surely rotting away, we can't let them rot away too quickly. Otherwise, they'd be nothing but skeletons (heh).

TOKONOSU CITY

Population: 1,000,000
A relatively large district considering the size of the school.
Will our heroes make it out of here alive?

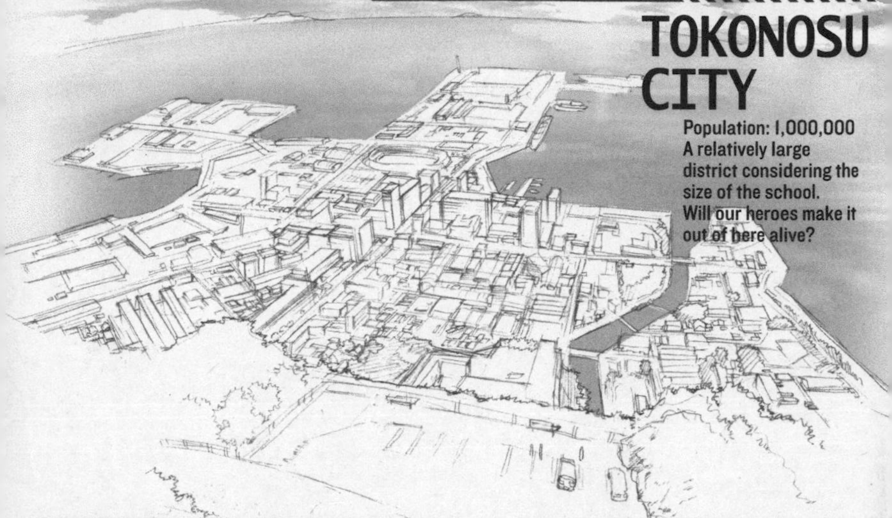

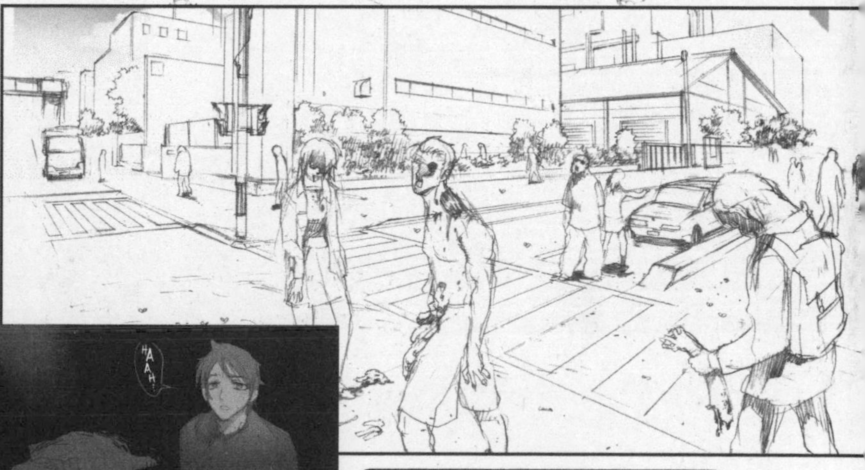

INITIAL CONCEPT MAP BY THE AUTHOR

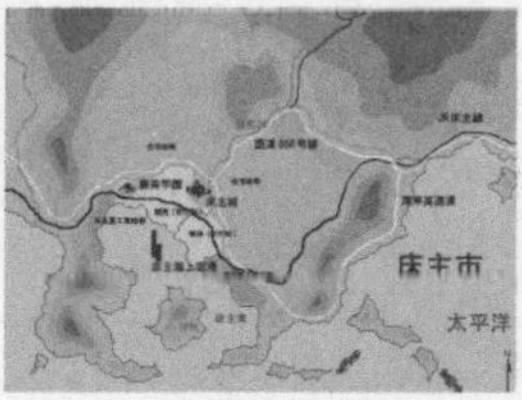
床主市
太平洋

COMMENT
DAISUKE SATO

Besides the fact that Tokonosu is in the eastern part of the country, we don't have much more detail or description for it. Of course, since it is the setting of this action-packed story, we're filling the gaps as needed to develop the story (heh).

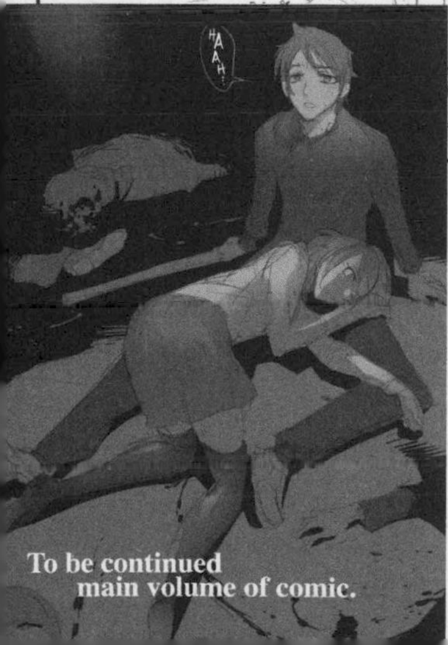
HAAH!

To be continued
main volume of comic.

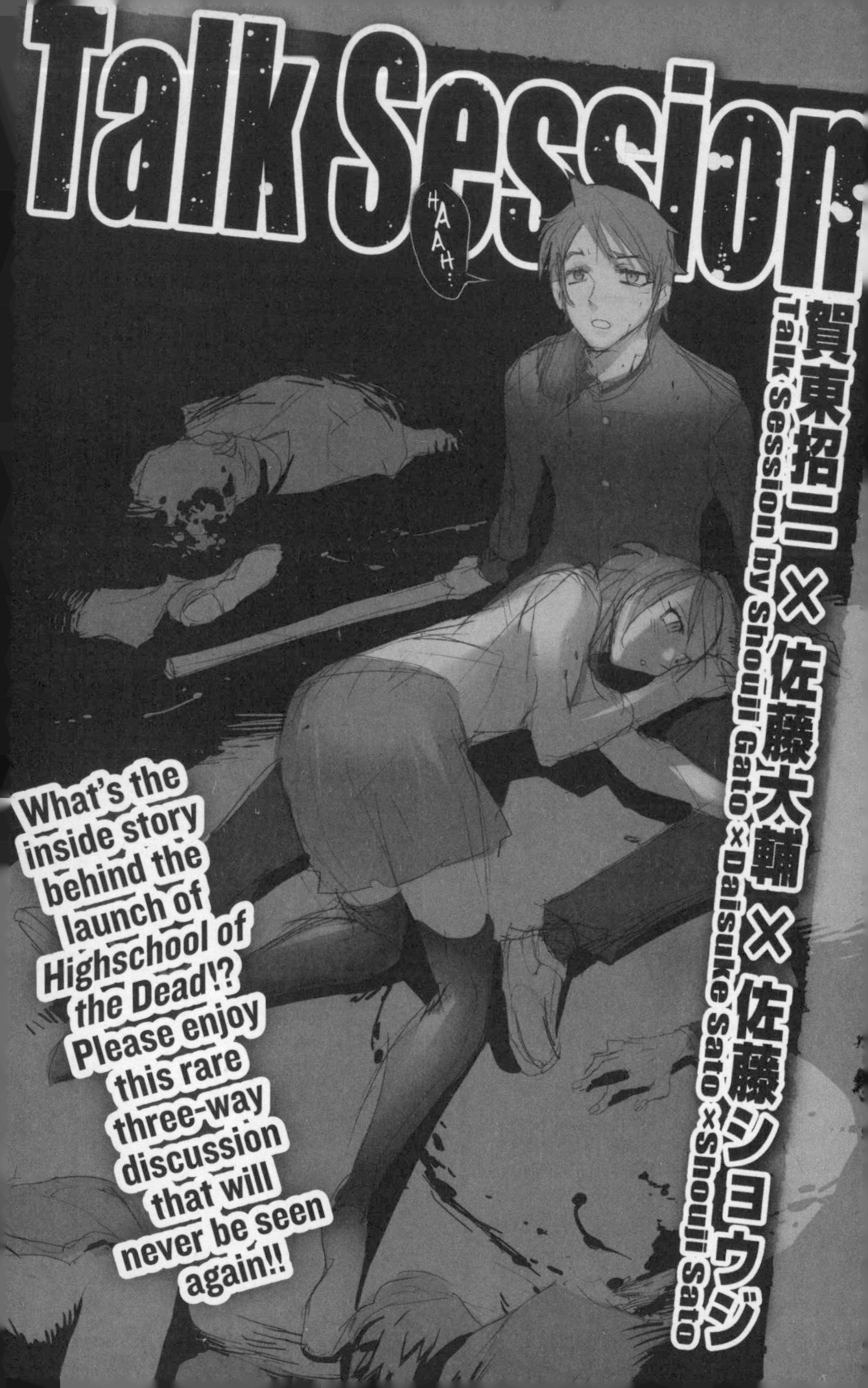
Talk Session
HAAH...
賀東招二×佐藤大輔×佐藤ショウジ
Talk Session by Shouji Gato×Daisuke Sato×Shouji Sato
What's the inside story behind the launch of Highschool of the Dead!? Please enjoy this rare three-way discussion that will never be seen again!!

SHOUJI GATO

While working part-time as a writer for the gaming industry, he contributed to a *Hourai Gakuen* anthology. After that, he made a big hit with *Full Metal Panic!* released by Fujimi Shobo. When the title was made into an anime, he also had a hand in the series' construction, scripts, and more. Besides that, he's also been active as a writer and series scenarist for episodes of *The Melancholy of Haruhi Suzumiya* and *Lucky Star*. In the video game industry, he's also headed the creation of original scenarios and supervised production. At the end of this three-way discussion, he saw an opportunity when the editor left, and, though the room was non-smoking, he cracked open a window and sneaked a smoke. His mischievous actions made him look just like a high schooler (eyewitness account).

Primary Works -
Novels: *Full Metal Panic!*, *Hourai Gakuen*, *Dragnet Mirage*

> ## "The collapse of society excites me."

Talk Session by Shouji Gato ✕ Daisuke Sato ✕ Shouji Sato

Sato: On the obi that wrapped around the Japanese edition of the fifth volume of *Highschool of the Dead*, we were able to include a recommendation from you, Gato-san, that said, "The utopia of every demented adolescent boy (myself included)!!"

Gato: When I was in middle school, I seriously used to daydream about this kind of scenario! I wanted to see what a post-apocalyptic world was like, or what would happen if terrorists occupied my school. In *HOTD*, I feel as though those daydreams have been fine-tuned at the hands of professionals.

Sato: So the dream of "school invasion by terrorists" is where you came up with the idea for *Full Metal Panic!*, I see. Using whatever the classroom has to offer to find an opportunity to fight back against the terrorists, be it firing guns or what have you... Pretty much reenacting *Die Hard* in the school was one of your dreams, eh? (heh)

Gato: I really wish I could have done that.

Sato: Since my school was near a river, every day I would ponder the likelihood of an army helicopter approaching from across the embankment and firing at our campus (heh).

Gato: That'd be awesome. But I'd never thought about the downfall of the world at the hands of zombies. Shouji-san, what about you?

Shouji: Nope. Sorry, I can't really relate to all this because I was a pretty optimistic kid. In middle school, I definitely wasn't daydreaming of ruin like you described (heh).

Sato: So what kinds of daydreams did occupy your mind? (heh)

Shouji: I really just wondered if I'd be able to draw what I wanted for a living. But these days, when I'm walking down the street, I find I'm always pondering, "Gosh, it'd suck if one of 'them' suddenly popped up here!" or, "It'd be scary if this place fell into ruin." I'm sure I have Daisuke-san's teachings to thank for that. (heh)

DAISUKE SATO

In early 1980, when he was still in college, he worked as a board game designer. His representative game was the *Red Sun Black Cross* series. In 1991, he debuted with his alternate-history novel, *Reversed Pacific War History*. After that, he tried his hand at a variety of genres, including fantasy, science-fiction, and action. His debut work with Kadokawa Shoten was the novel *Island of Revelation*, and it has many overlapping elements with *Highschool of the Dead*. When he saw Gato-san trying to sneak a puff, he said warmly, "Don't worry, it's fine. Let's all have a smoke!" and opened the window all the way. He took a long drag himself, making the two look like a real duo. Though it could have been Sato-san's tendency to want to make others feel comfortable (eyewitness account).

Primary Works -
Novels: Novel Version of *Red Sun Black Cross*, *Imperial Guards*, *Huckebein: Hitler's Final Order*, *Island of Revelation*

Shouji: You think this might be the seeds of a desire for destruction starting to bud?

Sato: The collapse of society excites me (heh). There's a phrase, the "convenient fall of society," that's been coined to ridicule apocalyptic stories where, for no explicable reason, food and water are easy to come by. But what's interesting about the theme of societal collapse is how the misery of lack of freedom becomes a source of entertainment for us. Since this story is featured in a magazine targeted at relatively young men, there are plenty of limitations on our creative license, but that's where I rely on the power of Shouji-san's drawings.

Gato: It's almost like, because the limitations put the brakes on and keep the excitement from reaching the highest point, there's this feeling of bittersweet tension when you're brought to the brink, but no further.

Sato: The sex appeal that comes out in Shouji-san's drawings is a perfect manifestation of his genius. He draws nudes that are the very embodiment of lust, yet somehow manages to keep it clean.

Gato: Yeah, you said it. Like they're slick and smooth. A good drawing of a pair of breasts makes you wanna feel it go "squish" under your fingers (heh).

Shouji: People say that I'm the one who's got my mind in the gutter, but the notes in the script expressly say things like, "Make this a fan service shot," or, "Sex it up, please." So, well, what I'm trying to say is it's not entirely my fault. Honestly (heh). But the fact that you said it makes you wanna feel them go "squish" means that what I'm trying to express has gotten across, so that makes me very happy.

Gato: When I read the chapters that come out every month, I can't help but think to myself how grueling a process it must be to create this final product. The detail to the drawings is just incredible!

Shouji: To get across the hyper-unrealistic parts of the story in the final product, I knew that only realistic backgrounds would do, so I work the hardest at making the backgrounds as hyper-realistic as possible. Though they're pretty warped (heh).

Sato: You take a lot of reference shots, though.

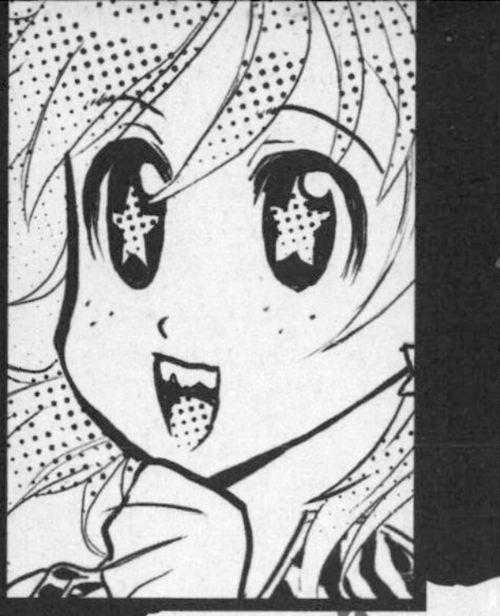

SHOUJI SATO

After working as an assistant numerous times, he presented his work through *doujinshi* circles and fanzines. He was awarded the *Young King OURs* rising manga award three times. When *Highschool of the Dead* was looking for its illustrator, Kouta Hirano-san recommended him, detecting that he showed potential for action manga, and so he was selected. He was born in Kyushu and lives there now. In this three-way talk, he was all nervous smiles when first meeting Gato-san. Sato-san explained that despite his sturdy physique, he is as sensitive as his drawings and terribly shy. To support that claim, even at the get-together afterward, the entire time he remained the polite and agreeable young man (eyewitness account).

Primary Works -

Manga: *Legend of the Two Alone*

"I don't care if you make me a disposable character (heh)."

Talk Session by Shouji Gato ✕ Daisuke Sato ✕ Shouji Sat

Shouji: Thankfully, since this story takes place in modern times, I just carry my digital camera around the neighborhood with me, taking photos for two to three days straight at a time. Since I figure people are watching and wondering what it is I'm doing, I try to go out infrequently (aside from when I'm taking photos). So I try to aim for the early morning hours, but I still look like a totally suspicious figure.

Sato: I write the scripts to make breaking the story down into panels as easy as possible, but Shouji-san has a particularly keen sense of understanding the script, and he'll construct the scenes even better than I had originally intended. He captures the mood with camera angles worthy of the big screen.

Shouji: But what's really the most grueling part isn't even the guns or backgrounds. It's the bicycles, motorcycles, and pretty much anything else the characters ride. Manga characters have certain proportions that simply make them not match up well to vehicles. Take Kouta-kun, for example. When he first hops up onto a vehicle, it makes for such a hyperspace design that when he's paired up with one of the taller characters, I end up having to cram both of them into a panel that simply won't fit them (heh). When the elements fail to complement each other, the drawing really gives off an incongruous vibe. So...I try to keep them to a minimum. Also, every time they come up, my assistants practically keel over (heh).

Sato: Either way, I appreciate all the effort you put into it. Shouji-san, you really are an incredibly straightforward kind of guy. You say what you mean, and you do what you say. Once you came on the project, I knew you were the type that does what he says and then some. You're a rare kind of person to come by these days.

Gato: As far as your drawings, naturally they were superb in Volume I, but they're also improving at an unbelievable speed. The detail in your work is incredible, but you're also very talented at knowing how much information to try to pack in. How do you guys arrange all this beforehand?

Sato: What I thought was genius was when we were deciding the characters' three sizes. Shouji-san went so far as to think of the size of their bra cups, and I got an e-mail from him saying he wanted that to be a specification.

●KOUTA HIRANO
A manga-ka. While still studying at his vocational training school, he debuted with the adult manga *Coyote*. His manga *Hellsing*, which is about the battle between vampires and vampire hunters, is his representative work and has been made into an anime more than once.

Talk Session by Shouji Gato × Daisuke Sato × Shouji Sato

Sato: Then when the drawings were complete, he had stuck to distinguishing all their specified bra sizes, so that even the way they swayed and jiggled were different. 99% of our e-mail correspondence is about tits (heh).

Shouji: It's true, we're always going back and forth over the boobs. Like discussing how to have them swing or be groped. Then there's deciding whether or not to make something a panty shot. We seriously have conversations like that (heh).

Sato: Funny thing is, neither of us even really question the kinds of conversations we have (heh). In this series, Alice is the only one who doesn't have a rack. Shouji-san was always saying "no way am I drawing a flat-chested woman!" so when it came to the police officer Asami-chan, I purposely had her appear to teach him a little lesson.

Gato: A lesson in what exactly (heh)?

Shouji: I have to say, since his writing exceeds my imagination to the nth degree, especially the variety of people's appearances, this is a something I could definitely not draw all on my own. During our collaborative discussions, I definitely feel the gap between what he's written and how I draw it (heh). Besides that, when it comes to the background set-ups, weaponry, and other things, I'm given specifications regarding the details, and master Kumi Misasagi, whom I have the pleasure of having on my staff, gathers the materials and puts them together for me. So it's only thanks to all that help that I am able to draw them as accurately as I can.

Gato: By the way, how did you end up becoming the artist for *Highschool of the Dead*, Shouji-san? This is your first serialized work.

Sato: At first, I was having a really hard time finding somebody to draw this story for me. That's when Kouta Hirano introduced me to an artist he highly recommended—Shouji-san. The sample he gave me was a single pencil sketch of a girl riding on a motorcycle, but it was really good. I'd read Shouji-san's works in the past, but they were all gag manga, so I didn't see the true skill behind them at the time.

●THE SPORADICALLY-PUBLISHED EIGHT-PAGE GAG MANGA.
"Legend of the Two Alone" wasn't much of a representative work since it was only ever commissioned when something went amiss with a work that was serialized regularly and they had to fill in the gap it left. Shouji Sato-sensei is the only legendary man who ever published a comic based off of a representative work like this.

Talk Session by Shouji Gato × Daisuke Sato × Shouji Sato

Shouji: I will always be grateful to Hirano-sensei for introducing us! And so...twice a year, in the summer and winter, I go to him to thank him in person (heh).

Sato: What makes Hirano-san so sharp is that, from just seeing a few pictures, he was able to visualize in his head how this person would draw this kind of title. At the time, he was with Koushi Rikudou, so I asked to let me borrow him.

Shouji: Suddenly, this e-mail arrives at my secret workplace (heh), and the one who actually told me about it was Rikudou-san's manager at the time, Kumi Misasagi, whom I mentioned before. It sounded interesting, so I figured I should try my hand at something that wasn't gag for once.

Gato: I'm sure you were pretty surprised at first.

Shouji: I was completely bewildered as to why he'd want somebody who's only representative work was some sporadically-published eight-page gag comic. And I was pretty much filled with anxiety. But since I knew I was willing to do whatever it took, I felt like I had the kamikaze spirit and would face my death face-first, if that was what this was to become (heh).

Gato: So that explains why so many of your characters are named after real people. Huh.

Sato: You want to join their ranks?

Gato: Yes, please! I don't care if you make me a disposable character (heh).

Sato: Maybe you could be on the Self-Defense Forces. "I won't let you! Over my dead body!" with machine guns going off in both hands as you meet your death.

Gato: "I'm not about to give up on Japan that easily!" A character like that would probably have a big scar across his face, don'tcha think? (heh)

Shouji: This is only my first time meeting you, but I can see that you're tall with a solid build, so I'd say that'd make you the dependable older brother type.

●THE RAMBO SERIES
A series of action films starring Sylvester Stallone. Rambo is an invincible soldier who has returned from Vietnam and now lives the life of an outlaw. The sequel that was released in 1985, *Rambo: First Blood Part II*, has him return to Vietnam to rescue POWs still detained.

●TOP GUN
A military action film released in 1986 starring Tom Cruise. The story takes place at Top Gun, the fighter weapons school that trains the best pilots in the American navy, and follows the main character, Maverick, in this story of love and maturity.

A pamphlet for *Highschool of the Dead: the Movie*. This was included as a bonus in the November 2007 issue of *Monthly Dragon Age*. If only *HOTD* were to become a movie... That's the kind of alternate reality this faux pamphlet suggests. The inside is packed with movie-loving Daisuke Sato-san's ideas.

alk Session by Shouji Gato ✕ Daisuke Sato ✕ Shouji Sato

Shouji: Of course, I'm sure Daisuke-sensei would write up a fabulous death for you. So I say we go for it and make this thing as grotesque as we can! With all this tension as he yells, "Choke on my guts, you creeps!" (heh)

Gato: Back in my college days, I used to appear in a lot of student films from the movie club, and I was usually the guy who died (heh). Like, I'd go to save somebody and immediately die right after.

Sato: I was always the perverted character in my school's student films (heh). In stories about zombies, it's the people's own stupidity that screws them over.

Gato: When it comes to zombies, you can't not talk about movies.

Sato: The movies I watch are all rated either R or X (heh).

Gato: It was just before the 90s when I started watching them almost religiously. The movie where I thought the military stuff was really the coolest was in Sylvester Stallone's *Rambo II* (heh). But as I come to understand more and more how the military really works, I see how laughable the whole *Rambo* series actually is.

Sato: Like, now you can point out how unrealistic it all is (heh).

Gato: But giving it another go around, it's interesting to me all over again. Like, really entertaining (heh).

Sato: That's what they call being able to enjoy something as an adult (heh).

Gato: Another one I really like is *Top Gun*.

Sato: Driving a motorcycle or a military aircraft and scoring against the enemy and with a girl...that really is a boy's dream. Like *Macross* (heh). In that movie, they fly actual military aircraft, but apparently the producer and those who have actually flown the aircraft had a slight difference of opinion that really caused some strife.

Gato: I heard that they'd show him the dogfight scenes in the *Macross* movie and ask him what he wanted to do about it (heh).

●DAWN OF THE DEAD
A horror film directed by George A. Romero that was released in Japan in 1979. Set in a shopping mall, the phenomenon of the "living dead" is never explained as we witness the struggle between them and the human survivors. From this zombie movie series was born the concept of infected persons eating people.

●DAY OF THE DEAD
Part three of Romero's zombie movie series. America's been taken over by zombies and one faction of militants and scientists hole themselves up in an underground storehouse where we see them struggle against the zombies and each other.

●SHAUN OF THE DEAD
A horror comedy film packed with homages to Romero's zombies. Immature Shaun works at an appliance store. He and his freeloading friend Ed try to figure out how to battle the zombies that are springing up all over England. There is also a romantic twist to this film.

●JOHN LEGUIZAMO
Born in 1964, this actor played Cholo in Land of the Dead. He often plays the independent role and has appeared in a lot of cult titles. In 2000, he won an Emmy Award for his acting talent.

Talk Session by Shouji Gato ✖ Daisuke Sato ✖ Shouji Sat

Sato: Even though the pilots apparently insisted that that was not how you fly an aircraft. In the end, *Top Gun* copied the *Gunbuster* anime, in terms of the flying, at least. The pilots really are skilled, so it's a shame that they copied something so unrealistic.

Gato: Nowadays, it'd be all CG.

Shouji: *Rambo...Top Gun...*hmm. To be honest, when those movies came out I wasn't even in elementary school yet, so I mostly caught them when they aired on TV. I don't know enough about them to say much on the subject, nor was I left with that deep an impression. Since they're such classics, it's a little embarrassing to have to admit that.

Sato: What kinds of movies other than action do you like?

Gato: When I was a kid, I was scared of horror films, so I rarely watched them (heh). As far as zombie movies go, since so many hit zombie video games have come out, I've gotten acquainted with them, and now I'm not very scared of them.

Sato: Even now, if I watch some of the older works from director George A. Romero late at night by myself, I'll get freaked out. Before I know it, I'm gripping a model gun as if my life depended on it (heh).

Shouji: I watched Romero's zombie movies when I first took this job. I didn't know much about the zombie universe (heh), and I love those deserted shopping malls and the corpses walking around dressed for the occupations of their former lives, along with that amazing background music that filtered over those surreal scenes. But the impact they had on me and the chilling vibe from the first time I watched them was out of this world.

Gato: Which zombie movie has left the deepest impression on you?

Shouji: I've seen plenty of films, but *Dawn of the Dead*, *Day of the Dead*, and *Shaun of the Dead* are the three best zombie films as far as I'm concerned. Oh, and I also loved Cholo in *Land of the Dead*. I fell in love with the looks of the actor who played him, John Loguizamo (hoh).

● **28 DAYS LATER**
A post-apocalyptic sci-fi British film released in 2002. The story follows London's fall to ruin when a virus turns humans into killing machines, and the lucky ones that survive battle against them. Naturally, the infected people were designed with zombies in mind.

● **THE DAY OF THE TRIFFIDS**
A post-apocalyptic science fiction novel written by John Wyndham about flesh-eating plants that can walk around and are cultivated for their vegetable oil. One day, an unexplainable mass blinding of the human population occurs, and the triffids escape their fencing, run wild, and threaten mankind.

● **THE DAY OF THE TRIFFIDS (FILM)**
The 1962 British movie adaptation of *The Day of the Triffids*, directed by Steve Sekely. It's a classic film that has been as influential as the movie *I Am Legend* and Romero's zombies.

Talk Session by Shouji Sato ✕ Daisuke Sato ✕ Shouji Sato

Gato: Looking at a more recent work, *28 Days Later* was pretty interesting.

Sato: That was really well done. That movie changes the classic science-fiction novel about killer plants taking over the world called *The Day of the Triffids* (adapted into a movie and television drama by the same name) into a story about an infection that turns people into zombies. The opening sequences are pretty much identical.

Gato: That work made the concept of the so-called "running zombie" popular.

Sato: Must be a British expression of realism (heh). But I also like Romero's staggering and trudging zombies too. Since they're so slow-moving, they look like they'd be easy to defeat, but the survivors are the ones who make poor decisions and screw themselves over. That's the interesting part to me. They're stories about how people who are supposed to be so fully capable let their inherent foolishness be the nail in their own coffins.

Gato: Like a natural disaster, zombies are a very simple phenomenon.

Sato: In a disaster, how the people react is what's interesting.

Gato: *HOTD* is also a story about human relations shifting and reacting in the midst of a disaster. In the story, there are those characters who exist just to really mess things up and make you wish '"if only he wasn't there!" but also to add a twist that's very enthralling. I'm really looking forward to seeing where the story goes from here.

Shouji: Personally, I can't wait to draw Rika Minami running amok... I mean, playing a more active part. Since she's such an invincible character, I'm sure it's hard to just pull her card any time, but since she's the kind of character I would definitely be unable to create, it's really a joy getting to draw her.

Sato: I also love her rack (heh).

Shouji: Like how we do up little vignettes of any characters who have died in the volume on the staff list at the back of every book, I wish I could draw other sub-characters in that space to reveal them more in a way that would appeal to the readers.

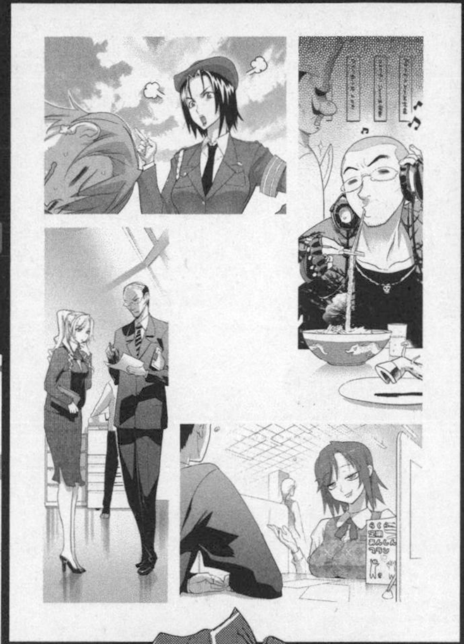

●END OF VOLUME STAFF LIST
After Volume I, this page shows the "good old days" of the characters who died in the volume as a way of eliciting tears out of the fans (heh).

T... suke Sato × Shouji Sat...

Shouji: I think it's that kind of thing that makes this world so believable, and urges the reader to wonder "what's going to happen to them after that?" Of course, I wouldn't forget the main characters' melons (heh).

Sato: Well, in any case, it's amazing that our middle school dreams are becoming reality now. That goes for everyone (heh).

August 2008 at the offices of Fujimi Shobo
Three-way discussion organized by Keita Nekoyanagi

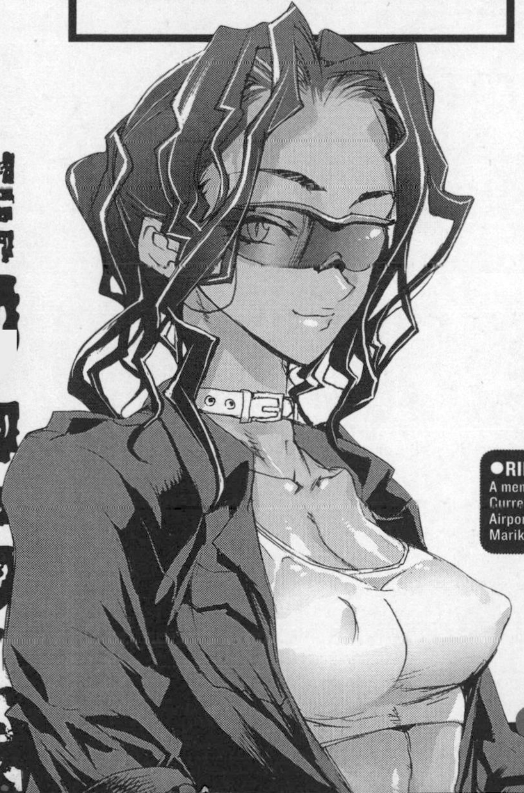

●RIKA MINAMI
A member of the Prefectural SAT. Currently working at the Tokonosu Airport. She's a sniper specialist and Marikawa-sensei's best friend.

Aug 2016

HIGHSCHOOL
OF THE DEAD ➏

DAISUKE SATO
SHOUJI SATO

Translation: Christine Dashiell

Lettering: Chris Counasse

GAKUENMOKUSHIROKU HIGHSCHOOL OF THE DEAD Volume 6 ©2010 DAISUKE SATO ©2010 SHOUJI SATO. Edited by FUJIMISHOBO. First published in Japan in 2010 by KADOKAWA CORPORATION, Tokyo. English translation rights arranged with KADOKAWA CORPORATION, Tokyo, through TUTTLE-MORI AGENCY, INC., Tokyo.

Translation © 2012 by Hachette Book Group, Inc.

Yen Press
Hachette Book Group
1290 Avenue of the Americas, New York, NY 10104

www.HachetteBookGroup.com
www.YenPress.com

Yen Press is an imprint of Hachette Book Group, Inc.
The Yen Press name and logo are trademarks of Hachette Book Group, Inc.

First Yen Press Edition: April 2012

ISBN: 978-0-316-20943-4

10 9 8 7 6 5

BVG

Printed in the United States of America